A Full-Orbed Christianity
The Protestant Churches and Social Welfare in Canada, 1900–1940

Challenging widely held views that religious institutions entered a period of decline and irrelevance after 1900, Nancy Christie and Michael Gauvreau argue that the Methodist, Presbyterian, and United Churches enjoyed their greatest cultural influence during the first four decades of the twentieth century. By examining the relationship of these churches to both popular culture and the emerging welfare state, the authors challenge the main tenets of secularization theories.

Christie and Gauvreau look at the ways in which reformers expanded the church's popular base through mass revivalism, established social work and sociology in Canadian universities and church colleges, and aggressively sought to take a leadership role in social reform by incorporating independent reform organizations into the church-sponsored Social Service Council of Canada. They also explore the instrumental role of Protestant clergymen in formulating social legislation and transforming the scope and responsibilities of the modern state.

The enormous influence of the Protestant churches before World War II can no longer be ignored, nor can the view that the churches were accomplices in their own secularization be justified. *A Full-Orbed Christianity* calls on historians to rethink the role of Protestantism in Canadian life and to see it not as the garrison of anti-modernism but as the chief harbinger of cultural change before 1940.

NANCY CHRISTIE, a former Webster Fellow in the humanities at Queen's University, is an independent scholar.
MICHAEL GAUVREAU is associate professor of history, McMaster University.

McGill-Queen's Studies in the History of Religion
G.A. Rawlyk, Editor

Volumes in this series have been supported by the Jackman Foundation of Toronto.

1 Small Differences
Irish Catholics and Irish Protestants, 1815–1922
An International Perspective
Donald Harman Akenson

2 Two Worlds
The Protestant Culture of Nineteenth-Century Ontario
William Westfall

3 An Evangelical Mind
Nathanael Burwash and the Methodist Tradition in Canada, 1839–1918
Marguerite Van Die

4 The Dévotes
Women and Church in Seventeenth-Century France
Elizabeth Rapley

5 The Evangelical Century
College and Creed in English Canada from the Great Revival to the Great Depression
Michael Gauvreau

6 The German Peasants' War and Anabaptist Community of Goods
James M. Stayer

7 A World Mission
Canadian Protestantism and the Quest for a New International Order, 1918–1939
Robert Wright

8 Serving the Present Age
Revivalism, Progressivism, and the Methodist Tradition in Canada
Phyllis D. Airhart

9 A Sensitive Independence
Canadian Methodist Women Missionaries in Canada and the Orient, 1881–1925
Rosemary R. Gagan

10 God's Peoples
Covenant and Land in South Africa, Israel, and Ulster
Donald Harman Akenson

11 Creed and Culture
The Place of English-Speaking Catholics in Canadian Society, 1750–1930
Terrence Murphy and Gerald Stortz, editors

12 Piety and Nationalism
Lay Voluntary Associations and the Creation of an Irish-Catholic Community in Toronto, 1850–1895
Brian P. Clarke

13 Amazing Grace
Studies in Evangelicalism in Australia, Britain, Canada, and the United States
George Rawlyk and Mark A. Noll, editors

14 Children of Peace
W. John McIntyre

15 A Solitary Pillar
Montreal's Anglican Church and the Quiet Revolution
John Marshall

16 Padres in No Man's Land
Canadian Chaplains and the Great War
Duff Crerar

17 Christian Ethics and Political Economy in North America
A Critical Analysis of U.S. and Canadian Approaches
P. Travis Kroeker

18 Pilgrims in Lotus Land
Conservative Protestantism in British Columbia, 1917–1981
Robert K. Burkinshaw

19 Through Sunshine and Shadow
The Woman's Christian Temperance Union, Evangelicalism, and Reform in Ontario, 1874–1930
Sharon Cook

20 Church, College, and Clergy
A History of Theological Education at Knox College, Toronto, 1844–1994
Brian J. Fraser

21 The Lord's Dominion
The History of Canadian Methodism
Neil Semple

22 A Full-Orbed Christianity
The Protestant Churches and Social Welfare in Canada, 1900–1940
Nancy Christie and Michael Gauvreau

23 Evangelism and Apostasy
The Evolution and Impact of Evangelicals in Modern Mexico
Kurt Bowen

A Full-Orbed Christianity

The Protestant Churches and Social Welfare in Canada, 1900–1940

NANCY CHRISTIE

AND

MICHAEL GAUVREAU

McGill-Queen's University Press
Montreal & Kingston • London • Buffalo

ISBN 0-7735-1397-3

Legal deposit second quarter 1996
Bibliothèque nationale du Québec

Printed in Canada on acid-free paper

This book has been published with the help of a grant from the Social Science Federation of Canada, using funds provided by the Social Sciences and Humanities Research Council of Canada.

McGill-Queen's University Press is grateful to the Canada Council for support of its publishing program.

Canadian Cataloguing in Publication Data

Christie, Nancy, 1958–
A full-orbed christianity : the Protestant churches and social welfare in Canada, 1900–1940
(McGill-Queen's studies in the history of religion ; 22)
Includes bibliographical references and index.
ISBN 0-7735-1397-3

1. Church and social problems – Canada – History. 2. Protestant churches – Canada – History. 3. Canada – Social conditions – 20th century. 4. Sociology, Christian – Canada – History. I. Gauvreau, Michael, 1956– II. Title. III. Series.

HN39.C3C47 1995 261.8′3′0971 C95-920892-5

Typeset in Old Style 7, 10/12
by Caractéra inc., Quebec City

For George Rawlyk, 1935–1995

Contents

Acknowledgments ix

Introduction xi

1 The "Urgency of Evangelism" 3

2 Reviving the Religion of the Vernacular 37

3 To "Complete the Circle of Scientific Theology" 75

4 A "Uniting Social Aim": The Protestant Churches and Social Work in Equipoise 131

5 The Protestant Churches, the Social Survey, and "Rural Planning" 165

6 The Social Service Council of Canada: "A Clearing-House" for the Modern State 197

7 The United Church and the "Revival of Personal Religion" 224

Conclusion: Encompassing the Modern Age 244

Notes 251

Manuscript Sources 355

Index 359

Acknowledgments

This book had a modest beginning in the spring of 1993 when Nancy Christie was preparing an article on social Christianity in the 1920s and its relationship to the wider culture. The consultation, at Michael Gauvreau's urging, of the marvellously extensive but hitherto untapped Hugh Dobson Papers, together with the infectious enthusiasm of George Rawlyk, persuaded us that a much larger monograph was desirable.

During the course of researching and writing we have incurred numerous debts. First, we would like to thank those readers who took the time from their hectic schedules to offer valuable comments and criticisms on earlier versions of this book. George Rawlyk and Carl Berger read the manuscript in its entirety and their acute insights were indispensable for rendering the argument clearer and more complex. We would also like to thank William Westfall for bringing his knowledge of popular religion to bear upon chapter 2, and John Kendle for his broad acquaintance with both progressive reform and Western Canada, which greatly sharpened our analysis in chapter 5. While the manuscript benefited enormously from their suggestions, all flaws and omissions remain fully our responsibility.

No acknowledgments would be complete without expressing our gratitude to the helpfulness and assiduity of a great many archivists. In particular, we wish to thank Ruth Wilson and Ian Mason at the United Church Archives in Toronto for making available to us the wealth of material relating to the early twentieth-century experience of the Protestant churches and for providing such a congenial setting for researchers. The valuable work of Jean Dryden and Ruth Wilson in refurbishing the archival record unearthed a vast array of new manuscript sources which in no small way contributed to the revisionist perspective of this monograph. We would also like to thank Harold Averill at the University of Toronto Archives for drawing our attention to the important S.D. Clark Papers; Richard Bennett and his staff at the University of Manitoba Archives; Phebe Chartrand at McGill University Archives for her help in locating material on the School of Social Work; Shirley Payment at the University of Winnipeg Archives; D'Arcy Hande and his staff at the Saskatchewan Archives Board for their patience in acceding to our constant demands on the Violet McNaughton correspondence; the staff of the Billy Graham Center Archives in Wheaton, Illinois, for having Christian trust in allowing us access to the J. Wilbur Chapman papers under difficult circumstances; and lastly, Patricia Birkett at the National Archives of Canada who kindly made available to us the records of the Canadian Council of Churches, which greatly facilitated our discussion of the Social Service Council of Canada.

The research for this book could not have been undertaken without the financial support of the Social Sciences and Humanities Research Council of Canada and of the Department of the Secretary of State of Canada for financial aid through the Canadian Studies Directorate.

Our greatest debt is to our series editor, George Rawlyk, whose own perspective on the past encourages scholarly debate and revisionism. He has, in recent years, been a great champion of the new social-cultural history, and we have benefited enormously from his extensive knowledge and his breadth of perspective. Nancy Christie, in particular, would like to thank him for his constancy and support during the research process. While the journey from manuscript to book is often a harrowing one, the path has been considerably smoothed by the shepherding skills of Joan Harcourt and the staff at McGill-Queen's University Press. This book has also benefited from Henri Pilon's attentive copy-editing and Len Kuffert's proofreading scrutiny.

September 1995

Introduction

This book reinterprets the conventional view that social reform went through a period of decline between 1918, when pre-war urban progressivism foundered, and the early 1930s, when a mature movement of centralized state planning emerged spurred on by the energies of an élite cadre of experts in the social sciences.[1] Historians have perceived the 1920s as a wasteland of reform activism largely because, by concentrating on university social scientists, business groups, and labour organizations, they have defined social reform as a purely secular process. By contrast, we have shifted our attention in this book to the Protestant churches to argue that until the late 1930s almost every facet of social investigation and social policymaking fell under the aegis of Christian leadership. In so doing, we challenge the easy assumptions of the secularization thesis that the decade of the 1920s was a period of drift for the Canadian churches and that social evangelism was the catalyst which ultimately led to the irrelevance of Christianity in the wider culture.

We have taken as our starting-point the injunction of Ramsay Cook and David Marshall, the most recent proponents of the secularization thesis in Canada, who have argued that because the process of secularization is a broad cultural and social phenomenon which occurs outside the individual's own loss of faith, it must be studied in terms of the changing relationship of the churches to other social institutions.[2] This book therefore examines the Protestant churches in the context of popular culture, social reform, the rise of the social sciences, and the growth of the modern state. Having analysed this broad terrain of twentieth-century Canadian social and cultural life, we advance a radically different interpretation of the interplay of Protestantism and Canadian society and argue that the period between 1900 and 1940 represented the apogee of the cultural authority of the churches.

Moreover, we take issue with the central assertion of the secularization thesis that any religious experience that diverges from a coherent system of theology constitutes a benchmark of spiritual decline. This, we argue, proffers an overly intellectualized and narrow definition of evangelicalism, a creed which had traditionally exalted emotions and experience over intellect. By giving due prominence to the important influence of popular piety in shaping the contours of evangelicalism in Canada, we demonstrate that what has been interpreted as evidence of theological, and therefore religious decline, was in fact an indication of a resurgence of popular forms of spirituality stressing a direct emotional experience of the Divine and antagonistic to élite religion as defined by the niceties of theological controversy and denominational identity. Interpreters of secularization have viewed social evangelism as tantamount to secular thought because of its rejection of theological dogma.[3] We argue instead that the emphasis placed by social evangelism on outward Christian experience as evidence of firm religious commitment resulted in a form of evangelical piety as coherent as the more intellectual adherence to the systems of Victorian theology. Just as nineteenth-century clergymen viewed historical theology as the means of preserving the tenets of evangelicalism from the incursions of modern science and philosophy, twentieth-century Protestant ministers saw in the exaltation by the social services of the practical day-to-day experience of the individual, which made religion accessible to ordinary men and women, the greatest safeguard of Christianity in a society increasingly characterized by the rivalry of opposing classes. The growing desire among young clergymen after 1900 to jettison what they saw as the socially irrelevant, denominationally divisive, and élitist dimensions of the Victorian evangelical heritage in favour of the experiential qualities of popular revivalism and social evangelism not only stimulated a resurgence in mass religious participation, but also marked a period of renewal of Canadian Protestantism and its unprecedented expansion into all facets of social and cultural life.

The exponents of the theological definition of religious vitality have taken at face value the prescription of the Victorian church colleges that only the intellectual rigours of a sound historical theology could preserve the authority of Christianity. Rather than functioning as an immutable standard, the primacy of theology was itself culturally conditioned and must be understood as a product of a specific historical context.[4] The equation of religion with theology, which characterized the Methodist and Presbyterian churches during the nineteenth century, has so dominated historical discussions of religion that it has beclouded our understanding of the role of the Protestant churches in the twentieth century in two important respects: on the one hand, supporters of the secularization thesis have used theological rigour to denigrate social evangelism, while on the other, historians such as Doug Owram and Mariana Valverde have adhered to a caricature of the antiquated and esoteric Victorian theologue to excise the churches from "progressive" currents of modern thought and social action.[5]

Between 1900 and 1930 the Methodist and Presbyterian churches envisioned their mission as nothing less than the complete Christianization of Canadian life. Richard Allen has defined the "social gospel" in terms of intellectual changes within Protestantism itself.[6] By contrast, we place the movement for social service, with its recognition of the increasing complexity and interdependence of modern society and its redefinition of the individual in terms of social experience, in the wider transatlantic context of the reinterpretation of liberalism in the early twentieth century.[7] That redefinition of the individual, which social evangelism represented, was not merely an intellectual phenomenon as some historians have claimed;[8] rather, this transformation cannot be understood apart from its direct links to the powerful current of pragmatic social action which marked the renaissance of the Protestant churches. Garbed in the optimistic millennialism of social evangelism, the Protestant churches expanded their popular base through mass revivalism, established social work and sociology in Canadian universities and church colleges, and aggressively sought out the leadership of social reform by incorporating independent reform organizations into the church-sponsored Social Service Council of Canada. Protestant clergymen were also instrumental in utilizing the most up-to-date methods of social investigation to pave the way for the application of expert knowledge to the formulation of social legislation, thereby helping transform the scope and responsibilities of the modern state.

Further, this book argues that the vacuum left by the failure of urban progressivism led by business and labour following World War I was rapidly filled by the Protestant churches which, between 1900 and 1920, underwent a marked transformation. Not only did they become national bureaucratic organizations, but novel ideas about the function and role of the minister in modern society existed within their new structures. The ideal twentieth-century clergyman, most aptly represented by the Methodist field secretary for Western Canada, Hugh Dobson, was a far cry from the image of the otherwordly cleric so evocative of Victorian Protestantism. Unlike his Victorian counterpart, the modern clergyman's purview lay beyond the walls of the institutional church, for he was expected to be a student of the social sciences and scientific agriculture, a coordinator and interpreter of community social surveys, a social activist, and a knowledgeable expert in the design of state social legislation, as well as a powerfully emotive revival preacher.

Although ideas of liberal collectivism had established a foothold in the few departments of political economy that were nascent in Canadian universities,[9] it was primarily through the Protestant churches, whose authority encompassed the interstices of cultural life, that the often radical tenets of the collectivist challenge to *laissez-faire* liberalism, with their emphasis upon social organicist views of society and an intrusive view of state intervention, permeated Canadian society. Until the advent of university-based social planning in the 1940s, the Protestant churches were the gravitational centre for a wide variety of social reform movements and the foremost sponsors of modern social welfare policy and the interventionist state. As such, this church-led alliance, with its strong links to local reform interests and its emphasis upon a largely maternal feminist agenda of social welfare measures centred on the expansion of government responsibility for the protection of women, children, and the family, represented a clear divergence from the American model of progressivism which was characterized by specialization, the cult of expertise, and the increasing influence of big business on government structures.[10]

More importantly, the prominence of the Canadian churches in the field of social policy during the 1920s and 1930s compels us to question the orthodoxy that Canadian progressivism was coterminous with the regulation of public utilities and the reconciliation of capital and labour.[11] Although enveloped by social evangelism, the views of the churches on the need to expand the role of the state into areas of child welfare, public health, mothers' pensions, unemployment insurance, old-age pensions, and the reform of rural life cannot be counted as a lesser species of progressivism simply because issues of importance to women and children were given priority rather than those of male-dominated business and labour organizations.

As this book makes clear, the enormous public authority enjoyed by the Protestant churches prior to World War II can no longer be ignored, nor can the view that the churches were merely complicit in their own secularization be justified. Although it has become commonplace to identify the churches as bastions of conservatism and traditional values – which, in part, they were – this book calls upon historians to reconceive the role of Protestantism in Canadian life and to view the churches not as the garrisons of antimodernism but as the chief harbingers of cultural change before 1940.

A Full-Orbed Christianity

[T]he more I think about such matters the more the distinction between sacred and secular diminishes. Theoretically, for me, there is no such distintion. It is artificial, false – the product of a narrow view of life and the product of a withered ecclesiasticism and a more wretched secularism. Practically, the two are so interpenetrating each other, that I am gradually atuning my theoretical position in actual life. A man is called *to live*. Life itself is the greatest responsibility and one which no one can escape ... for if we have the one spirit the difference of gift is a minor consideration. It seems to me that if one is in the true relation to God the question is "Where and how can I best serve Him" and this is generally determined by the answer to the question "For what am I best adapted?"

J.S. Woodsworth to C.B. Sissons, 14 Feb. 1902
National Archives of Canada
C.B. Sissons Papers, MG 27 III F3, vol. 5

COMMUNITY ORGANIZATION

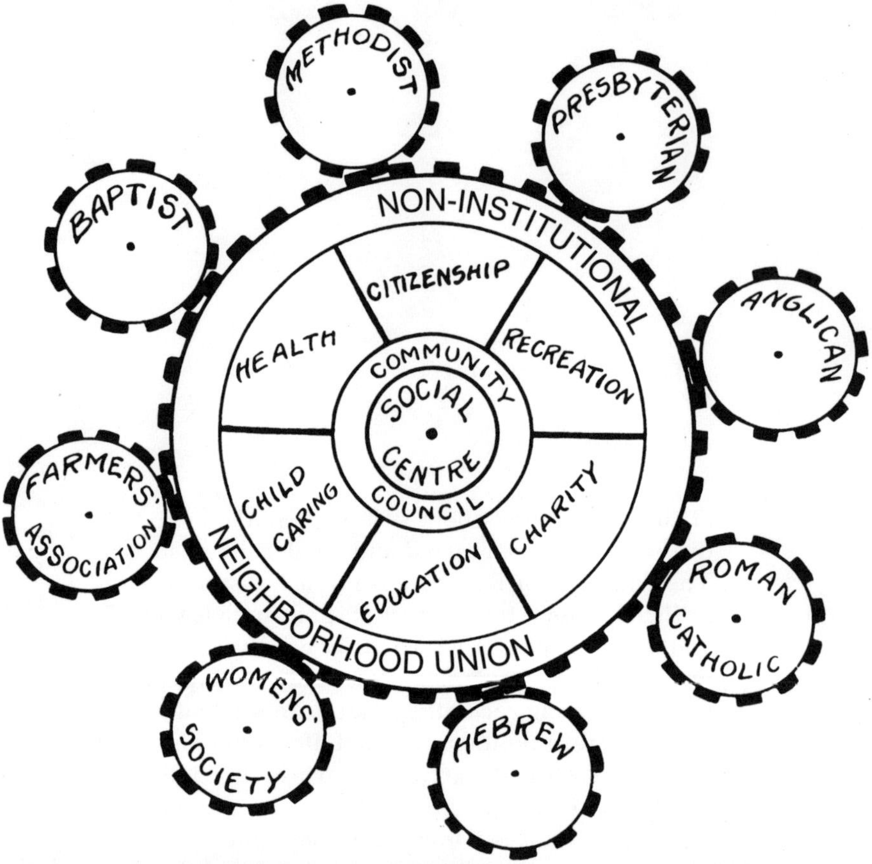

Today many an organization "makes things hum," but accomplishes nothing because it simply spins round on its own axis and does not "cog-in" with the community life.

Formal federation would not include all organizations and might "chain the wheels" of some that did unite.

In our scheme of Community Co-operation:

- **All may come in.**
- **Each is free to use all its power.**
- **The more progressive institutions may "speed up" the others.**

Cover of a 1916 pamphlet by J.S. Woodsworth summarizing the first year's work of the Bureau of Social Research. National Archives of Canada, James Shaver Woodsworth Papers, MG 27 III C7, 15; 8.

1 The "Urgency of Evangelism"[1]

Heralding the demise of the Victorian church and the emergence of a modern spirit of "social evangelism," Hugh Dobson, the Methodist field secretary from Saskatchewan, proclaimed in 1920 that "An 'Old Age' has passed and a 'New Day' has dawned." Far from greeting the twentieth century and such attendant social problems as urbanization, industrialization and class conflict, consumerism, and the rise of materialist ideologies with a sense of trepidation and defeatism, Dobson and a generation of young ministers saw in the challenges of modern life the beginning of an unprecedented spiritual awakening. Rather than decrying modernism, these critics of the Victorian church would have agreed with Alice Chown, a feminist and social reformer, when she asserted that it was indeed a "dead organism."[2] Ensconced in the new mainline Protestant organizations created after 1900 which were explicitly devoted to uniting evangelism with social service, these clergymen were eager to ensure that their brand of Christianity adapted to and dynamically interacted with changes in modern society. In so doing, reform-minded elements in the churches asserted a new leadership which challenged the intellectual exclusivity of the powerful church colleges and decisively shifted the cultural emphasis of Canada's Protestant churches from the preservation of a sound theology to a social action designed to address the problems of a nation in the process of transformation. Reflecting this new approach was the Methodist Church's Department of Evangelism and Social Service which was established in 1902. By 1906 Presbyterian progressives had been successful in erecting its counterpart, the Board of Social Service and Evangelism.[3]

"Perhaps never before," reflected Dobson, "have we had such an opportunity to quicken our whole national life with a new spirit." However, by reminding his fellow clergymen that "[r]egeneration in the realm of the spirit and reconstruction in the realm of politics, industry, education, and business must go together,"[4] Dobson emphasized that the new evangelism of social service must rest firmly on the recognition of individual sin and salvation, and he maintained that the departure from the traditional theological underpinnings of Victorian evangelism did not entail a wholesale rejection of the past. From this perspective the twentieth-century renewal of Protestantism involved the recovery of the very core of the evangelical faith, the direct personal encounter with the Almighty. Commenting on his department's campaign to establish social service as the dominant concern within the denomination, Dobson attempted to conciliate the Rev. William Sparling, the former head of Wesley College in Winnipeg, whose allegiance still lay with the Victorian evangelical creed. Dobson observed that "Wesley's emphasis on the authority of experience and the revolt against sin, or the seeking of holiness, is the real spirit of the Movement today."[5] The idea of social service, when viewed from the perspective of early twentieth-century Methodist and Presbyterian progressives, did not spring from what late twentieth-century historians have interpreted as a movement away from biblical verities to a "liberal" social ethic founded upon philosophy rather than religious experience.[6] What might be called "social evangelism" grew out of a perceived need to appeal to a democratic public and, paradoxically, it was underpinned by a very traditional, orthodox emphasis upon the divinity of Christ and human sin. It was this blending of a recognition of the demands of modern mass culture with a popular desire for traditional spirituality that explains why the Rev. C.E. Silcox, who headed the Social Service Council of Canada after 1935, found no anomaly in describing Ernest Thomas, one of the most socially progressive ministers, as a "conservative,"[7] and why such fundamentalist preachers as the American professional evangelist Billy Sunday were enthusiastically recruited by progressive leaders, who saw traditional revivals as the means of energizing the spirit of social service.

The insistence by the promoters of a more "modern" evangelism that theology should be expurgated from practical preaching and their championing of a more emotional and experiential religion did not imply a watering down of Canadian Protestantism. Nor did their critique of the inaccessibility of theology for the ordinary Canadian become the vehicle for an inexorable secularization of culture and society. By inflexibly linking systematic theology to the vitality of the church, the chief exponents of the Canadian secularization thesis[8] have unwittingly concurred with the outlook of the Victorian clergymen-professors, and they have thus perpetuated the very fallacy that the early twentieth-century critics of theology were anxious to dispel. According to Samuel Dwight Chown, sophisticated theology itself was the harbinger of secularization because "the ill-fitting garments of doctrine and dogma" eroded the authority of the church by severing it from popular culture and the wider social experience. The only way to rescue the church, in his view, was to destroy theology so that evangelicalism could once again command an authority founded upon direct popular appeal. "Theology is thought. Religion is life," stated Chown, who pleaded for a democratized and revitalized Christianity that appealed to all people by couching the experiences of Christ in simple terms of life and character.[9] Similarly, the Rev. C.W. Gordon, one of the leading Presbyterian advocates of a more popular social Christianity, disparaged the "abstract theological conception of truth" and, in response to the vicissitudes of modern life, encouraged young ministers to eschew dogma and sectarianism and to "look for new channels of access to the life of the world and to win the mass of humanity to a more uniform religious faith and purpose in life."[10]

It was democracy and not theology that was the major fault-line within twentieth-century Protestantism, and this division expressed itself in a conflict between intellectual and popular styles of religion, between a religion narrowly associated with the middle classes and one that attempted to recognize the implications of democratic culture. There was a tension between those ministers who sought to embrace and Christianize modern life and social conservatives like the Rev. J.W. Flett of Portage la Prairie, Manitoba, who saw in the spectre of the unchurched masses and their "extraordinary rush for pleasure"[11] the symptoms of Christianity's irrelevance. If there were pessimists who saw a declining role for the church in modern society,[12] they occupied an increasingly marginal position when the progressive advocates of social service assumed positions of leadership in both the Methodist and the Presbyterian churches after 1900. This clash, involving the definition of the relationship between church and society, in turn triggered an internal struggle for power between the progressive wing in each church, which the new boards of evangelism and social service inhabited, and the clergymen-professors entrenched in the church colleges.

From the 1840s Canadian evangelicalism had derived its cultural leadership and coherence from an inductive theology that sought a balance between spiritual experience and the rationalism of biblical study. The equation between theology and preaching was sustained largely through the church colleges, which by the 1870s had become the centre-pieces of the Victorian church. These powerful institutions were not only responsible for defining the very character of the authority of

Protestant Christianity, but were also instrumental in establishing a common outlook between the preacher and the professor and between the church and the college, whereby evangelicalism was interpreted as biblical study within the precincts of the church college. This consensus between evangelicalism and theology, which had helped forge the ideal of a college-educated clergy and a style of preaching animated by the intellectual certainties of historical theology, was clearly on the defensive by 1905. Not only had theology lost its pre-eminent status among the human sciences, but the increasingly esoteric scholasticism of the higher criticism had created a huge gap between the lecture hall and the local pulpit. In the first decade of the twentieth century Protestant clergymen could all too palpably appreciate the consequences of an overly intellectualized church by pointing with alarm to the unprecedented decline in church attendance.[13] Whereas the nineteenth-century inductive theology had enabled Canadian evangelicalism to fend off the incursions of modern thought for several decades and had in no small way contributed to the remarkable expansion of the Victorian church, its successes in creating a college-trained clergy had, however, led to an overemphasis upon the fine points of theological debate. A growing chorus of ministers began to believe, with some justification, that theology was, in fact, undermining the experiential essence of evangelism.[14]

The campaign against "the clouds of intellectualism" in the church colleges was first launched by Samuel Dwight Chown, the first head of the Department of Evangelism and Social Service. He believed that in the twentieth century ordinary Canadians were still drawn to experiential religion and that to endure in a democratic age Protestant churches had to embrace rank-and-file Canadians by returning to a "saving faith" based upon the actual experiences and personality of Jesus. Chown vociferously attacked the curriculum of the church colleges which in his view had become mired in an empty glorification of ancient theological systems. Chown's attack upon theology has usually been portrayed as a capitulation to the forces of secular social science, but his real concern was the removal of the dead hand of scholasticism which in his estimation had prevented true evangelism from feeding upon the renewing streams of the inner spirituality of each new generation. For Chown and his fellow progressives, the vestiges of the past and not modern life itself were responsible for the declining popularity of the church. Rather than producing "miniature theological professors," the church colleges had as their function to train ministers who would "enter into dynamic relation" with the forces of modern life and be attuned to rapidly changing popular religious sentiment.[15] The burden of Chown's critique centred on the higher criticism; he blamed it for cutting the church off from the "realm of sociology," by which he meant human social relationships. Of theological study, Chown caustically remarked:

> Then we took a balloon, for flying machines were not yet invented, and we sailed sublimely upward, landing upon the mountain of eschatology, or the science of the last things – the end of the world, heaven, hell, the judgment and hereafter. These subjects were illuminated by all the lamps which shone in the great field of speculation, and impressed upon us by a formidable body of bescriptured philosophy. In this way we were carried in our historical study of theology away up out of sight of the whole realm of sociology.[16]

Progressive Presbyterians like C.W. Gordon also rebelled against the stagnant nature of what he termed the "dead past" of theological authority, and called for a period of spiritual renewal based upon the warm emotionalism of evangelicalism, with its direct appeal to the masses who appreciated "the great questions of life." In Gordon's view the lifeblood of Protestantism was its marvellous ability to renew and adapt itself to a world in flux. Not only did the increasingly sophisticated advancement of knowledge demand an ongoing critical investigation of systems of belief, but in the new democracy, in which all individuals were a "law unto themselves," the church, more than ever before, had to present a non-theological gospel of Christ, one which would emphatically respond to the needs of all members of the local congregation. If the church was to survive, the message could not conflict with the "light of the present," nor could ministerial leadership be grounded upon the simple imposition of a faltering theological system over an unreceptive audience.[17] More succinctly, the Rev. J.A. Cormie, the superintendent of missions for the Manitoba Conference of the United Church, warned that if the church ignored the growing distaste among rural people for "polemical and sectarian preaching" and failed to minister directly to their real needs, its leadership would be usurped by other voluntary societies, such as wheat pools and cooperatives, that were not Christian in outlook.[18]

The call for a preaching that was responsive to the reality of everyday life did not entail the dissolution of Christian belief into a vapid consumerism and the empty experience of self-gratification.[19] Certainly, in 1920 W.H. Smith, a recent graduate of the Presbyterian Westminster Hall in Vancouver, saw in the rejection of a mechanical and static theology, as well as of a commercialized religion, a recovery of the true passion of evangelism as first articulated by George Whitefield and John Wesley in the eighteenth century. He viewed "real Christianity" as a blend of pre-Victorian traditions with a modern democratic ethos: the social forces of the age, as interpreted by the preacher, were to be combined with an older Christian enthusiasm founded in the "native and natural response of the soul of man to Jesus Christ." If theology was to come dressed in the garments of "every intellectual, moral and social springtime," then it had to shed its speculative abstractions that were, after all, but perversions of Jesus' simple biblical message of individual salvation. In short, preaching was to become simple, and it was to appeal directly to the emotions and be down to earth, just as Jesus had first articulated the Gospels. "To accomplish our great aim" of Christian renewal, Smith declared, "we must make spiritual realities interesting to the people."[20]

The concern with tapping into the essence of actual human experience was articulated by Chown's successor, T. Albert Moore. By imploring the church to modernize by becoming "more vitally related to the mass of the people," Moore was not simply caught in the morass of modern ideologies. He and other progressives did not conform to the image of the naïve and cloistered clerical moralist obtuse to social change; instead, they consciously and selectively embraced the modern spirit which they confidently perceived as being the leading edge of a rejuvenated Protestantism. Methodist and Presbyterian progressives felt greater affinity with social reformers outside the church than they did with the narrow Victorian clerics in the church colleges, and both attempted to undermine their influence. Moore dismissed theology as mere dogmatism, an archaic strait-jacket which confined the church to a static role in the face of modern social problems and impeded it from recovering its heritage of creative adaptability to cultural change. While he conceded that theology conferred a modicum of certainty, the church, he argued, had to develop a more open-ended evangelism, one anchored in experience and more inclusive of diverse social groups. In other words, the pluralism of the transformed church must mirror the increasing diversity of Canadian society: "It is our task to present the compelling personality of Jesus to men so that it will elicit its own response, leaving the new experience free to voice itself in language most appropriate to itself, rather than to gain acceptance of a certain theological system or to insist upon some uniform experience of faith or experience of salvation."[21]

J.S. Woodsworth, the "Saint in Politics," projected an image of himself as a "radical in theology," a renegade holding "unorthodox religious ideas" who, alone in the face of a monolithic conservative church, had embraced the modern spirit that aimed at making religion more meaningful to ordinary people. The myth Woodsworth had studiously cultivated of himself as a lone prophetic progressive does not accord with the actual development of his beliefs and testifies far more to his own extreme individualism and restiveness.[22] On the three occasions on which Woodsworth tendered his resignation from the Methodist ministry, his reasons for doing so dealt extensively with the strictures which the now large and bureaucratic church placed upon the freedom of individual ministers – hence, his continuous carping about the confining rules and regulations of the church. As Woodsworth informed his fellow ministers at the 1902 Manitoba Conference: "I still feel the call to service ... If it were possible, I would still be willing to work under the direction of the Methodist Church. But I must be free to think and speak out my own thoughts, and live out my own life." His attempted resignation of 1907 was a ploy to secure permanent appointment at the All People's Mission in Winnipeg. Upon securing his new position, Woodsworth frankly declared to his cousin C.B. Sissons that "I feel myself free to be myself."[23]

The Methodist denomination was not obdurate in the face of social reform, as Woodsworth contended, nor did it force progressive thinkers to pursue the ideal of Christian service "outside denominational lines."[24] Despite Woodsworth's own fulminations, the Department of Evangelism and Social Service, which had been the creation of the progressives, provided a ready forum for challenging the antiquated theological standards of the Victorian church and already offered a model of a more pluralistic and open church. Perhaps Woodsworth's perception of himself as a voice crying in the wilderness was more the product of his isolation in his first posting as a missionary in the north-western Ontario community of Keewatin, and bespoke his unawareness of larger movements within the Methodist Church. Moreover, his constant anxieties that he was becoming a heretic or agnostic were integrally related to his frustrations over his lack of prominence in the church and revealed a growing personal crisis about his future, both personal and professional. While stranded at Keewatin, where his education and middle-class moral standards precluded any affinity with the lumberjacks and millworkers who made up his congregation, Woodsworth, in the constant stream of letters he sent to his confidant, C.B. Sissons, reveals himself as a troubled and ambitious youth. In them, Woodsworth worried incessantly about whether he should marry, whether he would become a respected leader in his community, and whether he would attain what he considered the ultimate accolade, a theological professorship, preferably at Victoria College.[25] His expressions of religious doubt – what he termed "rationalistic unitarianism" – rose and fell with the degree of social and professional isolation he experienced. Significantly, when his call to Grace Church in Winnipeg offered him an enlarged social circle, intellectual stimulus, and a "recognized standing" in the community, Woodsworth's religious doubts were magically dispelled.

Later in 1902 he agreed to withdraw his resignation when he was told by the church elders that he was not a radical and that his ideas conformed to the progressive ideals increasingly in vogue in the church and when he discovered that he was no longer morally and spiritually isolated.[26] When Woodsworth refused T. Albert Moore's invitation to replace the Rev. Garbutt as field secretary for the Department of Evangelism and Social Service in 1913, the hollowness of his castigation of the church as hopelessly reactionary[27] was exposed for what it really was – the product of an unfulfilled personal ambition to replicate his father's status as a prominent church leader. Despite Moore's assurances that the department encouraged interdenominational activism as well as social rather than "illiberal" moral reform, and that he would be granted "considerable freedom of action,"[28] Woodsworth, ostensibly Western Canada's leading advocate of social reform, rebuffed the overtures.

In terms of Woodsworth's perspective on the need for transforming the church into an institution which fostered social responsibility, his program of reformation diverged little from the mainstream position advanced by Chown, Moore, and Dobson. Like theirs, his Christianity hinged upon making religion a way of life rather than theological dogma and in refashioning the customs of the church so that they were sensitive to the pace of cultural change.[29] In striving to remake Christianity into a religion of experience and practical social service, Woodsworth condemned "the intellectual standpoint with its historical creeds, confessions and standards" and a theology whose "phraseology is antiquated and its terminology almost unintelligible."[30] In believing that personal character and purpose rather than one's theology should define the modern minister, Woodsworth instructed Sissons to "run the theologs out of power" at the Toronto YMCA's city missions, "and thus enable the society to do more effectual work among those who need it."[31] This democratic impulse of Woodsworth's, what he called the transformation of introspective piety into a "socialistic" notion of individual responsibility, was founded, as it was in other progressives, upon a recapturing of the very origin of Methodism, Wesley's ideal of holiness. Although Woodsworth rejected the other-worldliness of eighteenth-century pietism, he maintained that holiness in its modern guise should combine personal piety with social work, education, and moral reform.[32] The social gospel, he declared in 1916, "means repentance of the old-fashioned kind ... It means a new birth – the entrance upon a new kind of life – the setting up of a new social order."[33] In formulating a more socialized religion, Woodsworth consciously rejected the notion that social responsibility was derived from Platonic social ethics – for in his view all Revelation had its source in God.[34] His advocacy of social service grew directly from his rediscovery of the riches of the "old gospel" of Christian service, even though it was intended as a response to modern social issues.[35]

Woodsworth's insistence upon personal holiness as the foundation-stone for modern social service derived from his extremely conservative upbringing by his missionary father. Although Woodsworth would state years later that he had never experienced directly the Almighty,[36] his diary reveals otherwise. On 10 August 1896 he wrote of a "friend" who knelt beside him praying for salvation: "there and then he took the step and gave himself to Christ, and there was joy among the angels in heaven as well as in our hearts ... Oh I have had too little faith but I believe there is going to be a baptism from on high in this community. May God give me grace and power to work for him – thank God for our midnight conversation. It has made me very happy." And at a prayer meeting three days later Woodsworth's evangelicalism was again evident when he recorded that he felt the presence of God.[37]

The mainstay of Woodsworth's preaching in the latter years of the nineteenth century reflected a powerful awareness of the personality of God and emphasized the importance of holiness and conversion.[38] His persistent self-doubt, what several recent historians have characterized as a gradual descent into unbelief, might be interpreted better as the traditional search for perfection that was so integral to the Methodist experience. Woodsworth's encounter with his first "confessed agnostic" led him not to abandon his faith but to try to become even more like Christ.[39] So powerful were the traditional imperatives of holiness and conversion that even when he had ostensibly left the Methodist ministry and turned to the "secularist" doctrines of political socialism, he continued to interpret his activities in explicitly religious terms. Writing to Violet McNaughton in 1925 about the vicissitudes of building a popular constituency for a party devoted to democratic socialism, he declared: "I feel like the early missionaries in the Southern Seas who before they could preach repentance had to teach people the idea of sin and invent a name for God!"[40]

In certain important respects Woodsworth's perspectives on theological questions were distinctly more "conservative" than those of his older colleagues, S.D. Chown and T. Albert Moore. What Woodsworth defined as "radicalism" in theology must be treated with some care: while at Wesley College in Winnipeg he considered John Mark King, an unimpeachably orthodox advocate of biblical theology, the most radical of his professors. More tellingly, in 1902 his fears concerning his faith were assuaged by a letter from Chancellor Burwash of Victoria College who, by bringing the young minister "into greater light," would certainly not, as a stout defender of biblical truth, have been directing him towards "liberal" social ethics.[41] In the wake of biblical criticism, what troubled Woodsworth, who had been raised on a literalist reading of the Bible, was that he would have to relinquish definite doctrinal conclusions in order to make Methodist doctrines consistent with modern "humanity." Despite his reservations that, with historical criticism, authority in religion now rested upon the less certain foundation of individual consciousness, Woodsworth assured Burwash that his "faith in God and in his personal guidance has not been, and I think, can never be shaken."[42] Even though Woodsworth had come to value the need for a Christianity concerned with society, this did not in any way impede his commitment to individual conversion that was so much a feature of the traditional evangelism of his youth, as was illustrated by the fact that in 1905 he was contemplating undertaking missionary work in China or Japan.[43] And, when he finally departed from the institutional church in 1918 his decision was based almost exclusively upon his opposition to the church's official defence of the war and did not mark a decisive loss of belief in God. Because Woodsworth maintained that the measure of one's religiosity was measured by participation in practical social service and that this meaningful behaviour of social responsibility was not limited to the institutional church, he viewed his resignation as a profound expression of godliness. In language reminiscent of his earlier descriptions of his relationship with God, Woodsworth recounted to the Rev. A.E. Smith that he "must obey God rather than men" by following the truth "that is revealed to me," and that by doing so he was experiencing "a growing sense of fellowship with the 'Master.'"[44] In the context of Woodsworth's relations with the Methodist Church, being a "radical" in theology, as he described himself, meant a rejection of scholasticism in favour of practical activism, and implied less a dilution of personal faith than an re-engagement with the Wesleyan evangelical experience that Woodsworth, and other progressives, believed provided the remedy for the social unrest of their democratic age.

It was because progressive churchmen clung so tenaciously to the bedrock of evangelical traditions that they beheld with surprising confidence modern culture, which seemingly encouraged the hedonistic pursuit of pleasure, self-interest, and the ruthless competitiveness of business. Quite imperceptibly, the values, attitudes, and language of twentieth-century life were integrated into the evangelical perspective. Emblematic of the ability of evangelism to adapt to modern culture without relinquishing its integrity was T. Albert Moore's reflection on revivalism: "When by our own endeavor and His Grace, we have been tuned to Him as the wireless receiver is to the transmitter, the revival will be here."[45] Here, technology merely served as a more sophisticated vehicle for expressing the individual's direct spiritual encounter with the Almighty.

A few ministers complained that their parishioners were not tuned to God but were interested only in skating, hockey, and movies. The Rev. James D. Orr, for one, was dismayed to discover an abiding disregard for churchgoing on the Prairies, where farmers had, he claimed, "drifted into utter carelessness about anything else except wheat and pleasure."[46] While urban ministers rightly deplored the introduction of the automobile, which drew middle-class parishioners from church services to country picnics, rural ministers saw a dramatic upsurge in church membership with the arrival of the inexpensive Ford.[47] More often than not, however, ministers responded to these incursions upon the church not with despondency but with an overweening confidence, as did the Rev. H. Whitely of Sintaluta, Saskatchewan. Buoyed by faith in their peculiarly evangelical belief that the modern obsession with popular amusements was characteristic of "the prophetic period preceding a period of revival,"[48] these clergymen believed that the challenges presented by modern culture formed just another cycle in their history. Evangelicalists had always seen in the record of human society a constant ebb and flow between periods of depression and of spiritual complacency, which undergirded religious awakening.[49] Indeed, many ministers actually welcomed the presence of such social problems as intemperance and other manifestations of public immorality – what recent historians have interpreted as symptoms of religious decline[50] – because they presaged a renewal of spiritual commitment. Hence, Woodsworth commented in 1901: "Sometimes I feel like praying for famine or pestilence or an earthquake to arouse the people."[51]

Many ministers discerned in the social instability that engulfed Canada between 1900 and 1930 a marvellous and unprecedented opportunity for the church. This attitude was not the disillusionment following a failure to stem the tide of secularization. While Hugh Dobson perceptively identified the various challenges presented to the church, he nonetheless expressed an unflinching optimism in the ability of the church to accommodate modern culture:

> There never was greater need of leadership along our lines of work than there is at the present time and I doubt if ever in the history of the church such leadership would bring greater results than it will bring today. I am not overlooking that the path will be beset with difficulties, but there is such a state of plasticity and instability of the public mind on many questions that now is the day to convert that mind to the point of view which is more distinctly Christian and social in its outlook. I find among people today, in their mental attitudes, a very high degree of convertibility. More than I have ever known before. That is our opportunity. The measure of our difficulty always exactly corresponds to the measure of our opportunity.[52]

Dobson witnessed in the social ferment of the period the elements creating a psychological mind-set favourable to mass conversion. The optimistic assertion of the progressive contingent within the Methodist and Presbyterian churches that true Christianity could provide a coherent middle way between passive capitulation and resistance to the vagaries of modern social trends was neither naïve nor an expression of self-delusion. Clergymen were not simply sidewalk spectators of the progressive age, but must be viewed as key actors who both witnessed and actively shaped the new mentalities and organizations which had developed to cope with modernity. In defining an outlook that balanced the notion of personal fulfilment with the ideal of social cooperation, these clergymen, by privileging experience and social action over introspection and by fostering a democratic view of community premised on social responsibility, participated in the vanguard of the transatlantic currents of thought that were transforming classical liberal individualism.[53] Far from observing their society through traditional lenses, these reformist clergymen in their lives incarnated the contemporary impulses they hoped to shape.

S.D. Chown was not unaware of the "great complexity of modern life" that compelled the church to undertake the ongoing study of "the social and intellectual conditions of our times," thus propelling Christianity towards a more social outlook.[54] Ernest Thomas, whose early ministrations had been conducted in the urban slums of London, England, witnessed the impact of industrialization in Canada, and concluded that the "simpler individualism" suited to a pioneering stage of society was yielding to the realization that the modern personality must now be conceived in terms of "new aggregations" of economic and political groups.[55] Similarly, Woodsworth pleaded for an understanding of individual behaviour in terms of the wider social organism and aptly likened the interdependence of urban life to a spider's web – pull one thread and you pull every thread. Like other progressive ministers, Woodsworth did not merely reflect upon the social repercussions that the extension of the franchise in 1897 implied, but he also placed the church at the forefront of change by ascribing to it the duty of tutoring the unleashed masses in the art of self-government and inner discipline that only Protestantism could provide.[56] This stood in contrast to the pleadings of the defenders of theological intellectualism, who concluded that the "future of the Church, especially its efficiency with the educated classes, rests upon the consistency of its Apologetics."[57] D.N. McLachlan, a Presbyterian advocate of social Christianity and later head of the Department of Evangelism and Social Service, formulated a very astute analysis of modern society. He argued that the sense of individual alienation and social disunity of modern life was the result of industrialization which, having eroded traditional craftsmanship of home manufacture, had destroyed the village community based upon uniform face-to-face social relationships.[58] One of the Methodist

Church's special workers, Beatrice Brigden, who is best known for her lectures on social purity, was also a keen observer of the impact of modern culture on local communities. Her interest in lecturing to girls and women on the competitiveness of modern business life was a direct, pragmatic response to the changing patterns of courtship which necessitated ever longer periods of work for single women before marriage.[59]

The reason why the mainline Protestant churches did not become irrelevant between 1900 and 1940 was precisely their ability to define social problems and respond constructively to them. Presbyterian Church activists consistently maintained that Protestantism was obligated to offer solutions to the complexities of modern living by applying the teachings of Christ to all human affairs, for it was Christianity which had been instrumental in uncovering social injustice.[60] The church's remarkable achievement was that, through the evangelism of social service, its cultural authority actually expanded in the changed conditions of modern industrial society. In the words of D.N. McLachlan, it successfully demonstrated to the archetypal "modern man" that he could be at once modern and also Christian.[61]

Although the modern consumer culture certainly contributed to a more pluralistic society, it was not, however, viewed by progressive clergymen as an insurmountable obstacle to the Christianization of society. When ministers assailed materialism they were not referring to the growth of popular amusements, but were pointing very specifically to what they considered their most dangerous ideological competitor for the allegiance of ordinary Canadians, Marxist socialism or economic determinism. T. Albert Moore denounced Bolshevism as "licensed immorality" because it made labour and not capital the basis of social organization and held out the real threat that the proletariat would dictate to all other classes and thus raise the spectre of an antidemocratic society. Moore compared Bolshevism to fundamentalist premillennialists, for they both opposed social reform.[62] The Rev. J.M. Singleton of Outlook, Saskatchewan, feared that these "modern cults" might lure people away from Christianity and thus incite social unrest.

While progressive ministers like C.W. Gordon encouraged the social equality implied by the new democracy because they believed it fulfilled the unselfish spirit of Christianity, they also feared that unless the church intervened to "mediate and direct" these social movements, socialism might win the allegiance of the masses.[63] As S.D. Chown bluntly informed his audience of Methodist ministers who were as yet unawakened to the necessity of social reform, the church had to choose between "an un-social religion, which cannot be Christianity," and "a system of social salvation, without religious impact or influence." Between the unpalatable alternatives of traditional élitist theology and materialist socialism lay the new spirit of social service. "We must Christianize our democracy," proclaimed Chown, "and democratize our Christianity at one and the same time or accept the failure of both."[64] Similarly, Ernest Thomas called for a new morality within the church, whereby ministers would take the lead in resolving questions of public health, class relations, and the building of a community life based upon cooperation, as the safe path between Bolshevism and reactionary capitalism.[65] Although often perceived as a radical because he advocated initiatives that would bring the working classes within the fold of the church, Thomas, in the aftermath of the Winnipeg General Strike, informed Woodsworth that he anticipated the "impending collapse of the whole Russian lie and deception" and a return to a more "reasonable state of mind."[66] In other words, Thomas welcomed working-class values as long as they evolved within the framework of a Christian culture.

It has become conventional to perceive the clergy's sympathy for working-class aspirations, especially during the Winnipeg General Strike, as confirmation of the adherence of men like Woodsworth, William Ivens, and Salem Bland to socialist ideology.[67] It should be kept in mind, however, that when many clergymen referred to socialism they actually meant social cooperation, which they believed grew directly out of a spiritual ideal of harmony founded upon Christianity. Thus, when the Rev. William Keal informed Hugh Dobson that more "Christian Socialism" was needed in the churches, he meant that a greater interest in social questions based upon the principles of Christianity had to be developed among the people in order to combat the "excesses of Bolshevism."[68] D.N. McLachan carefully outlined the subtle differences which the progressives discerned between socialism and a "socialized" Christianity: "There can be no doubt that the trend of to-day is toward socialization. Most people believe in some form of Socialism. It is the extremes they dread. Slowly the doctrine of the solidarity of Humanity is being understood and to the extent in which it is recognized, men are thinking, planning and governing in terms of this belief ... They realize that individual welfare must not be taught apart from social obligations."[69] It was upon the basis of this ideal of a wider social democracy that Chown could accept an increased role for the state in urban planning and the regulation of public utilities. However, in outlining his social critique, Chown firmly declared that there existed a vast gulf between a socialism that is "material" and one that was derived from Christian belief.[70]

Ultimately, most progressive ministers eschewed the political manifestations of socialism because they undermined the solidarity of the community by pitting class against class and because they struck at individual conversion, the very foundation of evangelism. "I am persuaded," wrote Chown, that "you cannot reform society on a secular basis. A regenerated society can come only through the influence of regenerated individuals."[71] Even among those clergymen who adopted a far more consistently "social" definition of religion and whose sympathies lay more overtly with the labour movement, community solidarity took precedence over socialist ideology. Prior to joining the Communist Party of Canada in 1925, the Rev. A.E. Smith stood at the forefront of the Methodist Church's efforts to reach out to a working-class constituency. As minister of People's Church in Brandon, Manitoba, Smith's preaching was anchored explicitly upon the biblical text of the Old Testament and aimed to awaken the modern church to the same social rifts that had characterized the history of ancient Israel. Smith informed his largely working-class audience that commercial and agricultural prosperity had created two distinct types of religion, one, little different from paganism, centred around the "official prophets" and the aristocracy, and the other, an older, purer religious tradition based upon the nomadic life of the Hebrews, expressed in the teachings of the "protestant prophets."[72]

The appeal to biblical history carried a clear lesson for both Smith's working-class congregation and the leadership of the church: the purest form of Christianity was expressed in the old popular revivalistic traditions of the common people of Canada. It was an undogmatic form of Christianity, based upon "personal experience" and participation in "Holy Communion," and through it Smith appealed to the still-lively popular memory of camp-meetings and seasons of religious revivals.[73] Smith's emphatic statement that "The Peoples Church has no creed and never intends to have one"[74] should be read not as a watering down of Christian commitment in the name of a secular socialist ideal, but as an urgent plea to the Methodist Church to recover its roots in the vital spirituality of the common people. Only by channelling popular revivalism into a social awakening could the churches bridge class distinctions, and by transcending their constricting heritage of dogma assert their spiritual freedom.[75] For Smith, the expression of a "socially-minded Christianity" was the only way to avoid social cleavage, which he considered the bane of true democracy.[76] William Ivens, the foremost champion of the Labor Churches in Winnipeg, endorsed Chown's view of Christian socialism when he stated "that for the Socialist movement to become divorced from its religious roots was for it to begin to die."[77] Writing to A.E. Smith from prison following his activities during the Winnipeg General Strike, Ivens stated his conviction that religion, not political socialism, was the way of salvation for Canadian workers:

[I]f religion for a period is not eclipsed, the Labour Church will have to keep the heart of the workers true to *Real* religion – if it does not then the spirit of materialism will presently sweep all before it like a raging storm.

What the world needs today, after its orgy of hate, destruction, and blindness, is *Brotherhood.* I mean, *real* brotherhood. The kind that includes an effective Brotherhood of Man. Until such is realized, the Fatherhood of God must be but an unrealized dream. Religion is Life, & Life is religion. Individualism with all its sordidness must be replaced by cooperation or brotherhood. But then, that takes us too far ahead for today.[78]

In keeping with the temper of debate on social questions in both the United States and Britain, progressive ministers grounded their defence of the public welfare and of a renewal of community life upon a notion of social solidarity that was at bottom fundamentally Christian in its outlook.[79] By so defining social cooperation in terms of individual Christian values and attitudes rather than of any specific economic and political program of working-class radicalism, progressive clergymen established a view of social reconstruction which, while spurred on by the ferment of doctrinaire socialism on the margins of political dissent, appealed most directly to a broad spectrum of reformist liberal sentiment. Because their position on social problems encompassed such a wide middle ground between unconstrained capitalism and economic socialism, and their moral ideal of the Kingdom of God on earth so invitingly held out the prospect that social equality could be realized, the inclusive concept of class relations espoused by these clergymen enabled working-class Canadians to participate in the wider evangelism. Although these debates, which revolved around the question of redefining the individual in terms of his social environment, were the product of discussions among a largely middle-class clergy, it must also be recognized that the churches actively sought the participation of labour in the reconstructed community.

While certainly responding to the labour upheavals of 1919, the Presbyterian minister D.N. McLachlan declared in 1920 that "it is a grave mistake to suppose that all labour men are irreligious because they are out of fellowship with the organized Church. The majority of those who are members of Labour Organizations are readers and thinkers. They have their own views of Christianity, which they do not call by that name." And, in order to harness this popular spirituality, he exhorted ministers to copy the methods of labour leaders by undertaking mass street-preaching rallies.[80] Despite T. Albert Moore's aversion to the violence of the Winnipeg General Strike, this labour protest did succeed in moving the Methodist Church towards a more open-minded recognition of their working-class constituency. Although the Methodists had made tentative overtures to the labour movement prior to the war, the events of 1919 in Winnipeg inaugurated a new engagement with labour interests and allowed the mending of the serious rupture between the Department of Evangelism and Social Service and those Winnipeg clergymen who defended the rights of the workers. This was demonstrated by the fact that in 1923 J.S. Woodsworth, William Ivens, and other labour leaders shared a platform with evangelical ministers and "worked heroically for Prohibition."[81] In 1921 Moore recommended that all Methodist preachers read *The Problem of Labor in the World To-Day* by the political economist Robert MacIver and the pamphlet *Christian Churches and Industrial Conditions* by A.E. Smith, the latter despite, or perhaps because of Smith's departure from the Methodist Church to establish a People's Church in Brandon, but even here Moore gingerly added the codicil: "We hope you will not think we are 'rushing' in where Angels fear to tread."[82]

Although church conservatives in the Manitoba Conference forced A.E. Smith, the most forceful advocate of the alliance between the churches and the working class, to leave the Methodist ministry in 1920, his later adherence to Communism was not indicative of hostility to Christianity. Indeed, until 1924 he continued to preach the tenets of social evangelism in both the Brandon People's Church and the Toronto Labour Temple, for he regarded Christianity as the means to unify a labour movement plagued with "apathy" and riddled with internal divisions between radicals and conservatives.[83] Just prior to joining the Communist Party, Smith was angling to find a way of returning to the Methodist ministry; he approached W.B. Creighton, editor of the *Christian Guardian*, with a proposal to write a series of articles on unemployment in Toronto, and, through the agency of the Sociological Fellowship of Canada, he delivered lectures on "Human Society" in various churches. Creighton's rebuff to his journalistic overtures was perhaps the chief catalyst in driving Smith irrevocably from the church.[84] Despite his "conversion" to the militantly atheistic Communist movement,[85] the consistent note of Smith's later career was expressed in his belief, articulated two decades after his conversion, that "[t]he world of the common man is filled with religious fervour" and that ordinary Canadians, "especially those who can be described as 'class-conscious workers' [are] possessed of the spirit of Jesus."[86] As a Communist, Smith saw his special mission much like the one he had while a preacher at Brandon, that of awakening the churches to their responsibility of providing effective leadership for the working-class Canadian. Writing to Mrs Mary Birchard in 1947, he declared that "[t]he day will come when a man will have to be a communist to be accepted as a Christian."[87] Despite her disavowals of the label "Socialist,"[88] Beatrice

Brigden, the Methodist social service travelling lecturer, was much concerned that the church should attempt to appeal especially to "our Socialist friends," in the belief that this would in turn strengthen their crusade to make social Christianity the dominant force within the Methodist Church. As one of the advocates of the broad centre of Christian reformism, Brigden was amused to find, during one of her social service recitals in Melfort, Saskatchewan, that she was caught between pietistic Holiness people seated on one side of the church and socialists who occupied the other. The symbolism of this was not lost on her. However, she was immensely pleased when the socialists responded enthusiastically to the new openness exhibited by the Methodist Church to all social classes. Her experience at Melfort provoked her to observe in a letter to her chief and mentor, T. Albert Moore: "what a pity so many of those really fine men and women are not using their ability in the church."[89]

Generally speaking, the Methodist Church lagged behind the Presbyterian both in offering a critique of industrial capitalism and in seizing the opportunity to enlist the sympathies of labour. Only after World War I did the Methodists regularly support an agenda of democratizing industry based on shorter working hours and a living wage, and concede the important principle that labour unrest resulted not from a failure of individual morality but was a symptom of a dehumanized capitalist system.[90] By contrast, as early as 1908 J.G. Shearer, secretary of the new Presbyterian Board of Moral and Social Reform, wrote articles on social evangelism for the labour press and introduced a series of motions to regulate child labour and the sweated trades and to establish shorter hours of work. That same year the Presbyterian Church initiated a series of conferences and round tables expressly designed to invite the opinions of working men on various moral, social, and economic questions.[91] This particular interest in the working people of Canada on the part of the Presbyterian Church was given deeper expression than in Methodism in so far as it engendered a wholesale reinterpretation of Jesus Christ as a working man. "The church that fails the working man," warned C.W. Gordon, "departs from allegiance to Christ." More importantly, by framing a style of preaching that focused directly on the interests and needs of the working class, the Presbyterians put into practice their belief that the worker and the capitalist should be treated equally. In 1914 the church arranged for the American Charles Stelzle, himself a worker turned clergyman, to conduct a series of shop meetings in the polarized labour climate of Winnipeg, and these at once beat back the inroads of atheistic socialism and provided a fillip to the fledgling social service movement within the church. As C.W. Gordon informed J.G. Shearer, Stelzle was at first heckled unmercifully by the "fiercest Socialists," but his message of Christian democracy soon earned him the warmest approbation of the workers who crowded into the Labor Temple in Winnipeg:

One man said if we had more meetings like these in the Churches there would be less distance between the Churches and the working people. Indeed it was quite pathetic to see the eagerness with which these men who the first night were so fiercely hostile and bitterly opposed to the church seemed to welcome even this slight appearance of interest on the part of the Christian people. Mr. Stelzle left our social forces here very much stronger indeed than he found them.[92]

Despite Stelzle's successes, progressive leaders knew that the struggle to establish a consensus around the ideal of social service was a formidable one. Ernest Thomas recognized that the authority of the church colleges was still powerfully entrenched and that "reformers and progressives" were often stifled "when they s[ought] to propagate their opinions."[93] It should be kept in mind that the Methodist Department of Temperance and Moral Reform, the forerunner of the Department of Evangelism and Social Service, had been created in 1902 for the express purpose of placing social Christianity on the same plane as evangelism. As S.D. Chown, its first secretary, stated: "The Church cannot stand divided against itself half slave and half free. It cannot stand in ethical slavery and evangelistic freedom."[94] The creation of this new department within the Methodist Church was not without controversy because it entailed a radical departure in establishing, for the first time, formal interdenominational links with the Presbyterians, Anglicans, and Baptists. Chown obdurately opposed the surrender of Methodist autonomy over the formulation of the agenda of reform, fearing a watering down in the priority Methodists traditionally assigned to temperance in the name of wider cooperation. Although he was a leader in advocating social service and pressed for the teaching of Christian sociology in the church colleges, he nevertheless gave pride of place to the more traditional moral questions, and in 1908 he opposed the constitution of the new interdenominational Moral and Social Reform Council of Canada because its mandate extended beyond the promotion of temperance and political purity and the battle against gambling and the "social evil."[95] Chown was thus viewed by less traditional reformers, such as Albert Carman, as an obstacle to the creation of interdenominational unity on social questions and as a brake to the expansion of church authority in the wider culture. Although an adamant opponent of the higher criticism,[96] Carman held clearly modern views regarding the need for an efficient and centralized church organization and for attention to be brought to a broad range of social questions appropriate for an industrial society. Carman therefore rejected Chown's more isolationist views, telling him that his outmoded vision of moral reform would have "disgraced" and "killed" Methodism. The Presbyterians, who also desired a consolidation of energies in the area of social reform, were ecstatic when in 1910 T. Albert Moore, with a more "national" outlook, replaced Chown as secretary.[97] Alerted to the American situation where secular social reform had displaced the churches from their position of leadership, Presbyterian progressives, such as J.G. Shearer and C.W. Gordon, urgently argued for centralized organization and unity of purpose, fearing that if social reform were left to individual churches, along the Victorian model, Protestant institutions would ultimately become "isolated" and irrelevant.[98]

When Moore took office in 1910 there was a decisive shift in emphasis away from narrowly conceived moral reform and that quintessentially Methodist concern with temperance, and this shift permitted an assertive interdenominational spirit. As Moore informed Woodsworth, because the General Conference had ratified his recommendations concerning the teaching of sociological questions in the church colleges, the Department of Evangelism and Social Service had decided to interpret its mandate in the widest possible manner. In fact, this decision on the part of the church as a whole gave the department a power base from which it grew exponentially during the next decade. "This action has been interpreted by us," observed Moore, "as giving us the widest possible liberty as to the subjects we would give attention in the conduct of our work. You will therefore see that the General Conference has dealt very kindly with us in the matter of allowing us to go into the broad field of social service and endeavour to bring forth the highest results for the cleansing of conditions, the uplift of citizenship and the betterment of humanity."[99] The department's role, which was initially intended to guide the church in addressing social problems, expanded to include all research on social policy and to advising provincial and federal governments in social legislation, thus establishing the very terms in which evangelism was interpreted within the modern church. In short, the Department of Evangelism and Social Service became the most powerful force within the institutional church and it attempted to reshape twentieth-century Protestantism in its image.[100]

It was after 1910 that the departments of evangelism and social service in both the Methodist and Presbyterian churches launched their programs of "aggressive evangelism." Their purpose was to stimulate the idea of service through a ten-fold increase in the number of social workers, of whom the most prominent were Beatrice Brigden (Methodist) and Miss Ratte (Presbyterian), William L. Clark (Methodist), a recent convert from Roman Catholicism who lectured on sex hygiene, and Hugh Dobson (Methodist), whose specialty was organizing national child welfare and social reconstruction exhibits. Recognizing that holding special social service sermons on Sunday was not sufficient to arouse the people to their wider responsibilities within the community, T. Albert Moore was instrumental in making "Evangelistic propaganda" more effective by creating a bureau of specialist lecturers who ensured that the message of social Christianity could be heard every day of the week. And because these lecturers met their own financial needs by fund-raising in each community they visited, this particular social agenda was free from interference from more conservative fiefdoms within the church, such as the boards of home missions. In addition to this network of social workers, the Methodist and Presbyterian churches established a series of special institutes, summer courses in social service training, labour bureaus, social surveys, redemptive homes, and settlement houses, and they promoted as well a broad program of social legislation ranging from workman's compensation to child labour and housing reform. Believing as they did that all social reform must be explicitly Christian, these churches aggressively absorbed a number of previously independent reformist agencies, such as the Young Men's Christian Association, the Women's Christian Temperance Union, Family Altar Leagues, and the Brotherhood Movement under their aegis. From the perspective of the Presbyterians, social work entailed "a positive, definite, aggressive, evangelical, evangelistic propaganda. The work must be correlated under one leadership and work to one great aim and purpose – to Christianize, definitely and consciously to put the Spirit of Christ into the lives of men, and to bring men into conscious and confessed relationship to Him."[101]

These grandiose ideals of "aggressive evangelism," however, depended for their realization upon a large phalanx of dedicated and energetic social workers, lay volunteers, and local clergymen. They were expected to emulate the heroic example of Hugh Dobson, the field secretary for Western Canada, who delivered on a peripatetic basis two or three sermons and lectures daily. Those, like S.D.Chown, T. Albert Moore, and J.G. Shearer, who mapped out the new strategy for social service from their headquarters in Toronto, exemplified this injunction to constant activity in order to achieve the Christianization of Canadian society. And, despite personally experiencing a great deal of psychological and physical pressure as a result of their obsessive dedication to ushering in the Kingdom of God, these social service leaders remained sharply indifferent to the impoverished working conditions of most local ministers, especially the young probationers assigned to rural parishes.

Dobson well expressed the overbearing expectations of the progressive leadership in one of his many directives intended to rally the district secretaries under his charge:

I doubt if any ministers of the past ever had the opportunity we preachers have today. One cannot have patience with Secretaries who cannot find anything to do. This was an excuse we heard much of three or four years ago, but anyone using it today, must be blind and without fitness for Christian leadership. Our religion is a religion of victory. We cannot fail if we do what is right. With man be the effort, with Heaven the success."[102]

Many of the rural ministers, who comprised the majority of the clergy well into the 1940s, found it difficult to maintain the enthusiasm necessary to awaken their congregations to the principles of social responsibility when, on meagre salaries of $1,200 a year, they lived a life of drudgery and penury. Often, young ministers were forced to supplement their incomes by peddling insurance, selling farm machinery, cattle dealing, or undertaking secretarial work, and they naturally balked at having to deliver addresses and sermons other than those their congregations expected.[103] Moreover, there was the persistent problem of ministers unwilling to surrender personal autonomy by working within the increasingly complex and demanding bureaucracy of the Department of Evangelism and Social Service. Even Salem Bland, one of the champions of social service, refused, just as had Woodsworth, to relinquish "personal arrangements" to work for T. Albert Moore.[104] Although most ministers quietly registered their protest against the unreasonable demands of the social service efficiency experts through passive resistance, one Saskatchewan clergyman, David Simpson, turned the "statesmanlike utterances" of the church on the subject of the relations of capital and labour against it. "I am waiting," he informed Dobson, "for the Social Service Dept. of our Church to first recognise the unfairness of the Church calling on men to give their lives and their best for the present minimum salary, and if this is recognised, rouse the conscience of the Church on the matter and *demand* a living wage for the ministers." He concluded his grievance with the sarcastic admonition that Dobson should "put your fellow-labourers on the same level that you do the booze-fighters, drug-addicts, prostitutes, [and] the unborn."[105]

The poor working conditions of the local clergymen were not the only obstacles to the fulfilment of the social service ideal. A more serious opposition to the aspirations of the departments of evangelism and social service lay in the persistent tension between the advocates of the wider evangelism, who envisioned a national and homogeneous church, and college-trained clergymen, whose horizons were bound to local middle-class élites upon whom they depended for financial support. These clergymen adhered to an older view of ministerial autonomy founded upon an élite education combined with a localist vision of social relationships, and this autonomy acted to check the incursions of the centralized bureaucratic impulse implied in progressivism. As late as 1919 the social service wing of the Methodist Church was still meeting considerable opposition from those ministers who wished to consign it to a safe institutional backwater. Drawing on the parallel of the defeat in 1919 of the "old parties" by the progressive farmer and labour coalition in Ontario, Dobson described the divisions within the church to his friend John B. Andrews, the secretary of the American Association for Labor Legislation: "We met a great deal of opposition in our Church in regard to the stand taken on Reconstruction at our last General Conference in Hamilton and for a time there appeared to be some ground for fear, but we are swinging again into control."[106] The conflict between the progressives and the church colleges within the Protestant churches also involved a gulf between those who defined the church solely in terms of its narrowly denominational institutional structure and the social service leadership which interpreted Christianity in wider cultural terms to allow the modern minister to fulfil his call in a vast range of professional guises and activities, from social worker to politician. As Dobson himself recognized, his course of action meant that Methodist doctrine would be eroded, for, as he stated, "we have risked the Church as an Institution itself for the sake of the cause of humanity."[107]

The difficulty in accomplishing the task of grafting the concept of service onto so large an institution as the church was poignantly revealed in the lengthy correspondence carried on between 1914 and 1921 between Beatrice Brigden, in her capacity as a special social service worker for the Methodist Church, and T. Albert Moore, the head of the Methodist Department of Evangelism and Social Service. In her constant travels to the small towns and villages of the Maritime provinces and the Canadian Prairies, Brigden was constantly confronted with the profound entrenchment of the Victorian model of the locally autonomous clergyman, whose frequent opposition to social service belied the vision of a smooth path towards consensus propagated by such official church organs as the *Christian Guardian*. The blandly optimistic catch-phrase uttered by Ernest Thomas in 1908 that "we are all social reformers now" was very much the statement of one of the progressive inner circle, whose task it was to inspire and rally in order to create that very consensus between traditional individualistic evangelism and the newer social Christianity.[108] Hugh Dobson's conclusion in 1917 that there was developing among ordinary believers a quickening interest in social evangelism must be read in a similar vein.[109]

Brigden's less than optimistic reports to Moore on the sometimes outright hostility with which local ministers and their congregations responded to social evangelism, as well as on their backwardness, accordingly reflected her position as one of the rank-and-file social workers who had to endure a daily round of criticism and rejection while receiving only half the wages of the most poorly paid male clergy.[110]

Although it is tempting to interpret the often grudging reception given to Brigden as a response to her sex, her role as a transitional figure between an antiquated "Victorian" moralism and later twentieth-century "secular" feminism should not be overstated.[111] Certainly Brigden's correspondence was punctuated with such observations as "I believe I would make a good suffragette"; however, these comments are startlingly infrequent given the conservative nature of her audience and were made only when, as in Alameda, Saskatchewan, a man particularly questioned the abilities of women.[112] Indeed, Brigden was often forced to endure the opprobrium of women's organizations such as the local branch of the Women's Christian Temperance Union in Manitou, Manitoba, which castigated her lectures as "immodest."[113] What is striking is that Brigden was not a suffragette and that, despite deriving immense gratification from her personal talks with young girls and women, she interpreted her role in the same terms as Hugh Dobson: to bring the whole community together in "the gospel of [a] full-orbed development"[114] which combined evangelism with social service. As Brigden herself bluntly stated the matter in 1915, "social service apart from religion is a failure."[115]

If anything, Methodism rather than feminism held pride of place in her thought. There are more frequent disparaging comments on the arrogance and élitism of Presbyterians peppering her correspondence than there are allusions to patriarchy. And, although she suffered frequently at the hands of small-minded male clergymen, the ever astute Brigden interpreted this ill-treatment from the perspective of ongoing tensions between conservatives and progressives rather than ascribing it simply to gender bias. Even one of the leading male progressives, Hugh Dobson, was severely criticized for his views on practical Christianity. At Grand Coulee, Saskatchewan, one member of the congregation believed that Dobson was "crazy," which elicited the rueful comment from Brigden that this was "no doubt complimentary to his breadth of vision."[116] In Manitou Brigden wrote of the Presbyterian minister, a Mr Rolston, that he "despises anything progressive – and even more so anything done by a woman – and if he dared would have refused me admittance to his church I know." In this specific case, Brigden made special note of the fact that Manitou was the home of the then famous suffragette, Nellie McClung, and so quite coincidentally the woman question had entered into the equation.[117] Moreover, despite her later protestations that she was at one with the working people of Canada, her sentiments clearly reflected the concerns of middle-class reformers. She was to remark rather patronizingly of Alameda: "what starved lives some people live [; there is] absolutely nothing in the town of an uplifting nature" outside of the school and the mission circle.[118]

The voluminous correspondence between Moore and Brigden provides a window through which to examine the difficulties that lay in the way of implementing social service at the local level. It also underscores the very personal nature of the relationships which sustained progressivism despite its bureaucratic ethos. Brigden used her weekly reports to Moore as one would a confessional, and thus fulsomely recorded the failures that social service was confronting in small-town Canada. At the same time, Brigden, who was given to recurrent bouts of depression and insecurity about her ability to stir people to action, sought the reassurance of her mentor, Moore, whose role it was to encourage her to continue in work that involved tremendous psychological strain.[119] Brigden had developed a close and trusting relationship with Moore, to whom she confided that "[t]alking the work over with you once in a while means much to me."[120] Not only did Brigden have to endure the stress of constant travel, but she was often billeted with traditional Christians who rudely informed her that she was of a "doubtful class of people." As well, she was constantly pestered about her marital status; one person thought that she had learned her social service principles in a redemptive home for fallen women, and in isolated communities starved for knowledge she was viewed as an encyclopedia and persistently hounded by eager questioners. And, in awakening Newfoundlanders to the cause of social service in 1918, Brigden had to bow to local custom and attend endless "flipper suppers," where the Newfoundland delicacy was served.[121] Moreover, it greatly troubled Brigden that her social purity lectures were often perceived as immodest and forced local women to talk self-consciously in half-whispers and to glance up and down the streets when leaving her meetings.[122]

These letters also demonstrate the subtle ways in which the central leaders adapted their methods and approaches to local conditions. By providing the department with vital information concerning the values and attitudes conditioned by class and region, as well as by ethnicity, Brigden's correspondence ensured that social Christianity was made "versatile"[123] and accessible to all Canadians. Paradoxically, by becoming more sophisticated in tailoring the social service message to various social groups, Brigden was also contributing to the solidification of a national and culturally homogeneous church. Over time, she developed different lectures for farm women and shop-girls; she proposed that advertisements be strategically aimed at farm men, and she often moved her talks from the churches to local theatres or town halls in order to reach non-Methodists and the poor and unchurched. A more telling example of the disjuncture between the centre and periphery was the error – conditioned by the urban bias of the church leaders – of beginning cycles of social service lectures during seed-time or harvest. Brigden constantly complained of poor attendance during these times and forced Moore to change her schedule. Obviously, the Presbyterian progressive leadership was similarly afflicted with these urban blinkers because the Rev. R.H. Lowry of Inverary, Saskatchewan, chastised C.W. Gordon for planning evangelistic campaigns in the middle of the autumn harvest. "Then we are here," complained Lowry, "in these country villages right in threshing time when our evangelist could help more with a pitch fork than with a bible."[124]

Progressive leaders soon realized that the major battle for establishing their authority must be waged against the local churches. The control exercised by the college-dominated Victorian church was formidable precisely because its power was diffused and was moreover sustained by the local clergyman who, by virtue of his theological training, was the representative of the undivided sovereignty of church authority. During her lecture tours Beatrice Brigden was forcibly reminded of the entrenched hold still exerted by the Victorian equation of religion and local power, and she complained to Moore that she could only reach the congregations through the compliance of local pastors.[125] The local clergymen were, however, often unreceptive to the social service message, an attitude particularly blatant in the Maritimes where Brigden's first social service tour began. On 2 June 1914, while speaking in a rural area of Nova Scotia, she was shocked, as a firm believer in the importance of the new social evangelism, to discover the degree to which others in the church did not share her vision. Protesting to Moore, Brigden wrote that "there are some pastors who have absolutely refused to open their churches."[126] This was particularly acute in the conservative rural parishes where the presence of a female social worker and a stranger would have seriously unsettled views of what should constitute a proper religious experience.

Brigden's lectures, even though they sought to remind her audiences that social ills fostered immorality, were nonetheless challenging to people reared on an evangelicalism of intensely private, inner spirituality. Recognizing that social work of this kind was a novelty, Brigden mused that "some folks will probably be many weeks regaining the perpendicular in their vertebral column."[127] To underscore the degree to which the new social Christianity won more ready acceptance in urban centres, she reported that in Halifax alone she received both the support of the clergy and ample subscriptions from their congregations.[128] However, when her lecture circuit shifted to rural communities the results were a devastating defeat for the cause of social service. Brigden found that male pastors not only refused to cooperate and to answer her queries regarding coordinating her speaking schedule with church events, but also regularly sabotaged her lecture engagements by feigning ignorance of the advertising material of the Department of Evangelism and Social Service, so that she blamed them for meagre attendance and financial contributions. On 12 June, the "last straw" occurred in Shubenacadie, Nova Scotia. There, Brigden experienced the dual ordeal of sectarian prejudice and of social and theological conservatism. The Presbyterian minister, Mr Burgess, had invited her to speak, but when she arrived he refused to give up his morning service for her. Brigden, who in the end had been given no time to deliver her social evangelistic message, told Moore: "I could stand the personal humiliation if the cause is being furthered." At another church, the Presbyterian pastor was absent on a fishing trip and, although she was allowed to speak, the congregation, without the active endorsement of the pastor, made no financial contribution.[129]

While one might expect this negative response to the novelty of social Christianity in the more traditionalist communities of the Maritimes, where religion had long undergirded conservative social values,[130] it was more surprising that Brigden's experience there was replicated in the Prairie West, the supposed crucible of the social gospel.[131] On the Prairies, ministers trained in the traditional evangelism of the church colleges were just as numerous and the battle to win the church to the ideal of social responsibility was just as hard-fought. This belies the view articulated by some historians that there was an immediate awakening on the part of ministers to the value of social Christianity. "Carnduff is the only town between Brandon and Estevan that made any attempt to open a church for our work," exclaimed a weary and frustrated Brigden. In 1915 only half the ministers in Manitoba and Saskatchewan even deigned to respond to her letters,[132] which induced Brigden to complain to Moore that "there has been some difficulty up this line in making the pastors 'understand,' just what my work is – and they have failed to advertise, and all made the announcements of later meetings as though they would like to apologize for so doing." In very palpable terms, Brigden experienced the larger intellectual divisions within the church between the "old fashioned type of Evangelist" and the new social evangelism. One minister, the Rev. Davis, turned her away because he assumed that she was a traditionalist, while the Rev. F.B. Richardson did so because she was not. Although as a Westerner she took these rejections as a personal slight, Brigden continued to believe in challenging the intellectual theology sponsored by the church colleges. Her faith in the importance of her mission to establish social Christianity was fortified by Moore's sympathy. In response to Brigden's experience of a poor showing in Saskatchewan, Moore consolingly wrote that he hoped "the good people of Lumsden may be less pious and more practical in their piety."[133]

Although often disheartening, these persistent rebuffs actually strengthened Brigden's resolve and provoked her to reflect: "I used to think it strange that some men should have disagreed with Christ – now I am almost glad they did – both the men and Jesus seem so much 'human' and 'twentieth century.'"[134] Indeed, the church colleges also did not meekly accept the presence of the new evangelism. On 29 October 1915 Brigden was to confront her most overt antagonist in one Rev. Smith who, because he had been recently appointed to Regina College, openly criticized Moore and Dobson and shamelessly demonstrated his disapproval of social service by flatly refusing to turn over the congregation's contribution to the Department of Evangelism and Social Service. Because Smith could use the college as an effective and public platform from which to attack social evangelism, Moore was made aware of the urgent need to silence him and to keep him "in the harness on right lines."[135]

Although Brigden could comment on 11 November 1915 that "the church is gradually awakening," her hopes for a rapid acceptance of the new evangelism were soon dashed in Alameda, Saskatchewan, where "the thought of the few church leaders [seems] to be repression not growth, the usual fatal mistake."[136] In Melita, Manitoba, the congregation was "indifferent" and the leading members of the church directly opposed her work; to add insult to injury, she was ordered to cancel her recital to make room for a Red Cross meeting.[137] However, Brigden was not confronted with unrelieved opposition from clergymen, and she praised the younger ministers, many of whom were from England, such as the Rev. Bray of Davidson, Saskatchewan, whom she described as "a live wire preacher."[138] Ultimately, each local minister could not act arbitrarily and was dependent upon his congregation. Often, the desire of the congregation to listen to Brigden's message of social evangelism, and in particular that of local women who appreciated her lectures on sex education and marriage, overrode the conservatism of recalcitrant clergy. At Metropolitan Methodist in Saskatoon, the Rev. Lewis was compelled to allow Brigden to speak because, as she sardonically observed, the minister would have been a brave man to have opposed the formidable Mrs J.H. Cairns.[139]

The central problem facing the promoters of the new social Christianity was, however, not simply the unfamiliarity of local congregations with the new direction taken by the progressive contingent. By 1916, even after Brigden had lectured in nearly every town and hamlet on the Prairies, in many instances congregations had become less rather than more receptive to social Christianity. "I have not worked in a single church in Alberta," Brigden remarked, "without the pastor giving me the impression that he, and of course his people too, viewed my work with considerable uncertainty and suspicion – and any minute might wash his hands of the whole affair and take to his heels."[140] While Brigden was well aware that Alberta, generally speaking, was more socially conservative than Saskatchewan, she was vexed to find that people in Prince Albert, Saskatchewan, held "a narrow and low vision of truth." Indeed, they had become so inured to the endless procession of social service workers that they had become "quite out of sympathy with our work and hold a chronic grudge against the Conference for afflicting them with such men as A.S. Reid, A.E. Smith, J.A. Doyle, and Clark Lawson, a young man who speaks about 'social things.'"[141] What Brigden's experiences both in Western Canada and the Maritimes demonstrated to progressive leaders such as T. Albert Moore was that the ideal of social Christianity could not be imposed upon people, but could become the centre-piece of modern Christianity only if it was seamlessly interwoven with traditional evangelism and revivalism, both of which commanded wide popular allegiance throughout Protestant Canada.

If the course of social service had been troubled by the entrenched conservatism of local ministers and congregations prior to World War I, the Winnipeg General Strike exacerbated these cleavages. Until 1919 the broad progressive core within the Methodist and Presbyterian churches was effectively able to embrace both the traditional evangelicals and the more ardent proponents of outreach to the working classes. Symbolically, in 1917 the Rev. M.C. Flett, an arch-conservative, and A.E. Smith, whose ministry in North Winnipeg was specially directed to the unchurched masses, together signed the Report of the Committee on Social Service and Evangelism which endorsed a broad spectrum of social reform.[142] This consensus was quickly shattered by the escalating tensions exposed during the strike. In a fulsome letter to Moore, Brigden explained how the strike had, more than the recent war, forced Methodists in Western Canada to take sides. A.E Smith's proposal to establish a People's Church in Brandon in cooperation with the Baptists was first articulated in 1918, when it was viewed as largely innocuous by the Methodist Church leadership, which welcomed the opportunity to create in it a working man's movement. But with the onset of the strike, during which charges of Bolshevism were attached to anyone interested in furthering the demands and in improving the living conditions of the working classes, the Manitoba Methodist Conference was no longer able to sustain the now fragile balance between traditional evangelism and the new social Christianity. By a very narrow margin of 36 for and 32 against, M.C. Flett, Principal Ferrier of Wesley College, and other conservatives voted down Smith's request for a one year's leave of absence. As a long-time friend of Smith, Brigden defended him as a champion of popular Christianity, but she bristled at the accusation that he was a Bolshevik when his only crime had been to instruct workers to stay home. Smith had consistently cautioned against violence and in his open-air address to 2,000 workers had merely led them in singing "Nearer My God to Thee." Brigden claimed that Smith was innocent of any radical associations and that he had been labelled a Bolshevik by Mr S.E. Clement and that "disgruntled politician," H.P. Whidden, the Baptist principal of Brandon College, because they feared that Smith's popularity both among the middle classes and the railway workers of Brandon might unseat Whidden, the Unionist member of Parliament.

In fact, Brigden was so disgusted by this blatant display of political manœuvring that she began to doubt that the Methodist Church possessed either the will or the idealism to reach the "millen[n]ium" of social harmony, and she also feared that it would repeat with the labour movement the mistake it had made in the 1880s of excluding from its ranks the Holiness Movement and the Salvation Army.[143] Although for many years Brigden had recognized the pervasiveness of conservative evangelism within the Methodist Church, her faith in the wider evangelism was shaken by her discovery in 1919 that Moore and other progressive leaders were prepared to compromise not only on the pace of reform but on the very principle of social inclusiveness and democracy that lay at the core of their progressivism. This was confirmed when Moore cooperated with the RCMP in their investigation of the labour churches and indeed facilitated it. As Brigden's respect for Moore was eroded, she brazenly informed him that the church was at a crossroads and that many Methodists "are thinking they see larger fields of service for the Kingdom outside the orthodox church." In the aftermath of the strike Brigden and other so-called "prophets of the new day" temporarily eschewed any social reconstruction founded upon individual redemption.[144] Brigden herself was tempted to join Smith's People's Church in Brandon. "I may say," she informed Moore, "I am greatly interested. Mr. Smith is attempting the thing I have thought about for the last ten years and talked about for five."[145]

Moore, for his part, did not share the views of his RCMP informant, C.F. Hamilton, the erstwhile biographer of Principal George Monro

Grant and a stalwart defender of both a conservative evangelism and a traditional social order. Despite Hamilton's portrayal of A.E. Smith, J.S. Woodsworth, William Ivens, G.L. Ritchie, and Carl Berg as unrepentant anarchists antagonistic to religion and the very notion of the divinity of Christ, it is apparent from his reports that their sermons accorded with a view of the church long advocated by the Department of Evangelism and Social Service. Woodsworth's only critique was directed at denominationalism, while Smith spoke on "The Growing Menace of Socialism" and "Can the Churches be Christianized," all hobby-horses of Moore's. The most radical event occurred on 17 July 1919 when Ivens read from Bellamy's *Looking Backward*. Despite this one departure from orthodoxy, the practice of singing from the "social hymnal," preaching the good news of social redemption, sermonizing on the sinfulness of poverty, and calling the workers to the wider communion of Christ, the services all fell within the purview of mainstream progressivism within the Methodist Church.[146] Brigden's own assessment of the People's Church was that it was no more radical in its social message than her work for the Department of Evangelism and Social Service had been; the only difference was that its activities no longer fell under the direct authority of the Methodist Church. Although the forms of its services were less overtly revivalistic than usual church practice, Brigden stated that every Sunday "there have been new voices heard in prayer at the moving Religious Education Service," what the "Orthodox" Victorian church would have called "so many conversions – praise the Lord."[147] Moore was not antagonistic to the religious views of Smith, nor did he perceive them as more radical than his own. What Moore resented was that Smith's successes were not occurring within the orbit of the church,[148] especially when the cause of social service was under such constant threat from the still lively conservative quarters. With the resurgence of conservative intransigence following the Winnipeg General Strike, Moore realized more than ever that the success of progressive social service required a critical mass of ministers who were committed to the ideal of practical Christianity, and he therefore was impatient with the Woodsworths and Ivenses who placed personal freedom of expression before their duty to the church. There was no division in either theology or social outlook between the so-called "radicals" and "progressives."[149] The disaffection of Woodsworth, Ivens, and A.E. Smith from the Methodist Church was not a reflection of church policy as a whole, but bespoke a visceral reaction to the peculiarities of political relationships within Winnipeg Methodism, where ultraconservative religious forces were temporarily ascendant. In any other context, the three would have gravitated to the church progressives. Indeed, Moore and Dobson were just as restive as Woodsworth with such conservatives as the Rev. Flett who in their estimation had poisoned the religious climate of Winnipeg, and Dobson maintained that "we must deal with Winnipeg with great firmness, but at the same time we must be kind and patient."[150] This was a reflection of their conviction that the struggle for the wider evangelism could best be waged within organizational confines and that the authority of Christianity in Canadian culture must be expressed through the institution of the church.

What the experiences of Beatrice Brigden and the tensions created by the Winnipeg General Strike so graphically demonstrated to progressive leaders was the depth of conservative feeling that prevailed among the local clergy. In response, these leaders initiated a concerted campaign to indoctrinate and re-educate reluctant ministers in the principles of the new evangelism, thus striking at the traditional power base of the church, the autonomous clergyman. As Woodsworth so succinctly stated the matter, ministers had to be "drilled in applied Christianity."[151] Dobson described the constant see-saw of power between the traditionalists and the progressives when he remarked in November 1919 in the aftermath of the strike: "it appeared as though for a while that our element in our Church that concerns itself with the Institution first had delegated us to a place where we would be safe, but the situation at present indicates that we have got the control of the strategic centers; that is, the conduct of field activities through our Church, and preparation of much of the literature."[152] In order to rectify the perceived lack of unity and clearness of conception of an evangelism for the times, one that dealt with civic, social, industrial, and ethical issues, social service leaders effected a transformation of the church bureaucracy, modelled upon corporate business practice, which ensured efficient and centralized control. Three field secretaries worked directly under the general secretary, T. Albert Moore, and each province was divided into ten to twenty-five districts within which there existed eight to fifteen circuits presided over by a social service committee. The field secretaries, like Hugh Dobson, wielded almost baronial power over their districts, in so far as they closely monitored each circuit and directed the taking of surveys of local social conditions, promoted cooperation between the church and other welfare bodies, preached special sermons on social service work, and distributed the latest literature by specialists in Canada, the United States, and Great Britain on the labour movement, child welfare problems, agricultural improvement, immigration, and the city beautiful movement, to name but a few. "In this way," Dobson informed the general secretary of the National Conference of Social Work in the United States, "we are trying to develop the ministry of our church and their churches in the habit of scientific investigation and persistent effort along social lines."[153]

Although this movement towards uniformity, specialization, and bureaucratic efficiency was perfected during the 1920s, it was first initiated by S.D. Chown who, as early as 1908, had called for specialized agents "skilled and competent to deal with the relations of economic problems to the Kingdom of God." He foresaw a disciplined organization led by a series of experts in social and economic questions, publicity, and legislative lobbying.[154] Likewise, the Presbyterian Church promoted uniformity among ministers by creating moral and social reform leagues in every presbytery.[155]

The promoters of the new social evangelism were not mere arm-waving visionaries, so much the staple of the literature on the social gospel. Rather, they were hard-headed, practical organization men – the Canadian counterparts of the American Progressives in their concern to create specialized bureaucratic organizations modelled on modern business efficiency. They were also experts in propaganda and publicity, and they skilfully exploited the advertising revolution then fashionable in the United States. Moore was, in his personal appearance and professional demeanour, indistinguishable from a modern business executive, and as soon as Hollywood became the mecca for filmmaking, he travelled to the United States with a view to instilling Christian values in Canadian mass culture and made a full investigation of the cost to the Methodist Church of entering the movie-making business. In order to undermine the conservative front line, Moore planned a wide-ranging strategy of attack: he took advantage of the harried and time-pressed local ministers by bombarding them with handy sermon outlines on social service work, he mailed out series after series of leaflets, circulars, and memoranda familiarizing ministers with the work of his department, he wrote and distributed both to ministers and government officials a wide range of pamphlets on the mechanics of practical Christianity, and he sponsored national travelling exhibits on reconstruction and child welfare. Here again, the pivotal role of the field secretary was in evidence. On the Prairies, Hugh Dobson was not only responsible for giving all ministers a reading course on social problems – thus circumventing the impact of traditional theological training – but through a torrent of letters responding to the mundane requests of local ministers, Dobson pertinaciously distributed a list of the most up-to-date social science literature. This stratagem implicitly created a new standard for modern ministers and thus rendered them increasingly dependent upon the knowledge of the social service fieldworkers. By 1920 the average minister's mailbox would have been stuffed with posters on reconstruction, lists of new social service hymns, pamphlets such as one entitled "Individual Regeneration and Social Reconstruction," and endless sets of stereopticon slides covering a gamut of topics from venereal disease to the life of John Wesley. When the church colleges were slow to implement recommendations favouring the teaching of Christian sociology, field secretaries were sent directly to the colleges to speak on the issue. And, to ensure that local ministers across Canada cooperated in celebrating Labour Day, Moore's Presbyterian counterpart, J.G. Shearer, set his publicity machine into high gear, and distributed 3,000 copies of *Social Welfare*, the journal of the social service departments of the Protestant churches.[156]

By so effectively controlling the minister's reading material after he left the church college, the Methodist and Presbyterian departments of evangelism and social service not only bypassed such traditional sources of information as church newspapers like the *Christian Guardian* but strategically minimized the impact of traditional theology upon the local minister. Although Dobson's estimation in 1919 that three-quarters of all clergymen had passed through that critical "transition stage" from traditional evangelism to social Christianity[157] was overly optimistic, by the 1920s very few Protestant clergymen remained untouched by the wider social ideals of the new evangelism. The real challenge for the promoters of the new social Christianity, however, ultimately lay not in persuading local ministers of its necessity but in making the social message of a "full-orbed morality"[158] harmonize with the demands of the common people, whose traditions of spirituality remained interwoven with the culture of revivalism. If the progressives, who believed in a wider democracy, clung to an idea of social reform that rested fundamentally upon individual conversion, they did so as a direct response to the ground swell of conservative Protestantism among the majority of Canadians.

2 Reviving the Religion of the Vernacular

Writing to the Rev. C.W. Gordon on 14 January 1912, E. de B. Ramsay, a young office clerk, confided to the celebrated Canadian author of the Ralph Connor novels how the reading of these popular literary works had brought him into close communion with God. For Ramsay, the message of "glad Christianity" expressed in the novels had not only relieved the tedium of office work, but also, in a consumer culture dominated by "material things," renewed his flagging faith in the power of "spiritual intangible things."[1] As this testimonial reveals, Gordon's popular religious novels, far from hastening the secularism of consumer culture, were for some Canadians at least potent inducements for personal conversion. This was especially the case among young, single males like Ramsay who were struggling to escape both their lower middle-class circumstances and the alienation brought on by routinizing and impersonal modern bureaucracies.

The theme of muscular Christianity which so pervaded Gordon's religious fiction was a deliberate strategy intended to attract the increasingly large number of men who, in the estimation of many clergymen, had spurned the conventional worship of the orthodox Protestant churches. More particularly, novels such as *The Prospector*, *Corporal Cameron*, and *The Sky Pilot*, set against the backdrop of the resource frontiers of Canada in the Prairie West and British Columbia, aimed at introducing Christian values to single, male workers who lived beyond the well-established moral and social norms of small-town Protestant institutions in the more settled provinces of Ontario and the Maritimes. That Gordon's novels were instrumental in converting numerous middle-

and working-class Canadians was revealed in the hundreds of letters from reborn Christians who thanked Gordon for the transformation his books had wrought in their lives. The observation of Alfred Fitzpatrick, who worked for the Canadian Reading Camp Association, that Gordon's novels had done much to "arouse interest in the isolated classes of laborers" in the lumber camps, was borne out by the personal experience of the workers themselves. For example, Frederick S. Hartman, a bush-worker from Melville, Saskatchewan, told Gordon how his books had converted him to Christ: "The new life imparted to me ... is constantly manifesting itself to me for I find life worth living now and everything seems sort of to harmonize with me." Not only had Gordon led this bush-worker to a new appreciation of his Galician fellow workers, but Hartman in turn became an evangelist, thus rendering the novels as effective as formal revival meetings in the Christianization of such remote frontier societies. "We read the bible daily," he informed Gordon in 1907, "and pray to the Lord, and I have no doubt that before many days there will be more here added to those that have found the straight and narrow road."[2]

Although Gordon wrote his books largely for a male audience, many women were also touched by them. Upon reading *Black Rock*, a Mrs Lambert confessed to Gordon that for the first time in many years she had "wept and prayed."[3] There were many Mrs Lamberts and there were many Frederick Hartmans. The phenomenal success of the Ralph Connor novels serves as a compelling twentieth-century illustration of the fact that the strength of evangelism had always been its inventiveness, in the absence of permanent institutional bonds, in tapping the well-springs of popular sentiment in order to revitalize Christianity. Where in the eighteenth century preachers used popular ballads and the vernacular language of the rank-and-file as the vehicles for Christianizing the common people, twentieth-century evangelists like Gordon turned to the medium of the dime novel to convert an audience of millions to the tenets of modern practical Christianity. Gordon's voluminous fan mail does not convey the image of creeping secularization;[4] rather, his readers interpreted the message of the novels to be essentially Christian despite Gordon's reliance upon romantic manly activity to provide the central dramatic action.

In North America the dynamism of evangelical culture flowed from a long tradition among Protestant preachers of appropriating popular sentiments and ideology. This fusing of evangelicalism with popular culture has been one of the most distinctive features of the American religious scene from the eighteenth century until the present. According to Nathan O. Hatch, this ability of religious leaders to capture the allegiance of the common people was principally responsible for the continued vitality of Protestant religion in both private and public spheres well into the twentieth century. The upsurges in the influence of popular religious sentiment from the periphery to the mainstream of American culture have taken place within the context of recurrent periods of religious revival referred to by American historians as "Great Awakenings." Each of these revival movements was led by one or more charismatic leaders, and by linking personal piety with public virtue they were responsible for making religion a powerful social force. What each of the great evangelists, from Lorenzo Dow and Charles Finney in the early nineteenth century to Dwight L. Moody and Billy Sunday, the pioneers of twentieth-century mass evangelism, had in common was their extraordinary ability to understand and embrace the popular idiom and to employ the most recent instruments of mass communication in order to make Protestantism more populist and so place it at the forefront of social change. Although revivalists may have consciously utilized non-religious methods, they were instrumental in infusing their society with the tenets of evangelicalism, thereby allowing Protestantism to claim a wider cultural authority than it would have had if it had remained solely within the purview of the social élites whose religious experience drew upon the tradition of intellectual theology.[5]

The intellectualist bias in the historiography of religion, so thoroughly castigated by Hatch in the American context, is an even more prevalent feature of Canadian historical writing. Because most Canadian historians of both the radical and conservative camps, apart from George Rawlyk, have ignored the vital connection between the religious experience and the common people, many recent historians who give pride of place to the intellectual features of Christianity have relegated the interaction of evangelicalism with popular culture to the margin of discussion by characterizing it under the negative rubric of secularization. By defining the strength of Protestantism in terms of its ability to create an intellectually coherent world-view, these historians have mistaken the loss of interest in theology and the resurgence of popular evangelism during the early twentieth century as symptoms of the triumph of secular attitudes. In the period between 1900 and 1930, an age of expanding democracy, the recognition by clergymen of the need to absorb ordinary working Canadians into their evangelical culture and their consequent reacquaintance with popular forms of expression, constitutes, when viewed within the context of popular revivalism established by George Rawlyk, not secularization but another phase in an equally powerful tradition of a religion shaped by popular values. The problem of analysing twentieth-century popular religion rests upon a difficulty of perception that grows out of its proximity to our own more secular age. If we jettison such a presentist outlook and show greater awareness of the historical context, Gordon's popular religious novels, the utilization of the techniques of modern advertising, and the introduction after the turn of the century of the anecdotal sermon appear no less religious than do eighteenth-century circuit-rider Nathan Bangs casting his message of redemption in republican language or Henry Alline writing New Light hymns based on popular ballads in Nova Scotia during the American Revolution.[6]

Between 1790 and 1830 evangelicalism expanded and was able to compete successfully with the Anglican establishment because it embedded itself in the social and political interests of the common people. In both the settlements of the Maritimes and the frontier districts of Upper Canada a strong shared identity was forged between the largely unschooled preachers and their audience of plain-folk by means of vernacular sermons that deliberately avoided theological subtlety in favour of forceful yet simple language and that stressed each person's direct emotional encounter with God. Early Methodists, New Lights, and Baptists closely followed the egalitarian spirit that was prevalent at that time among American evangelicals by incorporating the themes of popular democracy into their exhortations. This movement of religious dissent sought to flout the hierarchical social vision of the Anglican élites, but with the influx after the 1840s of settlers from Britain, where evangelicalism was fragmented by class identities,[7] what Rawlyk has recently called Radical Evangelicalism was forced to the periphery of English Canadian culture. Through the training of a clergy formally instructed in the intellectual conventions of theology, leaders like the Baptist Edward Manning in the Maritimes and the Methodist Egerton Ryerson in Upper Canada shifted evangelicalism away from its moorings in the world of the revival and the camp-meeting towards a preoccupation with institution-building and the promotion of a respectable middle-class, genteel society.[8]

Certainly, from the mid-nineteenth century onwards revivalism came under increasing attack from church leaders who were struggling to divest their church of its populist roots. Until the turn of the twentieth century, when a new group of progressive clergymen were reawakened to the importance of Protestantism's eighteenth-century tradition of class inclusiveness, the college-dominated Protestant churches remained enveloped in a matrix of intellectualism. The alliance between the local clergymen and the college professors strengthened Protestantism during a period of institutional expansion when its middle-class constituency was essential both for the influx of money and for the social prestige it provided. This class bias was rendered obsolete, however, by the social and industrial changes of the late nineteenth century, when the attendant broadening of the franchise brought into renewed prominence the desires and values of the long-neglected popular element. Beneath the concern about declining church attendance, especially of men, lay a profound recognition that Protestant institutions had traditionally failed to address the concerns of the socially disadvantaged. Not only had a newly conscious working class begun to challenge actively the economic establishment, but within the once unified culture of the middle classes new gradations of status and power began to reveal themselves. In traditional farming communities fissures appeared between the settled farmers and a younger land-hungry generation forced to seek land in Western Canada,[9] but even in that expanding Prairie agricultural frontier, class divisions developed with the arrival of thousands of British and European immigrants who often lacked both capital and access to prime agricultural land.[10] Moreover, in urban centres the struggle to achieve a respectable social status was becoming increasingly precarious. Individual initiative, once the key to upward mobility, was constricted by the burgeoning stratified bureaucracies in both business and government.[11] The promotion of professionalization and the support of labour unionism were strategies whereby both the middle and the working classes sought to obviate the effects of urban and industrial change, and the church adapted these methods and techniques to their work with these newly assertive groups. Clerks such as C.W. Gordon's correspondent, E. de B. Ramsay, along with the urban working classes, became the focus of this renewed Protestantism of the vernacular, which was consciously articulated by a growing number of progressive clergymen. Imitating their eighteenth-century predecessors, these dissenting clergymen sought to forge strong links between evangelicalism and popular mores in an attempt to expand the boundaries of nineteenth-century political liberalism to include modern social democracy.

The new revivalism was less flamboyant than eighteenth-century popular religiosity, which appears to have been far more controlled by the common-folk themselves. Although Nathan O. Hatch may have overdrawn the popular spontaneity of religious experience following the American Revolution and the convergence of social values between charismatic preachers and their audience, early revivalism stands in sharp contrast to its modern counterpart which was often controlled and carefully orchestrated from above by middle-class church leaders. However, it must be added that, in the Canadian context, social reformist leaders in the Methdodist and Presbyterian churches in the early twentieth century, by comparison with an earlier generation of genteel churchmen, were drawn from a much more humble social background. Among the progressive church leaders, A.E. Smith was the son of a Methodist church janitor, S.D. Chown was the son of a non-commissioned soldier, J.R. Mutchmor grew up on Manitoulin Island in impoverished circumstances as the son of a farmer and occasional mill-worker. In order to complete his training at the University of Toronto and later at Union Theological Seminary in New York, Mutchmor was hired by E.W. Bradwin of Frontier College to work alongside the Italian navvies on the Canadian Northern Railway. Even though Hugh Dobson had experienced the call to preach early in his life, he was compelled at first to work as a farm labourer outside Neepawa, Manitoba, and while attending Wesley College in Winnipeg he continued to work waiting on tables and chopping wood. Ernest Thomas, an immigrant preacher from Britain, experienced directly the poverty and social unrest of industrial London, while Richard Roberts, later known for his warm support for labour unionism, had grown up in a poor mining family in Wales. And even those like Beatrice Brigden, whose family's prosperous printing establishment had raised it out of the working class to middle-class comfort, claimed an identity with ordinary Canadians.[12]

Although revivals were encouraged by key Methodist and Presbyterian administrators from their central offices in Toronto, one must be wary of defining their *rapprochement* with popular ideologies as a mere stratagem of social control by which these administrators sought to contain social disorder. While their attitudes reflected middle-class concerns with the unpredictability of social change, it is nevertheless true that if their program of social reform constituted simply an imposition from above, it would have been articulated in a language unconnected to evangelism. Left to themselves, leaders such as T. Albert Moore and J.G. Shearer might have continued to inculcate the tenets of social service through their bevy of lecturers like Beatrice Brigden and M.C. Ratte, who believed in educating the congregations and not in converting souls.

If progressive churchmen had continued on the path they had followed prior to World War I, Christian social reform might have developed according to the American model, where the social gospel served simply as a conscience that fed secular movements of social engineering and was culturally disconnected from what became a competing impulse towards revivalism. In the United States revivalism became the primary expression of fundamentalism, while the ideal of social service veered towards a much more radical "social gospel" grounded in social rather than individual conversion.[13] In Canada the progressive clergy's reform of the institutional church permitted a blending, rather than the severing, of these two traditions. As Phyllis Airhart has convincingly demonstrated, the social Christianity promoted by twentieth-century clergymen remained intimately intertwined with an individualist piety that derived its social force from the tradition of revivalism.[14] This was so because progressive leaders chose to respond to a popular religiosity that demanded the reform of the social landscape to flow from the conversion of the individual. Thus, the ideal of social service was just as powerfully shaped by forces from below as it was imposed by mass evangelism upon large numbers of Canadians from above. The powerful ground swell of conservative religious sentiment from outside élite circles, which affected both the new and the old revivalism, prevented progressive social reform in Canada from developing into a cult of expertise divorced from popular democracy. Preachers such as the Rev. Harball, who daily confronted the conservative reality of grass-roots Protestantism in Canada, instructed the promoters of social reform: "You fellows are a way up in Social Service but way down on evangelism ... I think your message is greatly needed, and is a good preparation for a minister – it will give direction to christian effort when the love of God strains people to move."[15]

The power of popular Christianity, which was often very conservative and even, one might say, verging towards fundamentalism, was made evident by the degree to which by the early 1920s both the Methodist and Presbyterian leaders had yoked social service to the tradition of evangelical revivalism. The rediscovery of the power of revivalism in the the first two decades of the century by progressive church leaders was not only an attempt to convert the growing numbers of the unchurched, but also an attempt to tap into the reservoir of Canadian evangelicalism which had persisted since the mid-nineteenth century outside the "official" culture of the Protestant churches. But while its purpose in recapturing the popular idiom was to tame social forces, this effort did result in a renewed convergence between evangelical religion and popular culture. It was this efflorescence of popular spirituality unleashed by revivalism that ultimately revitalized Canadian Protestant churches heretofore swathed in an irrelevant intellectualism and on the path to decay.

The harnessing of revivalism by some progressive clergymen was only one facet of a much larger strategy to employ the technology and venues of popular culture to instil Christian belief. As early as 1915 both the Methodist and Presbyterian churches had established propaganda committees within their departments of social service and these overtly appropriated the latest advertising techniques to reinvigorate religion with meaning and vitality by means of a range of sophisticated pictorial presentations in posters, lantern-slides, handbills, and postcards.[16] So effective was advertising in promoting Christianity that Beatrice Brigden vociferously upbraided the central office of the Department of Evangelism and Social Service when it consistently failed to deliver the various pamphlets, posters, and window banners which were meant to herald her social service visits. In the absence of advertising, she reported distinct shortfalls in financial contributions.[17]

In their efforts to popularize social Christianity, Dobson and T. Albert Moore became experts in the most up-to-date gadgetry of mass culture. Far from seeing an irreconcilable opposition between the Christian message and secular entertainment, these progressives hailed the new technology as a great boon for extending the influence of the church into those interstices of society that had remained largely impervious to the orthodox sermon. In May 1920, following upon the tremendous success of the movie *Enlighten the Daughter* which, despite its moral message of sexual propriety, had been a hit in Prairie theatres in the previous year, Moore made a pilgrimage to Chicago for the specific purpose of inquiring into the expense of having films made for the church. The Protestant churches had also been successful in running a series of motion pictures on venereal disease in 1918, films which had been created by the Social Service Department at the University of Toronto.[18] But because of the almost prohibitive cost of making motion pictures, Moore and Dobson had to rely primarily on charts, cartoons, and diagrams to capture the attention of concerned Christians and to convey to them through graphic colourful pictures and snappy slogans both the perils of venereal disease and prostitution and the remedies to these miasmas of social degradation.

The ever-popular lantern-slide, introduced to the social service department by Dobson, became the pre-eminent tool of social evangelism. As field secretary for Western Canada, Dobson kept abreast of the latest refinements of the stereopticon projector, and ensured that these machines found wide use in church halls throughout the Prairies by personally instructing individual ministers on their use. He also established a circulating library of slides which covered subjects such as child welfare, social vice, prohibition, the city beautiful movement, housing reform, and the life of John Wesley.[19] The lantern-slide was one of the most effective and enduring means of popularizing the aims and ideals of the new social Christianity. In his quest to bring about social regeneration, Dobson perspicaciously searched out new ways of grafting evangelism onto popular culture. One of the most effective tactics was the incursion of the church into the circuit of well-attended summer and fall local fairs. In 1918 Dobson brought both his child welfare and social reconstruction exhibits to the fairgrounds of Western Canada in an arrangement whereby fair organizers paid the Department of Evangelism and Social Service $150 per fair in exchange for the "thousands of people" attracted to the event by his booth.[20] There is no doubt that these exhibits were instrumental in bringing Christianity into the lives of numerous Canadians through their emphasis on redeeming the child. This focus upon the child, so reminiscent of the nineteenth-century revivalists' insistence upon using the sentimentality of the image of the child Jesus and the Old Testament admonition that the child should lead the parents to conversion, undoubtedly appealed because of its obvious affinities with Victorian popular religion.[21] So successful were exhibits in awakening Protestants to the ideals of community service that in 1917 they were introduced at the great Easter season feasts of the Ukrainian settlements in Alberta.[22]

As these few examples demonstrate, Protestant progressives were extremely adept at entering into and exploiting the venue of worldly amusements in an attempt to ensure that Christianity remained within the mainstream of Canadian culture. While ministers may have beheld certain aspects of popular culture with annoyance, they did not react with either fear or a sense of hopelessness at the ability of the church to both contain and control popular amusements. When discussing with Hugh Dobson the unfortunate publication by the *Christian Guardian* of pictures of "half-dressed women" in their otherwise impeccable labour issue in 1920, Moore commented: "That will do for Eaton's catalogue but not for the 'Christian Guardian.'"[23] The generally benign reaction of the Protestant churches to popular culture stemmed from their belief that all culture outside materialistic socialism was either consciously or unconsciously Christian and therefore susceptible to their leadership. Such an unwavering faith in the capacity of Christian institutions to be in the forefront of changes in popular culture may appear hopelessly naïve to the modern observer. However, the conclusion of proponents of the secularization thesis that the churches, like other facets of Canadian society,[24] were deluged by a flood-tide of mass culture after 1900 presupposes both a fallacious assumption that individuals are passive in the face of impersonal social forces, and a highly tendentious argument that modern mass culture exerted a hegemonic influence in Canadian society as early as the turn of the twentieth century. Indeed, Canadian churches were able to Christianize popular culture easily because as late as the 1930s popular entertainments remained local and largely removed from the domination of American corporate mass culture. The only areas of popular leisure activity that the ever vigilant ministers cited as unwholesome and potentially dangerous to Christian culture were movies, magazines, and novels. Throughout the first three decades of the century the local saloon remained the most troublesome competitor of the church.[25]

The so-called "democratization of desire" which reinterpreted democracy in terms of equality of access to the world of luxury and unrestrained consumption was, by the early twentieth century, pervasive in American culture because of the powerful alliance that had been forged between between large-scale business, department stores, government agencies, museums, and the leisure industry.[26] However, even in the

United States this culture of consumption was confined before the 1920s to large cities such as Chicago and New York. By contrast, Canadian cultural institutions had not fallen prey to the new commercial morality which redirected the individual sense of personal fulfilment away from Christian duty towards the narcissism of consumer entertainments and amusement. Canada lacked the infrastructure of large corporations powerful enough to formulate an overwhelming ethic of consumer desire that would truly challenge the strong link between Christian values and the wider culture. It was only after 1900 that corporate mergers on the American pattern began to feature prominently in Canadian business life, and the culture represented by these large conglomerates would have had a very limited impact on the lives of the majority of ordinary Canadians, who lived outside the large urban and industrial centres of Toronto, Montreal, Hamilton, Winnipeg, and Vancouver.

Prior to World War II Canadian society lacked the essential attribute of mass culture. Where as in the United States the technology, distribution, and advertising of popular culture was financed and controlled by large business corporations,[27] in Canada the production of culture remained diffuse and local. The penetration of American culture in terms of mass-circulation magazines, novels, and movies was largely confined to large urban centres and to those who had both the wealth and leisure to consume. In short, luxury had not become democratized in Canadian society. Significantly, a mere two per cent of the Canadian population paid income tax when it was introduced in 1917.[28] In 1921 the Canadian census statistics stated that fifty-one per cent of the population lived in "urban" areas. But because the definition of urban included all incorporated towns and villages, this statistic belies the fact that a large majority of the Canadian people lived in settlements where economic patterns and social values were still fashioned by rural life.[29] In the still largely rural nation that was Canada, the only secular competitors to the church as a source of popular entertainment and education were dances, the saloon, and perhaps the occasional movie. So feeble was the incursion of American mass culture that the only form of popular amusement that consistently frustrated clergymen outside the cities was the craze in the 1920s for indoor skating and hockey.

Nor did American radio programing make much impact upon Canadians before the 1930s. In 1923 there existed a scant 10,000 radio sets in Canada, and in the next decade the number had not even reached the half-million mark.[30] This number dropped precipitously during the 1930s when many Canadians were forced to relinquish their radio sets in order to qualify for relief. So limited were the facilities in most Canadian towns and villages that even the church found it difficult to mount programs of wholesome Christian entertainment. Like the rural and small-town populations they served, few churches in Western Canada were electrified, thus slowing the introduction of new technologies like the stereopticon, let alone feature films. In the end, the importation of American mass culture was so slow that it was only by 1949, with the advent of television and the subsequent creation of the Massey Commission, that Canadian élites felt the need to protect Canadian culture.[31] In the United States the church had been relegated by consumer capitalism to a marginal voice of dissent, but in Canada, given the prolonged infancy of modern mass culture and the importance of rural life, the Protestant churches remained powerful enough to ensure that Christian values exerted a creative influence over the mainstream of cultural change until well into the 1930s. As a case in point, both the Methodist and Presbyterian churches invested in local radio stations as early as 1923, and later, through the medium of the Social Service Council of Canada, they were among the principal lobbyists for the creation of the Canadian Broadcasting Corporation.[32]

The immense popularity of C.W. Gordon's novels, which were suffused with the power of Christ's redemptive message, evoked the enormous vitality enjoyed by Canadian churches. "It is the *high uncompromising ethical* and *religious ideal* you keep steadily before the multitude of your enthralled readers. There can be no doubt that thousands will be saved from doubt and sin through these books."[33] So remarked J.G. Shearer when he exhorted the often doubt-ridden Gordon to keep writing his Christian fiction, which had so obviously become one of the most important vehicles for affixing Christian principles to the lives of ordinary Canadians. Not only had his novels affected the lives of bushmen, flax-millers, and gum-diggers in a country as far away as New Zealand,[34] but in the pluralistic social reality of twentieth-century Canada Gordon's books had, for many, replaced the theology-laden sermon as the medium of religious instruction. A prominent Baptist educator, Principal E.A. Hardy, placed Gordon's novels, which he called "a sermon in practical righteousness," on the curriculum of Moulton College, the Baptist women's institution in Toronto. Another Baptist, President Trotter of Acadia University, read selections from *The Man from Glengarry* to his students and commended Gordon's literary efforts in the following terms: "May you be strengthened and longspared to use your great gifts for the glory of Him you are serving so faithfully."[35] More importantly, novels such as Gordon's *The Sky Pilot* drew into the ministry a host of new recruits,[36] attracted by the new spirit of democratic evangelism which these books imparted with their emphasis on plain language and colourful storytelling. In his novels Gordon frequently returned to older themes of popular religiosity, including personal piety and conversion through revivalism, and blended these with such newer concerns as practical social service, the Canadianization of immigrants, the social uplift of good citizenship, and the purification of political life. But above all, his evocation of the individual heroic clergyman recaptured for a modern audience the personal nature of the powerful bond between God's servants and those entrusted to their care.

The progressive critique of the theological hegemony of the Victorian church colleges centred on the very problem Gordon's novels sought to redress – that theology interposed an artificial barrier between the clergyman and his congregation. J.S. Woodsworth told his cousin C.B. Sissons that young clergymen must discard old theological conventions and experiment with an uncomplicated preaching, based upon a direct emotional encounter with the personal love and guidance of God, to appeal to a popular audience. Like other progressive ministers, Woodsworth rebelled against the Victorian preoccupation with making the clergy an intellectual priesthood separated from ordinary people. Despite his own theological training, Woodsworth preferred the ideal of democratized religion because it would recapture the intimacy and fellowship between the clergyman and his flock. Needless to say, Woodsworth's praise of a religion of the vernacular was intended to maximize the minister's influence and leadership in the wider community. "As a minister," Woodsworth explained, "I occupy a kind of artificial and unnatural position which separates me from the people among whom I am supposed to work. They regard preaching and 'personal work' as my business and if I do get close to them it is in spite of rather than because of my position."[37] Although the desire among younger clergymen to rid the profession of these "unnatural" class divisions produced by an overly intellectualized theology may have sprung from a personal desire for social usefulness common among the middle classes at the turn of the century,[38] it did stimulate a widespread reorientation of both the content and style of preaching in the Protestant churches after 1900.

Foremost among the new strategies to attract previously unchurched social groups in both urban and rural areas was a renewal of evangelistic campaigns, or revivals. These were intended primarily to solidify the bond between the church leadership and grass-roots spirituality that had been rent asunder by the stress placed by the church colleges on preaching doctrine through the intricacies of biblical criticism.[39] The watchword of the new revivalism was the direct, colloquial insistence on the love of Christ for the sinner, and the consequent re-emphasis upon the individual's immediate, emotional understanding of Christianity. The renewed attention paid to both Christ's and the preacher's relationship with each and every individual conferred a new popular appeal to religion. "The meetings are beyond all my expectations," reported the Rev. Colin G. Young, Presbyterian minister at Prince

Albert, Saskatchewan, "and the joy of them is a new and strange thing to me ... I have a vision of Christ interceding for men. The image of His face will always be before me, and with this vision has come the emancipation for which I have long prayed. The weakness of my ministry has been the lack of personal work. I drew back from speaking to men, and lost so much in my ministry."[40]

Moreover, the message of practical Christian service which became increasingly embedded in these revival campaigns spoke directly to the everyday needs of Canadians. That the preaching of social service was instrumental in producing an upsurge in church membership was attested to by Beatrice Brigden, who informed T. Albert Moore in 1916 that "we cannot fail to notice that many who have become dissatisfied and drifted from the church" and "many who are thoughtful too, are being strongly attracted to the church again by the power of this newer program of the church."[41] Brigden's "racy, piquant style" at her recitals on social regeneration certainly contributed in no small part to the renewed popularity of the church among both men and women. One of her talks, "In the Beginning," covered topics such as embryology, eugenics, and feeble-mindedness; another, "She Buildeth Her Home," considered the implications of modern industrialism for the breakdown of the traditional family life; and a third, "The Alchemist Divine," was a practical discussion of sex hygiene. These talks were followed by a broader address on the women's movement and the place of women in modern society entitled "How Much Is A Woman Worth." To young girls and boys Brigden related the mystery of human reproduction through homely stories about frogs, fish, grains, and hen's eggs.[42] In Camrose, Alberta, her talks on marriage, child care, and reproduction introduced numerous farm women to the most pressing social problems of the day, while her recital there "ranked as one of the greatest treats of the season."[43] In a determined effort to appropriate the venues of popular culture, she regularly held her final mass recital in local music-halls or theatres even though the structure of her social service campaigns was unmistakably founded upon the tradition of the revival, whereby the charismatic preacher sought out listeners in highly personal, small-group encounters, which culminated in a climactic mass meeting. During her week-long sojourn in Davidson, Saskatchewan, Brigden, aided by the "live wire preacher" Rev. Bray, worked the community into a state of religious enthusiasm, which led to a final recital in the town hall where no seat was left vacant. As Brigden concluded, "So we reach numbers in that way we would not have in the church."[44]

Having acknowledged the failure of the churches to attract the urban working classes and new immigrants, the progressive church leaders, through the refurbished and democratized Christianity they promoted, pursued a variety of methods for reawakening the dormant religiosity of those constituencies they targeted for spiritual revival. In order to counteract the movies, slot machines, and vaudeville performances that had begun to invade urban centres, the Presbyterian Church's Committee on Amusements and Recreation sought to wipe out uncontrolled popular culture by introducing a series a of cheap concerts and lectures which emphasized religion.[45] In 1914 the Rev. R.J. Koffend, the superintendent of Evangel Hall, directly competed with the allure of consumer culture by converting an old store into a successful city mission where he instituted specialized classes for women and children on Bible themes: the mission complemented his vastly successful open-air meetings which drew a large urban audience.[46] The Methodists were no less successful in infusing popular culture with evangelistic purposes. In Winnipeg, J.S. Woodsworth, who in 1907 was appointed superintendent of All People's Mission, combined industrial education with evangelistic meetings in nine small institutes scattered throughout the city.[47] The creation of these institutes between 1907 and 1910 reflected a sophisticated understanding of the need for specialized approaches suitable to the pluralistic social experience of the modern city. At the social centre on Burrows Avenue, which served a large concentration of Polish immigrants, evangelists used the intimacy of the small cottage prayer meeting to replicate the close community relationships of Polish town life, while at the Maple Street Mission Woodsworth and his workers held two Gospel services on Sunday, three prayer meetings, Chinese classes, Brotherhood meetings for men only, and a series of special revival meetings, where forty-five adults and seven children were converted. At the Winnitoba Young Mens' Association, Methodist clergymen conducted "healthy recreation" through games and clubs specifically to combat "the mad rage for pleasure" among the urban youth.[48] And, in order to counteract the "radical" views of old-country British, Jewish, German, and Slavic workingmen, Woodsworth held a series of uplifting Sunday afternoon lectures at the People's Forum located in the Grand Theatre which were specifically designed for those whose Sunday had been "of no religious significance." Here, such topics as music, the single tax, architecture, the nervous system, and contagious diseases, although, as Woodsworth admitted, not in the narrowest sense religious, were supplemented by beautiful pictures, conversation, and good music to re-create the "religious atmosphere" of the middle-class home on Sunday.[49] The People's Forum, initiated by All People's Mission, was not the seed-bed of radical ferment: the talks by Chester Martin and Salem Bland on Canadian nationality and the British Empire, which were designed to break down national prejudices among immigrants, reflected its intended atmosphere of middle-class respectability.[50] This incremental strategy, initiated by the superintendents of urban missions, of slowly immersing immigrant workers in activities which appeared only incidentally Christian had an impeccably religious aim: as the Rev. S.W. Dean, the superintendent of the Toronto City and the Fred Victor missions stated, "These agencies act as very good bait for the Gospel hook."[51] In the final analysis the goal of evangelism dominated the new approaches of Woodsworth and his colleagues as they wrestled with the problem of Christianizing Canada's cities.

While the urban missions struggled to make the Protestant churches attractive to working-class people, some progressive clergymen remonstrated against those like J.S. Woodsworth and William Ivens who sought to define social service narrowly in terms of the interests of one class, namely, immigrant workers. T. Albert Moore, Hugh Dobson, and Beatrice Brigden held a much broader conception of modern social problems, believing that the middle classes, which they deemed equally crucial to the refashioning of the social order, were similarly dislocated by the effects of industrialization and urbanization. In St John's, Newfoundland, Brigden chastised local ministers for exclusively targeting female domestic servants as the locus of all social ills.[52] Often, progressives believed that the most recalcitrant group was the "educated and cultured" middle classes. The greatest opposition to social service existed among the wealthiest members of the church, who fought to retain the exclusive class meetings which, as the Rev. R.O. Armstrong of the Manitoba Sunday School Association caustically observed to Hugh Dobson, appealed to millionaires and were "not for the average Canadian like ourselves."[53] The leader of the social service activists within the Presbyterian Church, J.G. Shearer, believed that the middle classes, because of their greater access to wealth, were more consistently exposed to the blandishments of material goods which promised self-fulfilment and a sense of well-being.[54] The Presbyterian Church agonized much less over how to evangelize the working classes for, with the assistance of Charles Stelzle, an American who was a former labourer and an evangelist, campaigns led by Chapman and Alexander appealed directly to the labouring men of the Kootenays, especially the miners, among whom they were particularly effective. The success of these old-fashioned evangelistic campaigns contrasted sharply with the experience of the church in Nelson, British Columbia, where the direct emotional message of the Gospel had less influence among the more sophisticated audiences of middle-class Protestants who, Shearer declared, "will be as hard to catch as any class of people in the Metropolitan centre."[55]

The increased pluralism within the Presbyterian and Methodist churches during this period reflected neither confusion in the face of modern social change nor lack of knowledge of it. Rather, the wide-ranging employment by the churches of methods as diverse as family worship, cottage prayer meetings, social service lectures, urban missions, circuit spiritual conferences, and community surveys, together with mass evangelistic campaigns entailed a well-conceived strategy to increase the spiritual power of the church, one that was founded upon the recognition of specialization as the key to mastering the variegations of wealth, ethnicity, and gender, so characteristic of modern society.[56] The ongoing tinkering with the delicate balance of personal evangelism and social service was an immediate reflection of the interests and values of the various audiences which progressive leaders wished to enlist in the cause of the new evangelism. In advance of each evangelistic campaign, revivalists who specialized in particular areas fanned out to address specific groups, such as Masons, members of the Knights of Pythias, factory workers, and shop girls.[57] Where the Presbyterian Church used Charles Stelzle, whose emphasis on conversion through social service was deployed with great effect to try to convert workers, the Methodist Church employed Ernest Thomas, whose early reputation had been established as a preacher in the working-class churches of London. Thomas became best-known as an evangelist in industrial centres, where his stirring addresses at mass meetings were used with "splendid effect" to reach miners, lumbermen, and other workers. One anonymous worker observed of Thomas's message of social evangelism, "That was the best revival meeting I was ever in. If we have some more like this, lots of men would come back to the churches."[58] Presbyterians similarly adjusted the themes of their revival campaigns to address the needs of particular audiences. C.W. Gordon's two-week evangelistic mission in Minnedosa, Manitoba, closed skating, curling, and hockey rinks, as well as stores, in order to win over in particular the railwaymen who, ministers feared, were abandoning the church in favour of the fraternity of labour unions.[59]

In the more fluid and democratic Prairie West, Beatrice Brigden, with her refined and "womanly" demeanour,[60] appealed particularly to independent small farmers and local businessmen. Like Hugh Dobson, Brigden gained access to Prairie communities through such established middle-class organizations as the ubiquitous women's groups, the Women's Christian Temperance Union, and the Grain Growers' Association. Such alliances conferred upon her an aura of respectability crucial to offsetting charges often made that her eugenic talks on human reproduction, marriage, and relations between the sexes were "highly immodest."[61] Generally speaking, Brigden's talks on the social teachings of Jesus appealed to those members of the community who had long-established connections with vestigially Protestant institutions but who had drifted away from the institutional church because of their dissatisfaction with the increasingly esoteric preaching fostered by the church colleges. It was in these practical and intensely individualistic farming communities that the realism of Brigden's social Christianity won greatest favour. In 1915 one enthusiastic supporter told Brigden that "I am in full sympathy with your work. It's the kind of Christianity that counts."[62]

As part of their new commitment to specialization, the social service departments of both the Methodist and Presbyterian churches initiated programs of social purity lectures which were specially designed to convert the large numbers of women already active in church organizations to the imperatives of practical Christianity in the belief that they would function as spearheads to recruit their men-folk. Shearer had such an end in view when in 1910 he appointed Miss Marie Christine Ratte, a convert from Roman Catholicism whose experience in a large urban police department made her an ideal evangelist to warn congregations of the social degradation caused by the white slave trade. With a shrewd appreciation of the audience he wished to capture, Shearer observed to his colleague C.W. Gordon that she would make "an irresistible appeal to all people, but in particular to the women of the church."[63] In order to compete with this popular Presbyterian lecturer, T. Albert Moore appointed Beatrice Brigden, who, needless to say, enjoyed considerable success in winning women to the cause of social redemption. At Carnduff, Saskatchewan, her special women's meetings attracted a host of women from miles around.[64] Although Brigden's intention was to indoctrinate women in the benefits of companionate marriage to obviate the more open sexuality encouraged by modern novels, magazines, and film, her talks were often viewed as popular entertainment. During her week-long visit to one small Prairie town, Brigden was initially pleased that her womanly talks had gained her a large following of adolescent girls, but she was later appalled to find that these same "gum-chewing girls" attended her lectures because she spoke on the very things they had been discussing for years behind the schoolhouse and the barn.[65] Despite Brigden's discomfiture that the moral import of her lectures was lost, she was consciously aware and delighted that social Christianity did, nevertheless, often successfully compete with local popular entertainment on its own terms. In one town, where she denounced "social ills contributing to immorality throughout the land," the women begged her not to stop talking, but the young men of the community were less enamoured of her presence because she had succeeded in wooing young women away from the the local movie-house, where "Million Dollar Mystery" was playing.[66]

It appears that Brigden provided an outlet for many women who were isolated on remote and inaccessible farms, far from the social contacts of town life. So enriching were Brigden's talks on marriage and child rearing that these women were instrumental in circumventing the local clergy who were often unsympathetic to public discussion of these issues.[67] Because of their desire to hear a woman's perspective on contemporary social and family problems, some women in Western Canada seemed to be much less conservative than their urban sisters and displayed a greater readiness to accept the educative aspects of social service, even if the talks were not couched in more traditional evangelistic language and methods. For example, Mrs W.R. Woodman, who resided fourteen miles outside Denzil, Saskatchewan, amongst "quite a foreign population," beseeched Brigden to come and speak on her social purity themes because the traditional missionary work of three Moody Institute students in the area was not providing the necessary emotional satisfaction.[68]

However, Brigden's undisguised conformity to middle-class values often placed her at odds with newly self-conscious members of the working class. Her ideas on racial purity were so offended by the practice of the minister at Fort Saskatchewan, Alberta, the Rev. Charles Johnston, who invited "half-breeds" to attend services with the white congregation, that she termed him "a freak."[69] In "exploited" railway towns such as Innisfail, Alberta, the ideal of moral uplift which suffused her social service campaigns alienated the workers, who challenged her commitment to social change by grilling her on her opinions regarding Edward Bellamy's *Looking Backward*, a work that was clearly not viewed by Brigden as part of the church's social reform canon.[70] Despite Brigden's later professions, following the Winnipeg General Strike, of an identity with the common people, it was quite clear that during her social service tours she made little effort to seek out the very poor, whose self-consciousness at their inability to contribute financially to the church compelled them to avoid her lectures, at which a collection plate was passed.[71] While she believed that the church should, in theory, become more democratic and inclusive, she was, in practice, tied to the conventions of middle-class respectability; her attitude was forcefully demonstrated by an almost visceral recoil when one of her listeners assumed that her personal commitment to social purity derived from being rescued from the white slave trade.[72]

Ultimately, the ability of social Christianity to effect a spiritual awakening and instil the ideals of social harmony was circumscribed to a large degree by the narrowness of its class appeal. On the one hand, the emphasis which the new evangelism of social service placed upon the application of the lessons of the Gospel to daily life struck a resonant chord in those who had become inured to the irrelevant dogmas of the Victorian church. However, this same message of social regeneration was moored in the often judgmental language of moral uplift, and the implementation of its ideals depended upon the activity of a wealthy and leisured community leadership. That social Christianity often exacerbated the very class fissures it aspired to heal was revealed in Brigden's telling description of the miners in British Columbia as "so frightfully local, so primitive in every way"; Brigden herself fully recognized the limitations imposed on social service by the dual estrangement of class and ethnicity when she was compelled to admit that she understood neither their traditions nor their language.[73]

It soon became apparent to Dobson, Brigden, and other progressives that preaching the cause of social service often did not conform to the popular desire for a more traditional evangelism which rested upon a bedrock of sin, atonement, and redemption. More than once, local congregations instructed Brigden that she should convert people before introducing the novelty of practical Christianity, and not infrequently the vocal conservative elements in the church objected to Dobson's use of theatres, rather than the churches, to propagate his views regarding the reform of society.[74] Although Brigden tended to blame the unresponsiveness of numerous congregations to her message of social service on ignorance, especially among the wealthy, the inescapable reality was that the aims of the church leadership often conflicted with local public opinion, which was moulded by an older evangelical culture.

By 1919 even the optimistic Hugh Dobson was constrained to admit that social service had been preached far too aggressively and had failed because it had not been communicated in a fashion recognizable to people raised on the theological traditions of individual piety. In the midst of sending the Rev. C.B. Clarke the latest tracts issued by the British Whitley Councils on postwar labour reform, Dobson remarked:

> May I say, Mr. Clarke, it is scarcely necessary to say that you are not alone in having different people leave your congregation. I have had that occur several times, and all of us who are aggressive in these lines are giving some measure of offence. We appreciate very much the men who are not afraid of the faces of the people, and who speak plainly on the great issues of the day and interpret the Christian spirit in the light of those issues. We must, of course, always do it in a kindly spirit, but when we do it in that spirit, we can afford to leave the consequences with God. [75]

While Dobson's solution to the problem was to hammer away at modern practical Christianity until reluctant congregations caught up, others, such as the Rev. Bentley, who as a probationer in a rural settlement understood better the enduring and conservative nature of popular religion in Canada, saw that social service must be tempered with evangelism. As he confessed to Dobson, "I was a little too aggressive for the brethren and inclined to push things a little faster than public sentiment would justify."[76] When social service was presented within the context of traditional evangelism, the results were more impressive. After enlisting the most forceful and emotive evangelistic preachers behind the "progressive Movements of our Church," the Rev. E.D. Braden was able to report that the people of Vernon, British Columbia, were at long last "very heartily back of us" when they agreed to hold a child welfare exhibit in the local church.[77]

The entrenched conservative religiosity which progressive clergymen discovered at the core of local congregations compelled them to adopt revivalism as the means of reawakening the religious sentiment of ordinary people, which they hoped could later be directed towards social Christianity. In 1909 C.W. Gordon, the leading exponent of a more popular and democratic religiosity in the Presbyterian Church, told the Rev. A. Macmillan that preaching should centre upon personal salvation, and that only when such a revival of spiritual experience of God had been gained should the preacher introduce the gospel of personal service to others.[78] Gordon's own preaching, like his novels, was emotional and it also, by stressing the individual's direct relationship with God, harkened back to the rich traditions of nineteenth-century popular evangelical Scottish preaching. One visitor to Gordon's church in Winnipeg recounted that a woman, after hearing a sermon by the "full-whiskered" and physically imposing preacher, left with a handkerchief to her face; so wrenching was Gordon's sermon that a man, rough in appearance and one of the floating population of itinerant workers, was unable to choke back his feelings.[79]

The need to reassert the importance of revivalism in religious experience was impressed upon church leaders by the numerous ministers reporting on the traditional and conservative nature of Canadian Protestants. In Carman, Manitoba, the local Presbyterian congregation was won over to the new progressive vision of a full-orbed Christianity based on social service through the means of traditional evangelism centred on personal conversion. Writing to Gordon, the Rev. Francis Hall observed that "the people are of the old stock, set in their opinions, and rooted in prejudices hard to overcome. But when once awakened as they were last Sunday," through the appeal to personal piety, "they are the finest people one could work with." As ministers realized, the spiritual quickening brought about by evangelism was the most effective instrument for educating traditional Protestants in the outlook of the new Christianity whose dominant goal was social salvation. After several Sundays of spiritual preparation, "a great number … entered into the league of service." Not only were some women converted who then hosted cottage prayer meetings, but the "dormant energy" of Christian commitment that was awakened by evangelism resulted in the establishment of special men's meetings where the minister impressed upon those who were now spiritually inclined the new vision of personal work and its application to the wider society.[80] As the Rev. W. McNally of Pictou, Nova Scotia, explained, there was a great need for evangelism in the Maritimes, but he cautioned Gordon that "the people are ultra-conservative." In towns such as Pictou which were "spiritually dead," social service was likely to be ineffective unless preceded by a more emotional and personal brand of evangelical preaching. Through Gordon's simple appeal to the largely Highland Scotch congregation to forsake sin and accept the redemption offered by Christ, three young men, always the most recalcitrant group against any involvement with Christianity, "surrendered"; moreover, "the Holy Spirit could be felt" throughout his church and many people were in tears.[81]

In contrast to the early nineteenth century, when many of the participants at revival meetings were women, adolescents, and children, the more marginal members of the community,[82] twentieth-century popular evangelism was specially designed to draw men into the all-embracing experience of Christianity. The appeal of modern evangelism to men was amply demonstrated by the noteworthy success in Winnipeg, immediately following the conclusion of the Winnipeg General Strike, of the two-week campaign by the British preacher Gypsy Smith. Even though Smith's audience included workers to whom the appeal of practical social service with its emphasis upon labour democracy and urban reform should have won the most favour, it was the strong emotional strains of a heart-felt message of personal salvation that provided the "healing and comfort" necessary in the "psychological atmosphere" of post-strike Winnipeg. Surprised at the receptiveness of the working classes to religion, C.W. Gordon explained Smith's successes in terms of his reliance on simple "gospel facts" instead of "emotional acrobatics" or "hot air artistry," and the climate of "sanity and sincerity" which provided a much needed sense of order and stability to a so recently chaotic community.[83] In Amherst, Nova Scotia, the Rev. Anderson Rogers, a minister particularly concerned about the church's inability to reach men, told Gordon how working men in the industrial and mining centres of Sydney, Inverness, and Springhill were eager to be involved in revival campaigns that featured "stirring addresses" to win the conversion of individuals.[84]

The currently fashionable belief among historians that the popular culture of the working classes was a radical one[85] is belied by their receptiveness to traditional and even fundamentalist evangelism as well as by their dislike of the middle-class sentiments of Christian social service. In the case of the mission of Portal, Saskatchewan, on the Soo Line, the reaction of workers to social service was also characterized by gender conflict. There, the same workers who imbibed the themes of manliness in C.W. Gordon's novels found themselves temporarily allied with male members of the local business community who boycotted church services and the Sunday school after the local Women's Christian Temperance Union had effected a "Carrie Nation-like raid" on a moving-picture palace with some pious ladies wielding a fire extinguisher and others clinging to the projector to stop the show. The crisis was only resolved when the Presbyterian missionary, with a gift for both "prayer and hustling," persuaded almost all the workers and several businessmen to halt work in order to join in the final two days of his revival campaign. In all, thirty-one men declared themselves for Christ.[86]

However, it was in Winnipeg, well-known for its high level of trade union organization and its climate of polarization between capital and labour, that the conservative, evangelical character of working-class Protestantism was most evident. The working people of Winnipeg displayed a marked preference for the old-time evangelism that so predominated in the churches in their neighbourhoods north of Portage Avenue. While Winnipeg's middle-class congregations endorsed the new, modern tenets of social Christianity, working-class Protestants flocked to hear the procession of visiting revivalists who frequented Winnipeg between 1914 and 1920.[87] The special appeal of traditional evangelical preaching to the working classes was strongly evoked by A.E. Smith, one of the foremost sympathizers with the labour protest of 1919 in Winnipeg, in his unpublished semi-autobiographical novel, "The Passing Shadow." It told the story of one Roger Bilson, an apprentice printer who was converted beneath "the spell of emotional religious eloquence and passion" of the Rev. Charles Johnson. Although Johnson ministered to a largely working-class congregation and was dedicated to improving the material circumstances of his flock, he nevertheless shunned the liberal strains of ethical Christianity which had made such inroads among wealthier members of the community. Rather, his gospel was that of "the theology of Salvation from Hell" and his services were characterized by exhortation, song, and earnest prayer, and an "emotional fervency" that "everyone seemed to enjoy."[88] That this conservative piety was not simply imposed upon ordinary Canadian workers is best illustrated by the powerful control over preaching and spiritual life exerted by the North End working-class congregation at McDougall Methodist Church. In 1919, when their pastor William Ivens, editor of the *Western Labor News*, sermonized increasingly upon socialism and radical protest, his flock ousted him and appointed in his stead the Rev. J.O. Irvine, "a pronouced Premillenarian."[89]

The Rev. John Maclean's Bethel Mission and McDougall Methodist, both in the notorious North End, were not the only working-class churches in Winnipeg overtly committed to the fostering of traditional evangelism. Indeed, this form of spirituality was replicated in all the Anglo-Saxon working-class churches of north-west Winnipeg. Another church, Broadway Methodist in downtown Winnipeg, ensured a consistent working-class attendance by advertising that it was "a real Home Church ... The messages from the pulpit are spiritual and helpful, and Christ and the gospel are kept to the front." Even in the midst of the Winnipeg General Strike workers crowded into Zion Methodist to hear the old-time Gospel service led by the Rev. John Maclean.[90] And in the aftermath of the strike large numbers of workers were drawn to the warm emotionalism of the premillennialism of Pentecostalism which swept through Winnipeg after the immensely popular revival campaign led by Aimee Semple McPherson.[91]

This pattern of working-class religiosity was not restricted to Winnipeg but was also evident in newly industrialized towns like Brantford, Ontario, and in older urban centres like Toronto. There, the three-week long simultaneous revival campaign of January 1911 led by the American evangelist J. Wilbur Chapman attracted thousands of city dwellers, and many of his special meetings were explicitly directed towards working people. "Revivalism," trumpeted the *Toronto World*, "was in the air, and everywhere, in the business offices, the workshops, the factories, the stores."[92] At Chapman's opening service in Massey Hall an audience of 3,000 men thrilled to the evangelist's message of victory through Christ's crucifixion, and nearly 1,000 sprang to their feet at the end of the service to declare themselves for Christ. "[S]eldom," declared the *Globe*, "has Toronto seen the audience swayed by a speaker as was the great body of men ... Hundreds of men went down from the galleries and forward from every part of the floor to take the hand of Dr. Chapman or Mr. Alexander, and signed cards indicating their desire to lead a new life."[93] Daily attendance at the revival meetings, held in a number of city churches, fluctuated between 6,000 and 9,000, and bulged to 14,000 on Sundays,[94] but of greater significance was the willingness of Chapman and his associates to reach the common people by preaching in venues outside the institutional churches. Evangelistic services were held at the Christie, Brown & Co. cookie factory, which attracted over 250 people, and in a CPR railway car at the foot of York Street, where the sermon "Deformation, Reformation, and Transformation" secured the warm approval of an audience in which the "brass buttons of conductors, the white coats of chefs, the blue jumpers of grimy-faced car repairers" mingled.[95] At a special service held at the Taylor Safe Works, 150 men participated in gospel singing, conducted by a Mr Richard, "one of the mechanics."[96] Chapman's gospel of personal salvation and atonement, his firm opposition to the inroads of biblical criticism, and his willingness to castigate the institutional churches for their theological formalism were enthusiastically received in working-class neighbourhoods such as West Toronto, much to the concern of more liberal Canadian clergymen like the Baptist professor Joseph Gilmour of McMaster University, who feared that Chapman's presence would further disrupt a local community already polarized on the question of biblical inspiration and authority.[97]

In her recent study of early twentieth-century Canadian revivalism, Phyllis Airhart has argued, based upon a close reading of the Toronto-based *Christian Guardian*, that by 1915 Methodist piety had become non-revivalist, thus representing the full flowering of Methodism's engagement with progressive social service. The central assumption of Airhart's thesis is that the Canadian religious experience exactly replicated that of the United States where the fracturing of the Victorian evangelical consensus was occasioned by the increasing connection between revivalism and fundamentalism. In Airhart's scenario, even though the individualism of an earlier piety endured within the new progressivist paradigm, the embracing of social service by Canadian Methodists by necessity implied a concomitant abandonment of revivalism.[98] Her interpretation remains problematic, however, because of a semantic difficulty over the definition of revivalism. At one level, Airhart views revivalism in a highly amorphous fashion, as just an intellectual signpost around which Methodists could affirm their group identity apart from other Protestant denominations, most notably the Calvinistic Plymouth Brethren, but at another level, revivalism is narrowly employed to denote conversion itself. Both these definitions consign revivalism to the purview of religious debates among church leaders, disembodied from the historical events that were the revivals themselves. By using the *Christian Guardian*, which saw as its role the forging of ideological harmonies within Methodism, as the lens through which to discern the changing patterns of Canadian Methodism, Airhart naturally concluded that the entire denomination shared in the shift in consensus from revivalist piety to progressive social service.

Canadian Methodism was not fed only by this one official stream of evangelical belief emanating from the Toronto leadership; rather, at the level of the local congregation there also flowed a persistent conservative and populist evangelicalism which continued to feed the vitality of old-style revivalism. Not only did revivalism not peter out by 1915, as Airhart concluded, but because of its grounding in the emotionalism of popular piety it actually enjoyed a dynamic resurgence during and after World War I. Because of the Methodist progressive leadership's ideal of a revivified social democracy, together with its recognition of the power of conservative piety at the grass-roots level, the official program of social service became increasingly shaped by the culture of revivalism. Rather than diverging after 1900, revivalism and social service actually were drawn into an organic relationship in which mass revivalism functioned as the instrument that converted people to the newer tenets of social Christianity. Far from eschewing the older piety, Methodist progressives brokered this partnership between revivalism and social evangelism and thus ushered the older popular culture back into the mainstream of religious experience. In this way, revivalism became the core of the progressive creed.

Between 1908 and 1925 the desire of progressive clergymen to forge a stronger rapport between the Protestant churches and the people reinvigorated the somnolent tradition of revivalism and moved it once again into a central place in Canadian religious life. In the burgeoning urban centres of the United States, modern mass revivals had proven effective in recapturing the allegiance of working-class and middle-class Protestants alienated by the increasing dogmatism of mainline churches. However, revivalism in the United States was closely associated with the new fundamentalism, and because it competed with the social gospel movement which inspired urban progressive reform it was forced to the cultural fringes of Protestantism.[99] By contrast, even though Canadian church leaders actively sought out such prominent American fundamentalist evangelists as Billy Sunday and J. Wilbur Chapman, twentieth-century revivalism in Canada was not the manifestation of an evangelical culture in the process of decay; nor was it the symptom of a Protestantism besieged by secularism and dissolving into a welter of sensationalist advertising and crude fundamentalist passion. Because of its ability to articulate religious ideas in a popular idiom, revivalism soon became the cornerstone of the Protestant progressive agenda and functioned as one of the most effective vehicles for the promulgation of social Christianity. Even though J. Wilbur Chapman and the flamboyant Billy Sunday were best known in the United States for bringing large numbers of new converts into the fold of conservative Christianity,[100] they served quite a different purpose in the Canadian context. Moore welcomed Billy Sunday largely because his folksy brand of evangelism combined references to hell and damnation with modern advertising techniques that were powerful in assisting the church to compete with movies, magazines, and the radio. Most importantly, Moore envisioned Sunday's uncanny ability to win thousands to the cause of Christ as just the first step in persuading Canadian Protestants to begin a journey along the path beginning with personal conversion and culminating in social responsibility.[101] J.G. Shearer, Moore's Presbyterian counterpart, fully appreciated Sunday's usefulness in awakening urban audiences to the redemptive qualities of practical Christianity. As he told C.W. Gordon in 1914, "I believe, under God, that he [Billy Sunday] would do more for practical righteousness and for Bible religion and for prohibition than any other force we could bring to bear."[102] Similarly, Chapman's evangelistic campaigns were viewed, especially in mining and railway districts of Northern Canada, where even private religion had been submerged in the attractions of drink and gambling, as a spiritual barrage preparatory to the real work of the church which was social evangelism.[103]

Whatever the aims of progressive church leaders, old-style mass revivalism was extraordinarily popular in making the church relevant to the piety of ordinary Canadians. In order to capture the attention of new audiences, a whole gamut of familiar techniques of spiritual conversion were reintroduced into the Canadian religious landscape. Prior to World War I, camp-meetings, chautauquas, love-feasts, prayer meetings, and a host of revival campaigns were once again suddenly in vogue.[104] So effective were these in broadening the public profile of the Methodist and Presbyterian churches that the *Hamilton Herald* announced: "Camp meetings had been held, and will continue to be held." Apparently these peripatetic "spiritual conferences" attracted up to 500 followers at a time as they roved from town to town introducing the twin themes of individual regeneration and social justice.[105]

By all accounts the evangelists leading the "Truro Campaign" of the Presbyterians spoke nightly to a packed church of 600 people, and they even drew audiences of 200 at afternoon Bible-study meetings.[106] The Chapman-Alexander evangelistic crusade of 1908 averaged a nightly attendance of 3,000 during their fourteen-day revival held in the Orillia, Ontario, skating rink, and in 1906 the American evangelist R.A. Torrey filled a hall of 5,000 to capacity in Winnipeg with those who desired to be led to a Christian life. The combined impact of his 600-member choir, the prominent display of advertising posters, the skill of Torrey's advance workers who specialized in door-to-door evangelism, together with his colloquial sermons which spoke of the Atonement and of the redemptive power of the personality of Jesus, moved thousands to seek salvation in prayer.[107] An unprecedented number of 1,200 men and women in Sault Ste Marie, Ontario, surrendered to Christ during the 1914 "Union Tabernacle Campaign" led by the Rev. H.L. Stephens. This six-week campaign was followed by yet another successful four-week evangelistic mission in another industrial centre, Hamilton, which witnessed yet more "thrilling scenes" of individual conversion.[108] The incredible response to revivalism in these two steel towns demonstrated the explosive power of conservative evangelism when it was wedded to the newer gospel of social service in winning large numbers of new professed Christians to the mainline churches. In the aftermath of World War I, neither revivalism nor social reform languished; indeed, in combination they continued to attract large audiences. So large, in fact, that T. Albert Moore was compelled to requisition tents sufficient to hold up to 1,000 people from the Canadian Army.[109] The very success of the direct emotional appeal of reivivalism in attracting numerous new adherents to Protestantism persuaded progressive clergymen towards increasingly diversified methods to promote social service. They continued to draw upon the work of such American fundamentalists as Gypsy Smith and the anti-saloon evangelist "Pussyfoot" Johnson well into the 1920s, not because they agreed with them theologically but because of their enormous popular appeal.[110] Hence, despite his personal reservations about the efficacy of faith-healing, Moore endorsed the Price Evangelistic meetings, which in Vancouver drew 9,000 people, because his overriding concerns were that, at the very least, the previously unchurched would be familiarized with the Gospel of Christ and that this would lead them first to conversion and then to social service.[111]

Unlike their predecessors, progressive clergymen did not believe that the church's authority stemmed from learning and education, but rather that the vitality of the church in modern culture flowed from the popular consent of its audiences. Pulled by a democratic and populist orientation, this new generation of ministers attempted to recapture early nineteenth-century evangelistic traditions, which had represented a revolt against high culture and intellectual theology and the exaltation of the religious experience and language of the common people. Their constant harkening back to Jonathan Edwards, John Wesley, George Whitfield, Charles Grandison Finney, and Dwight Moody,[112] the great exemplars of the bygone age of popular evangelism, was more than mere nostalgia. By evoking these names the progressive clergymen were firmly placing their own democratic desires, encapsulated by the new social Christianity, within an ongoing tradition of respectable middle-class leaders who had sought to bridge the gap between the institutional church and the people. In his pamphlet, *The Challenge of Montreal*, the Presbyterian clergyman E.I. Hart commented on the problem of working-class men feeling alienated from the church because the usual learned, expository preaching lacked a relevant message. In order to rescue the nearly 200,000 workers in Toronto and Montreal for Christianity, Hart urged that "[w]e must cease to despise the Gospel waggon, the Gospel tent, and the street preacher."[113] The new evangelism thus tapped the practices of the older but still vital popular evangelicalism which lay outside the official structure of the churches and sought to use it to energize the expansion of Protestantism's activities in modern society.

Significantly, T. Albert Moore and J.G. Shearer excised the more anti-authoritarian, antinomian legacy of Lorenzo Dow and Henry Alline, whose views closely reflected the aspirations of the socially dispossessed. Modern revivalism was intended to make the church more inclusive of all classes,[114] and this meant appealing equally to the working classes and the "respectable" middle classes, who were often prejudiced against the noisy, spontaneous, and raucous outbursts that had characterized traditional evangelism. Progressive leaders hoped to tame the uncontrolled unleashing of emotion they had come to associate with the social unrest of the newly enfranchised workers by fostering a "sane" or "cultured" evangelism.[115] Moore sponsored the British evangelist H. Arthur Barton because, as a professional actor, he combined sophisticated dramatic appeal with the earnestness and simplicity of the stories of the "old gospel." As Principal A. C. Bernath of Huntsville, Ontario, observed of Barton's evangelical campaign, "even the conservatives have nothing to fear because he is not noisy, sensational or unduly emotional," nor was he "narrow or fanatical." In other words, Barton achieved that delicate yet somewhat bland balance, so avidly sought by the advocates of the new evangelism, between fundamentalism and modernism, between emotional release and orderly salvation.[116]

The struggle to compel the church to become more responsive to popular religious desires entailed a concerted attack upon the old-style doctrinal sermon. Increasingly, those ministers who, like the Rev. Rumball, possessed not "one evangelistic gift" found themselves criticized for their uninspiring though solid sermons for the simple reason that they could not grip those outside the immediate church membership. Like the Presbyterians of Elgin, Manitoba, progressive church leaders preferred ministers like Mr Fraser, a gifted evangelist who rescued Rumball's stalled evangelistic campaign by laying "hold of the people at once ... He made people think ... The *man* counts mightily."[117] The lack of talented evangelists who could preach in a familiar idiom, coupled with the growing emphasis upon the cult of personality which was seen as a necessary counterweight to the increasing alienation experienced by individuals who made the transition from rural to urban life, led both Methodist and Presbyterian church leaders to emulate the example of American professional evangelists whose charismatic, folksy style had already won impressive numbers of new converts to the ranks of organized Protestantism. More importantly, because they eschewed the role of the "pulpit buffoon," evangelists like J. Wilbur Chapman were deemed acceptable by the "prominent" and wealthy within the church. In fact, Chapman was upheld by the Presbyterians as the model of the modern preacher:

> Handled by Dr. Chapman, the old familiar texts seemed to become new again. No special knowledge of Homiletics was needed to enable one to see that the preacher had a clear perception in every sermon of what he wanted to do, and a burning desire to do it. His appeals were made to the reason, the heart, and the conscience of his hearers. There were no studied attempts to stir the emotions, nor any jaded rhetorical flowers to please a jaded imagination. In strong, manly, ringing sentences he sent home the truths of the old Gospel. In both quality and quantity he leans just a little to the good, old-fashioned ways, but he did the work, work which the new theology and a fifteen minute essay could never have done.[118]

The new popular evangelism, though it wished to strike a note of respectability and decorum, still privileged the emotions over the intellect, as was demonstrated by the Rev. J.W.A. Nicholson's account of a revival meeting in Cape Breton Island. Nicholson, who was best known for his later sympathies with left-wing movements in the church,[119] championed the style of preaching of the evangelist and ex-drummer William Matheson because it undermined the established theological orthodoxies founded upon the speculations of the higher criticism. Of this meagrely educated Highland Scot, Nicholson wrote: "he is generally aroused – full of emotion, earnestness, passion. A man who stands 6 ft. 3 and weighs about 250 pounds and speaks out of an awful experience of sin's power and the victory of grace, is a force on a platform even if his English is not grammatical." By presenting the Bible in such a way that everyone could immediately apprehend the spirit of God, Matheson broke down the barriers between preacher and audience, which resulted in the whole congregation of the industrial town of Inverness coming forward to declare themselves for Christ.[120]

The Protestant progressive aspiration was to re-create within the church the personal bonds that had characterized the face-to-face relationships of the earlier period of populist evangelism, which they feared had been lost in larger modern communities where the individual identity of ordinary people was increasingly submerged under the weight of impersonal organizations. In his address "Human Brotherhood," Moore struggled to redefine individualism in terms of an ideal of fellowship that would once again foster social cohesion and community. Here, the duty must fall to the clergyman to provide the role model for a warm, caring, and sympathetic fraternity of believers. This, in turn, involved a new, down-to-earth, colloquial style of preaching. "Our Gospel," Moore reminded ministers, "has become too formal, too conventional. We are too far from the people." Presbyterians like C.W. Gordon shared Moore's rebellion against a stultified formal and doctrinal form of preaching. In 1908 Gordon counselled local ministers on how to to recast their preaching so that the wooing or winning note of optimism and affectionate salvation dominated over the traditional emphasis upon doctrine.[121]

In making the Bible more accessible to the "common people" and thus allowing them to interpret for themselves God's grace in terms of their own experience of life, Moore was jettisoning the fundamental core of the Victorian church which rested upon the drawing of distinctions between the preacher and his congregation and between the Christian community and the rest of the world. "A narrow, individualistic Gospel," stated Moore,

> does not appeal to these people, and such a Gospel misrepresents Christianity. We must interpret the great ideal of Christ to men; we must show that the Gospel is a great passion for justice and brotherhood; we must make men know that Jesus Christ is interested in them, and we must translate our own love and interest in terms that men can understand.[122]

Following the example of the Salvation Army and of such British labour leaders as Ben Tillett, Moore in his attempt to refashion the church in more egalitarian terms was actually transforming the basis of authority, which he now believed lay with the audience rather than with a clerical élite. In contrast to the Victorian pastor who assumed that a hierarchical relationship existed so that his congregation would naturally obey the doctrinal wisdom on which his sermons were based, the modern preacher had as his principal task to keep his finger on the pulse of the people.[123] The modern church had therefore actively to seek out and enlist the sympathies of the unchurched – especially men – by organizing mass outdoor rallies where preachers who had specialized in voice training rather than in theology spoke the vital message of religious experience in plain language through a combination of humour and stories depicting real-life problems, all woven together by powerful testimonies of personal conversion and knowledge of Christ.

Although modern revivalism flowed less spontaneously from the audience itself and relied upon managerial techniques, it nevertheless carefully attempted to reproduce the close sense of community achieved through the shared emotional experience so characteristic of nineteenth-century protracted revivals. Well-organized gospel teams of lay workers who had caught the new "spirit of service" would fan out at these open-air meetings held in various urban centres, and through personal exhortation they helped unleash a great flood of emotion and trigger numerous public confessions. Personal contact was the watchword of the new evangelism, so much so that the Presbyterian Board of Moral and Social

Reform had to warn these newly "affectionate" ministers against "imprudent intercourse."[124] "They literally go out and bring them in," noted Moore. "Rarely are results obtained until the men get to work on the floor of the house." Moore instructed these modern-day evangelists to undertake careful community studies for determining the spiritual needs and social characteristics of their audience and to circulate an array of leaflets and tracts which underscored the progressive vision of Christ in its human and social terms. The popular appeal of this new evangelism was, in turn, furthered by the introduction of singers and musicians, in the belief that five short hymns strategically punctuating the new, abbreviated, and less formal prayers would, because of their entertainment value, not only attract larger audiences but also heighten emotional involvement and immediately stir the latent spiritual instincts of the people.[125]

Likewise, the Presbyterian Church promoted the new religion of the vernacular. In an address delivered after World War I, D.N. McLachlan outlined the new priority the church now placed on the active cultivation of the modern audience. Building on the example of modern marketing techniques, in "The Minister of To-Day" McLachlan instructed ministers that in the interests of obtaining new "customers" for God they should make a careful study of the "psychology of salesmanship." The first task of the modern clergyman, therefore, was to obtain a thorough knowledge of the people's point of view, their occupations, and their spiritual problems and weaknesses in order that they might interpret the Gospel in such a way as to immediately attract the attention of "customers." Like the best officers in war, the modern clergyman-salesman had not only to be in touch with the higher command but also to be in constant and intimate sympathy with his "men." Thus, modern sermons should not only rely wholly upon the appeal to sentiment, through ringing challenges to action and with constant references to the blood of the Atonement, but they should be short, punchy, and delivered in a conversational style. McLachlan earnestly advised young ministers to "burn your sermons" and "speak to the people." And, in imitation of the modern salesman who understood that the best way to get a sale was to create a positive desire in his customer to buy his products, the modern pulpit should become a platform for persuasion rather than the traditional tribunal where sins were judged. At all times, the minister must emphasize the blessedness of sins forgiven rather than speak of God's condemnation and punishment of human failings. "If the salesman regards it to be good business to make men feel that life is worth living," McLachlan stated, "is the Minister to be less enthusiastic in his endeavor to persuade men that the Christian life is the highest and truest life? Must he not try to make God real to them?"[126]

Not only were McLachlan's references to modern sales techniques meant to appeal to young businessmen and clerks, but they also represented a more fundamental mind-set that had been powerfully shaped by a general organizational revolution in American life, which itself was modelled on modern corporate structures and the impetus to centralized efficiency. The fact that the churches' desire for a democratized religious culture was forged from above by a small, middle-class leadership enshrined the very dilemma of North American progressivism, where the search for a more egalitarian society came to depend increasingly upon routinization, bureaucratization, and the leadership of specialized expertise.[127] Although Canadian Protestant social reform remained shaped to a great degree by grass-roots popular religious values, it was nevertheless, throughout the early twentieth century, rapidly developing the tendrils of organizational culture. Out of their desire to suppress the legacy of Victorianism and to establish their point of view as the dominant one within the church, the leaders of the Methodist and Presbyterian departments of evangelism and social service were impelled towards the use of modern advertising campaigns and centralized bureaucratic specialization, so well deployed by American corporations. Indeed, modern revivalistic campaigns had become so gargantuan and so peripatetic, and operated on such tight schedules, sometimes requiring ten to fourteen meetings per week, that a "systematized" approach was imperative. These thrilling "triumphs of the cross" were not the mere spontaneous products of effervescent religious zeal but were intricately orchestrated and well-disciplined occasions of evangelical awakening. As one Methodist minister observed, "Evangelism for this age" demanded a delicate balance of religious enthusiasm and efficient planning.[128]

Pamphlets such as the *The Methodist National Campaign* and the Presbyterian *The Conduct of a Simultaneous Mission of Evangelism*, drawn up in Toronto, were instrumental in producing a uniform assembly-line evangelism, characterized by the precise and minute description of tasks, procedures, and techniques all designed for producing predictable religious experiences. The goal of Moore, Shearer, and C.W. Gordon was that these well-tuned and finely organized revivals would not only take place simultaneously but also exactly replicate one another in every town and hamlet across Canada. According to Gordon revivals could be held either in churches or in town halls, local skating rinks, or opera houses; the public confession of personal sin by individuals was adamantly prohibited; and weekly daytime mass prayer meetings could be held profitably only in urban areas, while in rural locations the traditional locus of cottage prayer meetings, the neighbourhood home, was to be employed. The most important element in the ultimate success of a local three-week revival campaign rested with the physical comfort of the audience. Gordon cautioned ministers to ensure that, above all, the chosen venue be well heated and lit as souls could not be saved if one's feet were cold. "Let nothing stand in the way of the comfort of the audience. The Devil can, and often does, use a janitor to hinder the work of God." The evening meetings were to be wholly evangelistic in character and proceed along a tightly focused schedule, beginning on the first night with an appeal to backsliders; the second night was for reaching out to the previously unchurched through the use of popular hymns, and the climax of the third was to be a sermon on "the great fundamental and practical truths" of Christianity. The emphasis throughout was to be on Christ's love and on direct appeals to the heart. "The preacher must be living in the atmosphere of Heaven, filled with tender yearning for men, aglow with the love of God, if he is to bring his hearers to the crisis and win them then and there to decision ... He is God's ambassador. Eternal destiny for many hangs on how he does his work."[129]

While Methodist Church leaders were as punctilious as their Presbyterian counterparts in precisely itemizing the minute components which made up the ideal revival, including instructions on how to deliver sermons in "old Anglo-Saxon" words "easily understood by workingmen," their emphasis was upon the larger structure of organization and advertising. The key to any efficiently run revival was, according to Moore, a combination of personal power and planning: at the grassroots level Wesley's class meeting system was transformed into a modern "unit-system" whereby lay workers performed specialized tasks as part of a production team that was overtly modelled on the efficiency group methods then in vogue in modern business and on the athletic field.[130] Each campaign was to begin with a rigorous advertising assault to underscore the enthusiastic, optimistic, and positive elements of Methodism: by strategically placing human interest stories (such as that of the minister who scaled a roof to bring a telephone wire into the home of an invalid woman so that she could hear the church choir), photographs of leading evangelists, and accounts of church events in the major daily newspapers, the work of the church would be integrally linked to other "great names and big events."[131] As Dobson informed Moore: "There is a very great advantage in a little appeal to the eye in a certain type of leaflet."[132]

The Presbyterians were no less adept at applying modern business practices to the organization of revivals. Not only did they use newspapers, billboards, street banners, and invitation cards to popularize religion,[133] they were even more creative than their Methodist confrères by implementing the brilliant concept of the "King's Business" button, which became in essence a personalized walking advertisement for

Christ. Moreover, the buttons appear to have been amazingly effective in preventing backsliding, as one young woman from Fort Frances testified to C.W. Gordon: "After your service two nights ago I went to a party and I have never seriously faced the amusement question before, but when in the midst of the jollity I happened to look down at my 'King's Business' button I felt a great conviction come into my heart that for me the card party and the dance must be henceforth left behind. I spent the most unhappy night I have ever had, but my course for the future is clear."[134]

The growing emphasis upon the popular will expressed by the new evangelism was reflected in changes in both the style and the content of sermons. By the first decades of the twentieth century church leaders had observed a growing diffidence among most practising Protestants towards publicly confessing their conversion experiences.[135] As Phyllis Airhart has so well documented, there was a marked shift away from the evangelism which was based exclusively upon individual conversion and which drew a sharp distinction between saved Christians and a sinful world, towards a newer, more inclusive notion of Christian commitment which was expressed through ongoing Christian service.[136] Whether individuals wholly rejected the very practice of conversion, or, as the Presbyterian minister Alexander J. McIntosh observed of most of the people under his charge in Pipestone, Manitoba, they repudiated public declarations of faith in favour of private expressions of Christian commitment, is open to question. What was apparent, however, was a rising ground swell of popular resistance at about the opening of the twentieth century to older forms of community social control and religious discipline that revolved around the intrusive class meeting and the practice of surrendering oneself to God before the whole congregation.[137] Although it is somewhat unclear what these changes in behaviour indicated concerning larger shifts in social and cultural values, what did emerge was a multi-textured religious culture. While it sought at one level to safeguard private piety through the resurrection of closet prayer and family altars, it simultaneously conflated the expression of private piety with public social activity through the consistent application of the Gospel to social, industrial, and political affairs in Christian Brotherhood organizations and neighbourhood meetings.[138] The intention behind the prominence given to family prayer was to allow those individuals like J.S. Woodsworth who found the modern institutional church too bureaucratized and constricting to continue Christian worship, as Woodsworth in fact did in the privacy of his home after his resignation from the ministry. The strong support given by church leaders to family worship also had a class and an ethnic dimension. In Western Canada, family altars were erected where they had not before appeared so that "masters" could discuss the Gospel with their hired men and women who most often would have been recent immigrants from Europe and who did not as yet attend the local Protestant churches.[139] In the end, progressive church leaders began to interpret private and public morality in terms of a seamless web in as far as "personal morality is the basis of public morality" and community values in turn determine those of the individual.[140]

These changes in Christian behaviour, in turn, compelled ministers to shift the focus of their sermons away from sin and repentance towards the more inviting promise of Christ's redemptive love. Within this new dispensation, Samuel Dwight Chown proclaimed that the twentieth-century revival would be transformed and would not only be more optimistic in tone but deeper and more ethical in its spiritual awakening: "The preaching that shall produce it may not be nearly so dramatic as that of the past, and therefore the results may not be so sensationally and superficially striking. We shall not see an angry God laying upon His innocent Son punishment for our sins that we escape punishment, but we shall see a loving sin bearing God pouring out his life for us in the person of his Son."[141] Although T. Albert Moore experienced some reluctance in relinquishing the older evangelism with its emphasis upon sin, conversion, and the penitent bench, by 1920 he had come to share J.G. Shearer's view that sermons concerned only with "dying and going to heaven" were decidedly old-fashioned and actually subversive of the aim of the new evangelism, which sought to lead people into active Christian service.[142]

Revivalism in Canada was powerfully directed by these shifts within popular religious sentiment towards an acceptance of outward social action as the definitive mark of the individual's membership in the Christian community. What this new social evangelism confirmed was the "privatization of religious belief," for it was based on the idea that to be a Christian a person need not formally attend the institutional church[143] and that devotion to God's Kingdom on earth could be demonstrated through community service. This new broadly conceived cultural definition of Christianity was best articulated by C.W. Gordon, whose own books offered telling testimony to this new model of Christian behaviour: "Man is an individual and also a socius. He is born an individual but also into a family. He is organised an individual but into a community ... His salvation is that of an individual in social relations and there is no other salvation for him."[144]

This new outlook had a profound effect upon Canadian revivalism. Certain Canadian church leaders eagerly sought the assistance of prominent such conservative American evangelists as J. Wilbur Chapman and Charles Alexander, but their ultimate goal was in direct opposition to the direction taken by American Protestantism in the twentieth century. While American revivals led towards the rejuvenation of a militant fundamentalism during the 1920s, in Canada revivals such as the Chapman-Alexander campaign of 1911 were used by the Presbyterian Church to ignite public interest in the "higher spiritualism" that would ultimately build a consensus in favour of urban social reform.[145] By 1914 the spiritual cleansing and purification, which the individual experienced in revivals, had become so pivotal for the larger program of social Christianity that the Presbyterians expressed considerable doubt about the effectiveness of Charles Stelzle's gospel of unadulterated social service, preferring the more stirring emotional evangelism of Gypsy Smith, who in 1919 was instrumental in converting large numbers of workers. Of Stelzle, Gordon noted: "his evangelism is to be associated entirely with Social Service work. He is not an evangelist in the sense that he seeks to bring men to a personal knowledge of Jesus Christ. He does seek to bring men into service, more particularly social service."[146] The ideal was to combine revivalism with social Christianity. Prior to 1918 social service was quietly infused into evangelistic campaigns. At the Fort William Mission, social reform issues formed the basis of the concluding sermon, while in Vancouver a different strategy was employed by the Rev. D.N. McLachlan, who on alternating days interspersed his sermons on Christianizing the social order with traditional aggressive evangelistic techniques to bring in the masses of people from outside the church. Even love-feasts, those forms of Methodist personal piety most identified with the traditional holiness rejection of the outer world, were transformed into occasions for promoting the cause of moral and social reform. In Lunenburg, Nova Scotia, 4,000 people gathered for an old-fashioned Methodist love-feast where they were treated to S.D. Chown's modern optimistic sermons and T. Albert Moore's exhortations on the liquor question and the quest for child welfare and labour reform.[147]

By 1918 progressive clergymen had succeeded in transforming revivalism into a platform for social Christianity. While the war was being fought, it strangely had little impact on the debate within the Protestant churches at home and had little effect in altering the course of Protestant social reform until after 1918, when the notion of sacrificial service was elevated to mythical stature and transformed into the ideological engine that accelerated the pace of the acceptance of the new social Christianity into the broader culture. What was indeed a catastrophe for human civilization became in the eyes of progressive clergymen a positive life-force, redolent with God's beneficent intervention, to wring out of the "winepress" of human sinfulness "the pathway of redemption for the world."[148] The cataclysm of war offered a compelling demonstration, in the estimation of Protestant church leaders, of how Christ could be made more immanent through the direct application of the new gospel of individual service to the community and nation. As late as 1915 the view put forth by the spiritualist A.D. Watson that individual conversion was the crucial preliminary to developing a social conscience was still prevalent within both the Presbyterian and the Methodist churches.[149] By 1918 social service was no longer seen as simply the client of revivalism; rather, as Hugh Dobson claimed, social reconstruction had become the central avenue to personal conversion. By 1919 individual regeneration and social salvation had become interchangeable and mutually reinforcing.[150]

The idea that evangelism was complementary and even coordinate with social regeneration had been first enunciated by Chown in 1905. For this leading Methodist, personal evangelism and social service were the obverse sides of a single coin, that of faith. "Its in-take fills the heart," Chown declared, "with divine love for brotherly human service. Its out-put is a life organized in and for personal and social righteousness."[151] It was not unusual that Dobson could make the following observation: "I have found a great many occasions that the regeneration of the individual has followed the stimulus that came from a vision of society. Jesus presented to the minds of his learners the idea of the Kingdom. The Kingdom is always a society. That vision that He gave of the Kingdom led many to repent of their sins on their hearing of the Gospel of the Kingdom, to step out of their selfishness into a new consecration to the larger good, and to commit themselves to its program."[152] In his 1918 pamphlet, *What Delays the Revival*, Moore served notice that the spirit of progressive Christianity had finally captured the revival for its own ends: "The Revival involves Reconstruction in the fullest, deepest, widest, highest and most practical sense. Certainly, Soul-saving; but not merely in view of the hereafter; but the salvation of the whole man, here and now, in all his capacities and relations. The programme is immeasurable."[153] All the regional Methodist conferences followed Moore's lead, and in 1919 they issued their own declarations supporting the new-found notion that social Christianity was indistinguishable from the revival of individual spirituality. "God in Christ Jesus, through the power of the Holy Spirit *is awakening* in human lives an awareness of Himself," stated the British Columbia Conference in 1919. "The awakened individual, influenced by the spirit of the age, *is seeking* to Christianize all his social relations. This is *lifting him* into fellowship with Christ in service to his fellow men."[154]

While the new social evangelism became the dominant paradigm within both the Methodist and Presbyterian churches by 1918, it always remained in harmonious concert with the traditions of an older evangelical society. Compelled by the conservative nature of popular religious practice and in particular the tenacious allegiance of the people to personal piety, progressives within the church emphasized that the very act of applying the Gospel to social questions would replace the intermittent campaigns of mass revivalism. Indeed, social Christianity, with its "fuller consciousness of God," was in the view of many the key to ensuring an ongoing, enduring era of heightened spirituality. Ever responsive to the currents of popular religiosity, Dobson declared: "I feel quite certain also that the people are going to demand something more continuous and more thorough than the ordinary type of itinerant evangelism." With the growing popularity of social reform, Dobson believed that "we have commenced already in the greatest revival of the world's history: but it is not of the type of revival that wears itself out in three weeks or three months."[155] Hence, the directives outlined by such progressive leaders as Hugh Dobson not only received the assent of grassroots popular piety but were themselves the product of it. The Rev. H. Whiteley of Sintaluta, Saskatchewan, who, like many Canadian Protestants was converted during a protracted revival, distilled the views of his congregation when he stated that individual regeneration and social service were inextricably intertwined: "Accept Christ as the foundation and then line up the new experience to life in all its various phases. I think if we try to build up a righteous nation without accepting Christ we are trying to erect a fine building without laying an adequate foundation, and if we lead people to Christ and the life in Christ is not linked up to practical affairs, we have laid the foundation but failed to erect the building."[156]

3 To "Complete the Circle of Scientific Theology"[1]

Beneath the reorientation of the Canadian Protestant churches to the imperatives of social service lay a pragmatic desire to secure and maintain their leadership in social reform. The ability of the churches to take the initiative in building a strong and dynamic national coalition out of disparate local reformist sentiment drew directly upon the authority they derived from the expertise and specialized knowledge provided by the new social sciences, especially sociology and social work. In contrast to the American social gospel movement, which found itself overwhelmed and marginalized by the coincident rise of the social sciences in the universities during the 1890s, Canadian churchmen not only enthusiastically welcomed and readily integrated the new perspectives on modern social problems into their Christian outlook, but, in the almost total absence of sociology in the universities before 1920, also enabled the churches to serve as the primary vehicles by which modern social science entered Canadian culture.

This uniquely close connection between mainline Protestantism and the social sciences in Canada gave the churches a pre-eminence in defining the scope and method of the social sciences and thus lent a peculiar cast to the importation of specialized knowledge of social problems from Britain and the United States. The ultimate goal of the churches of creating the Kingdom of God on earth meant that they consistently eschewed the more objectivist forms of social science, such as behaviourist psychology and value-free sociology, in favour of social scientific investigation which, although empirical in its method, was firmly anchored to the pursuit of an ethical standard and the advocacy of a type of reform explicitly animated by the concerns of social Christianity. The power which the church continued to wield over the character and agenda of the social sciences extended not only to the training and employment of social scientists, but more importantly to the identification of the problems and to the very definition of a legitimate scope of activity for the social sciences in modern Canada. The authority of Protestant social Christianity in the sphere of the social sciences persisted well into the 1930s and was responsible for delaying the introduction of objective and technocratic social engineering into the key disciplines of social work and sociology. Only in the later stages of the Depression, after "economic management" and "planning" had become the watchwords of both the political left and right in Canada,[2] did university social scientists finally attain greater public authority *vis-à-vis* the churches. By 1940 academic social science was beginning to distance itself from its early development in close relationship with social Christianity in the name of a new alliance with a growing federal state bureaucracy.

The ambition of twentieth-century progressive church leaders to construct a reform coalition in which the Protestant churches would function as the central clearing-house for research, publicity, and lobbying for reform legislation had a profound effect on both the intellectual training and the social role of the rank-and-file minister. Where before 1900 biblical exegesis provided the intellectual foundation of a ministerial authority that remained largely confined to the institutional church, in the twentieth century the new ideal of the minister stressed his wider cultural role as a community leader. This necessitated the introduction of a new form of intellectual sustenance for Christian faith, modern social science. Ramsay Cook has observed that the central flaw of social Christianity was that it lacked a "systematic intellectual underpinning" and thus failed to acquire the authority of either traditional biblical theology or the supposed rigorous social analysis brought to bear by such radical and secular social thinkers as Stephen Leacock and Mackenzie King.[3] Not only were the majority of ministers enjoined to read Leacock and King at the urgent behest of vigilant field secretaries such as Hugh Dobson in Western Canada and Ernest Thomas in the east, but they were exposed to a wide range of British and American social philosophy to enable them to articulate a coherent and sophisticated Christian sociology which was instrumental in situating Canadian Protestantism on the cutting edge of the current transatlantic re-evaluation of traditional liberalism. The introduction of modern social science was believed to be particularly crucial in continuing to attract the best and the brightest young men to the profession in an age when the ministry was experiencing competition from the rising prestige of business, the law, and medicine. Increasingly, progressive church leaders identified the older theology as effeminate because of its preoccupation with other-worldly doctrines of piety and private morality, spheres traditionally assigned to women. Through the introduction of the new social sciences, progressives hoped to refashion the ministry into a more manly and activist profession whose arena would be the public sphere of politics, where the creation of social welfare policies was achieved through the scientific rigour of empirical investigation.

While the incorporation of the social sciences into Christian progressivism was intended to construct an expertly trained and gender-specific leadership for social reform, the church's ability to expand its reform constituency was given tremendous impetus by its formidable grass-roots support which drew almost exclusively on the tradition of middle-class female activism expressed by the vast network of local women's institutes, farm women's clubs, local chapters of the National Council of Women, and the well-entrenched Women's Christian Temperance Union. These groups articulated a maternal feminism that had as its goal legislation to protect the family and that sought to expand the influence of women in society not through politics but through their sphere of influence within the reform network. Maternal feminism has been consigned by modern feminist scholars to a conservative backwater because it ultimately failed, in their view, to promote the political and economic equality of women.[4] For those historians who have regarded as the *sine qua non* of modern feminism the achievement of suffrage and the expectation it held out that by entering political life women could shape public policy, the 1920s does indeed appear a bleak decade for Canadian women.[5] By privileging national political events over Christian social activism through voluntary organization, feminist historians have in turn lent credence to the interpretation that reform was in decline following World War I. But by focusing attention upon the alliance between the churches and women's organizations, a markedly different trajectory of social reform emerges, one that underscores the continuity of trends in place prior to and following the Great War. In the Canadian context, this continuity in turn suggests that the modern welfare state was less the creature of organized labour and government experts and far more the result of the energies of a progressive reform coalition composed of the mainline Protestant churches, middle-class women, and agrarian organizations, whose concerns reflected the direct impress of the rural hinterland and of social Christianity.

If one emphasizes the role of private organizations in the forging of social welfare policies, the 1920s becomes a decisive period in which, for the first time, enduring national coalitions, most notably the Social Service Council of Canada, were launched with the express purpose of formulating social policy at the federal level of government. A wide range of social reform groups sought out an alliance with this church-led organization, including farmers' organizations and the Trades and Labor Congress of Canada, but by far the most important component of this spearhead of reform was the contribution of women through the National Council of Women and the Women's Christian Temperance Union. The apparent paradox between the rejection of female ordination by many progressive male clergymen, such as Ernest Thomas,[6] and their overt attempts to enlist women into their reform coalition was not simply an attempt to restrict the role of women in the church. Rather, it reflected a recognition by church leaders of the power of women's reform groups at both the organizational and ideological levels of progressivism. Such an alliance was premised upon the need of male clergymen for a cohort of committed volunteers to work within or alongside the local church in order to mobilize permanently reform sentiment. On the other hand, female progressives, the majority of whom, even in the wake of winning the vote, shared the prevailing view that women must preserve a special moral role and thus avoid direct political involvement, enlisted the cultural prestige of Protestant Christianity to cultivate community support for their legislative program.

The strange alliance between the church and women's organizations was mutually beneficial, and because the new social Christianity conflated the private and public spheres it provided a respectable yet powerful vehicle by which women could gain public attention and support for issues that affected them and the family.[7] Indeed, middle-class women were very successful in utilizing the church to implement their women's platform at the highest levels of government. It is not coincidental that the platforms of the boards of evangelism and social service of the Protestant churches almost totally replicated that of the National Council of Women, whose program for social reform included child welfare legislation, prohibition, social purity, mothers' allowances, the eradication of sweated and child labour, and the establishment of a minimum wage for women. Moreover, the Protestant churches, especially the Methodist, were among the first groups to take up the plea of women for child welfare, and they were pivotal in lobbying for the creation of a federal government children's bureau. Thus, although the new social Christianity aspired to create a realm of male expertise, its equally powerful dependence upon an enduring tradition of localism and strong grass-roots reform sentiment drew it inextricably towards the female domain of the local women's groups, thus rendering the male-dominated progressive impulse within Canadian Protestantism the foremost champion of maternalist social policy.

TOWARDS A CHRISTIAN SOCIAL SCIENCE

Between 1850 and 1890 clergymen in Canada gracefully side-stepped many of the implications of Darwinism and social evolutionism by situating the well-springs of Christian faith in a historical theology that saw the development of human civilization not as a natural process but as the fulfilment of divine revelation.[8] This relative lack of interest in the relationship between religion and the natural sciences changed dramatically on the eve of the twentieth century. By 1900 clergymen had easily integrated social evolutionary thought into the tenets of evangelicalism largely through their reading of history, psychology, anthropology, and sociology, disciplines which after 1880 had incrementally absorbed Spencerian and Darwinian notions of human development.[9] The consequent blending of idealist philosophy with evolutionary science led to the breakdown of traditional compartments between science, morals, and religion. Once Spencerianism shed its dubious associations with positivistic science, its central metaphysic of society as an organism subject to the natural laws of development was quickly incorporated into all forms of knowledge that treated the development of the human mind and civilization.[10]

The popularization of evolutionary thought permeated the religious language of the progressive age. Darwinian thought was made accountable to religion largely through Lamarckian ideas of evolution, then in vogue among scientists and social philosophers, because these ideas were redolent of the older natural theology and preserved the centrality of divine benevolence and design in both natural and social evolution. Where Darwin had emphasized the randomness and the morally blind mechanism of natural selection to explain biological change, neo-Lamarckians such as Joseph LeConte and Henry Drinker Cope fell back on the theory of use and disuse, which implied that human agency was a critical factor in determining the direction of evolutionary change. This revision of Darwin made evolution palatable to an ethical vision of society because unlike Darwin it was hopeful in suggesting that evolution was purposeful and progressive.[11]

In a sermon to the First Congregational Church in Vancouver, the Rev. A.E. Cooke proclaimed that Protestantism must seek to unify science and religion lest it lose its influence by opposing modern culture. With the added weight of an introduction by Canadian anthropologist Charles Hill-Tout, Cooke elaborated on the ideas of the outstanding American neo-Lamarckian, Professor LeConte, arguing that the recapitulation theory of evolution was merely God's method of creation. Quoting LeConte, Cooke announced that the phenomena of nature were but the "objectified modes of Divine thought." He agreed with the nineteenth-century Scottish natural theologian and Presbyterian revivalist Henry Drummond that while the book of Genesis bespoke the problem of man's origins, evolution was merely the naturalized extension of divine fiat. "The laws of nature," Cooke observed, "are simply the ordinary way in which God works in the physical realm."[12] While in the United States ever widening fissures appeared after the turn of the century between fundamentalism and popular evolutionism, in Canada even a conservative evangelical like the influential revivalist French Oliver embraced evolutionary science and philosophy, claiming them as "God's messengers." More stunningly, Oliver applied the new evolutionary theories of the human mind and the anthropometry of the French surgeon Paul Broca to develop what he called the "psychology of prayer." According to Oliver, moral regeneration was akin to the Lamarckian theory of use and disuse, and he illustrated the happy convergence of science and spirituality by relating to an audience of 5,000 the story of an American blacksmith who, by quitting swearing, lost ninety per cent of his vocabulary and thereby was converted to Christ.[13]

In *The Church and Social Relations*, a pamphlet issued for the Methodist Department of Evangelism and Social Service, W.A. Douglas concluded that just as gravitation bound together the chaos of the universe, religion provided moral laws that were as inescapable as the imperatives of the natural world in serving to unite humanity in a harmonious brotherhood. In language resplendent with images borrowed from Victorian natural theology, Douglas described how "in the testimony of the rocks, in the wondrous mechanism of the heavens, in the sublimities and the harmonies of the universe, in the marvellous adaptations of the physical forces, in the ineffable potencies of thought and vitality" God's power was revealed to all classes, and from these fixed dictates of nature Douglas sought out the guiding tenets of twentieth-century social democracy.[14] The Methodist preacher W.W. Andrews was no less confident that by merging Darwinian science and Christianity, atheism would be banished altogether from modern culture. He deployed evolutionary thought to buttress the new social evangelism. By contending that human beings, like societies of plant life, do not "live for themselves" but are interdependent upon "various classes ... each performing different functions in the life of the community," Andrews, in his 1913 pamphlet, *Nature and Self-Sacrifice*, reworked Darwin's theory of the struggle for existence so that it ultimately refuted its author's central idea of competition and conflict over scarce resources as the mechanism of evolutionary change. Through what he termed "conscious self-sacrifice," human societies would evolve towards the highest form of life, classless interdependence characterized by social harmony.[15]

For many progressive social reformers Darwinian thought was made respectable because it was undergirded by eugenics, with its message of social efficiency. The Rev. Peter Bryce, a postwar champion of national efficiency, was likewise fascinated by Henri Bergson's theory of creative evolution because it harkened back to the supreme role of both God and humans in directing evolutionary social change. Bryce reached conclusions similar to those of Andrews by borrowing from Spencer's idea of the superorganic when he stated that "each member of society is a unit going to make up the whole of a complicated organism." For those evangelicals wishing to preserve individual piety within the new dictates of social Christianity, science provided compelling lessons that demonstrated the naturalness of the growth of individual responsibility flowing in the wake of social development.[16]

Because the assumptions and methods of the social sciences had, by the beginning of the twentieth century, become increasingly informed directly and indirectly by social evolutionary ideas, the acceptance of neo-Darwinian science by Canadian clergymen was an important intellectual hurdle for the mainline Protestant churches before they could advocate consistently the teaching of the social sciences as the essential equipment of the modern minister. Believing that evolution was not simply the product of natural laws but was also impelled by human intervention, ministers such as Hugh Dobson concluded that modern social progress could be assured by the application of scientific expertise. Hence, Dobson expounded on the need to study anthropology for the history of marriage customs, the science of heredity and environment, and modern social case work and sociology, for through these phenomena God taught us how to "adjust ourselves in the great class conflict" that now characterized modern industrial life. From Darwin, Dobson had learned that not all evolution was progressive, but by bringing modern social science to bear upon the foundations of faith, humans could initiate and control the direction of social progress. "[E]very plastic period," Dobson declared in 1927, "is an opportunity for higher forms of life to gain a predominance. Forms of life that are inadequate become casualties and the more adequately adapted survive. So progress is made."[17]

More generally, those Protestant clergymen who were committed to social Christianity were well apprised of the growing authority conferred on scientific investigation and the possession of specialized knowledge. The Presbyterian leadership, which was the first to advocate training in economics, sociology, and modern industrial problems, recognized that moral exhortation alone would not suffice in the modern world of rapid social change. To ensure their command over the direction of social reform movements, it was incumbent upon the churches to "be raising up a body of *trained and specialized workers*," for in the modern age "expert knowledge" was the only means by which they could garner public support. More importantly, Presbyterian progressives believed that the modern social sciences constituted the most crucial new departure to revivify the prestige of the clerical profession among ambitious young men.[18] Samuel Dwight Chown was astutely aware of how scientific methodology – what he termed the "inductive method" – had come to permeate all areas of modern life, and he impressed upon the Methodist Church colleges the urgent necessity of shedding their obsolete commitment to Old Testament theology in favour of courses that would put the minister in "sympathetic touch with the intellectual world" of the modern day. Only through the acquisition of modern knowledge, he argued, could young probationers be awakened to the wider social implications of their faith. In Chown's estimation, therefore, modern social science would preserve the church's autonomy because, rather than replacing Christian faith, it served to amplify the minister's search for those truths that had been revealed in the Bible.[19] As one Methodist, Mrs Alberta Gieser, stated, the theories of the social critic Henry George were telling evidence that "God is not dead" and that the study of the "exact science" of political economy would only demonstrate that "God stands ready to perform miracles greater than [in] the past."[20]

The Methodist Church had tentatively begun to sponsor the social sciences as early as 1898 when Nathanael Burwash had welcomed James Mavor's lectures delivered to the divinity students of Victoria College on political economy and the plight of the working man. Mavor was an exemplar of the conviction that the sciences did not displace faith, because he believed they could never occupy that sacred sphere which transcended all science and rational knowledge. From his training at the University of Glasgow, where he had studied with the idealist philosopher Edward Caird and with John Veitch, the late representative of Scottish Common Sense, both of whom identified faith as the primary element of knowledge which in combination with idealist tenets bridged the abyss between science and religion, Mavor derived a conception of the social "Good" that, by removing religion from its other-wordly monasticism, would challenge the currents of secularism.[21]

By 1908, as part of a wider program to promote the discussion of social questions within all church sponsored agencies, including the YMCA, the male-centred Brotherhoods, and various youth organizations such as the Epworth League, the progressive wings of both the Methodist and Presbyterian churches had strongly endorsed the teaching of

Christian sociology in the church colleges. A campaign to establish chairs of sociology in these institutions continued well into the 1920s, and in contrast to the American example, where sociology emerged as a discipline out of the urban crucible of the 1890s, Canadian sociology grew directly out of explicitly Christian concerns which were decisively shaped by the need to address the problems created by the perceived decay of rural communities.[22] The first Chair of Christian Sociology was established at Victoria College in 1919 and was occupied by the Rev. John Walker Macmillan, a Presbyterian minister who had studied political economy at the University of Toronto with W.J. Ashley, the English economist most closely identified with the Christian reformism of Arnold Toynbee and his social settlement ideal.[23] Macmillan, who attended Knox College and was ordained in 1891, served for twenty-five years as a minister in Vancouver, Lindsay, Winnipeg, and Halifax. He then became professor of social ethics and practical theology at the University of Manitoba. There he forged close links with Salem Bland and J.S. Woodsworth and became one of the chief lecturers in Woodsworth's Training Class in Social Work at the University of Manitoba which, although it included such civic leaders as newspaper editor J.W. Dafoe and welfare activist G.B. Clarke, was dominated by Protestant ministers.[24] It was this Winnipeg model of teaching the principles involved in applying New Testament Christianity to child welfare, relief work, the investigation of industrial accidents, and the development of modern social theories that formed the basis for his later sociology courses at Victoria College.[25] Although Macmillan is best known for introducing mothers' allowances in Manitoba and Ontario and for later chairing the Ontario Minimum Wage Commission,[26] his sociological views remained under the impress of Christian thought. While undertaking postgraduate work in social ethics at Union Theology Seminary in New York, Macmillan amplified his social outlook by reading Washington Gladden and Walter Rauschenbusch, prominent leaders of the American social gospel whose thinking was shaped by current sociological debates.[27] Despite the influence of Herbert Spencer and other American social Darwinists on him, Macmillan never doubted the tenets of Christianity or veered towards the secular ethics of modern philosophy. While he advocated the importance of modern social psychology, with its stress upon the interdependence of the individual and the social order, Macmillan's conception of social progress was grounded upon the individual mind as the primary mechanism of evolution, a process that in his estimation was wholly Christian because the highest form of the human species was Jesus Christ. Despite the fact that Jesus was a "socially-minded" prophet, the social gospel could never "devour the individual gospel," stated Macmillan, because the very progression of society towards increasing cooperation ultimately depended upon individual choice which was guided by the experience of the personal character of Jesus Christ.[28] Throughout his career Macmillan saw as his principal task the encouragement of sociology in the modern pulpit. In 1921 he spoke to the Methodist Ministerial Association on "Sociology and its Relationship to the Pulpit" and he later introduced the "Basic Principles of Sociology" to the students at the Canadian School of Missions. Even as late as 1930 Macmillan's growing espousal of government intervention in the sphere of social welfare remained tempered by his belief that a cooperative society was anchored upon the primary institutions of the family and the state, and that the church remained the critical linchpin between the public and private spheres.[29]

Another of Ashley's students, the Baptist A.L. McCrimmon, chancellor and professor of economics and sociology at McMaster University, promoted the new discipline of sociology within the larger parameters of Christian endeavour. Only through the study of modern social problems, what McCrimmon called the "much more virile mingling with the red blood of humanity," could the "selfish spiritual separatism" of the older theology be overcome and the true nature of God, His "divine Sociality," be asserted through the evangelization of industry, nation, and race.[30] Having graduated from the University of Toronto, in 1897 McCrimmon proceeded to the University of Chicago where he studied sociological theory with Albion Small, the founder of the university's Department of Sociology. However, it was under the tutelage of Small's colleague C.R. Henderson, who established the tradition of social investigation and the use of the city as a social laboratory which came to so define the Chicago School of Sociology, that McCrimmon developed his conviction that sociology's primary function lay in supplying the methodology for social reform and practical theology. Even as McCrimmon became immersed in the positivist tenets of Small's sociology, the "Conservative Envangelicalism" in his thought was evident and he eschewed Comte's "religion of humanity" because of its overtones of secular socialism. For McCrimmon the study of social problems implied the renewal of "the Glory of God" because "even in social work the far-off divine event is a lode-star to the Christian pilgrim."[31]

S.D. Chown's definition of sociology was much less immediately reliant than those of either McCrimmon or Macmillan upon the theoretical discussions of sociology then current in American universities, and instead it found its inspiration in those very problems of modern industrial life that had animated the ethical and social reformist tendencies of the formative phase of the social sciences in the United States during the Gilded Age. Chown was, in fact, openly hostile to the growing popularity among American social scientists of deterministic natural laws for explaining social phenomena because this signalled a shift away from the older connection between history and social science that emphasized individual free will rather than scientific social control.[32] Thus, although Chown had reservations about William James's *Varieties of Religious Experience*, which in his estimation overintellectualized the spiritual, he approved of James's "philosophical psychology" because, by reasserting freedom of the spiritual will over materialistic determinism, it staved off the unholy tenets of modern behaviourism and contributed to a general reawakening of "a new and greater evangelism."[33] Chown generally accepted the main outlines of Darwinian evolution but he was insistent on privileging the "divine natural" over the "naturalistic natural," arguing that the former preserved God's superintendence over his creation while modern eugenics, with its ironclad laws of heredity, removed morality and sin beyond the purview of individual responsibility.[34]

Out of this concern to preserve spiritual life in a world of biological determinism, Chown's vision of social scientific investigation verged towards a clearly historical conception of human evolution that he interpreted as spiritual development towards the Kingdom of God:

> Does not scripture teach us that we are to glorify God in the body? Does not biology teach us that we are at home in this world? Has not the whole evolutionary process (written above as historical development) been preparing us for our environment, and our environment for us? Do we not lose the measure of evolution (written above as spiritual development) we should receive in this world, and consequently fail in preparation for the next by thinking of ourselves as strangers here, as exotics, and not racy of the soil. The sermon on the mount is for here and now.[35]

Having thus situated himself within the idealist camp in the debate over evolution, it is easy not only to comprehend Chown's observation that science, Christianity, and human cooperation – what he termed "socialism" – were moving towards a point of convergence, but also why he conceived of sociology as the broad study of "man as a social being" or as the "science of living in brotherly conditions." Chown's definition of sociology, with its distinct moral bias and concern for an equitable distribution of wealth, owed much to the larger intellectual climate in which social philosophers and reformers redefined liberalism in collectivist terms in order to address the urgent problems of how to preserve human welfare and democracy in the midst of industrial unrest and monopolistic capital. For Chown, therefore, sociology was particularly valuable for the Christian minister because of its affinities with the generalist traditions of English political economy which, in the wake of

Alfred Marshall who turned economic study towards the problem of poverty, served to help awaken moral insight and increase sympathy for the condition of the people. Sociology, in Chown's view, was not meant to displace traditional theology; rather, its aim was to "complete the circle of scientific theology" by amplifying the minister's commitment to the new "social morality."[36]

Chown's insistence that social science must serve overtly Christian aims was echoed by Hugh Dobson who in 1925 exclaimed that "I believe firmly in the value of the earnest and devoted study of both theology and economics."[37] It was not Christianity that was altered by the social sciences; rather, Protestant church leaders determined the direction and methodology of the social sciences, especially reform economics, sociology, and social work, and they effectively made them tributary to the imperatives of social Christianity, because they and not the universities were the chief promoters of these new disciplines. The power of Protestantism to transform the social sciences imported from the academies of Britain and the United States was tellingly demonstrated by the title of an article by the Rev. Robert Connell: "Economics in Light of Christianity."[38] The introduction of the social sciences to the church college curriculum enabled the churches to respond more effectively to modern social change and it thereby actually strengthened church leadership, which resulted in the forestalling of secularization in Canada. The contention that the rise of the social sciences produced a new professional class which usurped the authority of the older religious leadership[39] is, it may be argued, an accurate description of the American context after 1914, in which social science revolted against its traditional alliance with social reform and out of this desire to free itself from ideology tilted irrevocably towards an objectivist outlook rooted in the natural sciences.[40] Where American social scientists embraced the ideal of technocratic expertise during the 1920s, Canadian social science remained firmly under the aegis of the progressive wing of the Protestant churches and thus preserved its close links with social reform and the goals of practical Christianity well into the 1930s. Indeed, the definition of social science as a form of Christian service was not confined to clergymen, but was enthusiastically embraced by prominent Canadian social scientists anxious to promote the authority and stature of their disciplines. Writing in 1883 Adam Shortt, founder of the Department of Political Economy at Queen's University, confided to his fiancée, Elizabeth Smith, that his reasons for preferring an academic career over a pulpit had little to do with religious doubt, but rather with what he saw as the most effective way of popularizing Christian ideals of social righteousness:

> At first I thought it could best be done through the Church & believe it so yet ... did the Church but take it up right. But I see there too great a tendency to impose the principles of righteousness ... upon the people as external commands given to them from without by a Law giver to whom alone they are responsible. And, although this may have been a natural & to some extent a necessary stage in human progress, yet it is far from being the highest or most efficient way of securing the elevation of humanity. They must be taught ... that there is within each & ever one a higher principle than that of the mere animal. A higher, & purer nature of which the other is merely a servant; and to which, as the essential characteristic of humanity, they are primarily responsible. That is, they are responsible to an internal principle – to themselves – more truly divine in origin & nature than external commands, which are but an imperfect expression of the dictates of this inner nature of man. This principle of humanity ... enables man to recognize that he is not an independent atom in the world of existence, but that he is essentially related to every thing else in the world, & especially to his brother man, without regarding whom almost equally with himself, he cannot perfect himself. Hence in seeking to elevate himself he is compelled to regard the highest interests of all others ... it is only when we get people to recognize this, that they will understand their duties toward their families & neighbours in its proper light, & see that in serving their own higher nature most faithfully they are likewise obeying God most perfectly ... You will thus see, dear Beth, how it is that I have chosen the teaching profession in preference to the Ministry as it exists at the present day.[41]

Although Shortt has been hailed as the progenitor of a "secular" political economy that owed nothing to Christian concepts of social reform,[42] it is clear that his conception of social science as a fundamentally Christian vocation firmly eschewed radical distinction between evangelical religion and modern social science. Rather than envisioning the displacement of religion by modern social science, the liberal ideology and social research espoused by Shortt and his disciples O.D. Skelton and W.A. Mackintosh, both later active members of the church-sponsored Social Service Council of Canada, rested firmly on the application of Christian service to the solution of problems raised by modern capitalism. Their outlook sustained a cooperative alliance between the churches, universities, and various reform constituencies which was only eclipsed after 1935 by the rise of expert social planning as represented by the League for Social Reconstruction and by the liberal-Keynesian economists who captured the attention of Mackenzie King.

Much of our understanding of social Christianity in Canada has been conditioned by the work of Richard Allen who, despite his immense contribution to the interpretation of the nexus of religion and social reform, has emphasized the influence of American social gospel writers such as Walter Rauschenbusch and Washington Gladden to the exclusion of almost all other intellectual influences. He thus unintentionally portrays progressive ministers as effete and somewhat out of touch with contemporary social analysis by comparison with university academics and secular social critics. Allen's attenuation of the learning of Canadian clergymen to a very narrow range of the American social gospel of the 1890s served his central aim of casting J.S. Woodsworth in the singular role of being one of the most "widely-read Canadians on social and civic subjects."[43] Next to such prominent clergymen of the 1890s as G.M. Grant, Woodsworth indeed does appear extremely widely read, given his sojourn at Oxford where he was exposed to the social ethics of James McCosh, Herbert Spencer, T.H. Green, and Andrew Fairbairn,[44] but by the early twentieth century his overweening reliance upon the early social gospel writings of Josiah Strong and Rauschenbusch and his lack of familiarity with modern economics and sociology placed him among the rearguard of the Protestant progressive contingent. It was only in 1913, five years after the Methodist Church established its reading course in social science, that Woodsworth read E.A. Ross's *Social Psychology*. And, when a host of young clergymen were already studying under the luminaries of American sociology and psychology, Woodsworth still clung to the belief that studying with the liberal theologian Francis Peabody, professor of ethics at Harvard, was the best means for acquiring both the most up-to-date knowledge of modern social problems and a professorship to teach social service in a Canadian university.[45] Certainly, Canadian clergymen avidly read works by Rauschenbusch, Francis G. Peabody, Harry Ward of Union Theological Seminary, and the Chicago school of liberal theologians represented by Shailer Mathews and Shirley Jackson Case,[46] but ministers were also instructed, after 1909, to read the latest works in both British and American social science, including those by J.A. Hobson and Sidney and Beatrice Webb, the Whitley Council reports, the reform economists, such as Alfred Marshall and W.J. Ashley, and prominent American writers like Richard Ely, John R. Commons, E.R.A. Seligman, Albion Small, E.A. Ross, Lester Frank Ward, and Franklin Giddings.[47]

As William McGuire King has so forcefully reminded historians, the boundaries between religion and social science were extremely porous in the United States well into the 1920s, and writers such as Shailer Mathews and Walter Rauschenbusch should be viewed less as cloistered theologians writing for a specific audience than as synthesizers of contemporary social science and as critical social thinkers who in turn influenced the shape of academic social science. Far from being isolated from contemporary social inquiry, Shailer Mathews spearheaded the reinterpretation of the individual in terms of that person's social relations, a conclusion that social scientists themselves were struggling towards in the same period. Mathews's emphasis on the "social mind" was a perspective shared by the philosopher John Dewey, the symbolic interactionists George Herbert Mead and Charles Horton Cooley, and the work in social psychology by E.A. Ross. "Religion," wrote Mathews, "is uncompromisingly functional, not only in adjusting the individual or the group to its environment, but also in the attempt to adjust the environment to person or community ... Religions are fundamentally social, the possession of some tribe, nation or church."[48] This interpenetration of religion and social science was no less prominent in Canada. The religious outlook of the conservative evangelical Baptist A.L. McCrimmon was redolent of Albion Small's organic conception of the relationship between the individual and society: "The God of the Christian religion is a societal Godhead. The man who is regenerated is a societal product ... Before regeneration he is a member of the human race; after regeneration he is not only a member of the human race, but also a member of the Kingdom of God. In both relationships he is inextricably related to a social economy."[49]

One of the first decisions taken by the departments of evangelism and social service of both the Methodist and the Presbyterian churches was to invite social scientists, including Robert Magill, professor of political economy at Dalhousie, political economists Adam Shortt and O.D. Skelton of Queen's University, and J.W. Macmillan and Robert MacIver of the University of Toronto, to recommend a reading list of the latest literature on economics, the history of trade unionism, socialism, and practical sociology.[50] This impressive reading course, containing the most outstanding works of British and American social science, was intended to form the basis of a curriculum in sociology which progressive leaders hoped to introduce to the church colleges across Canada. Although Shearer, Moore, and Dobson lobbied strenuously for the introduction of chairs of sociology at theological seminaries,[51] the United Church Commission on Courses of Study which sat between 1926 and 1928 revealed that the church colleges were recalcitrant in revising their traditional curriculum. United Theological College at McGill University, Victoria College at Toronto, and Wesley College at Winnipeg stood out as the only church colleges which directly taught sociology and psychology, and in this regard McGill was in the forefront with specialist courses in social ethics, urban sociology, and rural sociology at every level of the minister's education.[52] It was a testimony to the continued strength of church conservatives that the Report of the Committee on Curricula recognized the still compelling need for specialization in the social sciences in order to attract more than just the "less strenuously intelligent among the religiously inclined."[53] In addition, the Committee on Curricula continued strongly to recommend to the entrenched professors of biblical theology the value of courses in psychology of religion, sociology, and practical theology, with one year of fieldwork in the community for probationers.

Progressive clergymen effectively circumvented the refusal of the church colleges to incorporate the social sciences. The Presbyterians established a scheme of scholarships to enable students of the ministry to attend lectures on social questions in New York and Chicago, and in addition Shearer sent copies of the reading course to every Presbyterian minister in the field.[54] The Methodist Church was even more vigilant in ensuring that local ministers applied the insights of social science to practical Christianity by having the district field secretaries, like Hugh Dobson, establish informal reading courses. Out of their desire to forge a stronger religious leadership in the community, the Methodist Church not only founded its own reference library in current political economy, but it also urged the creation of a string of reference bureaus and lending libraries on social work across Western Canada to press the claims of practical Christianity in the wider community and to show people that they must repent their sins in light of "the changing circumstances of the industrial age and a new world order." To this end the General Conference of 1918 recommended that all candidates for the ministry, especially those in rural areas, read the most up-to-date textbooks on contemporary social problems.[55] Dobson was one of the foremost promoters of the introduction of sociology into the church colleges, and accordingly his reading course of 1918 reflected his own interests in the labour problem, public health reform, and rural development. Dobson, in fact, became one of the chief purveyors of the work of the American sociologist E.A. Ross, professor of sociology at the University of Wisconsin, whose own concerns for the closing of the American frontier and the diminution of Anglo-Saxon values under the impact of European immigration struck a responsive chord among Protestant leaders on the Canadian Prairies.[56]

Prior to 1920 progressive clergymen who were preoccupied with the "social problem" of poverty, industrial unrest, unemployment, and public health turned to the works of English social thinkers and economists, who were themselves attempting to reformulate traditional *laissez-faire* liberalism, then in decay, in order to reorient it towards the provision of general principles that could be applied to the solution of current social ills. The first breach with the old liberalism was struck by the work of Alfred Marshall, which shifted economics out of its theoretical isolation from human society and social values by overtly addressing the problem of poverty. The orientation of Marshall and the other reform-minded economists, in particular W.J. Ashley and Anglican divine William Cunningham, appealed to many Canadian ministers because of the new economy's emphasis on service, rather than greed, as the dominant principle underlying social relationships.[57] Just as Marshall's work employed Darwinism to show the ethical implications of social evolution, the thought of J.A. Hobson and such other new liberal and social democratic advocates of collectivism as G.D.H. Cole and Sidney and Beatrice Webb conceived of a new notion of the common good which, although it depended for its adumbration upon a synthesis of the ethical and scientific, nevertheless gave priority to the moral factor in both political and social development. British sociologists, new liberals, and Fabians shared a commitment to the empirical investigation of social problems that had as its goal the definition of social values. This was precisely what Canadian church progressives meant when they stated that ministers should follow the example of Arnold Toynbee, the British reform economist and the progenitor of the social settlement ideal, by investigating "the facts of life" in a manner that was "clear, accurate, unbiased, scientific."[58]

Although not explicitly Christian, the new liberal notion that the goals of the individual and society would evolve towards harmonious social cooperation based on self-sacrifice and altruism bespoke a moral fervour and a strongly ethical perspective. The organic view of society espoused by new liberals – what Hobson termed the "moral rational organism"[59] – and its emphasis upon the mutual dependence of individual and society, converged with the social evangelism of Canadian clergymen. Like Protestant progressives, new liberals such as J.A. Hobson adamantly rejected the Hegelian notion of the general will because it negated individual freedom, and they preferred to discern in the progressive movement of society towards cooperation the greatest realization of individual moral action. The new liberals, though they stressed collective behaviour, believed that this movement was derived from a harmonious convergence of the goals of individuals and their society that led to practical social reforms like the minimum wage, old age pensions, graduated taxation, and such schemes for labour democracy as the Whitley Councils which preserved the notion of voluntary action against state compulsion.[60]

In the aftermath of World War I, the influence of the British new liberalism reached its apogee and found its clearest expression in Canada in the reform programs of the Protestant churches, as outlined in their statements on reconstruction in 1918. These pressed for child welfare laws, minimum wage legislation, general social and health insurance, mothers' pensions, schemes of labour democracy modelled on the Whitley Councils, and the regulation of public utilities. The central tenets of the new liberalism were also reflected in the work of Stephen Leacock, prominent in the churches' reading course in sociology, who explicitly sought to revise the liberalism of Adam Smith and J.S. Mill. In a manner reminiscent of the British new liberals, Leacock called for a new "sense of social solidarity" founded upon the residually evangelical notion of public morality. And in redefining the individual in terms of society, Leacock, like Hobson overseas, framed a new idea of government intervention based upon the defence of equality of opportunity; he thus advocated the introduction of minimum wage legislation and old-age pensions which he saw as the natural outcome of the growth in social responsibility.[61] Likewise, progressive clergymen hastened to place Robert MacIver's *Labor in the Modern World* on their reading lists. MacIver's Christian social aims allowed him to introduce, in a less ideologically charged manner, the new liberalism's "radical" recommendations for collective bargaining, the establishment of a living wage, and schemes for social security which would "create order out of chaos," to the political economy curriculum at the University of Toronto.

Even though MacIver claimed that his proposals to make the state the arbiter of group interests reflected the "work of the Deity" and were barriers to syndicalism and Bolshevism, a view of social reform shared by progressive clergymen, the wedding of sociology and social reform aroused considerable opposition from conservative elements in Canadian universities.[62] MacIver's departure from Toronto for Columbia University in 1927, in spite of the strong support he had received from President Falconer, served as a powerful illustration of the reality that progressive social reform's strongest constituency lay not among the businessmen who controlled the inner councils of the university but in the Protestant churches. This immense popularity of British collectivist thought among Canadian clergymen rested upon the redefinition of social democracy and positive liberty it effected by establishing principles of social reform which not just incorporated the weaker classes but also laid the groundwork for a broad interpretation of the human condition that was inclusive of all social groups.[63]

The counterpart of new liberalism in the United States was progressivism and shared with it an ameliorative outlook and a focus upon poverty, delinquency, labour relations, and urban ills. Prior to 1920 these social problems acted as the central catalyst for the rise of sociology and the new economics, both of which were preoccupied with the search for order and sought through scientific knowledge the means to redefine progress in light of the social changes wrought by industrialization and immigration. This search for a harmonious liberal society imparted a particularly reformist and activist cast to the temper of American social science.[64] It was a sensibility that converged with the pragmatism of

Canadian social Christianity. As late as 1900 the reading of prospective ministers had been dominated by theological and philosophical concerns, but after 1910 the book lists of Canadian clergymen featured the works of Albion Small, Charles Henderson, E.A. Ross, Charles Ellwood, and Richard Ely, the very figures who established the modern discipline of sociology in the United States and who were responsible not only for deepening the already close alignment between American Protestantism and the social sciences but also for directing the endeavour of sociology towards establishing the Kingdom of God on earth.[65] Although the religious content of early twentieth-century sociology has been obscured by modern sociologists, who have combed the past for the purpose of affirming the "scientific" status of their profession,[66] the Christian overtones and the usefulness to practical Christianity of this early phase of American sociology did not go unheeded by Canadian clergymen. These men saw in scientific laws the orderly manifestation of divine power.

One of the first American social scientists to translate the social inequalities of the Gilded Age into a new vision of statist reform was Richard T. Ely. He effectively drew upon both the millennial optimism of Christianity and the Protestant emphasis upon the priority of the rights of the organic community over unrestrained individualism to articulate a rigorous critique of capitalism which made him, more than that of any other social critic of his age, sympathetic to socialism. Like his contemporaries E.R.A. Seligman, professor of political economy at Columbia, and, in Canada, Stephen Leacock, William Ashley, and O.D. Skelton, Ely dissented from classical political economy and sought to reorient the guiding principles of the discipline in the direction of the achievement of material abundance, which he viewed as the precursor to a truly harmonious social order.[67] In fact, Ely founded the American Economic Association with the central purpose of using historical economics as a salve for the conflict between capital and labour and as the scientific basis for Christian reform.

Ely's conception of a cooperative commonwealth, in which the positive state represented the hand of God, was shared by one of his students, John R. Commons, the founder of the subdiscipline of labour history in the United States. While at the University of Wisconsin, Ely and Commons collaborated in founding the Institute for Christian Sociology,[68] and in 1894 Commons published *Social Reform and the Church* in which he declared that the gross inequality of the labouring classes *vis-à-vis* monopoly capital was the greatest obstacle to the achievement of the Kingdom of God on earth. In a manner similar to the 1918 reconstructionist platform of the Canadian Protestant churches and to the related idea of group government elaborated by the agrarian Progressives Henry Wise Wood and William Irvine, Commons outlined a notion of social democracy premised upon the representation and mutual recognition of economic interest groups. Accepting the dictates of competitive capitalism, Commons argued that trade unionism and the principle of collective bargaining were a natural part of the evolution of the modern economy towards social pluralism.[69]

Another of Ely's students, Albion Small, a Baptist minister and founder of the Department of Sociology at the University of Chicago, brought his Christian outlook to bear upon sociology, which he viewed as the study of the process by which the conflict of social groups was resolved into a higher stage of accommodation and harmony. Small's conception of both social conflict and cooperation emanated directly from his evangelical belief in evil, the recognition of sin, and redemption. The consciousness of social sin was to be attained through the direct scientific observation of social groups in the urban laboratory of Chicago. While Small was best-known for his study of normal and abnormal social conditions and for providing the first holistic study of social forces, in his view theoretical sociology was but the first step towards empirical social investigation, which aimed to change the actual into the ideal wherein divine righteousness would pervade all social and economic activity. Thus, although Small was closely allied with Hull House and the urban charity movement of Chicago, the practical implementation of his sociological tenets was left to his colleague and fellow minister Charles R. Henderson, who to an even greater degree influenced Canadian clergymen. Through his courses in practical sociology given at the divinity school of the University of Chicago, Henderson developed the subdisciplines of criminology, the sociology of deviance, and rural sociology, and he was responsible for establishing the investigation of social groups in their natural setting, a later preoccupation of two more-celebrated sociologists of the "Chicago School," Robert Park and Ernest Burgess.[70]

However, the American sociologist whose views most directly mirrored the concerns of Canadian Protestant progressives was E.A. Ross, professor of sociology at the University of Wisconsin, whose theory of social control was an important counterweight to the dominance of the Smallian tradition at the University of Chicago.[71] Ross's muckraking exposé of monopolistic capital, *Sin and Society* (1910), held an obvious appeal for Canadian clergymen, as did his prescriptive writings on the dangers posed by non-Anglo-Saxon immigration. His greatest contribution to Canadian Protestantism, however, lay in his scepticism concerning the naturalness of man's social state. Like other sociologists, Ross applied loosely Darwinian ideas of evolution to human society. But to an even greater degree than either Ely or Small he was anxious to preserve the independence of individual behaviour within the overwhelming presence of social or group interests in modern society, what he called "social ascendancy."[72] Guided less by a faith in Christian idealism, which tended to see a confluence between the individual and society, Ross saw in the modern social state an artificial compulsion towards conformity. Having been raised a Presbyterian in the rural precincts of Iowa, Ross's sociology was a reaction against modern legalistic controls; instead he searched for the more natural and traditional bonds of opinion and custom, whereby those subtle psychological well-springs of community life drew individuals together harmoniously. Although Ross's conception of social control found later expression in the idea of technocratic social engineering, his intention was quite the opposite. Like Small and Ely his revulsion against the acquisitive individualism of modern capitalism was the central catalyst for his shift into sociology from economics, but the guiding principle of his sociology was the recapturing of the liberal millennium which safeguarded the sanctity of individual free will Ross feared was being extinguished with the closing of the American frontier. Ross's overweening desire to preserve individualism in the face of modern social pressures was an issue with which Canadian clergymen also wrestled. Although Ross had intellectually shed his evangelical origins, his notion that the chaotic drift of modern society could only be arrested through the inner psychological control located in the individual moral being had obvious affinities with the pietistic underpinnings of Protestantism. More importantly, his idea of social control founded upon public opinion and the example of extraordinary individuals led him to propound a definition of "social religion" beyond the confines of the institutional church as the pre-eminent sanction for a concept of community founded upon the unity of man and the fatherhood of God. Although Ross used social psychology to define modern social cooperation, his sociology was the ultimate expression of a Christian world-view shared by many Canadian clergymen in which the solution to modern social disorder lay in impregnating society with the ideals of Jesus.[73] Like Canadian progressive clergymen who read his works, Ross rejected theological disputation, but he retained a commitment to the beneficial agency of of social Christianity in preserving liberal values amidst the complexities of modern society.[74]

A SCIENTIFIC MALE LEADERSHIP

The growing emphasis which progressive leaders in the Methodist, Presbyterian, and Baptist denominations placed upon the scientific study of social problems was directly related to their concern that men did not play an active and organized part in Canadian religious life. The creation of departments of social service and evangelism coincided with the recognition by progressives that the charitable and community activities of the churches were becoming increasingly dominated by the better organized women's groups. Although this discrepancy between male and female participation was highlighted during revival meetings conducted during the planting and harvest seasons, by 1909 it was perceived to be a more fundamental problem. As the Rev. R.H. Lowry informed C.W. Gordon, "we have been dealing with women since we started. It is nearly a physical impossibility for men to be at the meetings."[75] As a response to the apparent lack of interest of men in religious activity, the Methodist and Presbyterian churches transformed evangelism by shifting it away from an emphasis on inner piety towards a social Christianity that highlighted the manly pursuit of public influence and community leadership. As the Scottish conservative Presbyterian minister James D. Orr stated, "I feel certain that the men of the Church are waiting for something to awaken them to their privilege and responsibility."[76]

The general cultural shift away from conversion towards social Christianity as the predominant expression of an individual's dedication to Christ appears to have also been a movement occasioned by a largely male rejection of public professions of faith, which came to be viewed as unmanly because they placed an overemphasis upon emotional display. In 1910 the Rev. F.J. Hartley commented on the changing behaviour of male parishioners: "The most striking thing was the Refusal of well brought up young men to accept Christ and yet the tenacity with which they attended the [men's] meetings."[77] The call to manly service apparently was successful in reclaiming the allegiance of "strong men" for Protestantism. The Kootenay and Minnedosa evangelistic campaigns which Presbyterians refurbished into mass exhortations for social service became models for male participation. Of them Gordon reflected, "it was a man's work from start to finish," and while women attended the meetings, "it was the manhood of the congregation and the community that was more particularly affected."[78] Similarly, the Methodist Beatrice Brigden who, during the course of her social purity tours was faced with the crying need for a form of evangelism that would appeal to the interests of working men and farmers, informed T. Albert Moore that the People's Church, because of the priority it placed on discussions of labour questions and social reform, had succeeded in attracting a congregation in which men comprised the unprecedented proportion of seventy-five per cent of adherents. "Surely," Brigden wrote, "the mere experiment would be worthwhile if only to see if a way could be found to hold a crowd of men together in a church."[79]

This movement to attract men into the precincts of church organizations began in urban areas, so that by 1910 fully ninety per cent of urban congregations had Brotherhoods, clubs especially designed to express piety through the Christian discussion of contemporary social evils. So successful were these agencies in encouraging male lay participation in urban churches that they were soon also deemed "the most vital and most hopeful" force for the renewal of country congregations, which lacked any special provision for male culture apart from the local saloon.[80] In 1908, as part of their general campaign to provide Christian leadership for social reform, Protestant progressives contributed the necessary funds that brought the Brotherhoods under the aegis of the church. The usurpation by the churches of the leadership of the immensely successful Brotherhoods, which had become the foremost centres for discussing social problems and in directing male energies towards public service, entailed a larger power struggle over which institutions would direct male social reform.[81] By the conclusion of World War I the independence of the Brotherhoods from clerical control became more difficult to sustain as the churches grew increasingly anxious over the problem of men in the church, an issue crystallized by the task of reintegrating into religious and church life soldiers as well as probationers who had returned. More importantly, the progressive leadership, which continued to battle against traditionalists to make social Christianity the dominant force in the church, needed a phalanx of dedicated social service activists. As a result they pressed for the complete control of the church over all men's organizations, including the Brotherhood clubs which even in 1916, before the postwar influx, had grown to 228 across Canada.[82]

Through the Brotherhoods, leaders of progressive reform within the churches, such as T. Albert Moore, J.G. Shearer, C.W. Gordon, Hugh Dobson, G.C. Pidgeon, and Mackenzie King,[83] aspired to create a male organization to rival the influence exerted by women. While church leaders were not averse to enlisting women in the new evangelism of social service – the Methodists invited Sister Margaret Saunders, a deaconess from Great Britain, to speak on the women's sphere in social settlement work, and J.G. Shearer sponsored the creation of Women's Moral Reform Councils, which were active at the local level and were dedicated to rescuing fallen women[84] – they neverthless ascribed separate spheres of influence to them. The inclusivity of the ideal of social Christianity invited the participation of both sexes in the cause of social reform. However, topics such as the labour question, industrial democracy, and political purity were areas of knowledge reserved specifically for male discussion largely because they addressed questions which the culture deemed overtly public,[85] while issues affecting the private sphere of family life, such as temperance, social purity, and child welfare, were identified as fit for women's social activity.[86] Certainly this division of labour was not hard and fast, for the Brotherhoods also regularly discussed the need for social legislation regarding minimum wages, mothers' pensions, and prohibition, issues which women social reformers had also initiated.[87] Women were discouraged from assuming leadership roles and were relegated to recruiting grass-roots support for social legislation, and it was the men, with their training in the broad principles of social science, who were assigned the more elevated task of undertaking empirical social research to diagnose the aetiology of social ailments. In the various men's leagues and Brotherhoods, laymen in local churches were encouraged to study American pathways of civic reform; as men it was expected that they would provide the necessary community leadership to enable the churches to lobby provincial and federal legislatures on the implementation of specific reforms.[88]

The mobilization of a ground swell of male lay participation was seen by church leaders as a crucial movement for recruiting new probationers to the ministerial profession. The institution of a formal commission in 1929 by the United Church to examine the declining interest among talented young men in the ministry as a career merely reflected a long-standing preoccupation with the inability of the ministry to compete with such other professions as law, medicine, and business which had greater social prestige.[89] By making the church more relevant to modern life and the minister's calling more scientific, activist, and broad, the introduction of the study of the social sciences was intended to rectify the popular perception of the minister as an effete and superfluous personage who occupied the rarefied and largely female world of private devotions. To this end, S.D. Chown summoned the modern minister to put on "the girdle of manliness" by entering the virile world of public activism and social reform, for, in his view, participation in the commonweal "save[s] the body from the effeminate languor and the soul from polluting thoughts. Labor is the economic basis of human fellowship. It is honorable as the Divine means of improving the material world ... There is no life worth living that is not industrial."[90] In a similar vein, D.N. McLachlan instructed each and every Presbyterian clergyman to "be a man who plays a man's part in a world of men. Wherever the place is, for a recluse living apart from other men that place is not the christian church of to-day."[91]

In order to promote the stature of the ministerial profession among men, Protestant progressives equated social Christianity with such male images as the Fatherhood of God, military generalship, and scientific rigour, and they used terms like "aggressive evangelism" to evoke male potency.[92] On the other hand, they denigrated traditional theology as other-worldly, pietistic, and effeminate. Thus, S.D. Chown called for a "strong muscular ethical religion" which could effectively challenge men to Christian service and withstand the rigours of modern public life.

"We can have it," he stated, "only by adding to our faith, manhood. Our very hymns are mostly feminine, and react upon our softer emotions, rather than our heroic life."[93] To implement those ideals of manliness, Chown insisted that clergymen be trained in the new "cement of righteousness,"[94] sociology, as were such modern-day statesmen as Mackenzie King. Only by being thus provided with a broader Christian social vision could clergymen dispel the devitalizing emotionalism, feminine passivity, and what Chown would have castigated as the spiritual onanism so characteristic of the ethereal metaphysics of Victorian theology. Modern social science, according to Chown, would

> show the young men of our country that the theological student is not a recluse, and that, in its essence, Christianity is ethical, altruistic, and aggressive. The associations of the preacher to-day incline him too much to the feminine side of religion. The minister should know the down-town life of men, and the message it needs. He should be a good mixer ... Ministers, in the best sense of the word, must be free to be men of affairs, promoters. The Church, to attract virile young men, must blazon forth the possibility of a career, which will justify their consecration to the ministry; and the outstanding fact is that their full equipment is impossible unless they know the world in which they live.[95]

The addition of the social sciences to the intellectual preparation of the Canadian minister was indispensable in carving out a new role for the clergyman as a community leader. And, by thus creating a strong civic leadership, that role extended the church's influence into all areas of public policy. Most importantly, the new disciplines conferred upon the Protestant churches an unchallengeable scientific authority which allowed them to capture the agenda and maintain the leadership of social reform movements. John A. Cormie, a persistent advocate of the study of rural sociology in theological colleges, warned church leaders that unless ministers exercised a "virile leadership" by keeping abreast of current scientific knowledge in both agriculture and community social problems, the church, especially in rural areas, would surrender its function as the moulder of public opinion: "A Church which has missed its opportunity of ministering to the social needs of the people cannot expect to retain its place of influence among them, still less to make a large place for itself in the life of the neighbourhood."[96] Reflecting also on the decline of the minister's status and authority in the rural congregation, Woodsworth observed: "[M]y world is different from theirs ... The smallest tradesman – the ordinary teacher – even the labourer has more real influence in the community than the minister."[97]

Out of the fear for the decline in the church's influence in the community, Protestant progressives consciously recast both the role of the minister and the function of religion in terms that were broadly cultural and extrainstitutional. According to Woodsworth, an anonymous minister from Bentley, Alberta, epitomized the new ministerial model of community activism when, armed with a university degree in social science, he left his college position in order to introduce social work and agricultural training to his congregation. In town this paragon created a library and a Mutual Improvement Society, and in the local Methodist Church he founded a club-room, a skating rink, a social centre, a Sunday School, night classes, and a special Bible class in which one hour was devoted to the study of psychology.[98] Likewise, C.W. Gordon and J.G. Shearer, who believed that religion was the central unifying force that mediated between the demands of the state, economic groups, and the individual, viewed the Rev. Dr W.A. Riddell's rural survey of Swan River, Manitoba, as a contribution to the building of Christ's dominion on earth, just as A.E. Smith stated what many progressives contended that the actual institution of the church was but a means to a larger religious end. Social evangelism, with its emphasis upon the application of the Gospel to the community, in turn required a broader role for the minister. The Rev. J.W. Macmillan's 1915 introductory lecture as professor of social ethics and practical theology at Manitoba College insisted that because the modern world was rapidly being "socialized," the modern preacher should be a man who "possessed personality and voiced his true convictions" so that he might "form an integral part in the activities of the community."[99] In a 1918 circular distributed to all ministers within the Methodist Church, T. Albert Moore outlined a much larger scope for the modern minister's activities. Under the rubric of the new evangelism, "the minister is equally spiritual when he is preparing a sermon, or when he is carrying a basket of food to a hungry family; when he is doing the work of an Evangelist, when he is preaching that sermon calling sinners to repentance, or when with a Committee on public welfare, he is considering the welfare of the community."[100]

By making the Kingdom of God coterminous with every facet of human activity and by defining religion in terms of experience rather than ecclesiastical dogma, progressive clergymen sought to break down all distinctions between the sacred and the secular. The imperatives of the new social evangelism now demanded that Christianity permeate all social relations and institutions.[101] This idea of a "corporate Gospel,"[102] in which all life was unified under God, provided the crucial rationale for the extension of the minister's calling into the fields of politics, university teaching, and social reform activism.

The Methodist minister Richard Roberts, a stalwart champion of applied social science, asserted that nothing in society lay beyond God's province and consequently there was no separate morality for business, culture, politics, or religion. "For the Christian," he declared, "there is but a single Kingdom, inclusive of all relations of life, a single law applicable to all its parts, a single spirit to govern all its activities."[103] In "The Wider Evangel" Woodsworth described the Holy City of the future as one in which there would be no temple, for "behold God shall dwell with men and they shall be his people":

> We should not only find the poor but should endeavour to change the conditions that lead to poverty. We should not only clothe the naked but find the means of clothing themselves. We should not only care for the sick but investigate sanitary conditions and work to prevent sickness. We should not only visit the prisons but save men from going to prison. Our scientific men taught us how far reaching is the law of cause and effect. It may sometimes be a Christian act to give a free dinner ... It is a better thing to find a man a job. It is good work to build hospitals. It is better to put in good sewers. It is a good thing to try to reform the criminal – it is better to train the child ... But I firmly believe in scientific Christianity – in performing our Christian duty according to the light that modern science has thrown on social conditions.[104]

In so outlining this prescription for an "intelligent, far-reaching Christian service," Woodsworth in 1902 conceived of all professions as fulfilling the minister's call because for him they fell under the guiding hand of the "one spirit." Thus, he could, with no trepidation, instruct his cousin C.B. Sissons to enter the "sacred" calling of teaching, and himself later fulfil his own injunction that the church should take the lead in public affairs by placing ministers on municipal councils and in Parliament.[105]

Like Woodsworth, Beatrice Brigden did not view her resignation from the Methodist Church as a rejection of Christian service. Rather, her departure was occasioned by frustration that her social purity work was not leading to ordination, which, when combined with physical and mental exhaustion from constant travel, led her to want to secure a more settled income. After years of sustaining a hectic pace of lecturing, Beatrice Brigden returned to her home town of Brandon, Manitoba, where she continued God's work within the People's Church, and she later joined the Quakers and became involved in socialist politics. As Brigden herself testified, there was no conflict between politics and her brand of religion: "Politics is working together to fulfill the needs of others as you would have them fulfill yours. Put that way it describes my religion as much as it does my politics."[106]

The view put forth by the Methodist and Presbyterian progressives that the broader social evangelism erased any distinction between the secular and the sacred was also advanced by Baptist minister C.A.

Dawson. In taking up his position as director of the McGill School of Social Service, Dawson, who also taught sociology at McGill University, was implementing his ideal that Christian social endeavour must "organically unite" the church with industrial organizations, schools, and government agencies, and in this way he reinforced the call for the creation of new extrainstitutional pathways which the application by the mainline Protestant churches of sociology to modern problems had established. "The church long ago realized," observed Dawson, "that the field of service and goodwill is more extensive than church organization, and that in social work as a separate institution it could discover a new ally in achieving the goals of a more abundant life."[107]

By the end of World War I the injunction to make the social sciences the centre-piece of the education of the modern clergymen was heeded by an ever growing number of young Methodist and Presbyterian men who sought the ministerial profession as a means to express their commitment to social reconstruction. The Presbyterian James Mutchmor, son of a Manitoulin Island lumberman and mill-worker, studied philosophy at University College in Toronto with the Rev. T.R. Robinson, a forceful advocate of the advancement of Christian social ethics and later head of the Social Service Council of Ontario. Influenced by the idealist ferment of the period, which saw the realization of the Christian life in the pursuit of the common good, Mutchmor turned to the realism of practical sociology as the vehicle to express his Christian belief after he found the biblical theology of Knox College too restrictive. As a student at the University of Toronto, Mutchmor had his social conscience awakened as a result of undertaking a social survey of the prostitutes at Simcoe and Queen streets. However, upon discovering that sociology was not held in high esteem by the "respectable channels" of the university he set out in 1913 for Union Theological Seminary in New York, then considered the leading liberal institution in the United States. There he "found God"[108] under the tutelage of Columbia University economist E.R.A. Seligman, the prominent social gospellers Henry Sloane Coffin, George A. Coe, and Harry F. Ward, professor of ethics, whose course on modern social problems introduced the young Canadian to a vision of social Christianity that incorporated industrial relations, social reconstruction, and the ethics of state intervention. Mutchmor's later career as minister of Robertson Memorial Church in Winnipeg, his service on the Winnipeg Central Council of Social Agencies, his leadership in promoting the professionalization of social work, and his study of old-age pensions for the Welfare Supervisory Board of Manitoba under Premier John Bracken proved the truth of his own adage that it was but a short step from minister to social worker to civil servant.[109]

Other young clergymen likewise viewed the appropriation of American social science as the route to advancement in the modern church. The Rev. Claris Edwin Silcox, a Congregational minister who later headed the Social Service Council of Canada between 1934 and 1940, made a pilgrimage similar to that of Mutchmor. Graduating from the University of Toronto in 1909, he proceeded to Brown University where he studied under sociologist Lester F. Ward, the chief interpreter of reform Darwinism in America.[110] At Brown University and Andover Theological Seminary, where Christian sociologist Francis Peabody taught, Silcox was exposed to the full spectrum of progressive social reform ideas. In Peabody's wide-ranging seminar Silcox studied the thought of Friedrich Nietzsche, Herbert Spencer, Auguste Comte, and Karl Marx, and he attended lectures on "The Church in Industrial Life," "The Church and Public Health," "The Individual and Society," and "Jesus as a Political Figure." Although he rejected Hegel's philosophical idealism in favour of the firmer empiricism of sociology, in 1913 Silcox nevertheless recorded in his diary that he had heard Dr Lyman Abbott speak on "Christ, Country and Social Science" and that he himself had preached "a la Rauschenbusch" on 5 January of that year. Moreover, by 1918, like many other socially conscious young clergymen, Silcox was influenced by the labour unrest which moved the problem of industrial democracy and socialism to the forefront of the reform debate. However, he wedded this encounter with radical thought to a new more social interpretation of evangelism that he outlined in the sermon "The Modern Conception of Christ" he delivered on 10 February 1918.[111] This harmonious reconciliation between Christianity, the social sciences, and social reform was later translated into his work for the YMCA and his study on church union for the Rockefeller-funded Institute for Social and Religious Research, which under the chair of John R. Mott conducted fifty studies of rural and urban churches.[112] Similarly, the Methodist Rev. J.F. Bentley, after graduating from Wesleyan Theological College in Montreal, attended Clark University where he concentrated on the study of the psychology of children, war, and religion with President G. Stanley Hall to obtain a doctorate which would qualify him to teach religious education at Wesley College, Winnipeg. Bentley, no less than the Baptist C.A. Dawson, envisioned a university professorship as only a more specialized and scientific path to the Kingdom of God. "The pulpit I love very dearly," Bentley explained to Hugh Dobson, "and have not wanted for success but it is the prevailing conviction that I am needed in other spheres that creates this spiritual passion for specialisation for the Kingdom."[113] Having targeted prohibition, immigration, and unemployment as the areas for social investigation in 1922, the Methodist Church obtained one of the Saskatchewan government's scholarships for study in Paris for the Rev. George Dorey. After studying sociology and political science for a year, he became one of the principal investigators in Hugh Dobson's social survey of Ukrainian immigrants.

Central to the progressives' goal of permeating culture with Christian values was their strong endorsement of social science training for younger clergymen so that as ministers they could provide Christian leadership to social welfare organizations and governments. However, the modern concept of Protestantism as a wider cultural movement, which the exponents of the new social Christianity articulated, often created a tension, particularly after World War I, with the church's equally powerful institutional aim of retaining under its direct auspices those most talented and most committed to forwarding the new social evangelism. While Protestant progressives realized that the wider cause of social amelioration required an explicitly Christian direction, they were also intent on keeping the most energetic advocates of social service within their own ranks. They not only wished to shore up the cause of social Christianity against the inroads of denominational conservatives, but they also sought to demonstrate to other social reform agencies that they were the premier institution for social investigation and for the formulation of social welfare policies. In short, their ideal of Christianizing the social order often conflicted with their overarching desire to extend the institutional power of organized Christianity.

On 25 February 1918 the Rev. W.J. Haggith of Banff, Alberta, wrote Hugh Dobson informing him that Henry Wise Wood, the president of the United Farmers of Alberta, had approached him because of the high esteem in which he was held as "a minister of the Evangel" and asked him to join the executive of the UFA. Wood's social vision dovetailed precisely with that of progressive churchmen in as far as he believed that "instead of Christianity being a helpless infant to be quarantined, it is the capable physician, able to heal all the ills of our social and economic body,"[114] and he shared with Dobson, himself a member of the Progressive Party, the conviction that "crass materialism" would be circumscribed by the presence of Christian ministers in farm organizations. Nevertheless, Dobson adamantly opposed Wood's proposition out of fear that if reformist politics were to slip out from under immediate church control it would result in the inevitable diminution of the church's authority in society. The fact that Wood was, in Haggith's words, "a Christian gentlemen and a lay preacher"[115] made little impact on Dobson, who was still anxiously trying to build up a reformist constituency within the church. Dobson therefore viewed with alarm any departure from the Methodist ministry, even when the person intended to serve overtly Christian purposes. In practical terms, Dobson believed that the only truly Christian service must emanate explicitly from the reformist program promulgated by the Department of Evangelism and Social Service and that greater opportunities for social influence could be realized within rather than outside the church. "Our friend Woodsworth," Dobson reminded Haggith, "thought he could serve best outside the church; I don't think that that is true ... You have to decide whether as Secretary of the U.F.A. you would be serving the public or preaching the truth, and interpreting life to the people ... I think that there is no age in all the past with such an opportunity for the true preacher as that which is upon which we are entering."[116]

That Dobson was merely employing pressure tactics rather than expressing any fundamental intellectual disagreement with young ministers who believed that by entering politics and government bureaucracies they were fulfilling the church's edict to Christianize Canadian society is best illustrated by his paternalistic admonitions to the Rev. Edward S. Bishop. Dobson had personally instructed Bishop in the new social science literature and had placed him as the principal advocate of child welfare reform on the Alberta Social Service Council, a church-funded body. Like other progressives, Dobson fervently promoted child welfare campaigns, with the intention of persuading provincial governments to create their own child welfare departments. However, when confronted with the prospect of losing the services of Bishop, one of the Methodist Church's most qualified experts in social welfare policy, to the provincial bureaucracy, Dobson prevaricated. He could not disagree with Bishop's contention that the Alberta government was at long last, after much prodding by the churches, assuming some responsibility over the welfare of the community by establishing its own parallel educational campaigns in the areas of public health, child welfare, sanitation, and venereal disease. Neverthless, Dobson used a not-so-subtle form of emotional blackmail on Bishop by citing T. Albert Moore's mental collapse, occasioned by having to bear the brunt of "clashing opinion on these social issues in our Church," to compel him to remain in the church. "I think we are about to pass through a period of great development," stated Dobson, "to be marked, by great difficulty, when there will be men persecuted for righteousness sake; but, at the same time, a period of great revival; and I was anxious to have, in the presentation of the message, which is the most fundamental thing after all, the largest number of workers who had both the technique of service and the spirit of evangelism. I think that is what will save our church and the people." And if this appeal to keep the church in the forefront of reform failed, Dobson threw Bishop the sop that he would be made the director of all Western Canadian social service work. Whether it was the conviction that he could help society better in the church or the realization that his personal ambitions could be better served there, Bishop eventually decided to heed his mentor's advice and pursue a career in the church. As Bishop confided to Dobson, his own Christianity rested upon the more traditional aim of reviving people's spiritual life rather than with more outward forms of social improvement: "I could not get away from the fact that the thing that most needs emphasis in the present critical juncture of the life of our church and country was the spiritual and evangelistic, and under such a conviction, I could not accept an appointment where I would be expected to soft pedal the religious and emphasise the physical, important though I recognize that to be."[117]

Dobson's fears that the church would become less and less essential to the management of social welfare were entirely justified in light of the American situation where, since the turn of the twentieth century, the reform program of mainstream Protestantism had become severed from Progressivism.[118] Although Canadian clergymen attested to the fact that the vast majority of social workers in the United States were professed Christians, they were not satisfied that the Christianization of society would be effected if individuals rather than the church itself were to infuse social reform with the spirit of Christian endeavour.[119] In reaction to the declining presence of Christian leadership in the United States, Canadian Protestant progressives aggressively set out to ensure that the institution of the church would not only insinuate itself into the reform network by placing ministers in strategic positions on social welfare bodies and by sending them to publicize the relationship between the church and social reform at a variety of conferences, but also that it would directly fund, manage, and define the agenda of national and provincial platforms for social amelioration.

When Hugh Dobson was appointed field secretary for the Prairie region in 1913, he was charged with the responsibility of leading the prohibition campaign and was instructed to enhance the public prestige of the church in the area of social reform by undertaking community social surveys and giving sermons and addresses on town planning, child welfare, commercialized vice and amusements, industrial democracy, the enfranchisement of women, old-age pensions, and mothers' allowances.[120] The Presbyterian Church, whose particular focus was urban social settlement work, was just as adamant in establishing an overtly Christian presence in social reform, and it eschewed the "thin, sentimental humanism" that had come to animate American progressivism. In the view of men like Shearer and Gordon, it was only the church as a public institution, by virtue of its newly acquired scientific expertise, which could bring the spirit of Christ to bear upon contemporary social problems. They drew a sharp contrast between the humanism of the American social settlement and the strong Christian tenor of their own settlement houses:

> The Social Settlement seeks to humanize and civilize; this is good, but it is not enough for our purpose. We must seek not merely to humanize but also definitely to Christianize. The Church must tackle this down-town problem as a *Church*. We are going into this work not merely inspired by a thin sentimental humanism, but because we are Christian people who seek the advancement of Christ's Kingdom, and the saving of men's lives. Any inspiration we have for this work we draw from Jesus Christ, and we shall not hesitate to say when we have received it: it is His Spirit. We must put Christ into the foreground and keep Him there; and next to Him, his Church.[121]

The figure of Jane Addams, who had come to epitomize the force of secular humanism behind the American social settlement movement, was reinvented by the churches, which used her mystique to enlist social reformers under the banner of Christianity. To emphasize his own Christian viewpoint, T. Albert Moore quoted Addams as saying that all settlement work "must be saturated with the religious sentiment if it is going to be successful."[122]

The implementation of church control over social reform was not simply wishful thinking on the part of the Protestant progressive leadership. In the area of social settlement work, for example, both the Methodist and Presbyterian churches were able to enlist the cooperation of wealthy citizens who provided the funds enabling the churches to hire settlement workers and thereby to control the entire network of urban social settlements.[123] By 1914 almost every social settlement and home for girls was under the direct sponsorship of one of the Protestant churches, a situation heartily endorsed by local governments which, like many social reformers, saw the wisdom of Dobson's perspicacious observation that social service could always be more cheaply undertaken through the church.[124] In 1921 Dobson declared that the "most aggressive agency on Child Welfare work has been the church, acting by themselves and also cooperatively through the Social Service Councils of the Province and of the Dominion. Our own Church Board has specialized in Child Welfare exhibit work, and now much of this work is being done by Social Service Councils." This was not simply an idle boast on Dobson's part, for he was, in fact, describing the very contours of the reform coalition which the church had built up in Canada. The powerful alliances which male church leaders had forged with the National Council of Women and other related local women's organizations were the engine that induced the federal government in 1920 to create a Child Welfare Bureau, headed by Dr Helen MacMurchy, within the Department of Health.[125]

THE FEMINIZATION OF SOCIAL REFORM

The alliances of the church leaders with women's organizations depended upon a mutually beneficial arrangement. On the one hand, the Women's Institutes, for example, provided the grass-roots organization that supplied the democratic ground swell of public opinion crucial for lobbying government officials, while the church, with its tremendous cultural authority and national prestige, provided women, labour leaders, and agrarian reformers with a public platform whose Christian character placed it above partisanship and therefore insulated the groups from criticism. Under the impress of Christian thought, even the most "radical social teachings,"[126] which in any other venue would have been perceived as a threat to the social order, were deemed legitimate forms of social amelioration because they were conducted within the respectable avenues of church reform. It was for this reason that the Trades and Labor Congress under Tom Moore and Jimmy Simpson so eagerly sought to align themselves with the Social Service Council of Canada when it was founded in 1914 by the Protestant churches. University professors, government officials, and leaders of local welfare organizations placed themselves under church auspices and thus endorsed the view of the Protestant churches that all social reform in Canada was ultimately Christian. Writing in 1912, Queen's University political economist O.D. Skelton, whom historians have touted as a prime mover in the rise of a secular, collectivist, and bureaucratic state, declared that the social problems of industrial society dictated a larger role for the church. Skelton, a prominent member of the Presbyterian Board of Social Service and Evangelism, believed that through the development of a social conscience among its members the church would play a powerful educative role in moving public opinion and the state in the direction of social reform. However, it was individual salvation, in Skelton's estimation, that would impel Christian believers to provide "the dynamic force needed to turn the wheels of whatever organization appeals to [them] as best fitted for the work of making the city the city of God."[127] Even the Commission of Conservation, which has been regarded as the precursor of a secular, scientific progressivism, deferred to the authority of the church. Not only did its chairman, Sir Clifford Sifton, speak of public health reform in language redolent with references to the "gospel," but he believed that this scientific movement towards the conservation of human resources should make its appeal from a firmly religious standpoint because the church in Canada was "supreme."[128] This sentiment was echoed by

Professor T.R. Robinson of the University of Toronto when he stated that it was incumbent upon Christian ministers to intervene in the discussion of industrial problems because all economic questions were ultimately moral.[129] Likewise, Winnipeg's architect of urban social welfare and later the first director of the McGill School of Social Work, J.T. Falk, contended that effective charity was impossible without the financial backing and leadership of the Protestant churches. Moreover, he stated that "[i]n the churches we find already existent the perfect organization from which to recruit the rank of volunteers."[130]

Like a juggernaut, the Protestant churches from 1906 through to the 1920s moved across the landscape of Canadian social reform, absorbing once-independent reform organizations. In 1906 the Methodists, in conjunction with the Anglicans and Baptists, annexed the Women's Christian Temperance Union and the Royal Templars of Temperance. Taking this first strategic objective in the campaign to dominate social reform prompted Albert Carman to exclaim: "It has been my success in uniting the Societies and Churches of the country."[131] In the aftermath of World War I, when the energies of social reform were at a low ebb, the Protestant churches were able to take advantage of the momentary weakness in the ranks of secular progressives in order to usurp control by underwriting their activities. More importantly, the churches tightened their grip on the direction of social reform by inserting new slates of leaders and organizers, young clergymen who had been trained in the social sciences. Historians such as Doug Owram have argued that in the wake of the war progressivism in Canada was dismantled because it could not resolve the tensions between moral and scientific conceptions of state intervention.[132] This opposition between the moral and the scientific is more apparent than real, and it can only be sustained by excising the church from the axiom of social reform. Once the church, with its confident integration of morality and scientific social investigation, is reinserted into the equation, then the continuities between prewar and 1920s progressivism can be delineated. Owram's view that social reform disintegrated in the 1920s is derived from his view that reform was merely secular. Social reform not only survived, but thrived under the dynamic leadership of the churches. In 1919 Dobson told the Rev. J.W. Wilson of Govan, Saskatchewan, that "[i]n the matter of cooperation in Church activities, there has been tremendous ground gained during the war as well as before. Our own Church's attitude towards 'union' has been defined and in the matter of cooperation, we stand ready so far as our Department is concerned to cooperate with any body and everybody that strive for similar purposes."[133]

As early as 1913 the Protestant churches had infiltrated and taken over the operation of almost every major organization and conference devoted to social welfare. In that year the Presbyterian Church was instrumental in bringing Methodists, Anglicans, Baptists, and the Polish National Catholic Church, along with Arthur W. Puttee and the Trades and Labor Congress, the Women's Christian Temperance Union, and the Sunday School Association, together in the Moral and Social Reform Council of Manitoba.[134] Meanwhile, the Methodists were expanding their social reform territory to include the Young Men's Christian Association and the male Brotherhoods. Moreover, T. Albert Moore and J.S. Woodsworth established the first Canadian Conference on Charities and Corrections, modelled explicitly on the American prototype, an organization that enlisted the cooperation of university social scientists, mental health reformers, and agrarian reform leaders dedicated to Christian social service.[135] In the new organization church leaders did not merely share the platform with secular social reformers, but through their control of the program committee the Protestant churches ensured that the reformist message of its annual conference was Christian in both its tone and substance.[136] Woodsworth had long envisioned the church as one of the "radiating centres" of community development, and he had used the evangelistic purposes of the All People's Mission as a vantage point from which to place himself at the centre of Winnipeg's social welfare activities. Combining his ministerial role with that of city welfare superintendent, Woodsworth ran the fresh-air camps, was a leading light in the associated charities, sat on the boards of children's aid, the playgrounds association, and the antituberculosis society, and was a member of the committee which investigated the relief of poverty. He campaigned for increased cooperation between the churches and civic institutions out of the belief that only in this way could a proper "spiritual vision" animate modern social ideals and thereby direct them into the "darkest parts of Canada."[137] Protestant ministers also dominated the Conference on Social Welfare and the Canadian Conference on Public Welfare, and by 1918 the churches had so entrenched themselves as the cornerstone of the social reform network that the Canadian Council on Public Welfare began to meet regularly under the Christian auspices of the Social Service Council of Canada.[138] Indeed, the Social Service Council was the institutional expression of the church-led reform coalition. At its annual meeting in 1919, University of Toronto classicist and reformer C.B. Sissons spoke on housing, Dr C.M. Hincks gave an address on mental hygiene and feeble-mindedness, J.T. Falk, the director of social work at McGill University, discussed mothers' allowances, Dr Helen MacMurchy stressed the plight of "defective" children, Hugh Dobson spoke on illiteracy and retardation, Charlotte Whitton addressed the problem of child welfare, Salem Bland elaborated the progressive farmers' platform, R.M. MacIver of the Department of Political Economy at the University of Toronto outlined his prescription for the democratization of industrial life, and the Rev. G.C. Pidgeon offered the keynote speech on Christ and Social Service.[139]

From the point of view of social reformers, the church was an indispensable force in organizing and publicizing their activities. At both the national and the local levels, it was the presence of the church which dictated the success or failure of reform campaigns. In Melfort, Saskatchewan, for example, it was the Methodist Church which brought the town council, the board of trade, the local grain growers' organization, and school boards together to discuss a wide range of issues that included mothers' allowances, the creation of minimum wage boards, free public health clinics, and the campaign against mental defectives and venereal disease.[140]

The Protestant churches were not only regularly consulted regarding the latest developments in the field of practical social reform, but they were also routinely approached by local government welfare councils, which relied upon the expertise of clergymen in the practical administration of orphanages, community centres, and public health clinics.[141] Some of the first large-scale studies of migratory labour and of homeless men in Montreal – a decade before Leonard Marsh and the McGill Social Science Research Project supposedly pioneered the field – were initiated by the Protestant House of Industry and the Central Council of Social Agencies. And not only did the Presbyterian and Methodist churches both sponsor the major social surveys of rural and immigrant problems, but they regularly worked alongside social scientists in establishing the fundamentals of municipal research into living conditions.[142]

Governments recognized the fundamental importance of the church in the local community, and they regularly sought out church leaders as channels of communication between federal and provincial governments in helping to generate information on social problems to aid in the formulation of social policy at both levels of government. There developed a close relationship between C.A. Hodgetts, the director of health statistics for the federal Department of Health, and Hugh Dobson, who through his close association with both the provincial grain growers and the local social service councils, was viewed as a pivotal figure in marshalling public support for health reform.[143] In a 1917 letter to Violet McNaughton, the prominent leader of Saskatchewan farm women, Arthur Wilson of the Saskatoon Department of Public Health testified to the dependence of his agency on Dobson's efforts in organizing public support for child welfare and broader health legislation which had borne fruit in a provincial act to fund rural district nurses and facilitate the establishment of public hospitals.[144] Both the National Council for Combatting Venereal Disease and the new federal Department of Health strategically enlisted the Methodist Church in 1919 to lead the cause of social purity because of its proven evangelistic experience at awakening a mass audience; Hugh Dobson was appointed to undertake their propaganda campaign, and he was instrumental in having 40,000 men and women in Toronto alone view the film "The End of the Road" at Massey Hall.[145]

The interest of the Protestant churches in industrial democracy was a direct response to the wave of labour conflicts following World War I and was immediately influenced by British reconstruction policies, which had as their centre-piece the creation of Whitley Councils, boards that offered a framework in which labour and management were accorded equal representation in the resolution of labour disputes. Moreover, the Winnipeg General Strike had effectively crystallized the need for research into industrial problems in Canada and the United States. In concert, the Presbyterian, Methodist, Anglican, and Baptist churches promulgated their own guidelines in which the democratization of industrial life would be secured by the modern churches acting as mediators between capital and labour.[146] In his pivotal position as field secretary for Western Canada, Dobson sought to convert local congregations to the church's official doctrine on labour relations, and to this end fought fiercely against the suppression by conservatives of the Methodist Church's Hamilton Resolutions of 1918, which had consolidated the labour platform of the other Protestant denominations and the Industrial Relations Commission of Canada.[147] Dobson's intense interest just after World War I in having the church become the principal forum for research into industrial problems and the designer of labour legislation was an immediate outcome of his association with John B. Andrews, a life-long colleague of labour economist John R. Commons and the secretary of the American Association for Labor Legislation from 1909 to 1943. With the motto "Conservation of Human Resources of the Nation," a phrase which occurred often in Dobson's plans for postwar reconstruction, the AALL spearheaded national campaigns for social and health insurance, and compulsory unemployment benefits, as well as workmen's compensation. Although tangentially and sporadically supported by American labour leaders, the AALL was created by university social scientists who fashioned the ideal of a welfare state around the priority of the male wage-earner. Its emphasis was clearly élitist, as it maintained that a modern interventionist state should be founded upon the expansion of administrative capacities through the expert recommendations of special industrial commissions.[148]

Although Dobson was initially impressed by the AALL's focus on labour research, its élitist and male bias and its overweening reliance upon university expertise, conflicted with the Canadian Protestant churches' democratic reformism based on local, grass-roots, and female support. Thus, after the initial flurry of interest in promoting labour legislation, the interest of the Canadian Protestant churches in Canadian labour issues dissolved into a primarily evangelical concern to bring male workers into a spiritual relationship with Christ. Hence, although Canadian Presbyterians clung more tenaciously to their prewar interest in labour reform,[149] by the early 1920s the bias of the social platforms of both the Methodist and the Presbyterian churches had shifted dramatically away from industrial democracy to issues of protecting the family through mothers' allowances, child welfare policies, health reform, social purity, and prohibition.

This shift away from a concern for labour activism has been interpreted by Richard Allen as synonymous with the decline of the social reform impulse in the churches, which in turn marked the waning of the churches' influence in Canadian society.[150] However, it was not that the power of the churches diminished during the 1920s. Rather, the temporary upsurge in the political strength of organized labour, illustrated by its fielding of independent labour candidates, dissipated in the five years following the war. Under the impact of economic depression and a vigorous assault by business, labour retreated to its traditional concern with the politics of shop-floor management and a restricted national political agenda of defending the interests of male, skilled craftworkers. Organized labour's central political concerns then revolved around the issue of political purity, the protective tariff, and immigration restriction,[151] and as in the United States it was left to organizations outside the labour movement to formulate a coherent program of industrial democracy.

Organized labour's record in promoting labour legislation was woefully inadequate, even when it enjoyed the advantages of participating in E.C. Drury's coalition government in Ontario between 1919 and 1923. Ultimately, labour simply followed Drury's lead in initiating protective legislation. In explaining the weakness of a national political movement representing the interests of urban workers, James Naylor has argued that the ideology of labourism failed to define the character of industrial democracy other than as an escape from the traditional party system.[152] The Trades and Labor Congress adhered to an essentially conservative view of government, and merely sought recognition of labour as an organized interest rather than the articulation of a broader platform of social reform. Nor did business reformers or university experts step in to fill the social policy vacuum left by labour.[153]

The halting efforts to create the modern welfare state have traditionally been blamed on the incompetence and political vacillation of probusiness governments. This argument has been most forcefully advanced in the Canadian context by James Struthers, who has laid the failure to enact a national scheme of unemployment insurance at the feet of Mackenzie King's fiscal conservatism and timidity in confronting the task of constitutional revision.[154] This line of interpretation rests on the tacit assumption that the rise of the modern social welfare state was the inevitable concomitant result of industrialization and the outcome of labour activism. In reality, the failure to implement social insurance schemes in Canada before the 1940s was owing to inadequacies in the labour movement itself, which, since the nineteenth century, had been committed to a pre-industrial ideal of craft respectability that stressed the independence of the male breadwinner.[155] What historians have viewed as the defeat of progressive reform in the 1920s merely reflected the decline of popular support for social welfare policies designed to protect *male* workers. Recent scholarship has effectively challenged both the Marxist and the modernization theorists by showing that the chief catalysts for state growth in the twentieth century were middle-class women's groups and agrarian organizations, whose aims often dovetailed. The scholars have also been highly critical of the assumption that the modern state was the expression of male interests. By extending the definition of what constitutes politics to include the important private lobby groups that were especially active in the decade prior to the New Deal, traditionally regarded as the point of inception for the modern welfare state, these historians have reinserted the women's perspective and argue that maternal feminists were crucial in fashioning social welfare policies expressing the needs of their female constituency.[156]

Their conclusions have even greater validity in the Canadian context. Voluntary organizations such as the Protestant churches, working in close alliance with the National Council of Women, were responsible for laying the groundwork of the modern welfare state which up to the late 1930s, instead of revolving primarily around the male-centred agenda of unemployment insurance, did so around issues that concerned women, such as mothers' allowances, minimum wage legislation, child labour legislation, and child welfare policies, and that served to protect the integrity of the family, such as public health and temperance. Given the power of women to promote their maternalist welfare proposals through the avenues of the Social Service Councils of the churches, it is not surprising that the essential element in achieving a consensus on welfare legislation after World War II was family allowances. What is particularly striking is that the Canadian labour movement was wholly uninterested in social issues that pertained to women. As Ruth Frager has demonstrated, male-dominated labour unions actually impeded the development of social legislation protective of women in the workplace.[157] Likewise, in her discussion of the creation of minimum wage legislation in Canada between 1910 and 1925, Margaret McCallum cites the almost complete lack of mobilization on the part of organized labour on behalf of women. Rather, it was the National Council of Women and, more importantly, the Protestant churches speaking through the Social Service Council of Canada that lobbied for minimum wage legislation.[158] This anomaly, that labour did not advance minimum wage laws, was even recognized at the time by university reformers like Professor T.R. Robinson, who headed the Committee on Industrial Life of the Social Service Council of Ontario. A minimum wage law, stated Robinson, "could not be made general in its application because organized labor is not willing to accept it." In the face of the conservatism of organized trades distrustful of legal wage-fixing,[159] Robinson sagaciously recognized the importance of such middle-class organizations as the churches in awakening the state to its responsibilities for the welfare of women.[160] In both the United States and Canada initiatives from the private sector laid the groundwork for the modern welfare state, a role which in France and Germany had been undertaken by state agencies and bureaucrats. However, whereas American middle-class women entered the sphere of welfare activism vacated by labour, business, and the universities, in Canada the Protestant churches became the principal player in the growth of the welfare state.

Although historians have focused upon the importance of the 1918 declarations of the Protestant churches on social reconstruction, they have not precisely analysed why the priority originally ascribed to the problem of industrial democracy shifted during the 1920s to questions of child welfare, mothers' pensions, social purity, child and female immigration, juvenile delinquency, and issues of divorce and birth control. Nor have they turned their attention to the question of the nature of the reform alliances struck with the churches over time. During the later stages of World War I labour temporarily sought the approbation of the churches in order to secure the legitimacy of trade unionism in the eyes of the state, and this accounts for the stress placed in the male-centred agenda of the 1918 social statements on Whitley Councils, unemployment insurance, and the nationalization of public utilities. Social Christianity's brief engagement with organized labour soon gave way to a distinctly female-centred preoccupation. After 1921 the contacts of the Protestant churches with male organized labour were maintained not through the advocacy of social legislation to protect male breadwinners but within the context of the more traditional individualist piety of the revival campaigns so integral to the progressives' vision of social evangelism. The adoption by the Protestant churches of a dual strategy of attracting men to the churches through the more traditional channels of evangelism[161] and of retaining the allegiance of middle-class and rural women through campaigns of social reform oriented to family-centred issues, explains in large part the sudden decline in the federal government's commitment to unemployment insurance and to a generous scheme of military pensions after the postwar recession ended in 1923. What historians have interpreted as a weakening of the link between Protestantism and social reform was in fact a strategic shift on the part of progressive church leaders away from dependence on a labour constituency, which in the aftermath of 1919 was hopelessly split between conservative unionists and radical socialists, to the construction of a far more powerful coalition based on the mobilization of women around the causes of protective legislation for women and children and the improvement of rural community life.[162]

Although the Methodist Board of Temperance, Prohibition, and Moral Reform considered as early as 1913 the establishment of recreational facilities, children's playgrounds and homes for delinquents, protective legislation outlawing child labour, and the promotion of sex education, issues that had long been advanced by local women's institutes,[163] by the 1920s Methodism's social program almost exactly mirrored that of the National Council of Women. This was hardly surprising: not only was the National Council of Woman the largest component of the Social Service Council's reform coalition, but since its inception in 1893 it had pioneered an increasingly influential tradition of non-governmental political activism upon which the church sought to model its own social reform campaigns.[164] In Hugh Dobson's 1920 annual report as field secretary, the social reform agenda was wholly woman-centred and included attention to mothers' pensions, minimum wages for women and children, and the establishment of venereal disease clinics, and the report also advocated mental hygiene surveys and the creation of provincial departments of child welfare.[165] By 1924 T. Albert Moore had committed the church to a women's platform for temperance, laws outlawing prostitution, the care of mentally defective and underprivileged children, the protection of the aged poor, and a selective immigration policy emphasizing children, and it pressed for the creation of courts for domestic relations in all the provinces and the coordination of child welfare under government auspices.[166]

Many historians of Canadian women have given lavish attention to the winning of female suffrage between 1916 and 1919 as the critical watershed in the construction of modern feminism. In so doing they have defined politics by the standard of male career patterns, which have traditionally interpreted political action in terms of holding office in Parliament and provincial legislatures. To this end some feminist historians have combed these male arenas for evidence of women's political activism, and, finding women's influence wanting, concluded that women were marginal to political processes and the formation of social policy during the 1920s because their names do not appear on the rolls of the federal Parliament or of the executives of either the mainstream parties or those of the left.[167] By stressing the history of political events and by viewing the activities of middle-class women in terms of social control of their working-class sisters, these historians have neglected the importance of local politics, the arena in which middle-class and agrarian women reformers were dominant, and they have therefore undermined the maternalist perspective, which emphasized reform activism outside the formal political structures. They have thus marginalized the influence of women in the creation of the modern welfare state. By broadening our understanding of what constitutes political activism to include local and voluntaristic pressure groups, institutions such as the Protestant churches and women's groups, which have been long ignored, become more central to the articulation of social policy.

While women did not occupy a large place in national political parties, by the early twentieth century women had nevertheless become a powerful force by virtue of their ability to develop sophisticated techniques of influence outside of mainstream male politics. Since the late-nineteenth century women had wielded immense influence through mass-based pressure groups, including the Women's Christian Temperance Union, the National Council of Women, and various farm women's organizations, such as the United Farm Women of Ontario, of Manitoba, and of Alberta, and the Women's Grain Growers' Association of Saskatchewan.[168] With some forty years of experience in these forums, women had developed a wide-ranging platform of social reform initiatives which included mother's pensions, minimum wage legislation for women, prison reform, maternity benefits and hospital care, care of the feeble-minded, and policies addressing public health, especially regarding women and children.[169]

Moreover, women reformers strategically utilized their organizations as important bridgeheads to consolidate links with such male-dominated reform groups as the Saskatchewan Grain Growers' Association and, more importantly, the church-sponsored Social Service Council of Canada. Although, as Cheryl Jahn has argued, women often remained secondary players within such reform alliances,[170] they were neverthless instrumental in shaping the policies of a wider progressive coalition. Some women continued to chafe beneath their demonstrable subordination to men. While many would have agreed with Mrs Walter McBain of Beadle, Saskatchewan, who observed that "[s]ome men will never get used to women being on an equality with men except in the matter of feeding swine and milking cows &c,"[171] most farm women continued to seek out alliances with male reformers, given that women's organizations were frequently plagued by divisions between rural and urban interests, regional differences, and religious beliefs. Thus, a farm woman like Violet McNaughton frequently found greater ideological affinities with her male agrarian counterparts than with her fellow farm women and their urban sisters within the National Council of Women. As the astute Violet McNaughton observed: "the men were glad to have purely rural women represented in this way for even in 1918 the W.I. [Women's Institute] organizations were to a large extent village as well as rural and at that time there was probably more class conflict between the two groups at least in the West ... It certainly gave us good scope to present the rural women's view points on other national bodies."[172] Not only did Western farm women ally themselves with such organizations as the Women's Christian Temperance Union, the Young Men's Christian Association, the Great War Veterans, and the Social Service Council of Canada to lobby for the creation of a Canadian Council on Women's Immigration for Household Service in 1919,[173] but their most successful political foray was their alliance with the Canadian Council of Agriculture. There, the Interprovincial Council of Farm Women induced the male majority to support women's social legislation on, for example, public health, municipal hospitals, domestic help, women's property laws, child welfare, and the creation of rural community centres; in exchange, women endorsed the low tariff agenda of the Progressive Party. This strategy was likewise adopted by Irene Parlby, the leader of the United Farm Women of Alberta and a long-time and vociferous opponent of the government-funded Women's Institutes, who actively sought the support of the male leadership of the United Farmers of Alberta to help secure provincial legislation regarding free maternity care, licences for midwives, free hospitals, and family allowances.[174]

The impact of women upon the social reform agenda of the church was more intense in rural Canada than in cities because the churches there were more dependent on such organizations as the Women's Grain Growers' Association, which was often the sole local organization concerned with issues of community improvement. By emphasizing the relationship between women's organizations and the Protestant churches, it becomes necessary to revise the standard account of agrarian progressivism in the first three decades of the twentieth century. As a result of the work of W.L. Morton we have come to see agrarian reform through the lens of the Progressive Party, a largely male organization. Its goal was to implement the platform of Western farmers who advocated a lower tariff and reduced railway rates, critiqued the old party system, and agitated for provincial control of natural resources. By linking the success of Progressivism with its impact upon federal politics,

Morton concluded that by 1925 this agrarian political movement had collapsed.[175] Morton's personal preoccupation with securing greater Western regional representation in Ottawa precluded him from examining the wider grass-roots and non-electoral dimensions of agrarian reform, which revolved around local community issues of improved education, public health, the creation of community centres, and the general uplifting of farm housing and working conditions.[176]

Progressive clergymen in the mainline Protestant churches aggressively courted the support of women's groups because they were the key at the local level to the mobilization of public opinion behind their program of social reconstruction. Not only did women form the backbone of the commitment of many local congregations to social Christianity, but as volunteer workers they were indispensable to the practical day-to-day operations of community social agencies. In an article entitled "Declares Church Must Eliminate its 'Dead Heads,'" the *Winnipeg Free Press* called for the creation of a "small army of women engaged in social work who are in closest touch with housing, factory and other problems affecting girls" "broad-minded, sympathetic, capable Christian women" who can go amongst single women who are in the most need of "definite Christian work."[177] In a similar vein, J.G. Shearer in 1918 addressed the Men's Grain Growers' Convention on "Women and Social Awakening." And, at the 1916 annual meeting of the Saskatchewan Social Service Council, where reforms pertaining to women and children were highlighted, the Rev. Reekie, superintendent of Baptist missions and later head of the Social Service Council of Saskatchewan, spoke on the theme of "Women in Social and Religious Life."[178] Protestant progressives had long divined that although mass evangelistic meetings were effective in inducing men to join the church, it was women who were traditionally more receptive to the somewhat novel tenets of social Christianity because of their experience in local women's clubs, sewing circles, Red Cross organizations, and temperance leagues, as well as in church charity work. Male church leaders recognized that without the active support and participation of women's groups, their social service program could not secure a hearing in local congregations.[179] Thus, in 1917 Hugh Dobson strategically offered his talks on food conservation through the Methodist Church's women's societies and sewing circles in order to reach the broader community. From experience, Dobson had learned that in advancing the practical application of the gospel of the Kingdom, the women's institutes must be the first port of call in any community.[180]

As a close observer of the American social welfare scene, J.S. Woodsworth was made acutely aware of the tremendous power which the women's club movement had brought to bear upon the creation of public social policy, and he therefore pressed Violet McNaughton to join the Canadian Welfare League and to sit on the Committee on Social Legislation of the Canadian Conference on Charities and Corrections. Woodsworth believed the special moral attributes of women could bring "a new spirit" to the league, which would become "a positive, virile force" of democracy, thus stimulating the creation of social legislation.[181] As president of the Women's Grain Growers' Association of Saskatchewan, McNaughton was sought-after by the male reform leadership because she was essential to marshalling powerful grass-roots forces, given that her organization represented more than 46,000 farm women.[182] And, in return for McNaughton's strong agrarian-based support, Woodsworth and other Protestant progressives supplied social scientific knowledge which would enable the Women's Grain Growers' Association to formulate more sophisticated policies regarding the rights of working women. In addition, her association with the Canada-wide constituency of welfare workers provided her with the opportunity to publicize women's issues at the national level.

Women reformers saw the Protestant churches as their natural allies largely because they shared with progressive clergymen the belief that politics and social reform were an expression of Christian service. As May Wallace of the United Farm Women of Ontario confided to Violet McNaughton, if she had not considered "the Political field as actual Christian service," she would not have been able to withstand the often unsavoury climate of contemporary political mores.[183] Maternalist feminists and the mainline churches held a common view that women, because of their attributes of selflessness and moral instinct derived from their role as mothers, were peculiarly suited to play a leading role in movements of social reconstruction. As Mrs Alice B. Richardson, a Saskatchewan farm woman, declared in 1916: "This coming of women to their own is one of the greatest events of the century ... The mother heart the mother instinct will be the means of redeeming mankind from the many bondages of today."[184]

It was the ideological consensus around the idea that women must be protected within society because of their special role as the mothers and guardians of a future generation which cemented links between women's groups, the churches, and labour organizations. The contours of this alliance were brought into relief through the passing of minimum wage legislation for women in Manitoba in 1918. The campaign was begun by women labour activists May Pitblado, Helen Armstrong, and Gertrude Puttee who investigated the wages of women for the Bureau of Labor, often by infiltrating dubious factories and shops in disguise. It soon gathered strength: January 1918 saw the "advent of women into the arena of public affairs"[185] when the National Council of Women, the Women's Christian Temperance Union, the Political Educational League, the Women's Non-Partisan League, the Civic League, the Women's Grain Growers' Association, and the Women's Labor League joined hands to support the concept of protective legislation for women. After a loud demonstration by hundreds of women in front of the Legislature on 12 February 1918,[186] Winnipeg's Protestant ministers unanimously recommended the adoption of a law. In turn, scientific authority was lent to the movement by the publication of both the Bureau of Labor's social investigation, sponsored by the Labor-Progressive MPP F.J. Dixon, and of the Rev. J.W. Macmillan's comprehensive report analysing the history of such legislation in Australia, New Zealand, Britain, and the United States. So powerful was the ministerial lobby within government circles in Winnipeg that Principal Riddell of Wesley College became the chairman of a special commission to draw up minimum wage legislation, while Macmillan was asked to chair the Minimum Wage Board charged with its administration.[187]

While all the supporters of the minimum wage were united by the ideal of a fair living wage, what lent particular urgency to its implementation was that it protected single women who would "inevitably" become future mothers. However, Macmillan, one of the most vociferous lobbyists for a minimum wage, was not primarily concerned with safeguarding women; rather, he saw its passage as a precursor to a comprehensive system of social and health insurance based on similar schemes in England.[188] Similarly, Principal Riddell's support for the concept of a minimum wage was as a prophylactic against sweatshops and as part of a larger campaign for a fair living wage. While the position articulated by these two Protestant ministers solidified the coalition between middle-class progressives and labour reformers in Winnipeg,[189] it was the pre-eminence of women reformers behind the campaign that was ultimately the crucial factor both in swaying reluctant conservatives within the legislature and in changing the meaning of the legislation from one based on individual rights and industrial equity to one based on protecting women's maternal role and on the survival of the traditional family. As Alison Craig stated in her weekly column, "Over the Tea Cups," the very welfare of the nation was at stake, for in the absence of a minimum wage, single women, "the mothers of the next generation," would be forced into dishonest ways.[190]

Maternal feminism was the linchpin of what was the dominant current in progressive social reform in Canada during the 1920s. This was so largely because politically sagacious women reformers adeptly allied their organizations with male-dominated federations, such as the Social Service Council of Canada which represented the national arm of local Protestant church boards of social service. Writing in 1919 the journalist

John Stevenson observed that the central conflict in the political life of postwar Canada was the struggle for supremacy between the business-oriented platform of the Canadian Reconstruction Association, centred on an urban agenda of high tariffs, improved housing, and reforms to industrial relations, and those reformers who "pin their faith in rural reconstruction."[191] Although business reformism failed as a result of the war, the 1920s was not a lost decade for progressivism. The coalition between social Christianity and maternal feminism was successful in putting the argument before governments that the maintenance of the social order depended upon the state intervening to protect the family. The reformism of the 1920s was pivotal, therefore, in laying the groundwork for modern welfare policies. The power of the agrarian-based maternalist alliance with the church was demonstrated in the social programs enacted first by the Manitoba Liberal Party between 1915 and 1922, and then by its successor, the United Farmers of Manitoba under John Bracken, a package of legislation which centred upon women's suffrage, temperance, mothers' allowances, the improvement of rural education, and new regulations on child labour.[192] A similar coalition lay behind the success of the United Farmers of Ontario under E.C. Drury, a member of the Social Service Council of Canada. While in office between 1919 and 1923, the UFO undertook a vigorous application of temperance legislation, the creation of a scheme for mothers' allowances and minimum wages for women, the establishment of public health clinics in rural areas, and legislation promoting the building of community centres.[193]

There exists an unwritten assumption that the modern interventionist state reflected men's interests and that it encroached upon and controlled the lives of women.[194] Maternalist feminists, however, believed otherwise. Speaking on behalf of the mainly agrarian women's institutes in Ontario, Emily F. Guest equated the expansion of the state into the areas of "scientific child culture" as the expression of the independence and growing abilities of women in the public sphere of the professions and also as a welcome addition to agricultural improvement, which thus far had been narrowly economic in its focus and pertinent only to men's work on the farm. Praising the recent establishment of the Department of Social Service at the University of Toronto, Guest informed President Falconer that "the last few years has changed the situation for us as women – we have in that time *proved ourselves* to *ourselves* in almost every line of professional and business life, and now, knowing that we can do all that men do as well as they can, we face the situation that there is our women's work that *only* we can do, and our trained hand and brain sees now that that work is being inefficiently done." Canadian middle-class women endorsed the cult of efficiency and scientific expertise which is usually identified as a predominantly male purview. Women championed the introduction of child care experts into rural communities because it would not only improve the quality of social conditions and community life in the increasingly disadvantaged country districts, but it would also provide a new field of endeavour for educated women. Emily Guest wanted women to participate fully in the new culture of science, claiming that "while there is an agricultural expert in every county for both schools and farms to refer to, there is no *home expert* to whom home-makers can turn, no place in Ontario that trains playground supervisors efficiently, nor specifically, school nurses." What she was criticizing was that the extension of state activities into such areas as scientific agriculture and technical education had thus far only benefited men. In Guest's view, the modern state must be transformed into an instrument of female interests. "The place of the home is the state," Guest argued; "[there] should be a state Department of Homes as well equipped and financed as the Department of Militia, or state recognition of *internal* defence as compared with *external* defence."[195]

In advancing a female-centred state, the first objective of the National Council of Women and of the Federation of Women's Institutes, both of which were primarily active within the church-led Social Service Council of Canada, was to secure the establishment of a Children's Bureau, preferably staffed by women, within the federal Department of Labour. Although the Protestant churches had been active since before the war in popularizing the cause of child welfare by instituting a Child Welfare Week which involved all clergymen across Canada in delivering sermons on children's rights and by using parades and baby contests to interest the public in the questions of children's health and the necessity of birth registration, by 1920 they saw the women's network as an indispensable public force in acquiring government recognition of this social issue. In January 1920 J.G. Shearer, the secretary of the Social Service Council of Canada, wrote to Violet McNaughton admitting that the women's lobby was critical in having the churches make child welfare the centre-piece of their overall conception of social redemption. "We approach you," wrote Shearer, "as a representative of a large organization which will have a tremendous power and influence in any such movement."[196] Under the impress of the popularity of eugenics, with its emphasis upon the mental and physical improvement of the race, child care had come to be viewed by Canadian reformers as of "inestimable value to every Social Activity,"[197] and it was seen as the critical thin point of the wedge for a broad range of government responsibility, including infant mortality, mothers' pensions, race degeneracy, child labour and immigration, old-age pensions, and state maternity grants.[198]

Speaking in 1920, Charlotte Whitton, Shearer's assistant on the Social Service Council of Canada and later head of the Canadian Council of Child Welfare, proclaimed that "[t]he greatest Philosopher and Economist whom history records set the child in the midst of His teachings, became indeed a Child Himself to enter the community of His own nation to whom He came, and made the understanding of the child, and the ability to place oneself in its position, as the requisite to enter the greater community of the Kingdom of Heaven."[199] Under the leadership of Methodist field secretary Hugh Dobson the Protestant churches aimed to unite voluntary organizations and the federal state bureaucracy with the ultimate goal of incrementally pressuring governments to shoulder ever greater responsibility for the social welfare of Canadians. The Protestant churches sought to parlay the popularity of the issue of child welfare among women into a vast expansion of the administrative state, which in future would include not only a Child Welfare Bureau but also a federal Board of Health, a Bureau of Surveys to correlate vital statistics and initiate national surveys in all areas of human welfare, and, at the apex, a Ministry of Social Reconstruction to coordinate voluntary reform groups and university economists and sociologists with government agencies in formulating welfare legislation. In expanding the scope of the modern state, the church's role would not be diminished, for as the repository of the Christian ideal of service it would continue to be instrumental in educating and rallying public opinion behind specific measures of legislation.[200]

The fact that the Methodist Church had, since 1914, publicized the larger problem of protecting the family and conserving human resources through its itinerant Child Welfare Exhibit was a victory for women's interests. It was natural that Dobson was chosen by the Methodist leadership to become the prime mover behind the national campaign to publicize the problem of child welfare, because as the field secretary for Western Canada he was the figure most directly connected with and influenced by the powerful agrarian women's lobby. Having been converted from viewing industrial democracy as the keystone of postwar reconstruction to placing the redemption of women and children at the forefront of reform, Dobson shifted away from the male-centred corridors of American progressivism, which had gathered around the American Association for Labor Legislation and the American Academy of Political and Social Science, and gravitated increasingly towards the orbit of the female-dominated National Conference of Social Work, Hull House, and the Chicago School of Civics and Philanthropy,[201] the leading American voices for regulation of child labour, mothers' pensions, and maternity and health insurance.

That Dobson was now moving within a progressive landscape shaped by women reformers who emulated practical sociology over the more theoretical orientation of male university professors was confirmed when he attended an American conference on the subject of immigration in 1919. There he shared the platform with Jane Addams, the notable director of Hull House, Sophonisba Breckinridge, who along with Edith Abbott had transformed Graham Taylor's Chicago School of Civics and Philanthropy into a formal department of the University of Chicago offering a rigorous and scientific program for the investigation of the American public welfare system, and Robert Park, a member of the Department of Sociology at the University of Chicago. All these reformers called for the application of social scientific data to the redress of urban ills and social unrest.[202] Although Dobson had advocated before the conference the reading of the latest theoretical treatises on social evolution by Small and Ross, after 1919 the recommendations for specific social legislation advanced by Dobson and a host of other progressive clergymen, including J.S. Woodsworth, Edward S. Bishop, Lorne Pierce, J.T. Falk, and Arthur Rose of All People's Mission in Winnipeg, were directly informed by the American female-led charity organizations and settlement houses. Not only did Dobson collect and distribute the publications of Breckinridge and Abbott, who wrote on women in industry, children's issues, delinquency, and housing reform,[203] but in 1919 Dobson instructed his student, the Rev. Edward S. Bishop, to visit the playgrounds of Chicago and to consult with two settlement workers, Jane Addams of Hull House, and his "personal friend," the Congregational clergyman Graham Taylor who headed the Department of Christian Sociology at the University of Chicago and its settlement house, the Chicago Commons. Taylor and Addams had both been instrumental in grafting the social sciences at the University of Chicago onto their own well-established networks of civic welfare organizations, settlement houses, and informal alliances of women reformers and social investigators, thus making the university the handmaiden of their practical aims of formulating social legislation. And in Taylor's case, the idea of viewing Chicago as a social laboratory directly served his aim of binding various civic, industrial, and cultural groups to the church in order to reinvigorate its ability to Christianize all aspects of human life.[204]

By the early 1920s Dobson was firmly ensconced in this American tradition of social investigation which stressed the centrality of women's issues. He was, for example, a close associate of Edward T. Devine, one of the editors of the *Survey*, the American journal devoted to promoting the unity of social work and reform, and one of the central figures in ensuring the establishment in 1912 of the United States Children's

Bureau.[205] In 1921 Dobson sat on the program committee of the National Conference of Social Work alongside the chief luminaries of children's reform, Grace Abbott, who later headed the Children's Bureau, Jane Addams, Mary McDowall, a leading social worker, and Julia Lathrop, who established the Charities Commission of Illinois, taught in the Chicago School of Civics, and later was one of the many female appointees to the Children's Bureau. It was from this close association with American women reformers that Dobson drew the inspiration as well as the concepts and methods that informed his child care exhibits and his later advocacy of a Canadian Child Welfare Bureau within the federal Department of Labour.[206]

Just as the local popularity of evangelism had lured the church leadership's social service ethos towards individual conversion and emotional piety, so the organized power of women's groups in rural and small-town Canada transformed the church's program of social amelioration away from an identification with élite, urban, and university-centred social science towards a more democratically inspired reformism. In it, male church leaders were persuaded to relinquish their early concern for the conciliation of the male workforce in favour of a largely female agenda that placed the redemption of children at its core. In the area of child welfare reform, the Protestant churches were the clear leaders. But, as Hugh Dobson reminded fellow clergymen, the National Council of Women was active at both local and national levels.[207] The churches were easily able to translate the concerns of women to social welfare agencies at the national level through the instrument of the Social Service Council of Canada, which the churches had established in 1914 to act as a clearing-house for all social investigation and reform. The council assumed the role that in other countries, including Germany, France, and to some extent Britain, was occupied by state welfare agencies; it initiated social legislation by interpreting local social problems that had been articulated through its affiliated provincial councils, and this legislation in turn was sustained by the diverse and minutely organized local welfare boards. The legislative programs formulated at the local level were hammered into national issues by the church, which publicized local reform agendas to high-profile organizations, such as the Canadian Conference on Charities and Corrections, the Public Health Congress of Canada, and the Canadian Conference for the Cure and Prevention of Tuberculosis, and ultimately to the federal Department of Health.[208]

Child welfare policy was not imposed from above by urban male medical professionals working in concert with the state. Rather, during the 1920s, prior to the entrenchment of professional expertise, it was the efflorescence of grass-roots reform – the expression of the convergence of interests between progressive clergymen and maternal feminists – which pressed the state and a reluctant medical establishment to give priority to child-centred reform. It was the churches that took the initiative in launching well-baby campaigns, where they educated not only the public but also male doctors on the need to examine for tuberculosis, on dental hygiene, and on the care of the feeble-minded.[209] Because child care legislation was grounded on a popular base that included local councils of women, church social service organizations, civic leaders, and welfare societies whose frequent child survey canvasses anchored its recommendations to local sentiment, it was attuned to a much broader range of influences and was more democratic in its formulation than it would be when child study became the exclusive purview of medical and university professionals during the 1930s, a development epitomized by Dr William Blatz's School for Child Study at the University of Toronto.[210]

Most of the church-sponsored child care initiatives were first implemented at the local level and only when there was sufficient pressure of opinion did the Social Service Council of Canada launch a national campaign to create a Child Welfare Department in Ottawa. As Peter Bryce and Charlotte Whitton informed Violet McNaughton, their coordinator of local women's needs in Western Canada, "[w]ith the digest of the replies to our various letters before us, the Committee met ... and the decision reached was that, in view of the very evident convictions, so widely held, that a Child Welfare Week for Canada would be of inestimable value to every Social Activity of the Dominion, it must be something for which a most thorough and comprehensive preparation should be made."[211] Since the well-spring of Western agrarian populism had called forth the idea of holding child welfare weeks, the increased government intervention that the creation of a federal children's bureau would signal was not inimical to ordinary Canadians, especially farm women who welcomed reliable information regarding child rearing. "I am sure," Dobson wrote Charlotte Whitton in 1920, "there will be a very hearty response to any action the Government may take in this matter from our western provinces, for the Provincial organizations, Churches and Women's Societies have been pressing for this matter for three or four years now."[212]

On 8 August 1918 Mrs S. Szapko, a recent immigrant to Canada, wrote to Dobson requesting the pamphlets on child care and motherhood which she had seen advertised in the Methodist Church exhibit at the local fair ground.[213] These pamphlets were similar to those issued by the United States Children's Bureau in Washington, which synthesized the most up-to-date medical and scientific knowledge on child rearing in a series of accessible pamphlets and articles in various national women's magazines. Molly Ladd-Taylor has recently argued that in the United States these pamphlets, far from being viewed as a form of social control by middle-class women, found hearty acceptance, particularly among poor and rural women who lacked other sources of advice to which they could turn. If the thousands of letters seeking advice regarding maternity and children's health is any indication, the majority of American women not only desired but demanded government aid for their families.[214] Rural women in Canada likewise desired increased intervention on the part of governments and the medical establishment on behalf of maternal and child health.[215]

This increased demand on the part of Canadian women for information pertaining to motherhood and children was a consequence of the immense success and popularity of Hugh Dobson's roving Child Welfare Exhibit which criss-crossed Canada following World War I. In 1918 the American National Child Welfare Association persuaded Dobson to duplicate in Canada the American National Child Welfare Exhibit, which consisted of seventy-five large panels of oil paintings, "the best on the continent,"[216] depicting various aspects of children's health, as well as twenty cards on the care of the mother, twenty-five illustrated cards on dental hygiene, and fifty cards and charts on the care of the feeble-minded. At each exhibit Dobson also circulated Helen McMurchy's readable pamphlets, such as *A Little Talk About Baby*, *The Baby Book*, and *The Canadian Mother's Book*.[217] This exhibit was then made available to local fairs throughout Canada at a cost of $300, a payment which was always recouped by the fair boards because the child care displays proved to be one of the most magnetic attractions for drawing people to these end-of-summer exhibitions. So popular was Dobson's Child Welfare Exhibit that he expanded its scope to encompass all facets of social reconstruction. To the original seventy-five panels were added 125 on such themes as slums and housing, an exhibit on tuberculosis, thirty photographs of Canadian social conditions, plus 300 lantern-slides developed by the Department of Evangelism and Social Service on child welfare. And, once Dobson had eight guaranteed fairs, he introduced the biggest crowd pleaser, the baby contest.[218] With great cleverness Dobson and his Methodist helpers interspersed these exhibits with evangelistic appeals as part of the Methodist Church's Forward Movement.[219] Inevitably, these large gatherings for Dobson's lantern-slide shows were converted into mass meetings for revivalistic purposes, largely because their proven ability to attract eight to ten large crowds a day provided the perfect outlet for his evangelistic message of social service.

By inviting the participation of various civic leaders, local businessmen, women's groups, and local doctors, Dobson used the exhibits as a means to promote the larger cause of community social service.[220] More importantly, the mass appeal of the child welfare displays served as the mechanism by which the church took the lead in forging local coalitions for democratic social reform. These occasions also acted as an opportunity to remind ordinary Canadians of the Christian spirit that sustained the cause of community improvement. During a four-day stint in Yorkton, Saskatchewan, Hugh Dobson effectively enlisted the support of the provincial health commissioner and the local mayor, who offered the City Hall which, as the venue for the flagship Child Welfare Exhibit, was later packed twice by men who came to view the Methodist Church's film on venereal disease. "They were a sober bunch of men when we got through," Dobson told the Rev. Manson Doyle. This was followed by five more film showings the following day. The popularity and importance of the Child Welfare Exhibit in nourishing the grassroots of Canadian reform soon made it the nucleus of a wider program of social service that included mothers' clinics and specialized talks to high schools students on the family.[221]

It has become commonplace for historians to interpret progressive reform as a largely urban phenomenon and narrowly the product of control by middle-class experts, a movement which then gradually radiated outwards to the benighted countryside. This perspective has ignored the persistence of the rural hinterland as a factor in initiating social change, and by doing so it has ignored the possibility that in early twentieth-century Canada the idea of national efficiency, which so characterized this era of reform, could also be informed by the rhythms of local democracy. If the campaign of the Protestant churches for greater government regulation of child welfare is any yardstick, it appears that much of progressive reform in Canada was first articulated and implemented in largely rural and agrarian settings, and from there was introduced to urban areas. Thus, it was the Prairie field secretary of the Methodist Church, Hugh Dobson, who took a leadership role in coalescing reform sentiment in Toronto around the profound social problems relating to children. In September 1918 he instructed the Rev. Peter Bryce on how to conduct a child welfare exhibit to be held in connection with the Ontario Branch Conference of Social Work. To Bryce, who later became the provincial director of child welfare and chairman of the Mothers' Allowance Commission in Ontario, Dobson enclosed a bulletin minutely itemizing the methods for securing and coordinating wide community support for the church's agenda which, as usual, not only included talks on the family and the importance of the child in realizing the Kingdom of God in Canada, but also covered a wide range of topics of both an evangelistic and social service nature. Dobson instructed Bryce to offer talks and sermons in Convocation Hall at the University of Toronto on "The Family – from the age of the homespun to the age of the machine," "The Marriage of the Unfit," "The Child in the Midst," "Growth in Religion," "The Living Wage," "The Triumph of Personality," and, in a manner reminiscent of a mass revival meeting, to conclude with a climactic sermon by the head of the Department of Evangelism and Social Service, T. Albert Moore, on "The Task of Canadianization." Of this extravaganza of reform, Dobson commented: "My idea is that we will make this the best exhibit up to date, in the city of Toronto, and represent, if possible, every agency that operates in the city for Child Welfare."[222]

In an age increasingly defined by scientific expertise, the integration of the social sciences into the theological training of Protestant clergymen was critical in providing the necessary intellectual authority for ensuring, following World War I, that the churches were not only able to capture but also to maintain their leadership of Canadian social reform. In order to forge a powerful reform coalition, Canadian church leaders sought alignments with a wide range of reform groups. Although many of these organizations were not overtly Christian, they nevertheless adhered to the widely held view of the Protestant churches as supreme in organizing and articulating a vision of social reform that would secure a wide public consensus. By seeking out the sanction of the churches the secular progressives greatly contributed to entrenching the power of Protestantism and its goal of Christianizing the wider culture. The paradox of Protestant progressivism is that although it hoped to employ the social sciences to emulate the model (generally characterized by male expertise) of American progressivism, the role the church had carved out for itself, as a body mediating between government bureaucracies, universities, national reform organizations, and popular values expressed through local congregations, rendered it much more susceptible to pressures from local and agrarian reform constituencies. And in Canada these constituencies were dominated by maternal feminists. While the leadership of Protestant reformism may have been male, the impetus behind its agenda was provided by the mobilization of vast numbers of middle-class and farm women. As a consequence, the reform platform of the Protestant churches was a direct expression of decentralized, populist sentiment. Initially, the Protestant churches' ideal of social reconstruction was shaped from above by the decisions of federal bureaucrats in the Department of Labour and their social investigators. However, the powerful forces of localism and the persistent pull of the Canadian rural hinterland, which still dominated the social experience of the majority of Canadians, soon transmuted the pattern of Christian social reform into one that reflected the needs and desires of women.

4 A "Uniting Social Aim": The Protestant Churches and Social Work in Equipoise

Writing in 1912 E.J. Urwick, later the head of the University of Toronto's Department of Social Service, celebrated the "uniting social aim"[1] of professors and priests which he believed must animate modern social work. Urwick's ideal of a harmonious reconciliation between science and religion in the common pursuit of a higher social good was nowhere more completely realized than in twentieth-century Canada, where the discipline of social work was founded and professionalized largely through the efforts of the Protestant churches. The fate of the McGill Department of Social Service, which was summarily closed on 4 August 1931 after the theological colleges withdrew their financial support, remains a telling illustration of not only the interdependent relationship between the church and the university but also the reality that Protestant social evangelism was the very engine sustaining Canadian schools of social work during the 1920s. The decisive role of the churches in determining the collapse of the McGill department compels a reassessment of Richard Allen's argument that in Canada there was a persistent conflict between moralism and science during the 1920s and that this conflict hastened the dominance of professional social work in setting the pace and direction of the modern public welfare system. According to Allen the development of modern social work disrupted the marriage between evangelism and social reform by forcing the church to accede to the demands of a secular society.[2] In Canada, however, the moralism sustained by social evangelism not only dovetailed with, but was also the prime mover in the emergence of a social scientific perspective. These strong bonds between Protestantism and the universities were particularly evident in the training of social workers, which until the mid-1930s was controlled by university professors who were either clergymen, like the Baptist Carl Dawson at McGill, or social scientists, like E.J. Urwick at Toronto; both groups reinforced the primacy of the churches because their social philosophy was grounded in Christian idealism.[3]

At the instigation of the Methodist, Presbyterian, and Anglican theological colleges at McGill, the Department of Social Study and Training was created in 1918 with J. Howard Toynbee Falk at its helm. Falk was a long-time advocate of the efficacy of placing the churches in a pivotal role in the development of social service work, and his appointment marked the fulfilment of the desire of the mainline Protestant churches for a body of scientifically trained workers for the burgeoning network of voluntary charities and social centres which the churches were then in the process of establishing. Falk had been trained in an evangelical social settlement, Christadora House in New York, by the redoubtable Sarah Libby Carson who was later brought to Canada by the Presbyterian Church.[4] As secretary of the Social Welfare Commission of Winnipeg in 1912, he was commended by C.W. Gordon for keeping the churches aligned with recent developments in social reform by effecting a "confederation of churches for social service work."[5] Although a champion of placing philanthropy upon a more scientific basis,[6] Falk, with his long experience within the ambit of church organizations in Canada, was perceived by Protestant progressives as an important Christian linchpin who would solder the connection between the growth of university social work and the social evangelism of the churches. Thus, Hugh Dobson wrote Falk upon his appointment to McGill in 1918 to say "I am glad our universities are beginning to see the necessity of more adequate training for social work."[7] An article entitled "Social Service and Theological Training," published in 1919 in *Social Welfare*, the national organ of the Protestant churches, underscored the special relationship that had been forged between McGill's theological colleges and the new Department of Social Service.[8] The primary purpose of the social work program was to train prospective ministers and church settlement workers in modern methods of scientific charity administration and casework, and to this end the theological colleges contributed over one-third of the annual budget of the department. While McGill University contributed a somewhat meagre $1,500, the bulk of the funds was supplied by a $7,500 contribution from the theological colleges. As a result, the Protestant churches had the whip hand in dictating the curriculum of the new department. Because of the need to foster practical training for clergymen, theoretical sociology was downplayed from the beginning in favour of courses that sought to introduce students to applied social investigation. The only broadly philosophical treatment of the principles of sociology was offered by William Caldwell, professor of philosophy. Long before the arrival of Carl Dawson, the supposed pioneer of urban social surveys and community studies, Falk taught a course on "The Social Development of an Urban County" for theological students and the Rev. Mr Dickie taught the "Social Development of a Rural Community."[9]

The balance of financial support was provided by the city charities, which were dominated by club-women and female case workers.[10] Even though it meant drawing in large numbers of girls and women "of leisure" into the program, which by necessity became more vocational in its tenor, McGill University officials actively courted community charities. They did so in the belief that in the afterglow of postwar enthusiasm for social reconstruction the quickest route for amplifying the profile of the university in the Anglophone community was to establish academically trained social workers who could take the lead in "co-ordinating the work of agencies." In this way, the leaders of McGill University aspired to make their institution the centre-piece in educating public opinion on issues of social reform and thereby preserve the always precarious solvency of their institution, which, unlike the University of Toronto, lacked access to public funds.[11] Like the broader culture of progressivism, the aspirations of McGill were double-edged, for while its promotion of the social service ideal reinforced its ties with the local community of middle-class reformers, the unintended consequence was that a daunting cohort of educated women began to gravitate to the professional opportunities offered by the new program in social work, and by 1922 they were displacing the male theological students for whom the program was designed. In the graduating class of that year, 86 of 140 students were female social workers, 58 were public health nurses, 14 were physical education students, and only 42 were male theological students.[12] The upsurge in female enrolment in turn prompted the nomination of Helen Reid, a prominent Montreal charity activist, as the first woman member of the department's Committee of Management, and some viewed her appointment as the precursor of increased female influence over the direction of the social sciences.[13]

This uncontrolled acceleration in the direction of vocational training in social work alarmed conservatives within the university, such as Stephen Leacock, who eschewed both women's rights to a higher education and a narrowly utilitarian curriculum because in his estimation these devalued the prestige of the academy.[14] In February 1922 Leacock issued a memorandum on reforming the department so that it might combine a broader philosophical understanding of social and economic forces with its already well-established emphasis on social investigation and practical social reform. Still influenced by the heady climate of postwar idealism, Leacock conceded that the ultimate goal of social work must continue to be the solution of social ills. "There is a great need," wrote Leacock, "for the application of intensive study and trained intelligence in the urgent social questions of the moment, and an open field for the kind of effort that only a university can undertake." However, Leacock was adamant that the academic standards of social work should be raised and that any practical endeavour must be preceded by intensive training in history and economics, which would place the Department of Social Service more firmly within the academic structure of the university and under the control of social science specialists such as himself. He recommended, therefore, that only after mental capacities were thoroughly developed through the taking of a BA should the well-rounded social worker study conditions of poverty, housing, immigration, prison reform, and public health. Leacock feared that the program unduly stressed individual casework and distracted the university from its primary mission of public enlightenment. By making the social work program more academically grounded in the theoretical social sciences, Leacock hoped to jettison the vocationally minded women and to restore the university's links with the theological colleges whose male students would form a scientific cadre trained to undertake and publish rigorous social surveys of Montreal. In seeking an accord between the churches, the university, and government, Leacock's perspective converged with that of Protestant progressives who, like him, believed that the development of a public consciousness was the imperative force that impelled practical social reform.[15]

In April of that year, the Committee of Management of the department, which was *de facto* the mouthpiece of the theological colleges, forced the resignation of Howard Falk, and enthusiastically took up the cudgels on Leacock's behalf regarding his plea for a sociological education that was "essentially humanistic."[16] Their model of the ideal director of social work was C.R. Henderson, a professor of sociology in the School of Divinity of the University of Chicago who instructed young clergymen on how to apply theoretical sociology to the task of civic reform.[17] The members of the Committee of Management had long fretted over the need to have economics, social psychology, and social ethics taught their department in order to offset the growing tendency, which they identified predominantly with women, of taking courses simply to further a career in social work. Thus, they quickly acceded to Leacock's and President Sir Arthur Currie's demands to hire a social worker who also possessed a higher degree in the principles of modern sociology. This fact notwithstanding, they still expected the prospective candidate to awaken the wider moral vision of both theological candidates and social workers and to preserve as well the university's close accord with community charities.[18]

In the hope of attracting a better class of student – read male social reformers – the representative of the theological colleges on the committee, Gordon Laing, advised Currie to secure a candidate to head the department who could meet the needs of the Protestant church colleges, which insisted that social evangelism be underpinned by sound academic learning in the social sciences.[19] The applicants for the position were S.A. Cudmore of the federal Department of Statistics, J.M. Wyatt of the federal Department of Labour, Dr R.F. Forester of Harvard University, the Rev. Humphrey Michell of Queen's University, who later taught social science at McMaster University, and the Rev. Carl Dawson of the University of Chicago.[20] Gilbert Jackson, a University of Toronto professor of political economy, was the leading candidate because of his strong connections with the church-based Social Service Council of Canada, but when he declined McGill's offer,[21] the committee focused its attention upon Carl Dawson because, apart from Michell, he was the only candidate who had intensive theological training and a strong Christian outlook. Significantly, Cudmore was passed over by Sir Arthur Currie because he was not deemed to be enough of a "booster" who could bind civic reform to university social science.[22]

Dawson perfectly fitted the requirements of the theological colleges which sought out a candidate strongly committed to the tenets of social Christianity. Not only had he been a student of C.R. Henderson, but as a postgraduate fellow in practical theology for six years in the Divinity School at the University of Chicago, this young Baptist minister had thoroughly imbibed the socially conscious liberal Christianity of Shailer Mathews and Shirley Jackson Case. Born in the pietistic Baptist religious culture of Tryon, Prince Edward Island, in 1887, Dawson had attended Acadia University, and as he matured his Baptist faith grew even stronger: upon graduation in 1912 he served as a minister in Lockeport, Nova Scotia, before proceeding to the University of Chicago for advanced theological training.[23]

Marlene Shore has portrayed Dawson's Chicago years as a period of increasing immersion in secular sociology culminating in the loss of his Christian faith.[24] As his own application to McGill makes clear, however, his sociological training took place entirely within the program of practical theology in the Divinity School, where his Baptist faith was reoriented towards an increasing devotion to the ideal of social redemption. Not only was Dawson an assistant pastor at the Englewood Baptist Church in Chicago between 1915 and 1917, but both during and after World War I his practical social work occurred within the Christian confines of the YMCA. Even his first teaching position was in the Department of Sociology at the YMCA College from 1921 to 1922. Rather than pursuing the "objective" social science of Robert Park, with whom he had taught from 1920 to 1921, Dawson was interested in the link between social investigation and local civic reform, and this interest reflected the older Chicago tradition of Albion Small, Charles Henderson, and Ellsworth Faris, who saw modern sociology as an extension of their Christian social ethics.[25] Moreover, during Dawson's sojourn at Chicago the sociology of Robert Park and Ernest Burgess, who in the late 1920s reincarnated themselves as apostles of objectivity, had greater affinities with the community studies of social reformers like Graham Taylor, Edith Abbott, and Sophonisba Breckinridge, who, like Dawson, worked in close association with the United Charities of Chicago. Thus, Dawson's career perfectly replicated that of his mentor, C.R. Henderson, and with strong letters of recommendation on his behalf from leading Baptist theologians, the theological representative on the committee, Gordon Laing, recommended his appointment.[26] Clearly outvoted by a committee heavily stacked in favour of the church college interests, William Caldwell protested to James Mavor that the job of finding a new director had been "ticklish" because of the enormous power exercised by "outside" interests, by which the disgruntled professor of philosophy meant the theologians.[27]

In the fall of 1922 Dawson arrived at McGill to teach on social economics, industrial and social legislation, poverty, social pathology, immigration, ethnology and land settlement, and urban and rural problems.[28] This program was not derived from the Chicago tradition of Robert Park, but instead had been laid down for Dawson by the church colleges. Under Dawson's directorship, despite the window-dressing of a change of name from "Social Service" to "Social Science" and new courses taught by Leacock and psychologist William Tait, the core of the program remained largely practical in its focus, and depended upon such vocational texts as *Social Diagnosis* by an American Charity Organization Society worker, Mary Richmond, Tuft's *Education and Training for Social Work*, and Steiner's *Education for Social Work*.[29] While some historians have insisted on viewing Dawson as a theoretical sociologist committed to an ideal of objectivity,[30] his entire career at McGill University was devoted to fostering the marriage between sociology and social reform. Upon taking up the directorship of the Department of Social Science and a position in the Department of Sociology, Dawson elucidated the connections which he saw between these two disciplines. "The new course to be outlined," he told social workers, "will have as its aim the provision of a larger background for the students intending to take up social work. Such an outlook is considered particularly desirable now that Sociology, which has been concerned to a great extent with the alleviation of social distresses and evils, is turning its attention to their cure."[31] Dawson emulated the work of the American Russell Sage Foundation which stressed advocacy over objectivity, and by inviting as lecturers caseworkers from the Chicago Juvenile Courts and Canadian social welfare agencies[32] he underscored his own commitment to an "intelligent social action"[33] founded upon the scientific collection of social data. When in 1927 Dawson called for the detachment of research from practical ends, he was not advocating the pursuit of empirical social science; rather, he was cloaking his ambition to move all social investigation from the purview of what he perceived as the unsystematic procedures of civic welfare agencies to the more methodologically rigorous atmosphere of the McGill Department of Social Science.[34] In fact, he was an enthusiastic champion of the overtly social reformist outlook of the Pittsburgh Survey, which he saw as a model for investigating the neighbourhoods of urban and rural Quebec.[35] His insistence that students collect social data and visit the railway shops, department stores, and factories in Montreal, and even his own social surveys of immigrants, which he contributed to the Canadian Pioneer Problems Series in the 1930s, had one goal in view: the subordination of social research to the progressive political goal of national efficiency and social redemption.[36]

Marlene Shore has argued that the most formative influence upon Dawson's approach to sociology was Robert Park at the University of Chicago. Park has been celebrated in quasi-mythological terms as the founder of the much vaunted tradition of empirical sociology represented by the "Chicago School" of sociologists, which included W.I. Thomas and Ernest Burgess. This interpretation of Chicago sociology, which discerns a sharp discontinuity between research for socially ameliorative ends and the later pursuit of objective social science, has been argued most consistently by sociologist Martin Bulmer who has relegated the earlier tradition of Albion Small, C.R. Henderson, and George Vincent to a stage of antiquarianism and religious amateurism preceding the true professionalization of the discipline after Small's departure in 1922.[37] This line of argument confers pre-eminent status upon Park's school of the late 1920s and has gathered its momentum largely from Park's own self-mythologizing which derived from his concern to distinguish himself from his predecessors whose sociological research he considered to be unscientific, reformist, and unduly moralistic in character. Thus, by the late 1920s Park asserted: "A moral man cannot be a sociologist."[38]

Bulmer's discontinuity thesis has recently come under considerable attack from historians who have protested against his ahistorical approach to the development of sociology in the United States.[39] These historians have rehabilitated the empirical rigour of the type of sociology and social investigation undertaken prior to the dominance of the Parkian paradigm in the late 1920s, and they maintain that because most of the urban and rural social surveys produced between 1890 and 1920 were undertaken by women, ministers, and social reformers, these have been unfairly marginalized and their contribution to modern sociology undermined. The revisionist scholars have shown the necessity of drawing a clear distinction between the work of Robert Park and Ernest Burgess prior to 1922 and their activities during the later years of that decade once they had emerged from the shadow of the Smallian legacy.

What has become evident is that during the years when Dawson studied at the University of Chicago, Park and Burgess, as junior and part-time academics, taught sociology thoroughly under the impress of the chairmanship of Albion Small, a Baptist minister and an outspoken exponent of the conjunction between social research and progressive social reform. It was actually Albion Small and George Vincent who first placed urban and rural community surveys, as outlined in their 1894 textbook, *An Introduction to the Science of Society*, at the core of sociology.[40] More importantly, the reputation of the methods of social investigation promoted in the Chicago School of Civics and Philanthropy by Edith Abbott, Sophonisba Breckinridge, Graham Taylor, and their female coterie of non-academic reformers, was clearly in the ascendant when Park and Burgess arrived in Chicago, as is clearly demonstrated by the indisputable influence of the Hull-House Maps and Papers on their approach to the diagnosis of social problems. In 1918 Park offered courses on the social survey which were attended largely by social workers and reformers. In them he expressed the view, indistinguishable from the one proferred by Jane Addams, Graham Taylor, and C.R. Henderson, that the true purpose of the social survey was to publicize social problems and thereby raise the consciousness of the community.[41] As late as 1929 Park linked his own urban studies to the tradition of social investigation established by the Hull-House Maps and Papers. Indeed, at the time of Dawson's encounter with Park in the early 1920s, it is debatable whether Park, whose later reputation was bound up with his pioneering of an "ecological" approach to the study of human communities, had actually developed a sociology that integrated the insights of natural history. In a 1922 review of the text book by Park and Ernest Burgess, *An Introduction to the Science of Sociology*, Lewis Mumford dismissed the volume as an "entertaining logomachy" containing little beyond a "diabetic flatulence of sociologies." Mumford's chief criticism, however, was that the sociology of Park and his protégé Burgess was inadequate because it failed to incorporate the work of geographers, and thus remained vague and abstract in its treatment of the human context. The analysis of the two Chicago sociologists could be sharpened, Mumford observed, through the study of "the ecology of the human community."[42]

Burgess made a similar observation in 1927.[43] Burgess's sociological views, more than Park's, were shaped within the context of civic reformism. In 1915, while at the University of Kansas, he conducted a survey of Topeka for the Russell Sage Foundation whose research program was exclusively dictated by the imperatives of social workers and civic reformers. Burgess was brought to Chicago expressly to replace C.R. Henderson, the sociologist who taught in the Department of Practical Theology within the Divinity School and whose philosophy of sociology was reflected in his observation that "God has providentially wrought out for us the social sciences and placed them at our disposal."[44] Although Burgess was not a Baptist minister like Henderson, because the sociological emphasis of the Divinity School was unerringly practical he taught in a manner not dissimilar from that of his predecessor. Not only did Burgess preserve his own strong ties with civic reform organizations, but like Henderson he assumed the critical function of placing divinity students in local social agencies.[45] He was a strong advocate of practical sociology and practical Christianity and he promoted the use of the social survey as data for the effective administration of local charity and reform.[46]

Dawson, as a student in the Department of Practical Sociology in the Divinity School, would not have been in contact with Burgess on the plane of theoretical sociology. They would have met during Dawson's search for a placement in the local YMCA, his chosen venue for applied Christianity. Every divinity student had to choose one of four fields of social service, and even though they received a thorough grounding in the principles of sociology, psychology, and social philosophy, this theoretical training was tempered by the practical imperatives imposed by the Baptist Church. All divinity students except doctoral candidates were thus limited to the number of courses they could pursue outside the confines of the Divinity School. Sociology was taught either by ministers or by philosophers, such as George Herbert Mead who still "felt the spirit of the minister."[47] Charles Henderson instructed Dawson on the relationship between the church and modern philanthropy, the labour movement, delinquency, criminology, and the sociology of the family; Albion Small taught the ethics of sociology; Professor Bedford introduced Dawson to rural community study; W.I. Thomas, best-known for his work on the Polish peasant, taught social origins, primitive social control, and mental development of the race; and George Herbert Mead taught the philosophy of nature.[48]

Thus, although Dawson obtained a doctoral degree in sociology, professional social work was seen by him as the natural expression of the call to social service, a largely Christian endeavour in which patience, sympathy, and "something we term religion" remained central animating principles.[49] Because he believed that university social work was merely an extension of the mission of social evangelism of the churches, Dawson surrounded himself with a host of dedicated Christians. "The church long ago realized," he declared in 1928, "that the field of service and goodwill is more extensive than church organization, and that in social work as a separate institution it could discover a new ally in achieving the goals of a more abundant life."[50] For example, Dawson placed May Reid, a woman of strong Baptist convictions and a graduate of Brandon College, the Baptist university in Western Canada, in a pivotal position as head of instruction in social case work and he promoted students like Muriel McCall, who later worked at the Social Service Council of Canada and the Montreal Children's Bureau and whom he glowingly recommended as "a young woman of fine Christian character and keen insight into social welfare problems."[51] Dawson was a regular speaker at the meetings of the Social Service Council of Canada and of various welfare organizations such as the YMCA and the Knights of Columbus, where he regularly shared the platform with other clergymen. And it is significant that when he established the Social Workers' Club at the McGill University Settlement he made the Anglican Rev. R.G. Burgoyne its founding president.[52]

Dawson lived for six years in what was considered the model urban social laboratory of Chicago, but his social vision remained firmly rooted in the conservative folk-ways of his rural Baptist upbringing in Prince Edward Island. Indeed, his doctoral thesis was an elegy to his nostalgic yearnings for the social discipline and rationality of the face-to-face relationships typical of a small rural Baptist community. Although it drew upon the currently fashionable crowd psychology of Gustave LeBon and Gabriel Tarde, Dawson's thesis was from beginning to end a diatribe against the irrationality and unpredictability of human masses at war or clustered in large urban centres. This outlook, together with his obsessive gardening of pumpkins in downtown Chicago, evoked Dawson's search for a simpler society.[53] The influence of Robert Park upon the young Dawson would have been tenuous at best, for Park only secured a full-time position at the University of Chicago in 1919. Given that Dawson continued to extol the moral superiority of a rural existence, it is doubtful that his own sociological interests drew upon Park's program to dissect the modern urban metropolis. It is more likely that when Dawson assisted Park as a junior instructor in 1920–21, he was influenced by Park's own personal search for a pre-industrial arcadian bliss characterized by neighbourly cooperation and a sense of belonging in which the individualist ideal of the independent farmer was harmoniously reconciled with community solidarity.[54]

Dawson's prescription for countering the social disintegration and loss of individuality wrought by industrialization was the discovery of new forms of social control to lead to the recovery of traditional values of intimacy, loyalty, and neighbourliness that had characterized rural and small-town Canada. Social work, he declared, "concerns itself with the problem of adjustment, when either individuals cannot meet the requirements of society for independent existence or society fails to fulfil its duty to the individual," and thus it must seek to investigate and ameliorate "all conditions over which the individual has no control but which tend to bring about maladjustment of the individual to society." Although a firm exponent of greater professionalism, Dawson still viewed issues of personal morality as central, and outlined such problems as cruelty, neglect, intemperance, divorce, commercialized vice, and "immorality" as the main areas of concern for the professional social worker.[55] Like the American sociologist E.A. Ross, who greatly influenced him, Dawson assigned to the Christian church a pivotal position in resurrecting individual self-determination. In a symposium entitled "The Christian Industrial Order," Dawson in 1923 addressed one of his favourite themes, the recapturing of traditional family ideals in the context of modern urban society. "We try to deal with the symptoms and not the disease in the body industrial," stated Dawson. "The churches can go far to help men formulate wider sympathies – to be interpreters of these new experiences in our time. They can inspire a new leadership on the part of capital and labor that they and we together may learn to control the machine that has caught us all and make it serve larger human needs."[56] In a similar vein, in a lecture to the Presbyterian Synod of Montreal and Ottawa on "The Church and Social Service," Dawson told the assembled ministers: "The vicious con the virtuous and so it is that the Church that is virtuous in itself must devise some means of vitalizing her powers to quell that vitiation." Dawson's recommendations for empowering the modern church was to wed it all the more firmly to modern social science, which would allow the church to more systematically isolate the "bad apples," the "mental defectives," and the "socially ill" so that they could be converted and redeemed. In language perfectly mirroring that of many progressive church leaders, Dawson argued that under guidance of a revivified scientific social service "the Church will know men and in knowing them will be able to redeem them from evil forces that surround them. That redemption will show men their part in the Kingdom of Christ."[57]

Far from diluting his Baptist convictions, Dawson's years of studying sociology at the University of Chicago actually reinforced his faith because he believed that he had found in the modern social sciences the key to restoring the church to its traditional place of authority as the guardian of popular piety. He castigated those who thought that social science was the adversary of the true functioning of the church. In his view social scientific investigation could not be sundered from religious faith: "One of the foundations of the Christian faith – one of its fundamentals – is service ... Social Science is one part of that service." Eschewing traditional theology, Dawson contended that the scientific rigour of sociology and social psychology, with their special knowledge of vice, crime, and all the human frailties, provided the most powerful means by which the social service ideal could become an integral part of modern Christian culture. Only by applying social Christianity through the endeavour of social work could the church become once again coterminous with the people and "be the relationship between man and his Maker and the foundation of the Social Order."[58]

During the 1920s the social work program became more firmly established, but it did not attempt to divest itself of its connections with the church colleges. Indeed, those people who sought to professionalize the discipline and place it on a more scientific footing were also striving to draw the Department of Social Science into closer concert with the social aims of the churches. At a monthly meeting of the McGill Social Workers' Club, which met with local church representatives, May Reid, Dawson's chief associate, spoke on the need for ever greater cooperation between professional social work, local welfare agencies, and the churches. Reasoning that because social work dealt mainly with individuals through family casework, it "had to turn to the church for spiritual ministration," and Reid accordingly recommended that the number of clergymen on executive boards of social agencies should increase.[59] Out of a firm belief that social workers should be professed Christians, in 1926 Dawson initiated a survey of religion in the program, and used this as a weapon to limit the number of Jewish students, despite the high profile of Jewish philanthropic organizations which regularly hired these graduates.[60] While Principal Currie scrambled to increase the enrolment of ministers in the Department of Social Science,[61] the social agencies and women's charity organizations strengthened their financial grip on the program, thus edging it further away from Leacock's idea of academic excellence and towards greater vocationalism and an emphasis on methods in practical casework.[62] As early as 1924 Dawson himself was beginning to shift the program towards a more career-oriented emphasis when he announced that "the school provides training for social workers who intend to take up social work as a vocation, and also for the girl and women of leisure. To all it aims to give the scientific point of view in social work."[63]

In 1929 the power of the advocates of vocational training became all the more evident when the theological colleges withdrew their annual grant. Even though Dawson attempted to mollify the principal of McGill, who above all desired to promote "systematic investigation" based on the academic social sciences, namely psychology, economics, and sociology, by recommending the raising of academic standards in social work through the implementation of a two-year college degree prior to taking up training in casework, his sympathies clearly lay with practical study. In 1930 he requested that the department become wholly oriented to social work and peremptorily demanded the addition of a supervisor of fieldwork to his staff.[64] This, however, placed Dawson increasingly at odds with the priorities of the academic leaders of McGill, who were seeking to buttress the research profile of the university while divesting themselves of responsibility for practical training in nursing and social work.[65] Belatedly realizing that the university administration had acquired funding from the Rockefeller Foundation for the McGill Social Science Research Project headed by British economist Leonard Marsh, who had published widely on the problem of poverty and unemployment in London, Dawson plaintively staked his own claim as a research social scientist. Despite the misgivings of staunch supporters of practical training, such as Charlotte Whitton,[66] he argued that social work should seek a broad profile beyond mere technical training in the established disciplines of economics, social philosophy, social psychology, and mental hygiene, and he sought to reintegrate the department into the academic structure of the university. It was to no avail, for with the withdrawal of the prestigious backing of the theological colleges, university officials could claim penury as a sufficient motive for closing the school. In 1931 Principal Currie appointed a special committee, which he stacked with powerful opponents of sociology and social work, to recommend cost-cutting measures to be applied to the Arts Faculty. As Dean Ira MacKay bluntly stated at the meeting of 27 March 1931, the faculty was no longer prepared to tolerate a department of sociology that in his estimation had usurped the subject-matter of other disciplines while failing to provide a solid undergraduate training. Further, he declared that "the School for Social Workers is not our job, there are no university requirements for admission. Unless the City or some of these social agencies pay for it, I do not believe we should spend money on it."[67] Faced with the loss of his program, Dawson was compelled to become a researcher under Marsh and was left to tend to his social workers in an institute funded by Montreal community social agencies that remained totally severed from the academic precincts of McGill until 1945.[68]

In contrast to McGill University, whose director of the Department of Social Science was a clergyman, the School of Social Service at the University of Toronto, established in 1914, four years prior to that of McGill, hired such British social scientists as Robert MacIver, J.A. Dale, and E.J. Urwick, and the latter presided over the school until the late 1930s. Paradoxically, however, the impress of social Christianity more powerfully shaped the Toronto school than it did McGill's, largely because its development was sustained by a university administration firmly attached to the belief that even within a modern university, ostensibly devoted to secular purposes, the true aim of higher learning was the expression of Christian belief through the cultivation of moral character and the idea of service. As President Robert Falconer, himself a Presbyterian minister, declared in 1907 in his inaugural address: "the highest type of citizenship cannot be permanently trained apart from a sense of obligation to and reverence for the moral order which is Divine. Religion is the crowning function of our manhood, for in religion we reach out to that which completes this fragment of the present."[69] Falconer, along with such other leading Canadian Protestant progressives as Hugh Dobson, was a member of the Religious Education Association of the United States and he was active in the Presbyterian Board of Social Service and Evangelism. As a result of his enduring links with prominent advocates of social Christianity, Falconer enthusiastically set out to create a School of Social Service that would scientifically address problems of poverty, philanthropy, and crime, as well as further the coordination of university, church, government, and civic social agencies, all within an atmosphere of Christian duty.[70] That the new school was intended to serve the needs of clergymen, missionaries, and deaconesses, along with public health nurses and female charity workers, was symbolized by the fact that in searching for a suitable director, Falconer consulted three American clergymen who had taught on the conjunction of Christian ethics and modern social science: Gaylord G. White of Union Theological Seminary, Graham Taylor of the Chicago School of Civics and Philanthropy, and C.R. Henderson of the Sociology Department and School of Divinity at the University of Chicago.[71] The positivistic views of Franklin Johnson, a student of Franklin Giddings of Columbia University, who held a provisional appointment from 1914 to 1918, were closely circumscribed by the presence in the school of a large number of professors who were either clergymen or sympathetic to social Christianity and moral philosophy. For example, the principles of social philosophy and psychology were taught by George Sidney Brett, who saw the study of psychology as a vehicle through which to analyse the Christian soul,[72] and by T.R. Robinson, a long-standing member of the Social Service Council and a Presbyterian clergymen. Practical casework was taught by Christian settlement workers, such as the Presbyterian representative, Sarah Libby Carson, and Methodist ministers, the Rev. Peter Bryce, the Rev. J.W. Macmillan, professor of Christian sociology at Victoria College, and the Rev. F.N.

Stapleford, head of the Toronto Neighbourhood Workers’ Association and formerly at the Divinity School of the University of Chicago.[73]

Franklin Johnson spent four undistinguished years at the head of the School of Social Service and was replaced in 1918 by Robert MacIver, associate professor of political economy, who had already established himself as a leading sociologist and philosopher. Born in Stornoway on the Isle of Lewis, Scotland, in 1882, MacIver attended the University of Edinburgh where, like Robert Falconer and many other Presbyterian progressives, he became a student of the idealist-realist philosopher Andrew Seth Pringle-Pattison, a late representative of the Scottish Common Sense tradition. Seth Pringle-Pattison’s teaching, with its emphasis on the uniqueness of the individual as opposed to the deterministic approach of Hegelian philosophy whose organic conception of social relations eviscerated the independence of both spiritual and personal responsibility in the development of human society, appealed to MacIver. While rejecting the authoritarianism, narrow denominationalism, and overweening Calvinism of Scottish Presbyterianism, MacIver wished to preserve an ideal of the small community wherein personal identity and spiritual growth found their fullest expression.[74] MacIver saw Hegel’s idea of the superpersonality as fundamentally anti-Christian. He reasoned that if God was the whole there would be no need to discover a higher absolute, “[f]or we are already in God and in every activity we are equally finding Him.”[75] While at Oriel College, Oxford, MacIver read the works of L.T. Hobhouse, J.A. Hobson, Vilfredo Pareto, Émile Durkheim, and Gustave LeBon, through which he developed his lifelong perspective that sociology was not a behaviouristic science but was integrally related to an religio-ethical study of human values.

Most important of all in framing his social philosophy was the German school of sociologists, in particular F. Tonnies and Max and Alfred Weber, who posited an important distinction between community and society; while receptive to naturalistic explanations of human evolution, they also preserved a realm of “spiritual need” and thus affirmed a creative role for the individual in shaping social customs and institutions.[76] Like the German sociologists, MacIver rejected the Spencerian view that ethical “instincts” were simply the epiphenomena of natural laws and the Hegelian notion that there existed a collective mind. MacIver was sceptical of the fashionable emphasis placed by sociologists upon the “operation of spontaneous social forces,”[77] for he adhered strongly to the view that human intelligence outweighed the environment in directing the evolutionary process.[78] Social interdependence, in his view, was not simply the outcome, as Spencer had argued, of deterministic natural laws; rather, the growth of social interdependence was equally an ethical phenomenon, and the progressive adaptation of human civilization towards a higher "good" was the expression of man's evolving relationship with the Divine presence. Thus, while Darwin's evolutionary forces explained the emergence of lower forms of life, MacIver, like many other idealists, still contended that as a higher animal human beings were capable of transforming civilization. "Life is the last creation," wrote MacIver, "which is the fullest expression of personality so that the first name man gives to God is that of the Creator."[79]

Because it remained grounded on the integrity of the individual personality, MacIver's synthesis of Scottish idealism and sociology did not function as a substitute for Christianity. Indeed, despite his chafing at the restrictive bonds of institutional Scottish Presbyterianism, MacIver's social philosophy adumbrated a critically important role for the church in modern society as the organization which most effectively defined and articulated the personal values he deemed vital to a healthy social development. Likewise, MacIver believed that religion was most intense and personal when it created not one but many churches, for all values were ultimately personal and individuals reached their fullest potential in serving the wider needs of the society.[80] Wishing to balance both pluralism and individual free will against community solidarity, MacIver eschewed the incipient totalitarianism suggested by such British Hegelians as Bernard Bosanquet, MacIver's nemesis, who conceived of the state as the pre-eminent institution of modern society.[81] MacIver envisioned a more complex interweaving of the individual within the web of society, and like E.A. Ross he even posited that throughout social evolution the individual must frequently come into conflict with the conformist imperative of group mores. According to MacIver, out of this need to reconcile the consequent social maladjustments caused by the endemic clash between individualism and social responsibility arose the profession of social work.

Because MacIver adhered to the belief that the ideal society was founded upon the principles of cultural and social pluralism, he likewise conceived of social welfare as the cooperative creation of the churches, voluntary societies, and labour unions working in partnership with the state.[82] Fearing the tyranny of the modern state, MacIver warned against the excessive professionalization of social work whereby its "historical dependence on religious organizations" would sever it from the larger sphere of values, which he and progressive clergymen saw as the ultimate goal of social reform. Although MacIver was an advocate of increasing the scientific stature of social work by grounding it more firmly to the "disciplined philosophy" offered by sociology, he argued that science was merely the intermediary providing the means of social diagnosis, a function clearly ancillary to the fundamental task of rebuilding the social order which rested in the final analysis on the enjoining of "the hearts of men" to a wider philosophy of social life.[83] Given the priority MacIver placed upon the emotional and artistic dimensions of social help, it is not surprising that he was also an enthusiastic defender of fashioning the new discipline into a vehicle that would promote career opportunities for women, in whose greater knowledge of family life, "social instinct," and traditional role as the guardians of social values, MacIver discerned the ideal qualities of the modern social worker.[84] Believing that social work was inspired by one's general social philosophy and the idea of service to humankind, MacIver designed a program which focused upon developing a "science of society" to introduce students to the "multitude of social relations." Hence, students at the Department of Social Service studied the distribution of wealth, the wage system, factory and housing conditions, social hygiene, women in industry, labour problems, rural conditions, and the history of such modern institutions as the church, social settlements, hospitals, and nascent welfare departments, as well as the structure of social legislation.[85]

It was upon this foundation that Professor J.A. Dale built when he arrived in 1919 from McGill University to relieve MacIver of his social work duties when he became chair of the burgeoning Department of Political Economy. Having already helped fashion the Department of Social Service at McGill, Dale was well-placed to leave his imprint upon the Toronto school until ill health forced his departure in 1927. Like MacIver, Dale had been trained at Oxford, and according to the famous English educator Michael Sadler, he had preached "Christian truth" from a Birmingham pulpit. Like many other idealistic young students at Oxford, Dale had fallen under the spell of John Ruskin's commitment to improved education for labouring men, and was thus instrumental in founding the Workers' Educational Association there.[86] In 1908 Dale was hired as the first professor of education at McGill University, where he was active in the University Settlement and inspired both the creation of the Department of Social Service and the Social Worker's Federation. During World War I he founded the School of Physical Training at McGill for instructing masseuses in the rehabilitation of injured soldiers.[87]

Dale's insistence that social work was no more than the practical application of the wider ideal of "service to the community" and merely the scientific development of one's innate sense of "goodness of heart, fullness of sympathy," brought him to the attention of Sir Robert Falconer.[88] Although more persuaded by the principles of British guild socialism and the necessity of the collective state than his predecessor, Robert MacIver, he neverthless interpreted socialism in largely ethical terms as the working out of Plato's ideal that it was the responsibility of each individual to serve the wider community.[89] As a socialist, Dale leaned towards an organic conception of social relations, but his Christian faith inclined him to a view of social work that was indistinguishable from MacIver's, in which a scientific synthesis of economics, psychology, and the study of the "social principles of evolution" served to uncover the ethical forces underlying the "rehabilitation of character," the true aim of all social reform.[90] Social service, declared Dale, "consists of the modern practice of the principles of the Good Samaritan, worked out in a scientific way, as the result of centuries of experience and study."[91] Because Dale believed that the social fabric was an interweaving of the scientific and the moral, and that the central dialectic of modern life was the pitting of the social good versus evil, even treatments advocated by modern practices of social hygiene that were ostensibly medical must be enveloped in a predominantly moral approach.[92]

The mainstream Protestant progressive leadership in Ontario had by 1920 forged a strong alliance between the churches, social reform organizations, and fledgling provincial welfare agencies, most notably those inaugurated under the premiership of the agrarian leader and member of the Social Service Council, E.C. Drury.[93] Through the creation of church-sponsored social service departments in such leading universities as McGill and the University of Toronto, the Methodist and Presbyterian churches continued to expand the field in which social Christianity found its expression. The appointment of such directors of social work as Dale and Dawson was pivotal in harnessing the professionalism of the modern social sciences to the task of forming a broad lay citizenship dedicated to Christianizing Canadian society. Dale's conviction that social work "is becoming conscious of a philosophy, a religion, which is permeating the mind of the community"[94] symbolized the general Protestant endeavour to bind together church, university, and civic reform. This conjunction of progressive interests, in which the Protestant churches formed the bridge between urban and rural reformers, was illustrated by Dale's appointment by Drury to head the Public Welfare Branch of the City of Toronto Health Department in 1923. There he was to work alongside the Rev. Peter Bryce of the provincial Mothers' Pension Board and the Rev. Stapleford, Secretary of the Neighbourhood Workers' Association.

Dale's nomination to the Public Welfare Branch roused a political furore and pitted conservative anti-Druryite aldermen against a progressive alliance of labour, church, and university public welfare advocates.[95] Fearing that the Health Department with Dale in it would become "an electioneering agency decided by Rev. Peter H. Bryce and other Druryite politicians in the pulpit," the Tory majority on the City

Council castigated Dale as "a parlour Bolsheviki" on the dubious evidence that he had invited American socialist Scott Nearing to speak in the Department of Social Service at the University of Toronto. In the face of this Red scare, Dale's appointment was voted down, but not without the deployment of the authority of both the Catholic and Protestant churches on his behalf. The Rev. Father Minehan of the Neighbourhood Workers' Association and the Rev. Dr Stewart of Parkdale Methodist Church spoke on Dale's behalf from their pulpits. More importantly, a special meeting of the Toronto Methodist Ministers' Association, led by Salem Bland of Broadway Tabernacle and R.J. Irwin of Bedford Park Methodist,[96] passed a strong resolution in support of Dale's appointment: they viewed it as a critical bridgehead into newly formed state social welfare departments for their progressive alliance, whose views on social reform were intimately bound up with the campaign of the Protestant churches to extend their institutional influence and educate public opinion on the value of scientific social work so that the tenets of social evangelism would permeate the wider community. University officials and Christian leaders concurred that if Dale was denied this important government post, "[t]he impression will be stamped on the public mind that the freedom of investigation of students of public welfare in the city of Toronto is subject to restrictions imposed by our civic rulers."[97] In this case, the claims of academic freedom were advanced to defuse the attempts by Tories to sunder the powerful alliance of academy, church, rural interests, and middle-class reform organizations,[98] from which the new Department of Social Work drew both its moral and its material sustenance. More tellingly, the resolute defence put up by church and university leaders underscored their commitment to the view that the social sciences in Canada should reject the American path towards so-called objectivity and remain firmly attached to the advocacy of social reform.

The battle line revealed by Dale's appointment persisted throughout the 1920s when the provincial Tories under G. Howard Ferguson, who returned the Conservatives to power in 1923, unleashed a barrage of assaults against the University of Toronto because of its strong Christian reformist sympathies.[99] It is significant that the focus of Ferguson's witch-hunts often fell upon those faculty members such as Gilbert Jackson, R.M. MacIver, and E.J. Urwick who were most closely identified with the Protestant Social Service Council of Canada. That universities and academics became the frequent targets of political opprobrium from the right indicates that politicians themselves viewed the churches, in partnership with the universities, as active players in the political arena, and that there continued to exist a powerful and well-organized movement for social and political reform in Ontario, despite the fact that the Conservatives remained in power until 1934. Although this alliance of urban and rural progressives, which gravitated to the progressive wing of the Protestant churches, was shut out of power at Queen's Park during the Ferguson regime, it functioned as a current nourishing the wider political process through local social reform movements. The progressive coalition occupied a crucial place as the ideological rival to what historians have suggested is a monolithic conservative society and political culture. Far from being a mere aberration in the political culture of Ontario, Christian-inspired urban and rural progressivism endured throughout the 1920s, and it dramatically resurfaced during the landslide victories of the former Druryite, Mitchell Hepburn, in the 1930s.[100]

At the University of Toronto, social reform remained the crucible of the social sciences and social work throughout the 1930s because of the appointment in 1927 as director of social work and head of the Department of Political Economy[101] of Edward Johns Urwick, who believed that "the true social ideal is always a vision of a City of God."[102] Urwick's social philosophy dovetailed with that of the social evangelism of the old Methodist and Presbyterian churches and the new United Church. Religion, according to Urwick, meant the persistent striving for a closer harmony with "God, Reality, or the Good," and he posited that all social aims and processes of the natural world were enveloped by a fundamental "kernel of spiritual power" because they ultimately depended upon the spiritual essence burning within every individual.[103] As he confided to his colleague and successor, Harold Innis, "No aim is true which is not spiritual – that is, which is not consciously directed to bringing nearer the attainment of the absolutely good end, the realization of the true individual as supreme over both society and self."[104] For Urwick, because the central problem of the modern age was "the riddle of social morality," its solution therefore depended almost exclusively upon the religious influence of the churches, whose evangelical tenets ensured a social order based on those Victorian verities of civility and self-control.[105] Urwick's sociology, which embedded the potentially secular canons of late-Victorian Platonic idealism and social ethics into Christian doctrine, not only earned him the respect of progressive church leaders but also secured him a permanent position on the Social Service Council of Canada. This gave him a leadership role on government welfare boards and a commanding voice as an adviser to the United Church's 1934 Commission for Christianizing the Social Order. The presence of such an internationally renowned figure as Urwick ensured that the bonds between Protestantism and university social science, far from dissolving during the 1920s as some have argued, were actually strengthened and remained solid until well into the 1930s.

The son of a Congregational minister, Urwick was born in 1867 in Cheshire, England, and in the late 1880s attended Oxford University where he experienced at first-hand the efflorescence of late-Victorian attempts to redefine and expand the contours of liberal individualism in terms of organic and idealist views that stressed society as a unit and not simply as a collectivity of individuals. Swept up in the Christian socialist revival of the period, Urwick closely followed the reformist economics of Alfred Marshall and J.A. Hobson, and like so many other social thinkers of his generation he earnestly sought to give concrete expression to his Christian ideal of social service by becoming a settlement worker at Toynbee Hall, founded in 1884 by Canon Samuel Barnett who believed that culture was the key to furthering understanding between classes.[106] Urwick was the sub-warden of Toynbee between 1897 and 1903, during which time it became the recruiting ground for social investigators, social workers, and civil servants, the most famous being William Beveridge, Urwick's successor, who later helped forge modern social welfare policies.[107] A vigorous opponent of indiscriminate charity, Urwick served as a Poor Law Guardian in Whitechapel (1896–1902) and on the Port of London Immigration Board (1897–1903) and was a very active member of the Charity Organisation Society, which brought him to the attention of one of its leading lights, Charles Stewart Loch. In 1904 Loch ensured that Urwick would be his successor to the Tooke Professorship of Economic Science and Statistics at King's College, University of London.[108]

In 1903 a joint committee of the Charity Organisation Society, the Women's University Settlement, and the National Council of Women Workers established the School of Sociology and Economics, the first training-school for social workers in Britain, whose two-year course was ostensibly intended to provide professional training for female social workers. Under Urwick's direction, the school escaped the narrow vocationalism demanded by women desiring work in the fledgling civic agencies of the modern welfare state by providing a theoretical emphasis in courses on social evolution, social economics, and social psychology.[109] In 1912 the school was absorbed into the London School of Economics, which, as early as 1903, had made overtures to the Charity Organisation Society to take over their management of the school. The offer had been rejected on the suspicion that there was insufficient ethical teaching in a program dominated by the bureaucratic rationalism of Sidney and Beatrice Webb, the dominant figures in social policy at the LSE. As Jose Harris has argued, events conspired to reduce the leverage that the Webbs could exercise in negotiations, for by 1908 not only was the LSE experiencing a financial crisis, but Beatrice Webb's Minority Poor Law Report had been subject to pointed criticism because its vision of the modern management of poverty depended for its realization upon a body of professional social workers which the LSE was unable to train. This compelled the Webbs to fasten once again their attention upon the School of Sociology and Economics, the creation of their rivals, Bernard and Helen Bosanquet. Negotiated under pressure by Urwick and L.T. Hobhouse, the terms of amalgamation in many respects favoured the Charity Organisation Society in as far as the integrity of the curriculum of the School of Sociology and Economics was preserved intact and its director, E.J. Urwick, was appointed to the staff of the LSE. That this turn of events was viewed as a disaster by the Charity Organisation Society was illustrated by Bernard Bosanquet's acid comment that the "confounded School of Economics has mopped up our little School of Sociology in London ... [W]e have made the best terms we could and are putting up the shutters with heavy hearts."[110] As a result, Urwick held the joint position as professor of social philosophy at the University of London and director of the Department of Social Science and Administration at LSE until 1927.[111] In 1916 this department secured important additional funding from the Indian textile millionaire Sir Ratan Tata, and with the participation of the Webbs, Hobhouse, and Urwick it emerged as the leading authority on voluntary and state welfare work and was the sponsor of numerous surveys of poverty and working conditions in England.[112]

Despite the tensions between the Bosanquets and the Webbs over the control of social work, they nevertheless participated in a common intellectual climate in which each side merely represented the outer edges of the complex and multifarious debate over the degrees of individualism and collectivism that would characterize the modern bureaucratic welfare state. Urwick's career and social philosophy epitomized the porous boundaries that existed among the constellation of ideas defining what has come to be called the new liberalism. Like his contemporaries Alfred Marshall and Arnold Toynbee,[113] Urwick was critical of the *laissez-faire* political economy that had sustained Gladstonian liberalism, and in order to stave off the dangerous tendencies towards state socialism, which he believed would erode the independence of the individual, he advanced a moral idea of socialism that saw collectivism in terms of mutual cooperation rather than the reorganization of economic life. Thus, although he shared with his mentor, Samuel Barnett, a commitment to "practicable socialism," which implied the intervention of the state in housing, education, and public health, Urwick remained a staunch indvidualist and baulked at the suggestion of state-funded old-age pensions and the idea of local governments using poor-rates rather than private charity to feed impoverished families.[114] Urwick was, in fact, an opponent of Lloyd George's 1911 reform of social welfare, for although he accepted the notion of "social interdependence" upon which these state initiatives were founded, he nevertheless wished to sustain the influence of such voluntary institutions as the church, social settlements, and clubs in welfare management.[115] On the other hand, Urwick was a great admirer of Hobson's organic understanding of the economy and his theory of underconsumptionism, and he was thus at the forefront of altering the perspective of the Charity Organisation Society, which by 1900 had shifted distinctly away from its former preoccupation with paternal control of indiscriminate charity and, through its sponsorship of a philosophical education for social workers, had become one of the most fruitful organizations contributing to the development of systematic social policy in Britain.[116] In fact, Urwick was one of the first new liberal thinkers to conceive of social work not simply as the uplifting of the poor but as a wider instrument of class integration in which the social worker must function as a more general "servant of society."[117]

Lecturing to female social workers at the School of Sociology and Economics, Urwick shared the aims of the Webbs and Bosanquets to train professionally future policymakers and welfare caseworkers by teaching the theoretical political economy of Adam Smith, Thomas Hobbs, Jeremy Bentham, T.H. Green, William Jevons, and Karl Marx, a curriculum that combined the traditionally rival philosophies of utilitarianism and idealism.[118] Similarly, at Toynbee Hall the program of speakers devised by Urwick reflected the broad spectrum of social critiques of traditional liberalism, and ranged from Tory unionist A.V. Dicey, imperial federationalist George Parkin, and Chamberlainite and Toynbee disciple W.J. Ashley, to the radical leader of the London dockers, Tom Mann.[119] Urwick's continued espousal of an individualist temper within a broader collectivist framework placed him in the mainstream of early twentieth-century British social thought and allowed him entrée into the most influential centres for the creation of social policy, notably the London Ethical Society, a club for social reformers and civil servants dedicated to transforming *laissez-faire* liberalism and attended by the foremost social investigators of the period, including Charles Booth, Beatrice Webb, C.S. Loch of the Charity Organisation Society, and such leading idealists as J.H. Muirhead and reform economists as J.A. Hobson and H.S. Foxwell, the founder of the club. In 1897 the London Ethical Society became the School of Ethics and Social Philosophy at the University of London, headed by none other than the ubiquitous E.J. Urwick.[120] Along with a colleague at LSE, L.T. Hobhouse, he was also a key founder of the Sociological Society which, as outlined in the presidential address by the political theorist and liberal elder statesman James Bryce, was committed to bridging idealism and empiricism by bringing the facts of social investigation to bear upon the traditional problems of the "moral and mental sciences." Clearly defending the ameliorative tradition in the British social sciences, the Sociological Society, largely at Urwick's behest, built upon Booth's survey tradition[121] by advocating the systematic collection of statistics regarding labour, cost of living, birth and marriage rates, employment of women and children, and industrial growth for the practical resolution of the "social question." This all-pervasive concern of British intellectual debate united all the social sciences in a common purpose.[122]

In his insistence that the central concern of sociology, or rather social philosophy, should be the adumbration of social values against which one could empirically discern the facts of social evolution, Urwick's thought closely resembled that of L.T. Hobhouse and Graham Wallas with both of whom he taught at the London School of Economics.[123] In common with Hobhouse, Urwick engaged in a life-long struggle with Spencerian philosophy. He accepted Spencer's organic conception of society as one progressively moving towards ever-increasing cooperation and individuation, as well as his reliance upon Lamarck's more benign notion of constant adaptation of humans towards the social state, what Urwick termed the unfolding of "moral adaptability,"[124] in opposition to Darwin's violent metaphor of struggle and the elimination of the unfit.[125] However, Urwick nevertheless rejected the conjunction between natural and moral law posited by Spencerians and the majority of idealist social thinkers. Rather, he leaned towards the view expressed by Thomas Huxley in his famous Romanes Lecture of 1893, *Evolution and Ethics*, that human good often ran counter to the dictates of the natural order.[126] Hence, while Urwick subscribed to Hobson's organic view of the economy, he also criticized him for failing to distinguish fully between the organic and the spiritual, the social and the personal.[127] Man's material condition could not be separated from his ethical and religious aspirations; nor could the achievement of the "social brotherhood" be deemed the product of blind economic forces, but rather it was the result of a personal search for a higher "good."[128]

Similarly, in a review of *Individualism and After* by Benjamin Kidd, Urwick castigated this extreme Spencerian for asserting that the social process completely controlled the individual mind. In Urwick's estimation, mind and spirit overcame the deterministic constraints of natural law as human evolution progressed. Thus, while accepting the program of modern sociology proferred by Auguste Comte, Urwick believed that society had now transcended the positive stage and had returned to an era in which metaphysical and theological forces were dominant and that these new social facts demanded a wider social philosophy rather than a narrowly objective sociology.[129] To the end of his career, he continued to warn social workers that social facts could not be treated like the data of the natural world. "The attempt to ape the physical sciences," Urwick bluntly stated, "is not good. You are not likely to bring history and politics into line with mathematical science."[130] Ultimately, Urwick saw religion, or the individual's transcendental "struggle towards an ideal," as the central dynamic of social change. Thus, he rejected the priority of science and the shibboleth of specialized social science as the interpreter of social reality and advocated instead the pursuit of a philosophy of social life and the continued interdependence of all the social sciences as the only means for understanding the complexity of human social experience. Objective social science was for Urwick a delusion because not only was all order and purpose supplied by God's grace but all social facts were created by an individual's spirituality.[131] Moreover, because society was a "spiritual organization," the regeneration of the world could not be realized through the manipulation of one's environment as most social reformers maintained. The antisocial behaviour that was inevitably caused by the clash between the interests of the individual and society was identified by Urwick as "original sin," and as a result its eradication depended upon the voluntary self-restraint that only evangelical piety and an ideal of service could provide. Thus, while sharing the new liberal faith that society was an interdependent unit, Urwick's organicism was but a metaphor for a higher cooperative individualism which he defined as the relationship between "you and I and God."[132]

Urwick's conservative, individualistic brand of new liberalism pervaded the Department of Social Science[133] at the University of Toronto throughout the 1930s. The central aim was identical with that of LSE which combined theoretical and practical skills under the rubric of developing a "social intelligence" through a broadly philosophical approach to social causation. Each graduate was to go forth armed with "social responsibility" cultivated through the study of social organization, the psychological basis of evolution, and problems of family and rural life.[134] Urwick's social philosophy functioned as a persistent barrier against the introduction of the American model of specialization and objectivity in the social sciences, and throughout his tenure as director of the Department of Social Science he adroitly blocked the appointment of American-trained Harry Cassidy on the grounds that he represented a narrowly materialistic approach to social casework.[135] As Urwick informed Falconer in 1929 in a lengthy memorandum, "The Education of Social Workers," the basis of training must be founded upon broadly theoretical perspectives offered by biology, psychology and most importantly social philosophy. "With regard to social philosophy," he protested to Falconer, "there is a tendency (especially on this continent), to reject this subject as being insufficiently 'objective,' and to substitute for it some branch of sociology. But it is hard to consider any social education satisfactory unless the student is made fully alive to the inter-relation of all forces, and to the supreme importance to those influences which we include under the terms moral and spiritual." Critical of the over-emphasis upon behaviouristic psychology in modern casework, Urwick inveighed against the danger "of social workers drifting into a materialistic attitude which is certainly not counteracted by exclusive attention to objective scientific method."[136] That the *rapprochement* between the Protestant churches and the social sciences at the University of Toronto was still powerful in the late 1920s is demonstrated by Urwick's ready agreement to the proposal by the theological colleges that all social work students undertake a class in Christian ethics, because like church leaders he believed in "the all importance of the spiritual foundations of social work."[137]

In 1927 United Church minister Ernest Thomas proclaimed that social evangelism provided the redemptive conscience for all social work and that the churches were "the agency of trained social workers."[138] Thomas's statement compels us to question the interpretation of some scholars of social work who have posited an endemic conflict between religiosity or moralism and the achievement of professional status. This dichotomy stresses that professionalization must necessarily involve the excising of religious ideas from the province of scientific social work.[139] This linear portrayal of the development of social work has recently been challenged in both the United States and Britain by historians who, in emphasizing the middle-class ideology and female character of social work, have argued that a great degree of negotiation between religion and science continued to animate social work even as it professionalized during the 1920s.[140] The conclusion of these scholars, that a moral apprehension of society existed hand in hand with the movement for professional autonomy, can be applied even more forcefully to the Canadian situation where social work was not only infused with religious idealism but was also directly shaped by the institutional authority of the Protestant churches, which employed the vast majority of social workers well into the 1930s.[141]

In Canada the original impetus for scientific professionalism in social work came from such progressive church leaders as Robert Falconer and the head of the Social Service Council of Canada, George C. Pidgeon, who had long frequented the annual meetings of the National Conference for Social Work in the United States.[142] Even J.S. Woodsworth, the supposed pioneer of secular social work in Canada, believed that the training of social workers should be modelled upon that of Sunday School teachers.[143] Far from being antagonistic to scientific social work, Protestant ministers like Principal James Smyth of Presbyterian College in Montreal were the most influential promoters of scientific inquiry and research among social workers, even though they they maintained that the goal of social casework lay in awakening the public consciousness of social sin.[144] The Rev. F.N. Stapleford, the head of the Neighbourhood Workers' Association of Toronto, a cooperative agency run by churches and settlements, estimated in 1920 that at least two-thirds of all social workers were hired by the churches and that fully ninety per cent of social work was linked directly or indirectly with the practical Christian endeavours of the churches. Anxious that the church should remain the "soul and inspirational force of social work," Stapleford vigorously urged the churches and philanthropic agencies to abandon vague moralism and concentrate on developing tools of social analysis and investigation in order better to affect the direction of public welfare legislation.[145]

All too aware of the increasing cleavage between social work and Protestantism in the United States,[146] Canadian ministers worked in concert with such university social scientists as C.A. Dawson, J.A. Dale, and E.J. Urwick to establish a Canadian Association of Social Workers to act as the fulcrum for "concerted social action"[147] among the churches, universities, and civic social agencies. One of the first to suggest the creation of a professional organization of social workers independent from the American parent body was J.H.T. Falk, who had long adhered to the view that social work must be dependent upon the churches because of its central role in "the transfusion of the spirit and power of God" to society.[148] With the goal of making social welfare more efficient and free from political interference – what Dawson defined as objectivity in social research[149] – the Canadian Association of Social Workers combined the energies of university social scientists and welfare workers and was sustained by a coterie of Methodists, Presbyterians, and Baptists from the Social Service Council of Canada, the Baptists most prominently represented by C.A. Dawson, M.C. McLean of the Social Service Council of Canada, and Winnipeg judge D.B. Harkness, later secretary of the Social Service Council of Ontario. With the ongoing presence of such strong Christian figures as Urwick, Dale, and the Rev. Peter Bryce, the association never gravitated away from its underlying tenets of practical Christianity to move towards a materialistic and objectivist scientific ethos like the one that progressively characterized American social work by the late 1920s. The new association was hailed by the Social Service Council as "a notable advance in the promotion of common ideals."[150]

Until the mid-1930s the "professional" and secular character of the Canadian Association of Social Workers remained in question, largely because of an unwillingness on the part of the new association to define separate spheres for clergymen and lay social workers. Between 1926 and 1938 the association lacked its own journal devoted to professional interests, and it was quite content to share *Social Welfare* with its parent, the Social Service Council of Canada.[151] More tellingly, R.W. Hopper, secretary of the association, advanced the idea of a "trained" social worker that was the very antithesis of the cult of professional specialization. Writing in 1926 Hopper stated that a social worker did not necessarily require university training in the discipline; rather, the term social worker could be applied "to all persons who have definite knowledge of social work but who may not have had any particular academic training other than that gained in the school of experience." This inclusive definition was explicitly designed to retain in the ranks of the Canadian Association of Social Workers the large number of Protestant clergymen and female volunteers who comprised the overwhelming majority of social welfare workers in the 1920s.[152] It is not surprising, then, that the fledgling association used the language of social evangelism, replete with terms such as "fellowship," "inspiration," and "devotion," to articulate a professional identity for social workers. As late as 1931 Jane Wisdom, a prominent Montreal social worker, could caution Charlotte Whitton against setting overly rigid standards for university-trained social work students as this would, she explained, discourage those who "follow the gleam."[153] The recurrence of this injunction among leading professional social workers and prominent social reformers of this period, which was but the contraction of the biblical phrase "follow the gleam, until we become like Christ, who gave Himself for us,"[154] serves as a forceful reminder that the Protestant churches and the tenets of Christian social endeavour continued to shape the identity of the new profession and demarcate the limits of its authority well after social workers had supposedly emancipated themselves from church control in 1926.

Thus, the observation by Peter Bryce of the Social Service Council of Ontario, that "to really appreciate and truly help in this work one must be a person of fine instincts and tender unselfish spirit," became the guiding principle of the social work profession.[155] Significantly, at the first meeting of the new professional association in 1928 in Montreal, the keynote address was delivered by Rabbi A.H. Silver of Buffalo, who spoke on the need for high idealism and religion in social work. This was followed by an exhortation by Catholic priest A.H. Desloges of Montreal, who called for the training of theological students in the fundamentals of social work as the prelude in launching a campaign to enlist the cooperation of 4,000 Quebec priests who were employed in the province's social and health agencies.[156] To assure the continued high profile of the churches in defining professional social work, the Social Service Council of Canada established an Employment Bureau which, in the words of Charlotte Whitton, would correlate the social agencies of the churches and social work.[157] With a similar aim in view, in the following year the Baptist executive secretary of the Social Service Council of Ontario, D.B. Harkness, established two scholarships for graduate students of social work at the University of Toronto, which he believed would ensure the church's sponsorship of mental hygiene.[158]

By the late 1920s fissures began to appear between progressive clergymen and professional social workers, the majority of whom were women. In 1925 the Social Service Council of Canada found it necessary to reiterate the Christian message of social work, and it rejected the suggestion from the Canadian Conference on Social Work for a joint annual meeting, fearing the eventual loss of church control.[159] The same concerns were echoed by the Rev. J.R. Mutchmor of Robertson Memorial Church in Winnipeg, who in 1929 became Manitoba's director of child welfare, in an article entitled "Is Social Work Inspiration Declining?"[160] The tensions emerging between clergymen and female social workers were exemplified by the open rift which developed in 1932 between Mutchmor and Charlotte Whitton over the issue of whether the identity of professional social work lay with voluntary social agencies or with centralized state direction.[161] However, not all women wished to sever the close connections between social Christianity and social work. Grace B. Cole and E. Phyllis Pettit, while pressing for more professional standards in church social work, nevertheless confirmed that no professional social worker believed in the separation of spiritual and material life.[162] Despite the prominence of Charlotte Whitton in federal government circles, the incipient challenge that professional female social workers presented to the churches was dealt a serious blow by the deepening Depression. As A. Ethel Parker attested, professional standards were undermined when trained female workers were forced to relinquish their jobs to unemployed men who were inexperienced in the methods of family casework.[163] Before 1929 the number of university-trained social workers in Canada had been miniscule,[164] and with the onset of the Depression the nascent professional ethos was quickly placed at a discount by church philanthropic agencies which immediately mobilized their traditionally well-organized and well-funded forces to usurp all manner of public relief. Hence, the older conjunction between evangelical faith and public assistance reasserted itself with renewed force when the Protestant churches strengthened their links with local social agencies by providing much-needed care of the unemployed, a task for which city governments were unprepared.[165]

The power that Protestant churches continued to exert in the wider society during the Depression was demonstrated by how they were instrumental in nominating ministers of public welfare in both Manitoba and Ontario. In 1930 the Conservative government in Ontario under Premier George Henry appointed the Rev. W.G. Martin, and as late as 1939 the city of Winnipeg chose the Rev. J.M. White to be director of public welfare.[166] With the withdrawal of the Canadian Association of Social Workers from the journal *Social Welfare* in 1926 – what Richard Allen has identified as the crucial benchmark of the secularization of social work[167] – articles by such progressive clergymen as J.R. Mutchmor, D.N. McLachlan, C.W Vernon, and Hugh Dobson once again dominated the pages of Canada's only forum for the discussion of social welfare policy. In this way, the Protestant churches were able to reassert their leadership over an increasingly conservative public opinion[168] which had come to view economic failure in terms of a deficiency of individual faith. Thus, Protestant church leaders were in a position to effectively recapture any terrain lost in the late 1920s to professional social workers by placing the problem of social and economic welfare within the religious and individualistic framework of evangelization.[169] As J.R. Mutchmor reminded the readers of *Social Welfare*, who included social reformers, church leaders, government officials, and professional social workers, all social welfare was merely the legacy of such evangelical reformers as "John Wesley, George Whitefield, Thomas Chalmers, Canon Barnett and Jane Addams."[170]

In 1935 the Canadian Association of Social Workers officially declared its independence from the church-based Social Service Council of Canada by inaugurating its own professional journal, *Canadian Welfare*.[171] Significantly, in that same year the first Church Conference of Social Work was held in Montreal, a direct assertion that the aims of ministers and social workers were no longer in harmony.[172] Some church leaders responded to this novel bifurcation in social work with equanimity. Most United Church progressives remained committed to fostering links between social Christianity, social reformers, and scientifically trained social workers and followed the example of J.R. Mutchmor, who continued to occupy a key role on the executive of the Canadian Association of Social Workers until 1938.[173] Witnessing the increasing gap between professional and voluntary social work, Anglican ministers Canon C.W. Vernon, who headed the Social Service Council of Canada until 1935, and Canon Shatford upheld the view that it was the purpose of the church to humanize social work and "to interpret and to inspire with that Spirit of the Master, without which its wells of elaborate machinery and developed method will in the long run prove futile." In their optimistic view, this breach could be healed by the traditional progressive method of widening the arena of spiritual work.[174] Even the Baptist Convention of the Maritimes, traditionally viewed as the preserve of conservative evangelism, in 1938 reaffirmed its dedication to the "redemptive character of social work" and the conjunction between Protestantism, the social sciences, and social reform by calling for the rejuvenation of church-funded social surveys and welfare policy research.[175] W.E. Taylor, professor of history and philosophy of religion at Wycliffe College, Toronto, offered a more individualist solution. He believed that the consensus between religion and social reform could best be preserved through the cultivation of a more private and personal role for the Protestant churches, whose task in the future must be directed towards sending individual church members into social movements where their indirect influence would effectively infuse the social order with Christian principles.[176]

The rapid uncoupling of professional social work from Christian social reform which occurred during the later stages of the Depression sent ripples of concern through the more traditional quarters of church progressivism. William Creighton Graham, principal of United College, Winnipeg, discerned in the increasing professionalization of social work the "alarming disintegration of Christian culture," and in 1939 he was the first Protestant church leader to posit a Manichean dichotomy between the "sacred" and the "secular" even though he still retained the conviction that the integration of individual and society, the traditional role of Protestantism, could be achieved by the renewal of social Christianity.[177] Similarly, although desiring to preserve the central thrust of modern evangelism – the curing of both individual and social ills – in 1935 Claris Silcox, the new head of the Social Service Council, who as a young minister had been one of the chief apostles of Christian social science, chided social Christianity for its implied pragmatism and scolded ministers who had come to interpret the problem of belief and faith during the exigencies of economic depression as simply "psychological adjustment." Despite his use of social Christianity as a technique for building consensus within an increasingly divided United Church, Silcox had himself made a decisive shift in the direction of religious and political conservatism. This was symbolized not only by his membership in George McCullagh's Leadership League, an association devoted to élite leadership by big business, but also by his espousal of an inner evangelical piety wherein the "unconscious mind" received the message of God, an experience divorced from one's day-to-day living. His position closely replicated that of the personalist religion of the Oxford Group.[178]

In 1939 Silcox attacked the alliance between Protestantism and social reform organizations represented by the Social Service Council, arguing that it had failed to preserve the distinctiveness of the Christian message because, in his view, its attempts to cooperate with bodies outside the Christian churches had left it in the invidious position of promoting religion through indirect means. Influenced by Catholic Social Action, Silcox maintained that the "*Church must remain the Church*" if it was to continue to be a force in Canadian society. In this regard, Silcox was the first to articulate a pre-progressive definition of the church in terms of its institutional presence rather than of its wider cultural mission, and in 1939 he changed the name of the Social Service Council to the Christian Social Council of Canada, in the belief that he alone was championing "*Christian* principles as the true solvent of social problems." Like Graham, Silcox enunciated a vision of two worlds, the sacred and the secular. "Let social workers everywhere recognize today," challenged Silcox, "the nature of the practical difference which separated the pure secularist from the devout and intelligent Christian."[179]

While at one level the attempts of Graham and Silcox to draw a sharp distinction between the churches and what they viewed as secular reform movements marked a sudden loss of faith in the possibilities of social Christianity, the relationship between the Protestant churches and the profession of social work in the late 1930s remained far more ambiguous. The conviction articulated by the mainline Protestant churches, in both their conservative and progressive wings, that social work should be animated less by technical expertise than by a wider social philosophy based on the tenets of Christian faith, was not an outmoded vision in the process of being rapidly eclipsed by secular approaches to social policy, as defenders of the secularization thesis have contended.[180] Indeed, the Christian view of social work endured throughout the 1930s and even into the 1940s because it was vociferously defended by a majority of university social scientists who, like clergymen, were suspicious of the materialistic tendencies within both sociology and social work. As early as 1927 R.M. MacIver had remarked upon the "spiritual loss" produced in the wake of an overly specialized and technical education of social workers.[181] Emboldened by the resurgent emphasis upon individual faith and character as a salve to the economic crisis of the Depression, J. Howard Falk in 1931 reminded professional social workers in Vancouver that their technical knowledge was inconsequential to the larger reform of the social order "if you have not within you love of your fellow-man and the feeling that life was given to humanity and not yourself; if that does not reflect itself in your personality you will never be effective."[182] Likewise, E.J. Urwick at the University of Toronto extolled the centrality of the individual as the antidote to the vices of modern sociology with its priority upon the social group.[183] Although Urwick was less socially conservative than Silcox, his proposal to transfigure the modern cult of specialization into an expertise of faith precisely mirrored Silcox's call for a return to the foundations of Christian belief. "There is the double authority behind most professional workers: the Bible and the Church," commented Urwick in an address to social workers in 1930.[184]

Urwick's proposal that to raise the level of community social work, social scientists should, like the Quakers, meditate upon the ideal of the "good life," was not intended as a negation of the achievements of social science or of professional social work. Rather, Urwick was seeking to find a *via media* between an entirely rationalist perspective, represented by University of Toronto sociologists C.W.M. Hart and S.D. Clark, and the equally distasteful prospect that social work would once again fall prey to the "half-baked sociologist-parsons" whom President Cody of the University of Toronto, himself an Anglican cleric, desired to appoint in the early 1940s.[185] What Urwick wished to recover, in the face of the increasing popularity of collectivist state welfare policies, was what he viewed as the Golden Age of social work in England, where state action was balanced by an equally vital voluntary ethos.[186]

It would be too simple to interpret the Protestant experience in Canada during the 1930s as the pitting of an increasingly irrelevant church against a rapidly coalescing new alliance of secular social reform interests. Rather, the fault line of debate was drawn between those clergymen and social scientists who proffered the ideal of a cooperative partnership between the church, university, and voluntary social organizations and a state-run social welfare bureaucracy, and those on both the political left and the right who advocated the attachment of professional social work to the emerging state-run social welfare bureaucracy. Thus, while Urwick was receptive to a limited growth in social planning at the provincial and federal levels, he still stubbornly defended his belief that the ideal communism was "an affair of the spirit." Therefore, he stated, the only true "social welfare consciousness" must be developed by a democratically inspired alliance between volunteers and experts. This would counteract what Urwick perceived as the oligarchy of state-appointed professionals surrounding the "political dogmatist" Charlotte Whitton, whom he, as well as a range of clergymen affiliated with the Social Service Council of Canada, came to despise because she had in fact breached the unspoken consensus between church, university, and social reformers that Christian reform must be apolitical and appeal to all social classes.[187] Worse, from the point of view of Urwick and his allies in the Protestant churches, Whitton was by the early 1930s attempting to circumvent the churches and the Social Service Council by seeking to professionalize social work through the centralized federal administration of relief. These conflicting views of the ideal relationship between social work and the state not only involved clergymen like J.R. Mutchmor, who peremptorily resigned from the Canadian Association of Social Workers in 1938 because of his opposition to the funnelling by Whitton of professional social workers, the vast majority of whom were women, away from the traditional arena of voluntary philanthropy into the burgeoning state welfare bureaucracy,[188] but also D.B. Harkness of the Ontario Social Service Council and his protégé, Harry Cassidy. Because of his later involvement with the League for Social Reconstruction, Cassidy has been portrayed as a "Canadian Fabian," a promoter of state collectivism and centralized social planning.[189] Certainly, Cassidy sponsored a greater centralization of public welfare administration in the name of financial efficiency and interprovincial uniformity, but his concept of an evolving "organic basis of life" involved a simultaneous growth in both public and private welfare, a view that ultimately simply restated the progressive reform notion of an equal partnership between church and state.

As late as 1940, in a lecture at the University of Chicago, Cassidy severely criticized social workers who abjured an important role for Christian social workers as intermediaries between private philanthropy and state public welfare. Like Anglican clergyman W.E. Taylor, Cassidy, in accepting a greater role for the modern state, likewise believed that Christianity's importance lay in educating the consciences of individual social workers who would, through their personal convictions, ensure the continued pre-eminence of Christian values within the formulation of public policy.[190] For his part, in 1939 Urwick spoke not only for clergymen but for many in university and government when he declared that social ills were caused by "sin or bad will or neglect of God's laws or wrong desire. And if there is any reality whatsoever in religion or goodness, then the solution of all social problems really begins and ends in the solution of the crust of evil which hardens the heart of each one of us and causes us to perpetuate injustice, poverty and misery in all their forms."[191] Despite the rising prestige of the democratic, socialist League for Social Reconstruction and of the liberal Keynesian economists who had, by 1938, moved to the inner councils of the federal Liberal party, the ideal of centralized state planning held by these groups did not simply eclipse the more individualist progressive notion of social welfare and social research as a partnership between church, university, and government. Indeed, because the presence of the Protestant churches in social welfare enjoyed the powerful backing of university social scientists, the belief that the solution of all social and economic problems lay in the moral as well as the scientific sphere remained in the mainstream of social policy debate until the onset of the World War II.

5 The Protestant Churches, the Social Survey, and "Rural Planning"[1]

In 1919, in an article he wrote for *Survey*, the leading American reform journal, J.A. Stevenson juxtaposed two divergent strands of Canadian social reform. One current was influenced by the urban interests of progressive businessmen and the other by those who "pin their faith in far-reaching rural reconstruction."[2] The latter was dedicated to the creation of cooperative agriculture and to the betterment of agricultural communities through the means of rural social centres. One of the most important currents in Canadian historical writing during the last three decades has been the focus upon the rise of urban-centred business, labour, and reform movements. It is argued that even before 1930[3] the Canadian city was the locus of the most dynamic and socially progressive forces that shaped contemporary industrial society. In particular, the strength of the work of H.V. Nelles and Christopher Armstrong has been to draw the attention of historians to the important problem of the relationship of business and government in forging modern public utilities. However, this scholarship has been detrimental to a broader understanding of progressivism in Canada because it has, through being inspired by American scholarship, wholly identified progressivism with the issue of state regulation of the activities of urban businessmen.[4] In contrast to the decisively urban emphasis of the American progressive paradigm,[5] Canadian social reform until the late 1930s was, it may be argued, forged in the crucible of rural underdevelopment and decay, and this crucible was first identified by the Protestant churches. Prior to World War I church leaders had begun to agonize over what they perceived as the decline of rural church-going because of the excesses of interdenominational rivalry. The difficulty was underscored by the oversupply of churches in the Canadian countryside. What began as an internal problem of church management soon blossomed, at the behest of social Christianity, into a full-fledged movement for community reconstruction and social planning of rural Canada.

In the 1920s the Protestant churches acted as the fulcrum by which the energies of agricultural scientists and social scientists and provincial and federal governments intersected around the issue of rural improvement. The churches thus played an important role in preparing the groundwork for the application of scientific expertise to the formulation of national social policies. This process culminated in the 1930s when rural relief and resettlement emerged as the centre-pieces of federal efforts to combat the economic Depression. This privileging of the agricultural sector cannot be simply attributed to what some have seen as the ineptness and backwardness of such politicians as R.B. Bennett and Mackenzie King, nor can the emphasis during the 1930s upon the countryside as the natural focus for economic recovery be dismissed as simple emotional nostalgia for a lost rural utopia.[6] Rather it was the product of a well-established scientific view of rural social planning, which during the 1920s formed the cutting edge of progressivism.

Some Protestant commentators, such as J.A. Cormie, seemed to articulate a rural nostalgia because of an overweening concern for preserving Anglo-Saxonism, which they believed rested in the sanctity of the family farm. Even though there were some exceptions, most Protestant clergymen were openly antagonistic to the back-to-the-land sentiment and consistently advocated scientific agriculture and a planned rural economy with the larger view of modernizing the countryside through what they viewed as more progressive ideas of social and economic cooperation. The majority of Protestant ministers were faithful champions of the extension of government intervention in rural social welfare, and nowhere was the conjunction of interests between church, university, and government better realized than in Manitoba where in 1926 Premier Bracken, himself a scientific agronomist who had conducted many rural surveys,[7] appointed R.W. Murchie, a Presbyterian clergyman and rural sociologist who taught at Manitoba Agricultural College, to conduct an extensive study of unused lands in that province, which in turn led to uncovering the more endemic problem of seasonal unemployment.[8] It was in fact the proliferation of social surveys undertaken for the most part by Protestant clergymen and the Social Service Council of Canada that established the idea of using the systematic collection of social data as the basis of government social planning. Not only was the church-based Social Service Council the prime mover behind the establishment of a federally funded Social and Economic Research Council – an initiative which saw fruition only in the 1950s – but its important Machine Age Series of pamphlets issued during the 1930s became the launching pad for the careers of such social planners as Eugene Forsey and Irene Biss. These two social scientists have come to be identified with their involvement in the League for Social Reconstruction, an organization touted as the originator of the idea of social planning in Canada. The tradition of social survey research was in fact established by the Canadian Protestant churches during the 1920s, and actually served to amplify the cultural prestige of Protestantism which was the central agent in transforming the modern state by bringing to bear the authority of scientific research and expertise upon problems of social and economic welfare.

The Protestant churches first enunciated their serious concern for the declension of religious life in rural communities in 1910 when Presbyterian minister R.G. MacBeth wrote "Problems of the Country and the City." In this article he stated that with a program of social reconstruction the "country church could be made ... the heart not only of the religious, but also of the best intellectual and social life of the neighbourhood."[9] The Methodist Church, which before the World War I was experiencing difficulties in replicating the Ontario model of congregational life on the Prairies,[10] in part because of intense competition from the Presbyterians, had developed a particular interest in eradicating denominationalism in favour of broad church alliances. By uniting country churches into large, multifaceted centres of community activity, they hoped to provide greater financial efficiency to poorly funded rural congregations. The Methodist Department of Evangelism and Social Service skilfully appropriated the public awareness of the problem of rural depopulation to invigorate its own aggressive campaign of converting the conservatively pietistic rural congregations to the tenets of social Christianity by arguing that the new evangelism offered the best antidote to rural decay. Through a torrent of books and pamphlets emanating from the desks of the regional field secretaries, traditional ministers in rural charges were constantly hectored on the ways in which conservative evangelism was contributing to both the impoverishment of rural social life and the weakness of the Methodist Church.[11]

Compelling illustrations of the postive wonders worked upon rural social life through the union of Protestant denominations under the banner of social Christianity were frequently published by provincial Social Service Councils to draw recalcitrant ministers to a recognition of the benefits of studying rural sociology, economics, agricultural science, and the principles of community social organization. One such report was written by Alex MacLaren, the secretary of the Community Centres Committee within the Social Service Council of Ontario.

MacLaren not only taught courses on rural sociology in the Social Service Department of the University of Toronto, but he also lectured theological students at Queen's University on rural sociology and economics. And, in order to further promote scientific rural reform among young clergymen, he conducted special summer schools for rural leadership at the Ontario Agricultural College in Guelph, where three-quarters of his students were country clergymen. As MacLaren himself testified, he had taught rural sociology in the university and at the YMCA and had joined the Social Service Council of Ontario so that "the whole power of the Council and particularly the churches might be put behind the rural movement, because I believe the church is the most vital factor of all." In his report in 1923 to the Ontario Social Service Council McLaren described the remarkable transformation wrought by Christian social work on small communities traditionally splintered by religious fissures:

> One day I received a letter from a small village in Ontario where the usual conditions of denominational divisions ... existed, and no worthwhile community life was being enjoyed. A week-end visit resulted in the appointment of a nominating committee which adopted our suggestions and started to promote community life, resulting in the bringing together in a short time of a Community Club with 400 paid up members. This Club has resulted in the wiping out of old feuds, and the increase of attendance at church.[12]

By 1914 the problem of the rural church had emerged as the focus for intense investigation in all the mainline Protestant denominations and it became a nation-wide movement of reform when the Social Service Council of Canada placed it at the forefront of its program of research. And, in that same year the first Conference on Charities and Corrections made the rural problem the centre-piece of its annual meeting. On this occasion, the Rev. John MacDougall, author of *Rural Life in Canada*, and President Creelman of the Ontario Agricultural College at Guelph spoke on the theme of rural depopulation.[13] The Social Service Council's goal of making the vicissitudes of rural life the core of their reform impetus was greatly enhanced with the inception of their publication, *Social Welfare*, in 1918. Throughout the 1920s the journal was used to parlay an issue that had begun as a local concern for dwindling church attendance into a reform movement of national significance. In order to provide further intellectual ballast for the Protestant church's preoccupation with the health of rural congregations, a preoccupation that in fact originated in a dispute between conservatives and progressives over the interpretation of evangelicalism, Methodist and Presbyterian leaders quickly identified their own campaigns for reforming Canadian rural church life with the American Country Life Movement. This organization had, by 1909, achieved national recognition when President Theodore Roosevelt in that year sponsored its cause by instituting a Country Life Commission to study farm economics, farm labour practices, and the disabilities facing farm women in isolated districts, as well as the weakness of the country church.[14] With the inclusion of the Rural Community Life Movement of Ontario in the Social Service Council of Ontario in 1918, issues concerning rural communities were given greater prominence and within the reform movement they achieved equal stature with such causes as mothers' pensions, minimum wage laws, and temperance.[15] The assiduous attention granted the problem of social regression in rural Canada by ministers of all the mainline Protestant denominations who formed the backbone of the Rural Community Life Movement, resulted in securing the commitment of university social scientists and experts in scientific agriculture to the movement, and this transformed a problem of the church into a broader church-led movement of social investigation and planning. As the Anglican clergyman and head of the Social Service Council, C.W. Vernon, commented in 1926, "[t]he great achievement of the Country Life Association is that year by year it gathers a representative group of thoughtful people really interested in rural life, but from the differing points of view of the farmer, the agricultural college professor, the editor of the farm journal, the rural social worker, the rural teacher and the rural minister."[16]

Very few Protestant ministers idealized the countryside as a lost Arcadia, nor did they conceive of it as the repository of moral and national virtue. For the most part, Protestant church leaders perceived rural life in remarkably negative terms and often with considerable disdain. The Rev. Dr John R. Watts, in an address entitled "The Rural Problem in Canada in Relation to Church Life," cited the isolation of farm life as the major obstacle to modern democracy, which he believed would flourish best within the context of social contact and cooperation. Judge Ethel McLachlan cited rural districts in Saskatchewan as the main breeding grounds for juvenile delinquency, while Judge Emily Murphy observed that the traditional two-room farmhouse, with its lack of privacy, was the major contributor to sexual immorality in Canada.[17]

Just as the Protestant churches had responded positively to issues such as mothers' allowances and child welfare, which were initiatives first mooted by various women's organizations across Canada, so by sponsoring the cause of rural reconstruction male church progressives were once again pursuing a course that greatly concerned the social and cultural well-being of rural women. In 1916, while head of the Bureau of Social Research for the Prairie region, J.S. Woodsworth paid tribute to the importance of rural women's groups in first arousing public discussion of the social isolation and cultural deficiencies of rural communities, especially as these pertained to women. Thus, Woodsworth credited farm women for broaching the idea of engendering community spirit in Western Canada through the instrument of the social centre. Although he was later to conceive of the community centre largely in terms of its efficacy in assimilating immigrants, he nevertheless viewed community organization and public spiritedness as merely extensions of the selfless duties of women in the home.[18] As early as 1912 the Commission of Conservation, an initiative of the Laurier Liberals and chaired by Sir Clifford Sifton, took up the cause of women's work on the farm.[19]

As the former minister of the interior, Sifton had a long association with the politics of Western expansion and he believed that the creation of a mature agricultural economy in Western Canada was the linchpin to the fulfilment of the National Policy. It is not surprising, therefore, that the commission's publication, *Conservation*, frequently reported on suggestions for modernizing the farm economy, in particular in introducing labour-saving devices that would alleviate the drudgery of women's chores on the farm. Thus, one of the first articles was entitled "Conserving Human Energy – Women's Work on the Farm – It Can, and Should be Made Easier."[20] After conducting its own survey of rural conditions, the commission concluded in 1916 that, along with improvements in such basic amenities as plumbing, electrification, and better telephone and mail service, the greatest incentive to keeping women on the farm would be the introduction of the automobile.[21] This position was heartily endorsed by the Protestant clergy who saw this modern innovation as the chief means of eradicating the isolation of farm families from their local church.

After the demise of the Commission of Conservation in 1921, marking the end of direct federal government interest in a broader program of national social and economic reconstruction in the wake of World War I, the Protestant churches and the women's groups that were affiliated with the Social Service Council of Canada took up the cudgels on behalf of farm women. J.G. Shearer, the guiding spirit behind the council, encouraged Western farm women like Violet McNaughton to enlighten the nation on the deplorable conditions faced by women on the farm by writing articles in *Social Welfare*. In 1922 Leona R. Barritt called for the protection of women in agriculture and advocated a comprehensive scheme for reform that included better medical and nursing facilities, the introduction of labour-saving machinery in the home, and, most importantly, the creation of a network of women's institutes and clubs and the sponsorship of cheap and accessible entertainment such as concerts and lectures.[22] At the 1923 meeting of the Social Service Council of Ontario, the theme of "The Church and Country Life" provided the forum for uniting the energies of such progressive clergymen as G.C. Pidgeon, social scientist J.A. Dale of the University of Toronto, President J.B. Reynolds of the Ontario Agricultural College, and representatives of women's institutes in pressing for improvements in rural recreation facilities and greater attention to religious education.[23]

The centrality of women's welfare in revivifying both the rural family and the wider community was a theme which the Presbyterian minister J.A. Cormie, later superintendent of missions for the Manitoba Conference of the United Church, returned to again and again in the extensive range of pamphlets and articles he wrote on the demise of the family farm. Indeed, all his solutions for improving rural life revolved around satisfying the needs of rural women. He recommended the modernization of the farmhouse, the beautification of the immediate landscape, the introduction of cheap electricity, the creation of church-sponsored social centres for leisure and culture, and, most importantly, the improvement of sanitary conditions in the hope that the incidence of infant mortality could be reduced.[24]

In an address to the Social Service Council of Nova Scotia in 1924, the Rev. Father Boyle, a Roman Catholic, declared that the "farmer's isolation, conservatism, indifference, individualism, antagonism and discontent all hamper his chances of keeping in touch with modern problems and movements. And yet Social Service will be lost on the farmer ... unless he participates in its contributions."[25] Here was the nub of the question for progressive church leaders. From their perspective, all the follies that befell rural districts – delinquency, poor sanitation, the lack of public health, poverty, crime, and social isolation – could be directly traced to their conservative evangelicalism. The result was inner piety and it sustained a notion of individualism that, in the view of progressive clergymen, remained hostile to modern ideals of social interdependence and cooperation. Within the broader evolutionary context which informed much of the social thought of these Protestants, traditional piety was deemed to be a feature of a less advanced social stage, and its persistence could quite possibly lead to the regression of the entire society into atheism, individualism, and economic atrophy. As the Alberta Progressive leader, Henry Wise Wood, put it, "[w]e cannot hope to permanently fix a mediaeval peasantry standard of rural life and a modern urban standard."[26] The Rev. Watts formulated the rural problem as that of "mounting from the lower level of frontier organization up to the level of modern life and institutions," and consequently his solution to rural backwardness was to "rurbanize" the rural mind. It was a process that would metamorphose the individualistic temper of the farmer into a more complete and modern ideal of socialization.[27] Salem Bland and J.S. Woodsworth likewise blithely advocated the introduction of urban modes of thinking to the culturally impoverished farming districts of Western Canada. Woodsworth believed that the social problems of the city and the country were two sides of the same coin. The problem had to be solved in tandem because of their interdependent relationship within the whole social organism. Bland concluded that if cities were to be ruralized through the creation of parks and suburbs, so the countryside should be raised up to urban standards through improved transportation, telephones, motor cars, social centres, and the eradication of tenant farmers in favour of independent producers.[28]

In the estimation of Watts, rural dwellers functioned within a lower social and economic stage of development than their urban counterparts, and had not entirely freed themselves from either the "process of inevitable law" or a religious fatalism whose omniscient idea of God precluded the exercising of human agency in altering the environment.[29] Social evangelism, therefore, was the all-essential key to rural social development. Only with a consciousness of "social sin" might the farmer appreciate the crucial spirit of cooperation that Watt believed must undergird successful farming under modern market conditions.[30] As the Social Service Council of Canada observed in its proposed outline for the conduct of community surveys, the farmer's independence and individualism had been essential in creating economically viable agricultural enterprises. But "at the same time" they had "retarded any parallel development of the farmer's interests in national life."[31] Similarly, another urban clergyman, the Reverend Lorne Pierce, book steward of the Methodist Church and chairman of the Committee on Rural Life of the Department of Evangelism and Social Service, castigated the "emptiness" of life in even the most prosperous rural communities, where "the slow, painful process of evolution is discredited." Rather than retreating from modern ideologies and technology, ministers like Pierce who deplored the backwardness of rural existence promoted the imposition of modern systems of thought upon the countryside. They especially wanted to apply the modern interpretations of the Kingdom of God in the belief that social Christianity was indeed the catalyst for social progress. Even though on one level progressive clergymen were well apprised of the obdurate resistance of rural conservatives to their brand of evangelism, many Protestant clergymen shared Pierce's patronizing view that through a persistent course of re-education and persuasion, rural piety could be recast in the image of modern progressivism.[32] "No community," Pierce reminded the Social Service Council, "but can sweep out every evil inheritance of the past in a few years by patient education and a sympathetic understanding of the spirits of men ... Here, then is the opportunity for a new Canadian Expeditionary Force that will show men what they are and, as Sons of God, what they might be, and then assist them to freely employ the services of the expert and co-operate with him in being re-shaped, equipped for self-expression." "The old evangelism," continued Pierce, "was hopelessly inadequate. It did not touch enough sides of a man's life." He went on: "The new evangelism seeks to develop the mind and to make it trained and alert, a quiver full of golden arrows for a body developed and strong as a perfectly-balanced bow to shoot, a spirit reverent and willing to make God's business in this world its chief concern ... and so we will not depend upon revivals and rescue parties, but we will put out the fire. We will not permit and then quarantine, legalize and then restrict. But we will employ all our powers in a thorough-going policy of prevention and prophylaxis and social sanitation."[33]

For progressives like Pierce, the primary agent for bringing about change in the countryside was to be the clergyman trained in rural sociology and modern agronomy. Much of the impetus behind the new interpretation of the minister's role put forth by the progressive leadership in the Methodist and Presbyterian churches flowed directly out of their concerns over the need for rural community leaders with scientific expertise. The new emphasis within the churches upon the preaching of "real life values" and upon a form of religious education that brought both the clergyman and the people in his congregation "to grips with the vital questions of the day," in turn called for a new kind of preaching that was to be both prophetic and practical.[34] In part, the insistence upon specialized training in sociology, social work, and agricultural economics for the minister was a strategy to make rural pastorates more attractive. As Pierce observed, "there is a general feeling that the rural work is not a man's job."[35] Although progressive clergymen often paid lip-service to the shibboleth of rural democracy and local control of community development, whereby the farmers themselves would "diagnose their own ailments, balance their own social accounts, mobilize their own resources," in reality, as Pierce stated, the ideal end was that they would eventually call in the expert, namely the local clergyman. One of these was the Rev. A.H. Robertson of Compton, Quebec, who after studying the principles of scientific farming believed he possessed the requisite knowledge to assume the mantle of community leadership. In 1912 Robertson organized a farmers' club and a women's institute, and he used his pulpit as the primary stimulus to awaken public opinion to the need for rural improvement.[36] Adhering to the view that farmers were far too individualistic in temper to organize themselves properly in terms of their group interests as modern society dictated, one writer for *Conservation* deprecatingly noted that "[f]armers, as a rule, do not lead farmers, and in that is the minister's opportunity."[37] In fact, most progressive clergymen considered the uniformity of country life, where the lack of social and economic barriers produced an environment in which "everything comes into contact with everything else," to be the ideal terrain in which the "trained social diagnostician,"[38] namely the local clergyman, could easily usurp the leadership of the community and thereby impose modern social values.

Despite the deep roots of conservative evangelism in the popular spirituality of rural Canada and the suspicion of "city interference"[39] often aroused by intrusive social investigations sponsored by the churches and the Social Service Councils, most progressive clergymen shared the view expressed by J.A. Cormie of Winnipeg that because the older, individualistic piety was more primitive and a weaker form of religiosity by its failure to address the practical needs of everyday living, "the country minister has a tremendous force, almost unknown to his brother in a down-town city church."[40] Even J.S. Woodsworth's identification with the cause of agrarian democracy could not adulterate his primary allegiance to the Methodist Church's goal of elevating the authority of Protestantism in rural Canada. Woodsworth contended that the modern rural minister, as the primary conductor of social surveys whereby classification led inexorably to a higher socialization, was the only "man in the community whose tastes are sociological" and who had the requisite expertise to dispense scientific knowledge of agriculture and the ideals of social and economic cooperation.[41] Here was Methodist postmillennialism at work, energized by the new gospel.

In 1918 the Methodist Department of Evangelism and Social Service appointed five people to a commission to study rural problems. It in turn recommended that chairs of sociology be established at all theological colleges, that the church encourage the creation of social centres in every rural parish, and that every local church become a centre for the discussion of public questions.[42] It was hoped that by serving the farmers' economic welfare and the social needs of farm women, rural society would eventually be brought within the pale of social Christianity and progressive reform.[43] In an article entitled "Training Rural Leaders," one writer concluded that "the churches are coming to realize the importance of providing special training for their rural ministers. It is being recognized that the most effective and lasting method of getting in touch with men and of serving them ... is to be able to help them with their everyday problems. To do this the rural minister, in addition to his regular training, should make a study of the conditions under which his parishioners live ... Then he can take an understanding lead in rural social betterment."[44]

Although the marshalling by the Protestant churches of their forces behind the issue of rural leadership may have at first stemmed from their aim of increasing rural church attendance, their growing absorption after World War I in a broader program of rural reconstruction hinged on the conviction that all true reform must be Christian. Beneath the rhetoric of revivifying the country church was to be found a more aggressive campaign to capture the leadership of the nascent Western agrarian political and economic movements which, after 1916, were rapidly garnering the widespread allegiance of Western farm interests.[45] "It seems to me, too," wrote A.D. Miller, professor of Old Testament at Alberta College and one of the leading advocates of reforming the theological curriculum in the direction of agricultural and sociological disciplines, "though this may be merely a prejudice, that the farmer's movement, fine as it is in some respects, is somewhat in need of guidance into a wider, fairer and more wholesome vision of our social structure as a whole."[46] By adeptly associating the cause of rural leadership with the tenets of social evangelism, the Protestant churches succeeded in drawing together, under their leadership, the United Farmers organizations from all the Western provinces, women's groups, and university professors. This convergence of interests was unveiled at the Rural Leadership Conference held at the University of Alberta in 1916 – symbolically, the same year in which the Canadian Council of Agriculture promulgated the New National Policy of the Farmers' Platform. At the conference Henry Wise Wood, Mrs Irene Parlby, and Methodist minister J.S. Woodsworth addressed an audience consisting primarily of rural clergyman on the urgent need to educate farmers on the application of the principles of cooperation to economic and social life. As the *Grain Growers' Guide* forcefully concluded, this 1916 gathering "was the most profitable social service conference that has yet been held in Western Canada."[47]

Because the resettlement of soldiers on unused agricultural land was seen as an extension of wartime planning and vital to postwar economic expansion, until 1919 federal policymakers conceived of the process of reforming the rural economy as falling within the ambit of direct state intervention.[48] Although the link between the problem of rural reconstruction, soldier settlements, and immigration was first mooted by the Social Service Council of Canada in 1917,[49] it was the federal government, through the Commission of Conservation, which undertook the first major study of rural conditions in 1917, Thomas Adams's *Rural Planning and Development: A Study of Rural Conditions and Problems in Canada*.

For the most part, the study by Adams, a British town planner, was a forceful critique of the unregulated land and immigration policies pursued by the federal government and the railways after the 1890s. Even though, as Adams attested, the pioneer stage of settlement was not completely over in Canada in the second decade of the twentieth century, he urged that the "crude methods of the pioneer stage" must be abandoned. "We must recognize that, in the future, science and clean government must march side by side with enterprise and energy in building up national and individual prosperity." In short, the management of the National Policy must in future fall under the imprimatur of progressive reform and be directed by agricultural experts, town planners, geologists, scientific foresters, and social workers. According to Adams the bane of rural society was speculation and absentee ownership, which only encouraged the natural inclination of the immigrant to be "migrating and unsettled in disposition," a restless but unproductive citizen alienated from those institutions such as the church that promoted cooperation and education – read assimilation. Although Adams recommended the intervention of the state in the reorganization of the relationship between country and city, he believed, as did most progressive clergymen and reformers, in a decentralized democracy nourished by strong localist sentiment. In this system, the extension of central government planning would be balanced by a vital voluntaristic impulse which would preserve self-reliance and initiative. Adams's notion of government intervention was necessarily limited in scope, for in his view the true spirit of cooperation resided in the individual and could not be imposed from without. Rather, it had to be inculcated through education and religious inspiration. "In any scheme of settlement," wrote Adams,

> there must be full opportunity for the exercise of individual initiative and enterprise and as little reliance as possible on the paternalism of governments. But, without undue interference with individual freedom governments of civilized communities must provide the impulse, direction and organization necessary to promote the successful enterprise of the individual citizens ... The land can be planned and settled in a business-like way, so as to facilitate co-operation and make social intercourse easy, without any greater restraint on the individual, or anything more artificial in the way of organization than we have at the present ... It may be harmful thus to create village communities by an artificial process and with financial aids from governments; it is not a harmful thing to so plan and settle the land that the village community will grow up in a natural way.[50]

Adams's prescriptions for rural planning had a great impact upon church progressives, especially Hugh Dobson, a vigorous exponent of social planning who made the treatise mandatory reading for all Methodist ministers, and J.W. Macmillan, the first professor of Christian sociology at Victoria College. As the necessary first step in alleviating the problem of rural depopulation, Macmillan proposed comprehensive "rural planning" through the creation of an expert government commission to undertake extensive surveys of all dimensions of country life.[51] Although in 1918 the federal government publication *Conservation* endorsed the implementation of federal and provincial government machinery for the planned settlement and development of agricultural land and the establishment of a comprehensive survey of the "social, physical and industrial conditions of all rural territory,"[52] after 1919 direct federal concern for rural planning and state reconstruction began to wane.

From its inception, the Commission of Conservation issued articles designed to arouse the interest of the churches in the reform of rural life,[53] and with the prominence accorded rural issues in the reform platforms of the churches and the Social Service Council by 1921, federal policymakers, in keeping with the philosophy outlined by Adams, were quite content to shift the responsibility for scientific investigation and planning of rural Canada onto the Protestant churches. Despite the propensity of historians to view the period of Union Government between 1917 and 1921 as a failed experiment in modern social welfare legislation, the experience of the Commission of Conservation suggests the necessity of a different approach. The Union Government did indeed intervene by nationalizing bankrupt railways, providing assistance to the re-establishment of veterans, and setting up a controlled system of grain marketing and a structure of employment exchanges, but these initiatives were clearly embarked upon as a response to wartime emergency and immediate peacetime readjustment, and they were never intended as representing a permanent widening of the scope of the federal government. Leading Conservatives, like Sir Robert Borden, and his Liberal Unionist colleague Newton Wesley Rowell clearly viewed voluntary institutions, and particularly the church, as better suited than the state in directing the complex psychological and educational task of permanent and enduring social reconstruction in both rural districts and urban Canada.[54] Doug Owram has read the retreat of the federal government from postwar reconstruction as signalling the collapse of the entire progressive movement[55]; however, the fate of the Commission of Conservation illustrates that the direction of social reform had merely shifted from the context of the state back to the voluntarist agency of the church. Indeed, Protestant social Christianity inspired a massive project led by local clergymen in surveying rural society, which ensured that social investigation and the idea of planning continued to flourish throughout the 1920s.

In the work of American philanthropic foundations and university social science departments, the community survey had become the *sine qua non* of up-to-date scientific social investigation. In the 1890s Jane Addams and her reform associates at Hull-House had instituted the survey as the central diagnostic tool of social problems, and by 1912 the survey idea had spread to the influential Russell Sage Foundation, which created a separate Department of Surveys and Exhibits, and to academe, where it became entrenched in the sociology departments at Columbia University and the University of Chicago. Not only did the community study form the basis of the 1894 sociology textbook by Albion Small and George Vincent, but at Columbia Franklin Giddings's program of graduate studies underscored the growing sophistication and specialization of survey research. One of Giddings's students, Presbyterian minister Warren Wilson, conducted numerous surveys of country church life in America and undertook the 1913 Huron County Survey for the Methodist and Presbyterian churches in Canada. The Institute for Social and Religious Research, for which the Canadian Congregational minister Claris Silcox worked during the 1920s, while best-known for sponsoring the Lynds's study *Middletown*, was in fact a lineal descendant of the social survey movement.[56] The Social Service Council of Canada's Social Service Bureau and Exhibits, which trained ministers in the investigation of general social problems such as child welfare, housing, intemperance, poverty, immigration, public health, and wife desertion, was modelled directly upon that of the Russell Sage Foundation. So tied were the Methodist and Presbyterian departments of evangelism and social service to American proficiency in social survey work that they had to call in such expert practitioners as Charles Stelzle to assist in the interpretation of data and for suggestions regarding practical applications.[57] The 1907 Pittsburgh Survey, which had been initiated by *Survey*, the leading American reform journal, established the methods pursued in Canadian religious surveys, and the community survey work of prominent rural sociologist C.J. Galpin set the contours of rural investigation during the 1920s.[58]

Despite the tremendous methodological influence of the American social survey upon Protestant progressives in Canada, the Canadian survey tradition diverged from its American analogue. Where in the United States the social gospel was wholly dependent upon academically trained sociologists for the gathering of statistical information for the Kingdom of God,[59] in Canada, where social science departments were underdeveloped and failed to become independent centres of social investigation until the 1930s,[60] the Protestant churches established the parameters of the social survey and clergymen remained its leading practitioners, even when these studies were sponsored by governments and universities. Upon assuming his position as field secretary for Western Canada in 1913, Hugh Dobson was charged with encouraging the scientific study of social and economic problems by Methodist clergymen. By making the social survey an endemic part of the local clergyman's duties, the Protestant churches became the dominant institution in the sphere of social investigation. In terms of both sophistication and number, the Protestant churches far outdistanced the universities, which only in the 1930s had sufficient funding to initiate ongoing programs of research. Dobson believed that the training ministers received in the practice and theory of social investigation was equal to postgraduate study at either Chicago, Columbia, or Cornell. Although Dobson's comparisons with American universities may have been inflated, his summation regarding the centrality of the Protestant churches in the field of social research was prescient: "If we add to the taking of a survey a carefully selected course of reading and a series of conferences on social problems, we have a course equivalent to what most of our best universities can afford, and ahead of any university in Canada at present in the department of Sociology."[61]

In order to control better the aims and methods of the social survey, the Protestant churches in 1920 issued a pamphlet by Charlotte Whitton, *The Community Survey: A Basis for Social Action*. In it, the themes and questions to be posed by the ideal social investigation, which was premised upon a coordination of local initiative and outside expertise, were outlined in great detail. As the author explained, "evolution in social work can come only when the knowledge of that which constitutes the good for the community, province, and nation can be popularized. That is the purpose of all social work, and the explanation of the methods of social work – to get the specialized knowledge of the few into the minds of the many. Then, and only then will action come in a democracy." However, the advocates of social Christianity were very precise and indeed almost dictatorial concerning the shape a progressive democracy should take. The list of experts deemed fit to conduct a social survey included first and foremost the local clergyman, teachers, businessmen, representatives of women's fraternal organizations and organized labour, local social workers, and at least one physician, one lawyer, and one member of the local Department of Health. Protestant progressives were very insistent that the outside social investigators conform to their own program of Christian reconstruction. They must be connected with country-wide social movements, and more specifically they must have been trained by such overtly Christian institutions as the YMCA, the provincial and federal social service councils, or the social service departments of the various Protestant denominations.[62] This document, which could be purchased from the social service departments of the Methodist and Presbyterian churches, the Social Service Department of the University of Toronto, and the Book Department of the T. Eaton Company, became the model for all community surveys, including those later instituted by Western farm women, public health groups, the National Council of Women, government agencies, and university-based surveys, including those undertaken by the students of the Baptist ministers C.A. Dawson at McGill and A.L. McCrimmon at McMaster University.[63] In fact, the church-authored questionnaires delineated the very boundaries of progressive reform, which included the conditions of industrial life, housing and town planning, the place of the immigrant in the community, public health, child welfare, juvenile delinquency, public morals, recreation, the administration of public relief and private charity, and the relationship of the church to the community.

The first systematic surveys by the Presbyterian and Methodist churches had been undertaken early in 1909 to measure the religious temper of local congregations and the readiness of ministers and their congregations to accept the new ideal of "Christian citizenship."[64] The clerical promoters of social investigation explicitly equated the survey with the older evangelical insistence that the human conscience must pass through an intense awareness of sin so that the soul might achieve redemption. The community, declared the authors of a social survey of Vancouver, "like the individual, may be the builder of her own destiny. She has only to set up an ideal for herself, pass through a period of introspection and self-analysis to discover exactly her present state and the steps that must be taken that she may become the ideal" human organization.[65] More tellingly, these religious surveys were intended to produce "heart-searching" in ministers whose preaching had grown stale and to awaken the conservative minister to the "social side of his field."[66] What progressives hoped was that through the unbiased collection of social facts, what Hugh Dobson termed "scientific pastoral theology," probationers would be able to relate their evangelical experience of incarnation, atonement, regeneration, holiness, Christian perfection, judgment, sin, and repentance to the present-day tasks of the church.[67] It was Dobson's conviction that the most important part of each local minister's task was to be engaged in an ongoing collection of social data as the means of thoroughly anchoring the church in the everyday life of the community.

Those social surveys that have been cited as vehicles of secularization were in fact intended as studious registers of the continued high level of church attendance and thus of the vitality of the church in modern society. The 1915 Pictou survey, for example, discovered that attendance at the rural churches had increased by sixty-one per cent, and could favourably report that in the countryside seventy-six per cent of the population went to morning services, with forty-nine per cent of those attending being male, and that evening service were even more successful by attracting fifty-eight per cent of men and boys. Still more revealing of the continued importance of the church in Canadian society, the Nova Scotia surveyors found that in the supposedly more secular towns, fully eighty-four per cent attended evening services; moreover, even that outmoded form of religious expression, the prayer meeting, drew twenty per cent of all church members.[68] The survey of the City of London, Ontario, happily recorded a similarly high level of active religious participation, and proudly boasted that the churches of this thriving urban centre were well attended by labour leaders and socialists who did not interfere in church work because they, too, were firm evangelical believers.[69] J.S. Woodsworth, the principal author of the 1913 survey of Regina, optimistically reported that it was "a progressive city in a progressive province, with public-spirited citizens, municipally-owned public utilities, well-kept streets and buildings." While the existence of a large immigrant district, "German Town," posed a potential threat to the cause of social harmony, Woodsworth reported that the Church Brotherhoods had had a positive effect in breaking down barriers between nationalities. As in the rural districts of the Maritimes, church attendance in Regina was high, averaging about seventy-three per cent.[70]

The overriding conclusion of these surveys was not that churchgoing was in decline, but that traditional piety, by isolating the church from the community, had created potentially dangerous religious and ethnic cleavages, which might in the long run weaken the authority of the Protestant churches.[71] This problem was explicitly posed by Woodsworth in his Regina survey. Although his data revealed that the churches had a powerful influence and were well attended, they tended to place their own institutional needs over those of the community to the detriment of the development of the new model of Christian citizenship so enthusiastically promoted by Protestant progressives. "It is a question," concluded Woodsworth, "whether self-centred organizations can develop unselfish men and women."[72] In Woodsworth's estimation, the crying need was for an organized system of popular recreation to bridge what he characterized as the growing class differences between professionals, businessmen, English-speaking skilled workers, and foreign-born unskilled labourers. The city government, he urged, should take over the theatres, and with the assistance of the churches transform them into a People's University to teach English to immigrants and, equally importantly, offer an alternative to commercialized recreation and the more dubious pleasures provided by hotels, poolrooms, and dancehalls.[73] The authors of a 1914 rural survey of Turtle Mountain, Manitoba, observed that while class distinctions were few among the mostly Canadian, Scottish, Irish, and English farmers of the district, social stress was evident both in the tendency of younger people to leave the farm and the rural church and in the presence of a large and transient pool of hired labour comprising sixteen per cent of Turtle Mountain's population.[74] The men who were hired labour, the investigators concluded, were a destabilizing element in the countryside because they were not rooted in either the community or the church. The problem in rural areas was thus the existence of a cleavage based upon ethnic and religious lines, a division that could only be remedied by the establishment of interdenominational evangelistic campaigns and social service committees by the churches, and by the promotion of Brotherhoods to provide both religious and recreational opportunities for men and youths.[75] In a similar vein, the investigators who studied London were troubled by the large number of inactive church members among skilled and unskilled workers, which raised the perilous spectre of class tension. This lack of church membership they blamed on the conservatism of churches, slow to encourage discussion of social and economic problems and reluctant to reach out to newcomers to the city.[76]

Extolling these investigations as models of modern science, progressive clergymen, anxious over the persistence of old-style evangelism and desiring to infuse it with modern social purpose, used the collection of factual data as part of their effort to establish social evangelism as the primary form of religious experience. Bryce Stewart, best known for his contributions to "secular" welfare state policy, began his career as a social investigator in the cause of social Christianity. While his survey of Port Arthur, Ontario, was one of the first systematic studies of the process of adjustment by immigrants and of living conditions in Canada, its principal intention was to convert the public to social evangelism. By adeptly establishing a link between, on the one hand, the failure of the church to establish a community presence beyond individual religious life and, on the other, the spectre of radicalism and the lack of assimilation among the Finns, who in his estimation constituted a "city within a city," Stewart concluded: "The church must be a conscience to the community upon its social problems, and must lead it into a neighborliness and brotherly kindness towards the immigrants of whatever nationality, towards the number of homeless men working in its industrial plants, and in the lumber and construction camps of the district."[77] Similarly, while attesting that the Protestant churches of Regina were well attended, J.S. Woodsworth's four-week survey of the city's immigration, labour, housing, and health problems provided factual evidence on the serious need of the churches to become the principal stimulus behind "civic regeneration."[78] Although it amassed voluminous new details and statistics concerning the general social conditions prevailing in rural Ontario, Presbyterian minister John MacDougall's survey, *Rural Life in Canada*, was in essence a compendious demonstration that the "organic character of social facts" demanded the joining of individual piety to social service and the church becoming the progenitor of the social welfare obligations to be assumed by the state.[79]

Although the Protestant churches had, as part of their in-house investigations of church adherence, collected data regarding industrial conditions, delinquency, infant mortality, housing conditions, feeble-mindedness, the "social evil" of prostitution, and ethnicity, it was not until 1914 that the churches, influenced by the popularity of surveys among American progressives, became conscious of the wider value of the social survey in educating "the popular mind [to] the collective sins of the community," and of its effectiveness in providing the scientific social facts needed to persuade governments to legislate in the social sphere. The broader implications of the usefulness of the social survey in promoting social reform was symbolized by the fact that a Survey Committee was established by the Canadian Conference on Charities and Corrections in 1914.[80] In the words of the authors of the Sydney, Nova Scotia, survey, their study was to function as a means of inoculation by which a "social serum" could be injected into the body politic.[81] This was not mere wishful thinking on the part of Christian idealists. Indeed, in 1922 the *London Free Press* reported that the United Farmers government of Ontario had utilized the statistics collected by the rural survey of the Methodist Department of Evangelism and Social Service as the basis for their legislation on rural reform.[82]

Throughout the 1920s virtually every community survey was either sponsored by the Protestant churches or actually proceeded under the immediate direction of a clergyman. The expertise of Protestant ministers in the area of social investigation was attested to by the fact that governments and other reform groups urgently invited them to undertake ostensibly "secular" investigations. The Saskatchewan government depended almost exclusively upon Hugh Dobson to organize all manner of social surveys, including a cost of living survey in Regina in 1918, sponsored by the Board of Trade, an investigation of the provincial milk supply and a survey of the feeble-minded, both in 1920, a housing survey of Regina in 1921, and various surveys of rural Saskatchewan focusing on immigrant conditions, health, child welfare, and sanitation.[83] For cost-conscious provincial governments, wary of increasing the scope of state involvement in social welfare administration through the back door of social research, the churches provided a cheap form of expertise while at the same time allowing government leaders to preserve a voluntaristic vision of public charity. Not only did such prominent Methodist clergymen as Peter Bryce, Lorne Pierce, and W.A. Riddell, later deputy minister of labour for the province of Ontario, undertake diverse social surveys, but Anglicans like the Rev. W.H. Adcock of Grace Anglican Church, Saskatoon, also became social diagnosticians. In 1920 Adcock initiated a study of "housing conditions in relation to family life in three typical areas," while the Salvation Army implemented its own surveys on housing and poverty. Even though they lagged somewhat behind the more energetic and invasive Methodist and Presbyterian churches, by the 1920s the Anglicans and Baptists did their share in classifying and interpreting the rate of Canadianization among Saskatchewan immigrants. And, as late as 1927 Baptist David B. Harkness, a leading light in the Social Service Council of Ontario, pursued the problem of agricultural failure in Northern Ontario, the newest belt of pioneer settlement, by surveying ten towns and cities.[84] Because of financial constraints, however, many local churches that wished to study community social ills scientifically were forced by mid-decade to rely increasingly on the church-funded Social Service Council of Canada. This should not be interpreted as the entering wedge of secularization, but rather as a transition from local effort to provincial and national control of social research, which nonetheless remained affirmedly Christian in its orientation. The studies proposed by Anglican divine C.W. Vernon for the Social Service Council of Canada on rural child labour in typical farming, fishing, and fruit-picking regions, and the Ontario council's ongoing investigation of community organization, public health, and the improvement of industrial conditions[85] were as much the product of social evangelism as was John MacDougall's *Rural Life in Canada*.

In no area was the church-held philosophy of social investigation as the means to cement social relations more evident than in their vigorous prosecution of a cluster of immigrant surveys between approximately 1916 and 1921. Here, the limits on the innovative nature of recommendations regarding immigration policy were more closely circumscribed because of the role of the churches as a private resource for government, and in this area they were more accountable to the government than in other fields of social and economic legislation. Unlike such areas as the formation of a child welfare bureaucracy at the federal level, which clearly implied the extension of state responsibility for social well-being, in the sphere of immigration the social surveys of the Protestant churches functioned largely as the simple application of data to reinforce with scientific precision the principle of identifying and classifying immigrant groups in terms of their economic viability, a procedure long enshrined in federal immigration policy. Whereas in other areas of social policy the Protestant churches endeavoured to lead often-reluctant politicians who defended the ideal of a limited state, immigration directly involved land settlement in Western Canada and the economic progress of that important regional linchpin of the National Policy. Consequently, both provincial and federal governments were much less ambivalent towards the social survey, which they viewed in this instance as an indispensable investigative prop sustaining the fulfilment of the National Policy. This more subordinate relationship of the Protestant churches to the state was not simply the result of a growing intrusiveness on the part of the state; rather, it represented a convergence of interests whereby the churches fully recognized the broad economic implications of the immigration question and the importance of this issue in galvanizing national public opinion behind the churches, thereby, progressive churchmen believed, confering upon Protestantism even more authority.

J.S. Woodsworth's 1916 survey of Ukrainian immigrants, which he undertook for the Bureau of Social Research, a body funded by the three Prairie provincial governments, symbolized this blurring of boundaries between church and state. While the survey was intended to provide the social facts that would underwrite future social legislation, its leading investigators were all clergymen and the central theme was the relationship of the church to the community. By his own admission, Woodsworth was not an expert in modern techniques of social investigation; as he frankly confessed to Violet McNaughton, his much trumpeted *Strangers Within Our Gates* had been written on the basis of impressionistic evidence and "some of the methods of work which I suggested are not what I would now advocate."[86] While Woodsworth's stated aim was to conduct a practical study of community problems in order to promote general interest in social welfare issues, much as had the Commission of Conservation, and to secure data as the basis of progressive legislation along the lines pursued by the universities of Wisconsin and Iowa, the overwhelming number of ministers participating in the survey ensured that its goal was in essence to monitor the vitality of the Protestant churches: "The contribution which it is hoped that this study may make," it was stressed, "is not the statement of the numbers that belong to this or that church, but the relationship of both this and that church to the entire community."[87] Indeed, the initial impetus to conduct this "intensive study of Ukrainian settlements" originated in the Conference for Rural Leadership, and because its intention was to seek "spiritual elevation" it was warmly endorsed by the Methodist, Presbyterian, Baptist, and Anglican denominations, as well as by the United Farmers of Alberta.

In this survey the Rev. A.O. Rose, C.W. Ross, W.H. Pike, J.S. Woodsworth, W.J. Sisler, Percy G. Sutton, and R.W. Murchie[88] undertook in 1916 three and one-half months of fieldwork in each of their districts, where they made at least 500 house-to-house canvasses of Ukrainian families. While the official questionnaire considered a wide range of social conditions, including the amount of hired help, leisure and recreational activities, sanitation, medical practices, agricultural techniques, and the general level of participation in Canadian public life, the conclusions of the report were overtly religious in their bias. "The sum of it all," Woodsworth stated, is that "the church and school are not leading and the people remain much as they were when they left Austria – ignorant and conservative. Indeed, in many respects they have degenerated. Societies for civic instruction and uplift do not exist." The clerical fieldworkers reported most consistently upon matters contributing to the diminution of church attendance: movies, poolrooms, gambling, baseball, comic books, the presence of soldiers, and berry-picking.[89]

At issue was the fear that the older religious customs of the Ukrainian immigrants were retarding the expansion of social evangelism, which ministers saw as the key to social, economic, and moral advancement. Thus, when Woodsworth expressed the desire to create "a new ideal" among the people of the Prairies, he really meant that the "Gospel Truth" should be preached more effectively in order to regenerate the rural conscience. Significantly, Woodsworth concluded his report to the Western provincial governments by quoting from the Rev. Percy G. Sutton who had stated: "I believe they will become good Christians and make their own peculiar contribution to God ... I believe these people have a capacity for suffering and self-sacrifice that, when devoted to Jesus Christ, will accomplish great things for the world."[90]

Prairie governments, like that of Saskatchewan, which itself had sponsored H.W. Foght's survey of the role of education in assimilating immigrants in 1916, encouraged progressive clergymen like Hugh Dobson, who during World War I began to fan out across Western Canada to investigate the culture, beliefs, and social conditions prevailing in immigrant districts.[91] The principal concern of these surveys was to determine the social causes underlying the volatility of nationalist sentiment and the assumed radicalism existing among certain immigrant communities, a particular preoccupation of a state at war. Employed to uncover new instruments of Canadianization, Protestant social surveyors like Dobson, who were closely attuned to wartime government policies regarding the increased need for efficient food production, closely examined the economic behaviour of immigrants in order to classify them according to an evolutionary scale of economic stages. With the social and economic incorporation of immigrants into national life in view, Dobson conducted his intensive door-to-door canvass, and immigrants were often buttonholed even while working in their fields. He hired a Ukrainian assistant, the Rev. Paul Crath, to map carefully and correlate statistically the degree to which recent immigrants had shed their "simple peasant habits" in favour of a more progressive "public-spiritedness." The investigators measured the latter by how much they read English-language newspapers, their willingness to send their children to school, their level of participation in the social life of the Protestant churches, and their involvement in farmers' cooperatives. Another principal researcher on this vast project of Canadianization was Presbyterian minister R.W. Murchie, professor of rural sociology at Manitoba Agricultural College, who had already become an expert in deciphering arcane data on farm management and their application to the problem of rural credit and indebtedness. The Protestant churches strategically co-opted such immigrant clergymen as the Rev. Richard C.T. Othen of Wakaw, Saskatchewan, who, having themselves converted to Protestantism, were naturally more optimistic regarding the ability of the churches to Canadianize immigrants. Because their Old World associations were thought to have been sanitized through their conversion, they were regarded as key spokesmen for the campaign of the Protestant churches to assuage public fears regarding the potential of immigrants to incite social unrest. Not surprisingly, after interviewing some 300 immigrants ranging across ten nationalities, these immigrant clergymen concluded optimistically that for the most part immigrants were becoming industrious and that their ties to the Old World, and in particular the problem of Ukrainian nationalism, provided no threat to the completion of the process of social "evolution" in Western Canada.[92] Despite the stated claim of Dobson and his associates that they were engaged in the impartial and "reliable" collection of information regarding the true character of immigrant communities, their studies were in fact prescriptive treatises designed to shape public opinion on the desirability of a more open immigration policy. By promoting the idea that socialization of community life was a natural process among the supposedly isolationist block settlements of Western Canada, these surveys upheld the national ideal advanced both by the Protestant churches and by the Department of Immigration and Colonization in the new Union Government.[93]

Mariana Valverde has argued that in early twentieth-century Canada issues such as social purity and immigration were controlled by a hegemonic exercise of power by the state and middle-class organizations. Because Valverde centred her discussion exclusively upon what she calls the "Toronto-Ottawa axis," an approach that necessarily excludes both rural and Western Canadian perspectives, she tautologically assumed that there was a consensus without examining either the scope or the factors that contributed to the "informational basis"[94] of these debates. By citing largely from the attitudes of the most conservative clergymen as her evidence, Valverde's analysis wrongly posits the view that given the hegemonic influence of the state, there was only one option regarding immigration policy – that of racism and the annihilation of immigrant culture.[95] Among the clergymen within the Protestant churches there existed, in fact, three divergent strands of opinion on the immigration question: first, the most conservative, the view of those who defended a rigidly exclusionist immigration policy; secondly, of those who, like J.S. Woodsworth and the Presbyterian D.N. McLachlan, endorsed a hierarchy of cultures defined by national character; and thirdly, of the majority of progressive Protestant clergymen, including Hugh Dobson and T. Albert Moore, who favoured an open-door immigration policy and accepted a modicum of cultural diversity.

Although it must be conceded that most clergymen and middle-class reformers wanted immigrants to be inculcated with the principles of democracy, a not unreasonable concern given that many recent immigrants were indeed unfamiliar with the franchise, having lived wholly under autocratic rule, the much-vaunted obsession with an Anglo-Saxon superiority that was founded upon a hierarchical classification of racial characteristics did not feature prominently in the views of the majority of Protestant clergymen. The view that moral and social characteristics were hereditary and therefore ultimately unassimilable, which was enunciated by D.N. McLachlan and which closely mirrored J.S. Woodsworth's obsession with the intractability of racial traits put forth in his summary of the immigrant dilemma, *Strangers Within Our Gates*, was, surprisingly, a minority voice among progressive clergymen.[96] What A.J. Hunter disparagingly described as the "old-fashioned missionary attitude" was vociferously attacked by most progressive Protestants as unchristian and unbrotherly.[97] More typical was the support for an open immigration policy expressed by Hugh Dobson and the National Council of Women; both reacted vociferously to the suggestion of the Imperial Order of the Daughters of the Empire that all immigration should be halted.[98] Indeed, Dobson and T. Albert Moore were apoplectic over what they regarded as S.D. Chown's extremely racist comment that immigrant communities would remain "a conglomeration of unassimilated nationalities." Where Chown desired a total cultural assimilation of immigrants, Moore and Dobson were more sanguine that the looser bonds of law and commerce were sufficient bridgeheads between the Old World and the new.[99] As Dobson outlined in a memorandum entitled "The Immigration Policy of Canada," the churches must resist the popular demand to restrict immigration to Anglo-Saxons, and he vociferously protested against the policy of deporting "undesirables." Recognizing the need for a rural population to further the task of economic and social development in Western Canada, Dobson reminded his readers that prejudice was a segregating rather than an assimilating factor, and though supportive of strict medical regulation to prevent the entry of "defectives," he urged the Protestant churches, in the interest of a "united progressive, law abiding country," to sponsor the publication of foreign-language books describing Canadian life and an active program of child care exhibits in immigrant districts in order to reduce social divisions between new and old Canadians.[100] Like Adelaide Plumptre, former president of the National Council of Women and a prominent member of the Social Service Council of Canada, most progressive clergymen in the Methodist and Presbyterian churches, while conceding the need for regulation, accepted immigration as a natural force which could become a blessing, rather than a curse, for national social development.[101] Certainly, progressive clergymen like Dobson and Woodsworth championed the creation of social centres as instruments of Canadianization,[102] but on the whole the Social Service Council of Canada aggressively defended the principle of open immigration and strongly endorsed Charlotte Whitton's "Some Aspects of the Immigration Problem," which concluded that the greatest solvent for national economic growth was the expansion of the admission of both agricultural settlers and labourers for farms and the burgeoning natural resource industries of Western and Northern Canada.[103]

Social Christianity in Canada was upheld by a powerful strand of individualism which preserved a large degree of independence for private culture within a broad ideal of community citizenship, in contrast to the United States where the social gospel and progressivism more directly privileged the communal above the individual, so that the notion of the private and public were almost wholly conflated. This peculiarity of the Canadian concept of social service had direct implications for the way in which Protestant clergymen cast the idea of assimilation. While they were adamant that immigrants conform to a public culture – that is, by participating in the civic polity through voting, by the cultivation of economic growth through the application of the principles of scientific farming, and by upholding an ideal of community cooperation – clergymen were amazingly flexible on the range of private beliefs, habits, and traditions immigrants could preserve within the larger framework of Canadian social life. Dobson fought against coercion of immigrants and was a consistent exponent of the need for clergymen to learn the language, history, and customs of Western Canadian immigrants, as he expressed in his pamphlet, *The Immigrant's Point of View and His Objective.*

Another publication of the Methodist Department of Evangelism and Social Service, *The Problem of the Melting Pot*, illustrated the dangers of racial prejudice through the Bible story of Ruth, which Protestant progressives believed provided divine confirmation of their view that intermarriage was a positive factor in building national loyalty.[104] The Rev. H.D. Ranns stated that an immigrant has "a love of freedom and a social idealism that are assets to any national life that assimilates him,"[105] and the Rev. H.G. Forster, who would become superintendent of non-Anglo-Saxon work in the Niagara Presbytery of the United Church, saw immigrant culture as a positive stream in Canadian life: "They bring to us great traditions – traditions of a Bach, a Beethoven, a Garibaldi, a Shevchenko, a Kossuth; traditions infinitely greater and richer than our own Anglo-Saxon traditions. It was their ancestors who bared their bodies to the onslaught of the Turks and Tartars in the Middle Ages, and with spear and pruning-hooks, died by the thousands, but they saved European civilization."[106] In attempting to create what R.H. MacDonald termed a "rural cosmopolitan democracy,"[107] many clergymen defended the evolution of a Canadian citizenship defined by a "fused race," which was neither Anglo-Saxon, Polish, Ukrainian, Italian, or Finnish, rather than the simple racial dominance of Anglo-Saxons.[108] In fact, most clergymen vociferously deprecated the excessively racist views of the Anglican Bishop of Saskatchewan, George Exton Lloyd, as did H.E. Wright, a student of Baptist sociologist A.L. McCrimmon at McMaster University, who by placing immigrants within the same social evolutionary continuum as all pioneering peoples, including the Anglo-Saxons, made them integral participants in Canadian national life. "The less we hold ourselves aloof from our New Canadians," Wright contended, "the more we appreciate and understand them, the deeper we shall see into the soul of them. The sooner we demolish the walls that separate us and become conscious and cognizant of their worth as potential Canadians, the sooner will they see deep into the souls of us. Then and only then will we build more stately mansions." Utilizing the concept of the pioneer fringe, first articulated by the Australian and American geographers Griffith Taylor and Isaiah Bowman, a theme that later found its way into the immigrant surveys of McGill sociologist C.A. Dawson, Wright stated: "We recognize in the immigrant the lineal descendant of the forgotten pioneer and like the pioneer he will achieve competence and prosperity."[109]

Not only was there a divergence of opinion concerning immigration policy, but there was another central line of cleavage dividing Protestant progressives. It arose not over the issue of race, but over that of hired labour, which in turn reflected differing attitudes to the National Policy between Eastern and Western Canadians. While Charlotte Whitton saw immigration as the key to the revival of the nation's prosperity because of its supposed ability to reduce unemployment through the expansion of improved arable land on the Western frontier,[110] Western Canadian writers, such as J.S. Woodsworth and the Rev. John Cormie of Winnipeg, considered immigration to be a minor factor in population growth and, more negatively, they viewed it as the central cause of economic stagnation and degeneration on the wheat-growing frontier.[111] The lower standards of living, coupled with the greater attachment to the soil demonstrated by immigrants of continental European origin, were, according to Cormie, forcing Anglo-Saxons to leave the family farm, a process that resulted not only in "a sort of social sterility,"[112] because it compelled women to abandon the farm, but also in actual economic deterioration. Cormie's objection to unregulated immigration did not stem from racial categories. Like other progressive clergymen, he believed that the church should stimulate a general public appreciation of the history and traditions of the "other" so that derogatory and racist terms like "bohunk" and "dago" could be eradicated from the Canadian lexicon. In fact, Cormie foresaw "a mighty commonwealth of races" living on the Prairies in the spirit of fellowship and goodwill.[113]

Cormie's opposition to the current government immigration policy focused on its cardinal principle, that immigration should function largely to provide a labour pool. What industrial Canada saw as a positive economic force, Cormie perceived as the introduction of large numbers of "marginal people," groups of migratory and seasonal hired men and women who had no real stake in the community and thus no real desire to contribute to the economic growth of the Prairie provinces. His was an attitude echoed in the 1930s by A.J. Hunter and Professor Eugene Forsey.[114] The problem of the tenant, wrote Cormie in 1928, "is the problem of the temporary dweller in either town or country. He does not remain on one farm or even in one district long enough to get deeply rooted anywhere, and his interest in the community is limited by the loosely tied bond which binds him to his neighbourhood."[115] For clergymen hoping to promote immigrant conformity to a national culture, the localism enhanced by farm tenancy and hired labour was disquieting and illustrative of the potentially regressive tendencies already characteristic of even the Anglo-Saxon rural mentality, as displayed in an overweening individualism that was subversive of social evangelism's ideal of cooperation as the foundation of economic prosperity.

Cormie's conservative evocation of the country home as the foundation of national unity and social progress was echoed by J.S. Woodsworth, who likewise feared that "marginal people"[116] – the foreigners and the hired men – were contributing to the dismantling of his utopian yearning for an arcadian rural bliss. Though Woodsworth recognized that the presence of farm labourers rescued Canadian women from the farm drudgery which threatened always to cast them down to "the stage of the peasant women of Europe,"[117] and though he supplied immigrant labourers to Anglo-Saxon farmers in Manitoba while he was superintendent of All People's Mission,[118], he continued to adhere to the belief that "in the farm-home family life has perhaps reached its highest development." "The common task, the united family circle, life-long friendships, democratic relationships, genuine neighborliness, high moral standards, simple healthful pleasures, deep personal religion, a religious community consciousness – happy memories, a haunting yearning for the lost paradise," he asserted, "these are all the issue of the country home."[119] In part, Woodsworth, like Cormie, feared that the uncontrolled growth of farm tenancy would eradicate Western rural independence and render Western Canada an impoverished resource milch cow for Eastern industrial interests.

Beneath these more narrowly economic arguments lingered Woodsworth's personal visceral fear and dislike of Old World intruders who, in his estimation, had done so much to arrest the full flowering of Protestantism in Western Canada. Referring to the importation of skilled British and unskilled European labourers, Woodsworth identified the central dilemma of Canadian immigration policy when he wrote in 1913 that "[t]hese two classes imported into this country are absolutely essential to our newer and fuller life, yet they threaten the old order. They might be termed the danger zone."[120] And although his reflections were suffused with the promise implicit in evangelistic conversion that this danger zone might become the "brightest light which will prove our national salvation," Woodsworth's social Christianity was nevertheless still informed by an "old-fashioned missionary attitude," with its assumption of Anglo-Saxon superiority so disdained by leading Methodist progressives, which impelled him to utter the phrase "we are true born English people and not dirty foreigners."[121]

Although the Protestant churches continued to study immigrant adjustment and the social problems attendant upon the rural pioneer economy into the 1930s,[122] increasingly the social survey became anchored to university departments of political economy and sociology. Leadership in social investigation did not pass from church to university in opposition to church interests, however, for it was church-based institutions, such as the Social Service Council of Ontario, that often underwrote scholarships resulting in the acceleration of the study of rural sociology in university social science departments.[123] The mammoth surveys of the agricultural frontier undertaken in the 1930s were often led by clergymen, of whom the most noteworthy were R.W. Murchie of the Manitoba Agricultural College and C.A. Dawson, Baptist sociologist at McGill.

Murchie's career symbolized the continued harmonious coordination of interests between church, university, and government that so characterized progressive reform in Canada. Born in Scotland in 1883, Murchie immigrated to Canada in 1906 and began theological training at Manitoba College. After serving as a pastor for six years, he became a professor of theology at the University of Manitoba, a position he translated in 1918 into a professorship of rural sociology at the province's agricultural college as part of his mission to bring social Christianity to rural Canada. Murchie's experience in conducting rural leadership courses for ministers and their wives not only brought him to the attention of Protestant progressive leaders, who frequently employed him in their own surveys, but also to the Bracken Progressive government, which in 1927 appointed him chair of the committee inquiring into seasonal unemployment. Apart from being a consistent advocate of the importance of scientific settlement and tighter public regulation of land use, themes underscored in the writings of American geographer Isaiah Bowman, Murchie, through government surveys such as *Unused Lands of Manitoba*, reinforced the definition by the Protestant churches of assimilation as a process in which the history, customs, ideals, and standards of living of each group provide equal contributions to a redefinition of Canadian national life.[124]

Although Murchie was later celebrated as one of the authors in W.A. Mackintosh's Canadian Frontiers of Settlement Series published in the 1930s, which utilized the concept of the pioneer fringe as its central thematic framework, his concern for the relationship between older urban settlements and newer, peripheral rural economies was an immediate extension of his discussions of the factors contributing to the maturity and eventual stability of pioneer life that he undertook for Methodist and Presbyterian rural surveys during the period from 1913 to 1925. In an article written in 1919 for the *Grain Growers' Guide*, Murchie wrote:

> Just as agriculture must pass through various stages so must the development of the home have three definite stages, following closely on the development of the farm. The three stages … are: – the "Pioneer" stage, where a new settler comes in to clear and break up the land; the "Exploiter" stage, in which the farmer seeks to get from his farm all he can, to lay up a modest competence and retire to the country town or city; and the "Husbandman" stage, in which the farmer realizing that farming is a profession, and a worthy one, and that country life is worthwhile, seeks to develop his farm, to run it as a business,

and to educate his family that they, in their turn, may take his place in the development of community life.[125]

Fifteen years later, in a similar vein, W.A. Mackintosh explained in his foreword to *The Settlement of the Peace River Country: A Study of a Pioneer Area* (1934) by C.A. Dawson and R.W. Murchie that this survey of rural life was intended to show how, on this new agricultural frontier which recapitulated in Canada the economic stage of the eighteenth century in Western Europe, the process of development from the premature era of land boom and speculation was groping, through its search for suitable products, to reach a higher level of evolution as defined by mature and stable settlements.

Having imbibed the view of the university social scientists promoting the Frontiers of Settlement Series that their research was of a pioneering nature, Marlene Shore and more recently Barry Ferguson have narrowly situated this type of social investigation in the context of the university, thereby ignoring the important and long-standing concern for rural problems that were the focus of the earlier voluminous church surveys.[126] In many ways the later projects of rural scientific investigation, immediately replicated earlier church surveys: Dawson and Murchie copied the earlier investigations by examining 400 farm homes, focusing on the needs of women in rural society, and, most strikingly, evincing a marked concentration on religious organizations as the central forum of mature social cohesion. The close affinity between the latter-day university studies and the earlier church surveys can best be demonstrated by their shared view that the church should become the fundamental social centre in these "fringes of settlement." "Religion, or an emotional substitute for it," remarked Dawson and Murchie, "has become an integral part of life in every region, but without organization its expression is errative and discontinuous." Despite the veneer of social scientific terminology, the recommendations of the studies were remarkably similar, even though they had been penned almost two decades apart. Obviously the progressive paradigm had endured because Dawson and Murchie informed policymakers that the churches, farmers' movements, and the women's institutes, those "great channels of human idealization," must take the lead in drawing people together "with an enthusiasm for sacred aims in a secular world."[127] Even as late as 1942 university social scientists continued to write in the service of the United Church. In that year Alexander Brady of the University of Toronto Department of Political Economy was requested by the Board of Evangelism and Social Service to write on "The Farmer in National Life." In this study he affirmed that while problems of rural credit, regulation of markets, and rural electrification were suitable responsibilities for the modern state, the more fundamental contribution to ensuring the health of rural communities – the fostering of attitudes of mind and a sound philosophy of life – must remain the purview of the church. "Finally, there must be created among farmers," Brady stated, "a sense of interdependence relative to other members of the community whether trade unionists or merchants. It is easy for the farmer to develop a feeling of isolation from the townsmen but such isolationism in any class is a menace to the solution of problems in a democratic way. The unity of social life must be grasped if the problems of that life are to be genuinely solved."[128]

The most important precursor and the primary rationale driving the creation of the modern welfare state is the systematic collection and interpretation of social data that serve as the basis for legislative change. In the absence of direct government-sponsored research bureaux – apart from the short-lived Bureau of Social Research in the Western provinces and a small Dominion Bureau of Statistics – during the 1920s this unoccupied terrain of social investigation was filled by the energetic Protestant churches. Church campaigns to survey social conditions, although originating in the more narrow identification of the problem of declining church attendance, were fuelled by the promise of social Christianity and the fulfilment of the Kingdom of God, and these goals for the modern progressive clergymen had to be achieved through the application of scientific techniques. Although the social survey, the newest and most sophisticated method for the study of social conditions, drew the intellectual networks of church and government into close proximity, the fact that the churches only became quasi-governmental agencies over the question of immigration policy had important implications for the unfolding of the modern welfare state in Canada. In other words, the institutional context for the information undergirding social legislation is as important to an understanding of the welfare state as the legislation itself. Because the impetus for social investigation, and hence social reform, resided with the churches and not government bureaucracies, the creation of a full-fledged welfare state in Canada was necessarily incremental and halting. This gap between the social investigations by voluntary institutions and by governments meant that the collectivist liberal ideas the Protestant churches often enshrined in their legislative recommendations were not immediately acted upon by provincial and federal governments. The Protestant churches, through their preoccupation with rural social declension, first articulated the idea that scientific data should form the basis of modern social planning. However, because this notion of "social engineering" founded upon the deployment of expertise was vested in the churches, whose power was dependent upon local support and was thus decentralized, and not in the federal government, their ideal of social planning was far less coercive and intrusive than would be later welfare policies, which had their roots in the federal bureaucracies. Moreover, because the central dynamic of Protestant social investigation lay in rural Canada rather than the city, where concerns of industrial and organized labour were at the forefront, welfare policies in Canada, especially during the 1930s, grew along a different tangent, but one no less progressive, than in other modern states.

6 The Social Service Council of Canada: "A Clearing-House" for the Modern State[1]

Through their tradition of social investigation the Social Service Council of Canada and the Protestant churches established the empirical basis for the public discussion of social welfare legislation in the 1920s and 1930s. They were the crucial catalysts in creating a climate of opinion conducive to an increasingly interventionist state. The importance of the contribution of private bodies to the rise of the modern state has been generally neglected by Canadian historians who, by focusing their attention almost exclusively upon the spate of welfare legislation introduced in the late 1930s and 1940s, have conceived the arena of policy-making too narrowly in terms of the legislative process. Even those historians, most notably Doug Owram, who have sought to broaden the debate by examining the contribution of university social science experts to the process of policy creation at the federal level, still perceive the initiative for new departures in government regulation as emanating principally from the elected politicians and the Ottawa civil service mandarins. By privileging economic research as the natural precursor of the modern interventionist state, Owram identified the relationship between university experts and the federal government, a partnership that emerged most emphatically during the decade of the 1930s, as the pioneering achievement supplying the impetus for the managerial state of the 1940s.[2]

While the production of empirical knowledge of social and economic conditions was an indispensable factor in stimulating the modern expansion of state responsibility – what Gianfranco Poggi has termed "the scientization of politics"[3] – this process in Canada not only began a decade earlier than some have estimated but it also occurred outside the immediate parameters of government control. During the 1920s, prior to the formation of the League for Social Reconstruction and the movement of liberal Keynesian academics into government circles, the church-funded Social Service Council of Canada functioned as the primary instrument for the investigation, interpretation, and publicization of such social problems as child welfare, immigration, rural planning, housing, penal reform, family law, old-age pensions, and unemployment insurance. These endeavours occurred largely because of the alliance of the churches with women's groups and other social reform organizations, and thus provided the fundamental infrastructure of knowledge necessary for the creation of modern social welfare policy. While not as integrally linked to the federal government as the later generation of social scientist mandarins in Ottawa, the Social Service Council of Canada in fact served during the 1920s as the main vehicle by which university social scientists journeyed towards their later role as members of a government brain trust.[4] In addition to acting as the foremost organization lobbying politicians, the council was important for its educative role: through the wide circulation of its journal *Social Welfare*, its many pamphlets and circulars, and its close association with the local pulpit, it was a powerful force in guiding the popular mind towards an acceptance of the state's wider responsibility in fostering the general welfare of society. Indeed, because the Protestant churches and the Social Service Council of Canada adhered to a notion of social Christianity that interpreted social responsibility as the expression of a fuller individualism, they viewed the expansion of state responsibility as commensurate with the needs of an evolving and increasingly complex social organism. By thus dissolving earlier notions of the disjuncture between public and private, this conception of the social order allowed such voluntary organizations as the Protestant churches a powerful voice in shaping public policy. But, more importantly, it meant that the Social Service Council of Canada and its constituent provincial bodies were the first to enunciate systematically the idea of the liberal positive state. There is no better illustration of the contribution of the Social Service Council's program of social investigation to a reformulation of traditional liberalism and of its role as the progenitor of modern social welfare policy than in the way it identified its brand of scientific policymaking with that of President Hoover's Research Committee on Social Trends of 1933, which Michael J. Lacey and Mary O. Furner have ranked with Keynesianism as "the outstanding twentieth-century examples of new liberal theoretical reflection and comprehensive social description."[5] This statement makes clear that the route to the modern welfare state was a bifurcated one: one current, Keynesianism, centred upon economic investigation and central banking, while the other no less significant tangent, scientific policymaking, grew out of the type of systematic social research that in Canada was first sponsored by the Protestant churches.

The advocates of social Christianity emphasized "group thinking and group action"[6] and maintained that only in the community could the individual attain the highest degree of both self-realization and salvation, and thus the churches, which acted as society's conscience, would impel the community towards social reform.[7] Social Christianity's real function was, however, a far more pragmatic one. Its search for practical solutions to modern social problems, implicit in the phrase "applied Christianity," was enshrined in the Social Service Council of Canada, created in 1908 as a central clearing-house for inquiring into modern social and industrial conditions and thus for supplying the basis of knowledge to allow the Protestant churches to mediate between the government and the people.[8] C.W. Gordon characterized the Social Service Council as a "loosely organized army" of provincial intelligence corps whose investigations of social conditions formed a rallying centre around which progressive reformers prepared for war and whose ultimate object was to pressure government to pass social legislation.[9] In providing what Ernest Thomas called "a co-operative control of the Government," the church sought to transform the state in such a way as to bring into closer harmony the goals of government, of agencies such as the press, and of other hitherto independent social reform organizations, all under the rubric of a full-orbed evangelism. As Hugh Dobson wrote in 1920, "[t]his increasing co-operative practice of Christianity, in governmental and voluntary activities, has been, and is, an evangel of increasing power, awakening the people to an interest in saving humanity in all its aspects."[10]

According to C.W. Gordon, the roles of the state and the church were identical, for both were anchored by individual consent and both sought to reconcile the inherent conflict between the rights of individuals into a higher ideal of social cooperation.[11] And although he was an advocate of the expansion of state responsibility in the field of social and industrial welfare, Gordon nevertheless believed that it was the individual who ultimately determined the "quality of the State."[12] Queen's University social scientist O.D. Skelton shared the view of progressive clergymen that the modern idea of collectivism implicit in growing state responsibilities must preserve a balance of power between state and church, because in his opinion the consciousness of interdependent social relations, which undergirded modern state expansion, was but the expression of the individualistic tenets of evangelicalism. The interventionist state, for Skelton, was thus premised upon individual salvation, what he identified as "the dynamic force needed to turn the wheels of whatever organization appeals to him [the Christian believer] as best fitted for making the city the city of God."[13]

Believing that society was composed of three great entities – the family, the state, and the church – and that the state itself was merely a social organism that grew out of familial relationships,[14] Protestant church progressives naturally perceived the church as playing a central role in fostering that ideal of social cooperation and social service that must, in their estimation, eventually inform the responsibilities of the modern state. "The Social Service Congress is a great religious institution of Canada," declared the Rev. Canon Tucker in 1917, "and it gives to all its services a religious impress ... Our lives are not our own; the State claims them now for service. Service for others is the only thing that counts."[15] By devising an interpretation of the state as just the collective expression of individual self-sacrifice and service and thus grounding the goal of the common good upon a moral basis of social unity, Protestant clergymen ensured that increasing state intervention in political and social reform would necessarily reflect the interests of the churches and so combat any tendencies towards an idea of state socialism founded upon economic materialism. And, while the primary function of the modern church was to develop a "corporate conscience" that would not only awaken the body politic to its wider social responsibilities but more particularly transform politicians into "preachers of righteousness," the new interventionist state, as implied in the sermons of S.D. Chown, was to evolve along the lines dictated by "[t]he natural laws of the spiritual world" in order to stave off the monopolistic and materialistic visions of statism promulgated by political socialism. Fully supportive of the expansion of the state in the ownership of public utilities and in social welfare, Chown wished to define socialism not as the embodiment of narrow economic interest but as the incarnation of personal development realized in the practice of social service. "Socialism," he declared, "needs the steady, untiring consecration and the dynamic power of the most vigorous type of Christianity attainable; and Christianity would be helped by the outlook of Socialism to attain a practical social objective. Linked in this way, they may become fellow-helpers to the truth which makes men free."[16]

In positing a notion of social cohesion inextricably intertwined with the realization of individual rights and a view of the civic state reliant upon the essentially moral criterion of service – what Chown termed "the perfect social state[17] – Protestant progressive clergymen held a concept of the state that was commensurate with a transatlantic intellectual climate devoted to the redefinition of liberalism into a socially conscious current of political thought. Although closely identified with

British new liberalism,[18] Canadian social Christianity more closely paralleled its American counterpart, progressivism, by adhering more closely to the political centre of liberal thought. In Britain, where organized labour had achieved a powerful position in political life, new liberal interpreters of the state felt compelled to respond to socialist arguments, but in North America, where labour interests remained enmeshed in the internal politics of the work process, progressive reformers were far less constrained to integrate the socialist critique of capitalism into their notions of social reconstruction. This spirit was evoked in the phrase of Ernest Thomas that "we are all social reformers now,"[19] a more palatable dilution of the now-famous British dictum, "we are all socialists now."

The ruminations by Protestant clergymen on the coordination of church and state activities regarding social legislation were not mere theoretical posturings, but were informed by practical experience from their attempts, during the early twentieth century, to awaken all levels of government to assume a wider burden of social responsibility for improving the conditions of modern life. As early as 1907 S.D. Chown, J.G. Shearer, and L.N. Tucker, respectively the representatives of the Methodist, Presbyterian, and Anglican denominations, presented a resolution on unemployment to the federal minister of public works on behalf of the Associated Charities of Toronto.[20] The confidence of the churches in lobbying government accelerated dramatically during and after World War I, largely as a result of the Union Government with its creed of service and its efforts to promote state action in the name of wartime national efficiency. Buoyed by the fervour engendered by government-sponsored postwar reconstruction programs, the Methodist field secretary for Western Canada, Hugh Dobson, drew up his own broad program that would have greatly expanded the scope of state responsibility for public health, child welfare, social research, and the general "socializing of community life." Dobson's program, in turn, would have greatly extended the still-embryonic social welfare bureaucracy by creating a new ministry of Social Reconstruction and by expanding the Dominion Board of Health to include a new Bureau of Child Welfare and, to correlate social legislation, a new Bureau of Surveys.[21] Wary of what they viewed as the overweening influence of businessmen on the Union Government as well as in innumerable municipalities, Protestant clergymen like Dobson unceasingly pressured governments throughout the 1920s to take up their plans for social regeneration, which revolved principally around the maternal feminist concerns for improved family and child welfare.[22]

Indeed, the Protestant churches and their allies, the women's institutes and organized labour, had every reason to fear the entrenched power of more conservative elements in Ottawa, for in 1919 the Social Service Council's proposed Children's Bureau, whose responsibilities would have pertained to a broad range of reform issues, such as sweated labour, immigration, education, and recreation as well as public health, was sabotaged by the medical establishment and its allies in the Unionist cabinet, who opposed the incursion of public health and social reformers into their professional domain. To demonstrate the political acuity of the social reform network which was embodied within the church-led Social Service Council of Canada, in 1920 this network was successful in establishing the Canadian Council of Child Welfare, a quasi-public organization sponsored and funded in part by the federal government and staffed by Protestant social workers and representatives of women's groups.[23] As Dobson confided to Charlotte Whitton, assistant secretary to J.G. Shearer: "I am sure there will be a very hearty response to any action the Government may take in this matter from our western provinces, for the large Provincial organizations [the Social Service Councils], Churches, and Women's Societies have been pressing for this matter for three or four years now."[24]

Like the Rev. George Pidgeon, minister of Bloor Street Presbyterian Church in Toronto, who believed that "[a] policy of drift" characterized the public policy of Canadian governments which, because of their unhealthy dependence upon the privileged classes, he castigated as indifferent to the people, the Protestant churches aggressively campaigned to transform the process of governing by making social legislation the manifestation of scientific investigation rather than of party favouritism.[25] Indeed, it was with a similar view of freeing Canadians from their "slave masters" and perpetrators of party warfare, the politicians, that the Rev. Edward S. Bishop was urged by his Methodist brethren through the head of the Department of Evangelism and Social Service, T. Albert Moore, to accept a position in the Alberta government's new Department of Social Welfare. Moore viewed this as a particularly "strategic post" and a great opportunity for Methodism because of the free hand Bishop would have in shaping the policy and activities of this new government department.[26] The Methodist leadership fully endorsed this government initiative because the department's efforts in public health, child welfare, sanitation, and venereal disease would parallel, rather than wholly displace, the church's own efforts. In short, the Methodist Church welcomed the expansion of the state into social welfare administration and education, for as the funding capabilities of the Protestant churches, and hence the Social Service Councils, became more straitened, it believed it was increasingly incumbent upon governments to relieve private institutions and to shoulder the burden for sustaining the common weal. Moore urged Bishop to accept the government position because it would "speed up this wonderful movement with all the prestige and support of the government behind it" without relinquishing its Christian tenor.[27]

Although the churches often took on the funding and management of social welfare initiatives, they were extremely critical of politicians who failed to recognize that the churches were simply pioneering social institutions and programs in the expectation of them becoming part of an expanded state machinery in the future. Thus, in 1919, even though the churches had for some time been teaching English to immigrants in their social settlements, they vociferously encouraged private agencies like the Toronto Board of Trade to establish their own classes; this step, they believed, would lead to the ultimate responsibility being "taken by federal and provincial governments."[28] While C.W. Gordon feared that "whenever the Christian Church has sought to control governments it has ended up by being controlled by governments," this apprehension over the growth of government was a minor problem for most Protestant progressives and seems to have been related to Gordon's more traditional concern for the compact theory of the state with its extreme defence of individual rights.[29] By far the most commonly held attitude articulated by progressive clergymen on the subject of the increased presence of the state was that of T. Albert Moore and Hugh Dobson. While insisting that homes for delinquent girls should be managed by the churches in order to preserve their redemptive and Christian character, Moore and Dobson were all too aware of the terrible drain such initiatives in applied Christianity placed upon church coffers. In 1922 a frustrated Moore wrote to Dobson: "I took the ground very strongly that such homes ought to be provided by the Government, which should be very pleased if the churches render assistance in oversight and maintenance … The Church must influence the Government to create and conduct these institutions in such a way as will secure the application of the principles of the Gospel to the lives of these girls."[30]

Grandiose generalizations have been offered by historians who have argued that the displacement of the churches by government-sponsored social welfare programs constitutes irrefutable evidence of secularization, on the assumption that the churches were antagonistic to such government initiatives.[31] Nothing could be further from the theory of the state or which most Protestant churchmen espoused in the early twentieth century. Far from worrying that it would lead to the demise of the church as a public institution, clergymen eagerly welcomed the assumption of responsibility by governments for social welfare. Believing that the central mission of social evangelism was an educative one, Hugh Dobson maintained that having awakened governments to the need for the provision of social welfare programs the churches must withdraw as soon as possible in order that they might concentrate more effectively on the very core of the Christian experience – personal evangelism. Dobson expressed his relief at the ever increasing interest of government in the sphere of community reconstruction to Ernest Thomas in 1920: "This progressive legislation and the assumption of responsibility by the Government for the care of dependents and needy children and of the diseased is more and more relieving our Church for the direct appeal for the changing of men's minds towards the Gospel way of living."[32] Writing to T. Albert Moore, Dobson was even more emphatic on the merely temporary exigencies that compelled the church's management of social reform, and the urgent need to redress the weakness of the state in Canadian life:

> I pointed out that the potential progress in social legislation and adjustment and in that thought of the people had been so great that it had in effect cleared the ship for action in the matter of Evangelism. That is, that the Unemployment Organization of the Government, Mothers' Pensions, Minimum Wage Board, Care of Feebleminded, Health activities and the potential development represented in the interests of the people in social development today was as such as to take away in a measure from the Church the burden that always rested upon us as a night-mare of difficulty to absorb the energies of our Church in helping the drunkards and other derelicts, the dependents, the unemployed, and so forth. The effect of all this is that we are clearing ourselves of the detailed burden of these things and are ready to give ourselves better than ever before to the one clear goal of bringing about repentance.[33]

What the Protestant churches feared far more than the expansion of the state in social welfare in the years immediately following World War I was the entrenchment of conservative attitudes hostile to increased state responsibility for social recovery. Against this nemesis of social Christianity, progressive clergymen like Hugh Dobson effectively lobbied for a Bureau of Public Welfare in Regina. In 1918, however, this bureau was summarily closed by a new alderman who, as Dobson complained to J.H.T. Falk, the head of the Winnipeg Council of Social Agencies, had no notion of the value of modern social work.[34] Well apprised of the need to arouse "the masses of the people" from an attitude of indifference on public questions, the Protestant churches and their reform allies established specific committees on social legislation as part of the Canadian Conference on Public Welfare and these regularly publicized the necessity of government legislation in the areas of housing, mental hygiene, rural planning, juvenile recreation, and the standardization of hospitals.

Despite the necessity throughout the 1920s of lobbying recalcitrant politicians on the need to consider the solution of social problems rather than the politics of railways and tariffs as the touchstone of national prosperity, the Protestant churches and their Social Service Councils saw themselves primarily as educative agencies rather than as "a political fighting machine." "Our function," stated D.B. Harkness, secretary of the Social Service Council of Ontario, "is not in meeting a particular social problem, but rather the application of the scientific method to the question of how to bring the specific service to bear upon the specific need in the community life. We are interested ... in discovering and making known the social needs, secondly in knowing the most approved services for dealing with the needs and where these services are obtainable, and thirdly in encouraging the development of those agencies in each community which are best adapted to bringing needs and services together." In particular, the Social Service Council of Canada desired to build the conditions for a "constructive co-operation and scientific social engineering" coordinated with government departments, which they were glad to announce had come to view the council as the source of "expert service" and an "authoritative source of information and counsel."[35] This central aim of moulding public opinion was carried on through a variety of means. The Social Service Council published the newest principles of sociology and social investigation through its journal, *Social Welfare*, which it began to sell openly at bookstalls in 1920 in order to secure even wider circulation. Reformers and clergymen read papers at the annual meetings of the council and at various conferences on public welfare. They published articles in the *Canadian Churchman*, the *Presbyterian*, the *Christian Guardian*, the *Canadian Baptist*, and the *Maritime Baptist*, and they secured various specialists to author leaflets for public consumption. Perhaps the greatest success at capturing a wide public readership was achieved in the 1930s when the Machine Age Series of pamphlets, published by the Social Service Council of Canada, reached a circulation of 12,000 copies, and this during a period of financial stringency and retrenchment.[36]

In 1918 the Social Service Council of Saskatchewan outlined the essentials of a public campaign for social reform that involved the insertion of brief weekly articles in local newspapers and the enlistment of editors favourable to the cause to include a social service page in their papers. Large numbers of leaflets for distribution through various affiliated organizations and the provincial departments of education and health were designed to reach a mass audience. Having prepared the ground, the council would then orchestrate a series of public meetings, speakers bureaux, and district conferences, the whole structure coordinated by the "systematic itinerary" of local secretaries with a battery of lantern-slides, charts, and photographs. This campaign would culminate in an annual provincial congress which would then submit resolutions to the government on the subject of social legislation.[37]

The ultimate goal of the churches, however, was that this barrage of propaganda would so excite public opinion that it would induce the intervention of federal and provincial governments in the field of social welfare. Thus, in his 1920 report Hugh Dobson dwelt at length upon his cultivation of government officials and saw as a particular mark of his success that "[o]n several occasions governments have asked me to prepare special memoranda on special legislation or administration all of which demands sympathy, careful study and time." "Those who have devoted themselves to social guidance," continued Dobson, "know even better than their critics the danger of giving a wrong direction to social development in days like these, when discontent and hope are so pronounced and the human will is insistent and sometimes reckless and ill advised."[38] And, although they believed that governments and municipalities should eventually assume the largest share of all social service work, Protestant reformers, faced with the task of pacifying those who were more conservatively inclined and who seemed to form the majority of the Canadian community, adroitly urged the preservation of voluntary social agencies whose work might continue under government sponsorship.[39]

Under the leadership of Hugh Dobson, a strong advocate of the nationalization of railways and coal mines, of a graduated income tax, and of unemployment and social insurance, the Committee of Social Legislation of the Canadian Conference on Public Welfare orchestrated a nationally organized campaign to collate information on social conditions in order to secure new social legislation by the dominion government.[40] In 1919 the Methodist Church's recommendations for a program of community centres was adopted by the government of Saskatchewan, and in that same year Dobson campaigned alongside the provincial women's institutes to have the British Columbia government organize a Department for Neglected Children.[41] In 1920 the Methodist Department of Evangelism and Social Service was responsible for inducing the Saskatchewan Department of Health to establish eight free venereal disease clinics in Yorkton, and in 1921 the Presbyterian Board of Social Service and Evangelism lobbied Premier Martin of Saskatchewan for the creation of homes for delinquent girls. In 1922 J.G. Shearer recommended federal maternity benefits legislation based on the ongoing study of the Child Welfare Committee of the Social Service Council on female employment patterns and Australian models of social insurance.[42] So dominant had the Protestant churches become in the sphere of caring for wayward girls that by 1923 it was commonplace for representatives of the churches to attend meetings held by municipal governments on the subject.[43]

After years of diligently impressing upon governments that the Protestant churches and their social service councils represented the leading edge of social investigation and reform, by the 1920s government leaders had become more receptive to their new style of lobbying which was based upon the systematic collection of social facts. So open had the lines of communication between church leaders and federal politicians become – and indeed, so strong was the public authority wielded by the churches – that upon reading about the Saskatchewan government's intention of releasing men jailed for liquor offences, not only did an outraged T. Albert Moore write immediately to Prime Minister Mackenzie King, but more signficantly King responded with even greater alacrity to refute the allegations.[44] More than any other politician in Canada, King was convinced that any enduring social reform must be founded upon Christian social service and that all benevolent government action was premised upon the nurturing power of the church to change the individual human heart, convictions that made him particularly receptive to the blurring of lines between voluntary and state institutions, between private and public endeavours.

Indeed, even as a youth King did not differentiate between the Christian ministry of the church and the ideal of practical service which he believed was implicit in a career in politics. This belief, that he could serve his "Master" equally well in the church, university, or politics, remained with King throughout his lifetime, and it continued to animate his personal commitment to reform as well as his belief that the state's primary role was that of mediator between social classes and interest groups.[45] Imbued with the spirit of social salvation, King arrived at a similar perspective regarding the growing complexity and interdependence of modern life to be managed ideally through a congeries of private and public interventions. In this way, social cooperation could be achieved without relinquishing the very foundation of liberalism, the independence and responsibility of the individual. Like Protestant progressives, King eschewed the materialist socialism advanced by the most radical Fabians,[46] but at the same time he recognized the increasing necessity for government responsibility in protecting human welfare in both economic and social spheres. These same themes concerning the coordination between voluntary and state action in the arena of social betterment were adumbrated by King when he spoke before the Presbyterian Board of Moral and Social Reform in 1908. Appealing to the wisdom of that venerable liberal thinker Goldwin Smith, King attested that politics and the Christian ministry were interchangeable callings.[47]

In turn, he charged the church with providing suggestions to the Labour Department regarding such questions as the employment of navvies on the transcontinental railways and the problems of seasonal labour among lumbermen in Northern Canada, child labour, and sweatshops, declaring that not only would such social investigation enable the church to serve the masses more effectively, but that "no work could be more truly Christian."[48] It was precisely on this basis of preserving both Christian and voluntary effort that the Presbyterian Church concurred with King's aversion to having governments fund directly economic and social research.[49]

Because King believed that the teachings of Christianity provided the best foundation for the resolution of all industrial problems, he effectively eradicated the barriers between church and state. By insisting on their concerted study of provincial laws regarding social improvement, and indeed their systematic investigation of all social problems, King was in fact employing the churches as quasi-public research agencies with the aim of securing uniform national social legislation. And, as part of this foray to dissolve the distinction between private and public institutions in the field of social redemption, King requested that the churches in turn open their pulpits to representatives of the state, and allow him, for example, the privilege of speaking to congregations on such issues as "the Church and Labor." With a similar end in view, King importuned clergymen to sit on government boards and committees;[50] when they did so it in fact represented a precedent for the deployment of scientific expertise in the legislative process and created the first quasi-official think-tanks to function as the primary pipelines through which university specialists gained their first foothold in government structures of policymaking.

The Social Service Council of Canada held its first meeting on 26 December 1907 and its constitution was ratified on 1 October 1908.[51] Initially called the Moral and Social Reform Council of Canada, this cooperative venture of the Presbyterian, Anglican, Methodist, Baptist, and Congregational churches was founded primarily with the intention of pressuring governments to pass temperance legislation. However, as George Pidgeon later testified, many clergymen, including J.G. Shearer who occupied the key position of secretary of the new council, purported to subscribe to the temperance cause largely because of the strong allegiance it commanded among ordinary Protestant Christians, and they believed this widespread support for temperance would push both local clergymen and their congregations to participate in a wide range of social reform activities.[52] Despite its rhetoric in supporting the Dominion Alliance, from its very inception the Social Service Council sought to transcend a narrow moral agenda in favour of broader social issues, and its intentions were signified by the presence on its executive of Jimmy Simpson of the Trades and Labor Council and W.C. Good of the Dominion Grange and Farmers.[53] By 1911 its program of reform had moved decidedly beyond moral matters of temperance and social purity and concerned the conditions of sweated labour, accommodation for single women in cities, town planning, and housing reform. Moreover, at the prompting of the Baptist W.C. Keirstead, a committee was struck in that year to interview Sir Charles Lucas of the Colonial Office regarding the settlement of the land claims of the British Columbia Indians.[54] Proclaiming in 1912 that "the Son of Man is the final authority over all human life, in its social as well as its individual aspects," the Social Service Council began to apply Christian principles to its campaigns for the equitable distribution of wealth, the abolition of poverty, the arbitration of industrial disputes, the care of the feeble-minded, the control of contagious disease, and the preservation of international peace.[55]

The picture of harmonious consensus between the mainline Protestant denominations over the goal of Christianizing Canadian life was belied by the political tensions that surfaced around the issue of which Christian body would direct and control the temperance cause. Almost immediately, fissures developed between the Methodists and their ally, the Lord's Day Alliance, on the one hand, and the very powerful Presbyterian forces that were linked with the Trades and Labor Congress on the other. To the dismay of the Methodist Church, it was discovered that ninety per cent of the Toronto labour representatives on the council opposed temperance, which quickly alienated the representatives of the Dominion Alliance of temperance reformers. At first, the Methodists feared that the Presbyterians and those "dancing, card-playing, smoking" Anglicans would consistently "shut out any matter" raised by the Methodists.[56] What S.D. Chown really feared was that the Methodists would have to relinquish control of such pet issues as temperance: "What will be left to me?" asked the chagrined Chown. "I am to work away only upon such issues as for the time being are hopeless, or thought to be, and when I get them into a hopeful condition, I am to hand over the fruit of my labors to the Moral and Social Reform Councils and as a Methodist, to step down and out."[57] Because the Methodist Church so clearly identified itself with temperance, Chown adamantly refused to allow the Presbyterians and Anglicans to give the fillip to a cause which he deemed to be within the purview of Methodism. Not only was the issue of temperance thereafter greatly downplayed in the Social Service Council, but as a result of Methodist Church protests each constituent unit or church body allied under the umbrella of the Social Service Council was allowed considerable administrative autonomy in making representations to government on the subject.[58] Largely through the influence of Albert Carman, the shared recognition that the Protestant churches must cooperate if they were to ensure that social reform remained under the guidance of Christian institutions won out over what many now viewed as the old-fashioned denominational querulousness. Sensing that the impulse to unite the social reform activities of the Protestant denominations would only intensify, Carman accused the recalcitrant Chown that he would be killing the Methodist Church, which would be left "dead and disgraced," if he failed to make it appreciate the modern need for the institutional cooperation of Christianity to offset the power of organized labour and capital.[59]

J.G. Shearer's vision of a centrally directed national organization of Christian social reform was further eroded by the very character of Protestant social reform whose core support remained at the regional and local levels. During the 1920s the progressive leadership of the mainline denominations faced considerable resistance in harnessing provincial social service councils to the Toronto headquarters of the national body. In 1923 Shearer attempted to subvert provincial autonomy when he proposed that the provincial and dominion councils be collapsed into one unfied office.[60] On this issue, the Methodists, who had themselves once been the advocates of decentralization, strongly supported Shearer's agenda. They sought to reduce the financial independence of the provincial councils which they insisted should be funded solely by the departments of evangelism and social service of the churches. Not only did the churches wish by so doing to eradicate bodies which would compete with them for the collection plate, but they would also effectively bring control of all social reform under the direct auspices of the mainline Christian denominations.[61]

The endemic tensions between the centre and periphery in Canada were graphically illustrated by the persistent failure of the Saskatchewan Social Service Council to bend to Shearer's will. Although just as overtly Christian in their attitude to social reform, the provincial social service councils were far more responsive to the influence of local women's institutes, and so they tended to concentrate more of their energies upon the care of the feeble-minded and the general problem of child welfare than did the national council, whose original focus was on labour conciliation.[62] Moreover, in the case of Saskatchewan, the council's head was the Rev. W.P. Reekie, a Baptist minister who was not appreciative of the incursions of the Presbyterians, Methodists, and Anglicans who dominated the Toronto offices. Reekie's wife was the president of the provincial Women's Christian Temperance Union, a body likewise reluctant to divest its authority over a powerful arm of the reform network. Of Reekie's stubborn defence of his local reform bailiwick, Shearer astutely observed that he "is laying his wires carefully and will have his back to the wall fighting for his official life."[63] Under the pretext of the positive ideal of cooperative social reform lay a much less benign spirit of institutional aggrandizement by the Protestant churches, which sought to divert the energies of all reformers into channels under direct church control. Thus, Moore challenged "the establishment of over-head organizations which tended to become competing rather than co-relating forces," and stated "that we were opposed to any system that had the tendency to take the actual burden of social service activities off of the Churches. We were anxious to get the Evangelistic spirit linked up to the social service activities in the churches, and in order to do that the Churches themselves must be set to work. They are the permanent institutions."[64] After a series of "most unpleasant" meetings, the Social Service Council of Saskatchewan agreed to join the national organization but only on the condition that the Social Service Council of Canada redefine itself as a clearing-house for the separate organizations under its aegis. Thus, rather than dominating reform interests from the centre, the council became the ultimate mediator of social reform initiatives that sprang either from local churches or from local and provincial social service councils.[65]

Sustained by the energies of these local and regional reform movements, the Social Service Council of Canada broadened appreciably its program of social research and reform during the 1920s. Although still wholly engaged in the application of Christian principles to the identification and solution of social problems, it gradually incorporated a wide spectrum of reform organizations which thereby acknowledged the leadership and cultural authority of the Protestant churches. Between 1917 and 1929 the council, reflecting its variegated composition, enshrined three distinct emphases in social legislation. Until 1921 the council's concerns expressed its engagement with organized labour, and then between 1921 and 1925 a second phase of endeavour was dominated by a female-centred agenda that kept questions of child protection and female immigration at the forefront of its social research. During the late 1920s the presence of university social scientists on council committees moved the organization towards the examination of large-scale economic forces affecting Canadian social development.

The Trades and Labor Congress was the first "secular" organization to join the Social Service Council of Canada, largely through the prompting of the Presbyterian Church. Since the first decade of the twentieth century the Presbyterians had invested much energy in considering the problem of the unjust treatment of loggers and navvies in Northern Ontario and the general need to improve working conditions.[66] During the immediate aftermath of World War I, the TLC powerfully shaped the reform program of the council, which was absorbed in debating the merits of the British Whitley Councils and other reforms to the system of industrial relations. In 1921 the TLC reached the apogee of its influence when it induced the Social Service Council to issue a resolution prohibiting the immigration of all labour from Europe with the exception of farm workers and also calling for the permanent exclusion of all Orientals.[67] This policy flew in the face of the generally more open attitude of the mainline Protestant churches. However, between 1921 and 1925 the predominant influence of labour was eclipsed when the Social Service Council added to its original base by gathering into its fold the Dominion Grange, the YMCA, the Women's Christian Temperance Union, the influential National Council of Women, the Victorian Order of Nurses, the Federation of Women's Institutes, the Canadian Council of Agriculture, the Canadian Prisoners' Welfare Association, and the Salvation Army.

From approximately 1911 the Social Service Council of Canada had controlled the program committee of the Annual Conference of Charities and Corrections, a reform organization which by 1914 had become the foremost advocate of a broad range of social insurance schemes – mothers' pensions, industrial insurance, workmen's compensation, and the minimum wage. And, in order to secure the maximum exposure for such unprecedented experiments in state intervention, it invited Lloyd George, the architect of Britain's 1911 unemployment insurance legislation, to speak at its 1914 convention. Although he was unable to attend, the Canadian Conference on Charities and Corrections continued to sponsor speakers like Robert MacIver, the University of Toronto political scientist and member of the Labour Relations Board who defended the Whitley Councils and other reconstruction proposals involving a drastic expansion of state activities. Because of the conference's particularly forward-looking views regarding state supported social welfare, the Social Service Council of Canada was eager to secure its allegiance to its own Christian endeavours. This coup occurred in 1918 when the Canadian Conference on Charities and Corrections became a unit of the council.[68] Similarly, in 1919 the Social Service Council united forces with the Canadian Conference on Public Welfare and in 1921 J.G. Shearer joined its executive.[69]

This new alliances reinvigorated the churches' attitude to full-fledged state intervention in the field of unemployment relief, which had been more quiescent, and may very well have been the inspiration for the report of the Committee on Industrial Life of the Social Service Council of Ontario in 1923, which produced the most advanced and cogent rationale for state care of the unemployed. While it has become commonplace to portray church-sponsored reforms as both facile and moralistic, the 1923 statement of the Ontario council, authored by the Rev. T.R. Robinson, had radically divested itself of the Victorian belief that poverty arose from the inadequacies of individual moral character. Robinson's report, while it echoed in part the 1916 Ontario Royal Commission on Unemployment by recommending that governments must plan ahead during periods of prosperity for cycles of depression by instituting programs of public works, went much further. Not only did it consider the problem of unemployment in terms of world-wide trade patterns – a hallmark of the 1935 treatise, *Social Planning for Canada* – but it also defended a far more overt national government responsibility in protecting "its industrial population from the risk of periodic hard times and enforced idleness" by introducing the notion of contributory social insurance. This, Robinson contended, would remove the social stigma of the "charitable dole." Robinson's analysis of unemployment insurance, which he considered within a broader government plan to ensure full employment, far surpassed Lloyd Georgeism, whose centre-piece of social welfare remained the dole, and in many ways it presaged the later social analysis of William Beveridge.[70] Although Robinson admitted that unemployment insurance was at best only a palliative, he concluded: "perhaps the best that can be done by insurance, is to preserve the worker from absolute destitution when out of work. But a system which could do that, and do it without the demoralizing effects of the dole would be well worth trying. The accumulation, therefore, under Government control or supervision, in times of industrial prosperity, of a fund which would be available in times of depression for the relief of the unemployed in a systematic way seems a necessity." Moreover, Robinson recommended the institution of state pensions which would relieve "the industrial veteran at once of the haunting fear of want and the stigma of charity."[71]

By 1925 the internal structure of the Social Service Council of Canada, with its proliferation of research committees and discussion groups, reflected its increasing specialization and dedication to creating a more scientific foundation for social legislation. The growing presence of university social scientists on these committees had produced a shift in attention from the maternal feminist agenda to the structural problems of the Canadian economy, in particular seasonal unemployment. Although the council's members believed they were still working "in the spirit of the Great Head of the Church,"[72] their examination of the Canadian economy together with their attempts to diagnose modern social problems involved, in their words, the application of more "modern methods" of analysis. Symbolically, the striking of a new Committee on Research coincided with the death of J.G. Shearer in 1926.[73] The Ontario Social Service Council had in fact paved the way for the formalization of the traditional conjunction of interests between social Christianity and university departments of social service when the University of Toronto, represented by the psychologist E.A. Bott, joined the council. By 1929 the regular presence of such university social scientists as E.J. Urwick, T.R. Robinson, Humfrey Michell, W.E. Blatz, J.A. Dale, and W.C. Keirstead consolidated the links between church and university, and at the same time in no small way contributed to enriching the research profile of the council.[74]

This process of integrating university specialists into the efforts of the Social Service Council to further the "intensive Christian conquest of Canada"[75] and to enlighten public opinion through the publication of rigorous social investigation was replicated at its headquarters. There, as early as 1919 a host of university academics joined the Industrial Life and Immigration Committee. Between 1919 and 1922 the Rev. Hugh Dobson, the Rev. Richard Roberts, the Rev. J.M. Shaver, and Nellie McClung were joined by the Baptist A.L. McCrimmon, chancellor of McMaster University, by University of Toronto professors J.A. Dale of the Department of Social Service, Gilbert Jackson of the Department Political Economy, and the Rev. T.R. Robinson of the Department of Philosophy and Psychology, by Professor John Line of Mount Allison University, by Professor Humfrey Michell of the Department of Political Economy at McMaster University, and by J.W. Macmillan, professor of Christian sociology at Victoria College. This committee established a quasi-official relationship with the federal government when, in 1921, at the behest of Gilbert Jackson, J.G. Shearer interviewed newly elected Prime Minister Mackenzie King regarding the need for a scheme for unemployment insurance.[76]

Although the first studies by the committee centred on that traditional aspect of the national economy, immigration, in the early 1920s the focus of its economic research shifted decidedly towards the general problem of "social wealth," with such publications as Jackson's "Co-Management Experiments in Canadian Industry," W.R. Taylor's study of resource and land development, and Michell's report on the employment of women and children in Canadian industry. Perhaps the most path-breaking publication was J.W. Macmillan's "Relation of Wages and Standards of Living in Canada," which centred on the right of the worker to share in surplus wealth, a notion first advanced by the British new liberal thinker, J.A. Hobson. In this publication, Macmillan not only defended the Whitley Councils and the concept of British guild socialism, but he also outlined a broad program of social insurance that included legislation on minimum wages, health insurance, and old-age pensions, and he placed for the first time before the Canadian public the need for governments to address systematically the problem of the unfair distribution of wealth, what later became the guiding concern of all future generations of social planners.[77] In 1922 W.A. Mackintosh of Queen's University joined the Criminology Committee, and in conjunction with E.J. Urwick of the University of Toronto sent recommendations to Prime Minister R.B. Bennett in the early 1930s regarding the reform of the Canadian penal system.[78] Professor Hubert Kemp, a young political economist at the University of Toronto, joined the Committee on Industrial Life, where in 1925 he and Jimmy Simpson of the Toronto Labour Temple interviewed jobless men in a survey modelled on an American report, "One Thousand Jobless Men." Using modern sampling techniques, their study attempted to investigate the "normal" patterns of unemployment among skilled, semi-skilled, and unskilled workers. Although less sophisticated perhaps than later inquiries into joblessness, it remains nevertheless one of the first studies to cite the problem of seasonal unemployment.[79] A similar study of labour needs in agriculture was drawn up by the Rural Life Committee, comprised of Professor W.T.R. Jackman of the University of Toronto, Professor W.C. Keirstead of the University of New Brunswick, and the Rev. John MacDougall.[80] The only committees continuing to reflect strongly the influence of the maternal feminist constituency on the Protestant churches were the Child Welfare Committee, which recommended maternity benefits modelled on Norwegian legislation, and the Committee on the Maintenance of the Integrity of the Family, whose report, although quoting extensively from anthropologist Edward Sapir and sociologist William F. Ogburn, reasserted the traditional Christian prohibition against divorce.[81]

Throughout the 1920s the Social Service Council of Canada generated and published a host of research projects ranging from the Rev. J.W. Macmillan's *Out of Work* in 1925 to town planner A.G. Dalzell's *Housing in Relation to Land Development* and *The Housing of the Working Classes*.[82] In 1927 the Industrial Life Committee published *One Thousand Jobless Men*, undertook research on prison reform, and published *Canada's Child Immigrants*, whose introduction was written by Professor Gilbert Jackson, and Charlotte Whitton's "Child Welfare in Canada in Light of International Discussion."[83] At the Conference on Social Welfare held at Knox Church, Regina, in 1927, the Rev. J.R. Mutchmor presented a paper on "Urban Unemployment." Based on work done in 1925 by the Protestant House of Industry and the Montreal Central Council of Social Agencies on homeless and migratory labour, Mutchmor's study cited the work of British Fabians Sidney and Beatrice Webb on the problem of destitution.[84]

Protestant clergymen continued to identify pressing social problems as the Social Service Council's program of research cohered during the late 1920s, but the council's published studies were increasingly undertaken by such university experts as R. St.J. Macdonald, professor of hygiene at McGill University who wrote *Housing and Health*, and Toronto political economist Hubert Kemp, who penned a number of reports regarding old-age pensions. In 1927 the Committee on Research requested Kemp to undertake a study of "Canada's Old Age Problem and the Homeless Single Man," and later that year he wrote a report comparing the old-age pension schemes of Great Britain, New Zealand, and Australia, for which he also canvassed labour opinion on how best to administer such state welfare initiatives. In 1928 the same committee, in cooperation with the Social Service Council of Ontario, studied the problem of the dependency of the aged in rural counties. This research was collated in the *Preliminary Report on Old Age Pensions*, published in April 1928, which recognized the principle that social security should become integral to any future definition of the standard of living and lent its support to compulsory, universal, and contributory old-age pensions.[85] Having cut his research teeth by formulating social legislation under the auspices of the Protestant churches in the 1920s, Kemp was naturally one of the first members of his department to be sought out by the federal government in the 1930s when it was scouting for experts in the application of knowledge in the social sciences to government policymaking.[86]

Because of the dearth of Canadian and American funding for ongoing social science research and publication in the universities prior to the 1930s,[87] the Social Service Council of Canada functioned as the primary initiator, financier, and publisher of a broad range of social science literature. In a 1928 address, "The Place of Research in Social Service Work," Canon Vernon declared that in order to have business and government value their scientific knowledge, in future all policy recommendations were to be founded upon a well-planned program of research in the most modern methods.[88] The 1928 Committee on Research thus outlined a future agenda that balanced the rising influence of university specialists with that of the council's female reform constituency. Research, the committee declared, should centre on studies of child immigrants, the seasonal unemployment of male workers, mental defectives, Canada's relationship to international labour organizations, and world child welfare work. Indicative of the ground-breaking spirit of the churches, Dobson and Vernon proposed the creation of a Council of Women for the purpose of studying the problem of female immigration.[89]

By providing scholarships for research in the universities at the Master of Arts level, the churches in fact became the initiators of much of the research work in the social sciences that had previously been deemed merely "secular" in its inspiration. A five hundred dollar fund allowed Alburey Castell, one of Hubert Kemp's students, to study "Seasonal and Permanent Unskilled Unemployment in Toronto" in 1930, and another University of Toronto student, Miss Edith M. Martin, to complete her thesis on "History of Delinquency in the Province of Ontario."[90] In 1929 one of C.A. Dawson's sociology students at McGill, Miss Phyllis Heaton, penned a "Study of Income, Standard of Living, and the Normal Amount of Employment in Families of Unskilled Workers in Montreal" at the behest of the Social Service Council, research which she parlayed into an MA degree at McGill, awarded in 1932. Heaton personally visited the homes of workers for the two-fold purpose of assessing current social programs by comparing the social conditions of these families with those of families receiving relief from the Family Welfare Association, and of establishing a floor for normal standards of living upon which to base future social security policies.[91] As a result, in 1931 the Research Committee advised Dawson to begin publishing a collection of studies on a range of social conditions in Montreal.

The Social Service Council of Canada continued to adhere to an all-encompassing Christian world-view in which the promulgation of social reform rested upon both the Christian message of social service and modern social science. Nevertheless, the recognition by Protestant clergymen of the efficacy of expert knowledge in the transformation of the modern state combined with their well-placed concerns over the diminishing financial resources of the churches to sustain a comprehensive program of social research compelled them to summon the federal government in 1930 to establish a Canadian Council on Social and Economic Research on the model of the National Research Council. Significantly, this idea was most actively mooted by the former Methodist field secretary, Ernest Thomas. He was a pertinacious advocate of scientific research on social and industrial problems,[92] and throughout the 1930s an insistent voice urging the United Church to affirm the importance of personal evangelism and the spirit of revivalism.

The vast research program that had characterized the work of the Social Service Council during the 1920s was severely curtailed during the Great Depression by the disastrous shortfall in funding because of the increasingly penurious state of local churches, which had always been the mainstay of the provincial and national councils. For example, contribution to the councils of the Methodist and Presbyterian churches of $2,575 in 1922 had dwindled by 1935 to a meagre $100. As a result of the impoverishment of the main Protestant denominations, the provincial social service councils literally collapsed during the Depression.[93] Although some people, like the Rev. Peter Bryce, attempted to keep the issue of old-age pensions before the Social Service Council of Ontario,[94] and the Social Service Council of Canada not only advocated a uniform system of national relief administration but also recommended laying the foundation of permanent measures to stabilize unemployment,[95] for the most part the attention of Protestant clergymen devolved from the theoretical question of national social security to the more pragmatic and local concern of how best to provide relief to destitute individuals, including their own ministers. The ever present concern for sustaining individual morale which suffused the Social Service Council throughout the Depression not only emanated from clergymen, but the resurgence of interest in the well-springs of individual faith also engulfed social scientists, including Harry Cassidy, whose proposed remedy for unemployment centred upon establishing club life along the lines of wartime YMCA work and the use of special radio broadcasts to rally the morale of the army of unemployed men.[96] However, there was no clear dividing line between clergymen and social scientists on the question of "moral" or "scientific" solutions to the social problems of the Great Depression. Cassidy, who sat on the executive of the Social Service Council, supported the view of clergymen that the unemployed must be presented with high ideals. However, his own plan for using direct relief methods, which revolved around the long-standing social work practice of individual casework, centred upon identifying deserving and undeserving poor,[97] and thus diverged from the position of the mainline churches that the concept of social welfare should replace the older idea of charity. In 1931 Canon Vernon wrote: "[w]e must create such conditions in society as shall make it possible for every life to grow up strong, pure and fit – a vast undertaking calling for a synthetic, scientific, sociological, and Christian programme."[98]

More tellingly, the final collective effort at social research sponsored by the Social Service Council was the Machine Age Series of pamphlets, published during the mid-1930s. With the exception of the work by D.L. Ritchie, dean of United College in Montreal, who contributed *Youth and the Machine Age*, the volumes in the series were written by social scientists, including Irene Biss and D.C. MacGregor of the Department of Political Economy at the University of Toronto, W.M. Drummond, professor of rural economics, also at Toronto, Mossie May Kirkwood, a lecturer at Trinity College in Toronto, George Britnell of the Department of Political Economy at the University of Saskatchewan, and Eugene Forsey of McGill University. While never overtly acknowledged by the collective authorship of *Social Planning for Canada*, the concept of the "Machine Age" developed by the Social Service Council frequently found its way into the policy prescriptions of the League for Social Reconstruction.[99] Opening with an analysis of the process of industrialization in the century since 1833, in her work Irene Biss asserted that Canadian society in that period had achieved political democracy and nationhood and had experienced many of the benefits of advances in science and the resulting efficiency in industry, with the result that even those workers on relief during the depths of the Depression probably possessed a higher standard of living than had the pioneer backwoodsman. However, the economic insecurity characterizing the lives of many Canadians constituted an indictment of the industrial order, which had brought no permanent benefit to the ordinary worker,[100] and worse, had negated democracy by dividing society into the propertied classes, who dominated government, and workers, who were paid a wage.[101] As D.C. MacGregor bluntly informed clergymen and social scientists, there now existed in Canada a "proletariat" which numbered about two million people or sixty per cent of all workers. The potentially explosive character of these masses of economically insecure workers was, for MacGregor, telling evidence that "the present chaotic order of things cannot be endured much longer, not even by capitalists."[102] Likewise, Ritchie warned that the Depression had, by dashing the hopes of Canadian youth, made them prey for Fascist and Communist movements.[103]

Despite this arraignment of the inefficiencies and inequalities of capitalism, the authors of the Machine Age series stopped well short of proposing political socialism. Their prescriptions for social change were characterized by a nostalgic yearning for the independence and self-sufficiency of the small farmer. Both W.M. Drummond and G.E. Britnell sought to awaken social scientists and government to the need to stabilize the economic position of the small family farm as the basic remedy for the Depression. Echoing many of the concerns of the earlier church-sponsored rural surveys, they lamented that farming had ceased to be a way of life and that the farmer was now dependent upon cities and factories.[104] As Britnell stated in *The Western Farmer*, there was a real danger that the precarious nature of the wheat economy, graphically illustrated during the Depression, would compel the Western Canadian farmer to lower his standard of living in the direction of that of the European peasant. This, in turn, would have dire consequences for Eastern Canadian industry, which depended upon a healthy demand for manufactured goods for its own economic health.[105]

Although each of the Machine Age Series pamphlets recognized the complexity and alienation of modern society and industrial working conditions, all of them except Forsey's, which proposed noncontributory unemployment insurance through a graduated income tax – a clearly socialistic solution to the machine age[106] – sought to extend the scope of state regulation of the economy in the name of preserving capitalism and the cherished values of individual freedom.[107] The belief that society rested in the final analysis on what Britnell termed individual "moral fibre"[108] meant that any demand for state intervention was cast in terms of preserving an older ideal of community founded upon individual fulfilment. This frame of reference characterized both Britnell's call for more scientific land management and settlement policies and MacGregor's vision of "a more stable and more skilfully regulated system" in which economic security would be achieved through combining steady and productive employment with a comprehensive system of unemployment insurance.[109]

Irene Biss, later a member of the League for Social Reconstruction, concluded that the ideal society was one in which social harmony was created by the possession of common ideals – rather than legislative intervention – and where personal development was realized by "joining joyfully in the search for higher values and finer interests."[110] And like D.L. Ritchie, Biss promoted pensions and unemployment insurance with the aim of recovering Canada's lost innocence and the self-determinism of the now receding frontier age. "The social group has grown so great," wrote Biss, a devotee of new liberal thinker Graham Wallas, "that the friendliness of a small community is lost in a sea of acquaintanceship, and in the 'artificial brotherliness' of service clubs."[111] Mossie May Kirkwood, a student of the philosopher George Sidney Brett and a self-proclaimed disciple of new liberalism and American progressivism, sought like the Protestant clergymen to balance the claims of individual and society. "A social order or economic system that denies any individual the fulfilment of self-realization," according to her, "denies God."[112] Her pamphlet, *Women and the Machine Age*, a paean to the rights of women, adopted an individualistic perspective similar to that of Biss: "When with blood and tears the parts of society are all become individuals, there will be a new and fuller co-operation than has ever been possible for our race."[113] The increasing insistence that individualism must balance "social control" was evident in the 1934 meeting of the Canadian Institute on Economics and Politics, whose membership comprised Biss, F.H. Underhill, F.R. Scott, H.M. Cassidy – all members of the League for Social Reconstruction – Professor John Line of the Fellowship for a Christian Social Order, C.B. Sissons, and Hubert Kemp of the University of Toronto, when it agreed to invite Reinhold Niebuhr, the Neo-Orthodox American critic of the social gospel, to conduct the institute's course on "Objectives and Methods in Social Reconstruction" as well as its Sunday morning devotional service.[114]

Although the Machine Age Series was immensely popular, with a sale of 12,000 copies which raised considerable funds for the ailing Social Service Council,[115] this was to be the last major publication project of the council, for after 1935 it entered a period of increasing internal divisiveness and rancour. Alluding to an article by W.B. Creighton in the *New Outlook*, entitled "A Christian Social Service Council for Canada?"

in March 1936 a disenchanted Hugh Dobson remarked about Creighton's disingenuous attempt to resurrect the council: "of course he knows well that the Social Service Council is dead in western Canada," except for a single local branch, the Vancouver Social Service Council; as he protested to the Rev. Hugh Rae, if the church was unable to sustain its own work, it would be a pipedream to expect it to fund the Social Service Council.[116] These obvious financial disabilities encumbering the smooth operation of the Social Service Council of Canada were further compounded by the appointment in 1934 to the executive secretaryship of the council of the Rev. Claris Silcox, a Congregational minister whose experience as a researcher for the American Rockefeller-funded Institute of Social and Religious Research had brought him to the attention of Canadian progressive clergymen who believed that his skills as an "outstanding social engineer" would further amplify the important research profile of the council.[117] After the lacklustre leadership of the little-known Rev. J. Phillips Jones, who had succeeded the outstanding Canon C.W. Vernon, Silcox, with expertise in social psychology and sociology which had secured him the attention of prominent American social scientists, was expected to confer greater national prestige upon the Social Service Council.[118] Despite his impressive credentials, Silcox was perceived by many progressive clergymen as an outsider, an assessment strengthened by Silcox's domineering desire to impose his own pet research topics upon the social agenda of the council, most notably the study of Catholic-Protestant relations. Rather than acting as an intermediary between churches and government on social issues, Silcox, out of his concern for eradicating religious prejudice, became, for example, consumed in the fruitless task of writing to Adolf Hitler on the need to restore religious liberty in Germany.[119]

As it turned out, Protestant leaders had not appointed a fellow progressive. The rise during the Depression of the aggressively secular political ideologies of Fascism and Communism had pushed Silcox towards the far right and towards a world-view that severed the progressive equipoise of Christian social endeavour by irrevocably pitting the "purely secular" against "the totalitarian spiritual life."[120] In a statement that clearly turned its back on the path towards increasing government management of social security paved by the council during the 1920s, Silcox remarked in 1935 that the government should regard people as one family whose "moral and spiritual good must be ministered to by industry and finance."[121] More tellingly, Silcox sought to turn the council away from social research and towards an agenda of moral reform,[122] which placed him in decided opposition to the program fostered by J.G. Shearer and Canon Vernon. As a powerful illustration of Silcox's breach with the traditions of Christian social science, the hallmark of the Social Service Council of Canada, was the fact that despite pressure from E.J. Urwick, a strong defender of the harmonious relationship between churches and university, Silcox intervened in 1934 to prevent the council from accepting the invitation of the lieutenant governor of Ontario to participate in the very important Royal Commission on Housing.[123]

Moreover, by attempting arbitrarily to appropriate the temperance campaign from the United Church, Silcox alienated the council's most important constituency. Thereafter, key progressives like Hugh Dobson fiercely defended local church control against the incursions of the council, by using the argument that it had abandoned its earlier concern for the "whole gospel." In Dobson's estimation, all social service work must be reclaimed by the church boards of evangelism and social service, which alone would ensure "full Evangelical activity."[124] As a result of Silcox's meddling, church progressives began to bypass the Social Service Council, and in 1937 they were determined to issue their own Labour Day messages in response to the conflict between Premier Mitch Hepburn and the Committee for Industrial Organization (CIO) in Ontario.[125] Since the early 1930s, mainly because of an awareness of the immense financial outlay involved in social research, many clergymen were anxious to devolve responsibility for such work to independent specialists.[126] However, Silcox's militant and other-worldly attitude that religion must be removed from contact with secular forces succeeded in alienating whole reform organizations that had once willingly collaborated under church leadership. As a result, in 1935 Charlotte Whitton and Howard Falk led an unfriendly campaign to have their Canadian Council on Child and Family Welfare take over the leadership of the Social Service Council.[127] Thus, Silcox's warning that the churches would falter unless they formed a united Christian front against all secular forces became a self-fulfilling prophecy. Just prior to his departure from the council to assume a position with the ultra-right-wing Leadership League of Canada, Silcox declaimed upon the decline of the church that he himself had been so instrumental in bringing about: "The future of the Church depends upon its capacity to make a clear testimony to the implications of its gospel for the whole of life. The spiritual task today has become social, as the social question has become, *in esse*, spiritual. We venture to affirm that if the Church fails in providing the necessary leadership in this field, no success in other departments of its work will free it from the stigma of universal failure."[128]

After shattering not just the consensus between social reform and Christian endeavour but also the balance between provincial and federal legislative issues, and after withdrawing the vital succour that evangelism had always provided Christian social activism, the Social

Service Council of Canada, now a hollow organization renamed the Christian Social Council of Canada, was entrusted to the care of the Rev. J.R. Mutchmor. Although a defender of the idea of government planning for social security measures along the new liberal lines of Beveridge, Keynes, and Leonard Marsh, Mutchmor was forced to relinquish much of the council's sponsorship of government legislation, and it was henceforth confined to addressing only those issues that remained outside the purview of the now more powerful Canadian Welfare Council.[129] The Social Service Council of Canada, once the clearing-house for the entire spectrum of social reform, was forced to reclaim what public influence it could by joining the Canadian Council of Churches in 1940.

Although the intensive research program of the Social Service Council of Canada came to an abrupt end in the waning years of the Depression, it had nonetheless contributed to the transformation of the modern governing process by establishing the practice whereby social legislation was formulated on the basis of the systematic collection and interpretation of social data. This tradition, which is usually associated with the university experts who flocked to the federal bureaucracy during World War II, actually began under the auspices of the Protestant churches during the 1920s. The Social Service Council of Canada certainly helped in fostering this transition towards a more élitist and specialized form of social policymaking by being the first private institution to funnel university social scientists into the corridors of government. What is significant, however, is that despite the increasing presence of social scientists within the various research committees of the council throughout the 1920s and 1930s, the Protestant churches continued to assume the crucial leadership role in the identification of social problems and the funding of research. Until the mid-1930s the balance of power still lay with progressive clergymen and their diverse network of reform groups that were firmly connected to local and provincial interests. Thus, this early impetus for the creation of modern social welfare policies was not only more accessible to public discussion and therefore less élitist than its reincarnation in the 1940s, but it remained inextricably wedded to a Christian world-view.

7 The United Church and the "Revival of Personal Religion"[1]

By the late 1930s an increasing number of Protestant leaders began to view the Great Depression as not only the result of a man-made international economic disequilibrium but also as a great spiritual crisis. They were responding to the powerful resurgence among a majority of ordinary Canadians of a desire to rediscover the well springs of individual Christian piety and inner faith. Like the social scientists H.M. Cassidy, who interpreted the worst ravage of the hard times as a psychological erosion of inner faith, and Gilbert Jackson, who in 1933 identified the root cause of the economic Depression in terms of human sin and located its solution in the transcendence of selfishness through inner contemplation,[2] Protestant clergymen, while often divided over state-directed remedies, unanimously agreed with the call of the Board of Evangelism and Social Service of the United Church for "an inner transformation divinely wrought" and a regimen of private prayer and self-discipline as the prelude to a new age of religious revival.[3] In so doing, church leaders like T. Albert Moore sought to give concrete expression to a renewed, spontaneous popular interest in the individual spiritual life. Writing in 1933, Moore noted with pleasure the increased attendance at church services and the general revival of interest in family and private prayer, Sunday observances, and Bible reading. More astonishing to this veteran clergyman, however, was "the remarkable freedom with which people generally on trains, in hotels, and other unusual places, discuss the place of Jesus in their lives." Unsolicited, strangers would speak to him "of their comfort and strength [they received] from our Heavenly Father, through prayer and faith, in their special times of trial and need." Even in this, the worst year of the Great Depression, Moore emphatically concluded that the Christian faith "is certainly winning a notable influence in the lives of the Canadian people."[4] In a startling re-ordering of the relationship between social Christianity and individual conversion, D.N. McLachlan, head of the Board of Evangelism and Social Service, instructed ministers to harness this pervasive ground swell of the popular search for an immediate heartfelt experience of God's presence by reinstituting the revival meeting. As he announced: "It has been said that if religion ends with the individual, *it ends*. A truth more far-reaching is the fact that unless religion *begins* with the individual, it *never begins*."[5]

It has been argued that the 1930s were a disheartening time in the United Church of Canada because of its supposed inability to foster religious revival. The new church could neither articulate a coherent theological statement nor formulate an acceptable course of social action. Such an argument confuses the vitality of the religious experience with the achievement of doctrinal consistency. Even though mainstream Protestant evangelicalism continued during this period to be defined in non-theological and strongly experiential terms, the 1930s were nevertheless characterized by a tremendous efflorescence of religious commitment among a vast number of Canadians who, like their pastors, interpreted economic difficulty in terms of spiritual crisis.

Hugh Dobson reported after a tour of drought-stricken Saskatchewan that ordinary believers were eager as never before to participate in evangelistic activity because they considered economic catastrophe to be the inevitable outcome of a failure of "human atonement" and therefore wished above all to reclaim the "sacredness of human personality,"[6] The fact that social Christianity became a contentious issue for Protestants because of the spectre of political socialism, Communism, and Fascism has led some scholars to the rash conclusion that the consequent questioning of the ability of social Christianity to provide a ready solution to the Depression meant that Canadian society was declining into secularism.[7] The decade of the 1930s was in fact one of intense religious activity which took the form not of the direct application of Christian principles to social reform, but of the revival of pietistic spirituality. It was from this inner contemplation of God alone that, in the estimation of both clergymen and their congregations, any true outward improvement in the social order would be accomplished. In other words, social policy was but the outer, and secondary, expression of the more concrete inner evangelical apprehension of God. Even the most socially radical clergymen, Ernest Thomas, for example, who belonged to the Fellowship for a Christian Social Order and who adhered to the statist vision of social planning promulgated by the

League for Social Reconstruction, insisted that the present crisis could not be wholly solved by the external reorganization of the economic structure. Thomas explained his reservations concerning the manipulation of social policy by technocratic experts to the Rev. J.W.A. Nicholson, a member of the league, by observing that no "radical changes" could be effected without "a change of mind and heart" brought about solely through repentance of sin. Thomas endorsed the view of the Rev. John Line that the promotion of state intervention by the Fellowship for a Christian Social Order was of "limited influence," and he affirmed that the Depression was first and foremost an "ethical issue" to be solved by the campaigns of evangelization of the churches, which would inspire "a newness of thought, conviction and life."[8]

Rather than declining during the Depression, the Protestant churches experienced a momentous upsurge both in church membership and in the number of people openly declaring their commitment to evangelical and orthodox Christianity. Even ministers who expected a high level of church adherence were surprised at the extraordinary demonstration of religious sentiment among ordinary Canadians and at the public demand for revivalistic services, especially among Canadian youth who were particularly receptive to preaching animated with "profound conviction."[9] The Rev. Charles Daniel reported to his fellow United Church ministers in 1935 that in Peterborough, Ontario, the evangelistic meetings of the Rev. H.L. Stephens, who had conducted a series of successful mass revivals after World War I, were so large that the Sunday services had to be moved to the local theatre. More stunning still was the fourfold increase in attendance at prayer meetings.[10]

Nor was this religious movement confined to rural areas and small towns; from Alf Bailey's account of the marvellous spiritual occurrences in Winnipeg, it is clear a strong popular demand existed for a style of preaching that would induce a definite moment of conversion. Indeed, it appeared that Dr Bonnell's message at Winnipeg, which "thrill[ed] with its appeal for complete surrender," was the reason why Westminster United, one of the largest of the city's churches, was bursting at the seams well before the start of the Sunday morning service. Here, as Bailey noted, Protestants took their church attendance very seriously indeed.[11] Similarly, the Rev. J.W.H. Milne of Ottawa reported a dramatic increase in attendance at Bible classes and prayer meetings full to overflowing, a situation that was so encouraging he urgently pressed church leaders to launch a mass evangelistic crusade from coast to coast in order to tap this unprecedented popular yearning for a personal relationship with God through Christ. As he stated in 1933, "[t]here is no other explanation but the hunger of hearts for the Word of God begotten by the Spirit of God." He noted that because of the swelling ranks of committed Christians, the congregation was compelled to move its prayer meetings from the Ladies' Parlour to the more capacious Sunday School Hall of Chalmers Church.[12] Such revivals of personal spirituality had become commonplace in many local churches by the mid-1930s. At Shaughnessy Heights United Church in Vancouver, the Rev. G.P. McLeod was awestruck at the distinct and rapid shift in popular piety towards more spiritual and overtly biblical preaching. "It was surprising to find that the sermons on the Holy Spirit and the Resurrection brought more response than any I have preached for some time. I can only attribute this to a rapidly deepening conviction of the reality of the 'Living Christ,' not a concept for study & teaching, but as a personal presence in my own life."[13]

As a result of the demand of numerous Christian people for "real spiritual fellowship,"[14] as early as 1930 the United Church had begun to divest itself of its emphasis on practical Christianity, the defining principle of the Protestant progressive leadership throughout the 1920s. Indeed, the new denomination sought to recapture and bring to national prominence the powerful stream of local evangelism that had quietly simmered beneath the official promotion of social Christianity.[15] Just as popular piety had so forcefully shaped the attitudes and methods of the Protestant progressives, so in the early 1930s the subterranean stream of evangelical Christianity again resurfaced. However, amidst the vicissitudes of economic collapse, this current even more powerfully determined the official agenda of the United Church, which took steps to strengthen the forces of evangelization to such a degree that the tenets of social Christianity were eviscerated from the definition of Christian experience and absorbed into the primacy of personal evangelism and the essential experience of conversion. Indeed, it could be argued that the United Church had returned to the religious paradigm of the 1890s, when the goals of social reformation were fulfilled by the endeavours of individual Christians rather than accomplished under the auspices of Christianized institutions. As D.N. McLachlan, the secretary of the United Church Board of Evangelism and Social Service, confided to George Pidgeon, chairman of the Committee for the Evangelization of Canadian Life, "[l]aymen at the last General Council stated it was never so easy to talk religion as to-day. In addition to the efforts of the Church, Statesmen, Economists, Educators and Sociologists have frankly confessed that beneath the special form of disorder which confronts each of them, there is the acknowledged fact that in modern society its members lack that peace and courage derived only from life in God."[16]

There was no better barometer of the quickening movement among Canadians for personal evangelism than the success enjoyed in the early 1930s by the Oxford Group, an interdenominational society devoted to fostering spiritual renewal and public conversion through small fellowship meetings held for the most part in private homes. Like progressive clergymen, the Oxford Group leaders gave priority to religious experience rather than to theological or doctrinal questions, which were deemed divisive.[17] In common with the United Church's own prescription for personal evangelism, the Oxford Group believed that the key to resolving the social and economic problems wrought by the Depression was a changed heart and spirit.[18] Rather than being a right-wing lunatic fringe, the Oxford Group, at least in the early 1930s, occupied the broad centre of evangelical culture, as seen in its insistence upon a definite conversion experience and upon its "quiet time" in which the individual, through inner contemplation of personal sin, was brought into closer intimacy with God.[19] The Oxford Group movement eventually secured the warm endorsement of the United Church: more than any other technique of revivalism, it rekindled the spiritual fellowship with God that had so pervaded early Methodism. The Rev. J.W.H. Milne's description of the moving of the spirit among his Ottawa congregation was strangely evocative of the pietistic strain of early nineteenth-century Methodism, especially its power to stir women to acceptance of God's grace: "There was not a weak link in the chain. Everyone had liberty and spoke with earnestness and power. There was such a pleasing balance such a delightful harmony that one could feel the Divine guidance."[20]

In the early 1930s, it should be stressed, the United Church had itself experienced a quickening of inner spirituality among ordinary churchgoers. This tremendous emotional release translated itself into a renewed commitment among leading clergymen to the value of evangelization through a combination of small fellowship meetings and mass revivals. D.N. McLachlan saw the Depression as a great opportunity for a great "spiritual awakening" and he instructed ministers to organize revivals and institute "the clinic idea" of the pastor attending to the personal crises of each member of their congregation.[21] In order to give this inchoate movement of popular piety a permanent institutional expression, the United Church established a Joint Committee on the Evangelization of Canadian Life in 1931.[22] The increasing porousness of the boundary between the Oxford Group and the United Church's campaign of evangelization was demonstrated by George Pidgeon's leadership role in both movements.

Many United Church ministers who admired the Oxford Group's ability to touch "the heart of the masses,"[23] including Pidgeon, were won over to its encouragement of a decisive moment of emotional release and conversion. Almost the entire cohort of progressive clergymen who were active during the 1920s lent their weight to Pidgeon's campaign of personal evangelism. J.R. Mutchmor, James Shaver of All People's Mission, S.D. Chown, T. Albert Moore, Richard Roberts, and D.N. McLachlan all supported the evangelistic aims of the Oxford Group. Even that "apostle of radical economic change," Salem Bland, gave his unqualified support.[24] The only leading progressives to dissent from the Oxford Group were Hugh Dobson and Ernest Thomas. T. Albert Moore, the perennial head of the church's Department of Evangelism and Social Service, praised the Oxford Group for its devotional quality. "My impression is that a visit to Toronto would be of great spiritual helpfulness," he wrote Pidgeon in 1932.[25] His only reservation about forging closer links between the Oxford Group and the United Church was the large financial responsibility that would be incurred.[26] The Rev. Richard Roberts, who was involved with the group, admired its preoccupation with Bible study and prayer, and in fact he promoted many of its methods, most notably "the quiet time," in his column in the *New Outlook*, "The Quiet Hour."

In short, there was little to distinguish the group's methods from the traditional evangelism familiar to both United Church clergymen and their congregations. Many ministers even approved of the group's practice of public confession, because they too identified this as the true benchmark of Christian commitment; however, they were nonetheless leery of the process of "confession" or "sharing" because it depended upon the concept of "absolute honesty," which was often far too explicit concerning sexual sins.[27] Despite the opprobrium levelled against such a complete baring of the soul, seen as offensive to middle-class sensibilities, the priority given to public confession remained the core of the Oxford Group movement and it was "essential to multitudes of people."[28] The Rev. Albert E. Jones, pastor of King Street United Church in Toronto, saw nothing objectionable in either the methods or the doctrine of the Oxford Group, and was indeed abashed to discover that the influential Ernest Thomas and W.B. Creighton were so critical of what he believed was a respectable and effective form of evangelism.[29] Supporters of the Oxford Group were particularly aggrieved by the negative response of the *New Outlook*, because they perceived Creighton as squelching evangelistic zeal. So completely had the piety of the Oxford Group, with its emphasis upon personal repentance of sins and conversion, captured the hearts of United Church congregations that by 1936 Creighton was ostracized from every United Church in Toronto and was forced to seek refuge there at Yorkminster Baptist Church.[30]

This new emphasis on intense inner piety thus accorded well with the views of many United Church ministers, most notably D.N. McLachlan, who thought that the Oxford Group had been responsible for the greatest spiritual renewal among United Church clergymen in many years.

Although McLachlan was somewhat perplexed by its style of evangelism, which lacked the traditional sermon, hymn-singing, and exhortation, and was wary of its practice of public confession, he nevertheless observed to Pidgeon that "rarely have the Ministers of this community been so completely stirred to deep heart searching," or had so many Protestants experienced such "a glow and release which brought radiant joy and for the time, marked ethical change." McLachlan's statement regarding the Oxford Group movement represented the official position of the United Church, given his position as secretary of the Department of Evangelism and Social Service. "The Oxford Group has shown quite clearly that people can be spiritually influenced by a direct appeal," he informed Pidgeon in 1933. "The Church is ... challenged afresh to procedures which she has neglected. It has been demonstrated that great numbers of people are waiting to be challenged personally for complete decision; and it is clear that the general desire for needed social changes will be fruitless without changed persons."[31]

As early as 1932 McLachlan was instructing ministers that the valuable qualities of the Oxford Group movement should be "conserved and utilized." Indeed, by the mid-1930s the United Church had quietly integrated the Oxford Group's approach to personal evangelism into its discipline of preaching and prayer meetings, and it thus avoided the financial drain which direct association would have entailed. So successful was the incorporation of the movement into the United Church's campaign for evangelization that even Pidgeon conceded that there was no longer a need to mention the Oxford Group by name, for its influence had so suffused the United Church "many religious folk" were now stirred to give either public or private testimony which lifted them into fresh experiences of God's saving grace. Speaking before the United Church's Committee on Evangelism and Social Service, Pidgeon stated: "Testimonies are being given in our churches of the power of God now present to save ... Out through the country people are inquiring into its meaning and longing to hear for themselves of these wonderful works of God."[32] Here was telling evidence that the time was right for a massive national campaign of religious revival, which did in fact occur all across Canada during 1935.[33]

The Oxford Group's appeal lay largely with the middle classes;[34] nevertheless, it held the allegiance of a vast number of Canadians who responded positively to its message of the certainty conferred by absolute personal and direct surrender to God's will. The Oxford Group has frequently been dismissed as a shallow and banal religious phenomenon whose appeal was confined largely to Toronto and south-western Ontario.[35] While it did excite Christian enthusiasm, particularly among university students,[36] it also won favour among a wide constituency of men and women of all ages and social backgrounds who were united in their need for Christian earnestness. So overwhelming was the demand for personal religion that even when the Oxford Group evangelists were having an "off morning" at Knox Church in Winnipeg, and in their own estimation were failing to make a large dent in the congregation, they still attracted 1,800 people to their evangelistic services. At this particular church, even the small fellowship groups boasted an average attendance of 100.[37] Despite its decided emphasis upon inner spiritual life, the group even appealed to those who, like Mr and Mrs J.C. Fletcher, were "keenly interested in the social problems of the day, and [were] endeavouring by a study of economic history to arrive at the cause & possible cure for these ills, as far as individuals can do so."[38]

In 1933 the Rev. Milne attested to the widespread influence of the Oxford Group meetings throughout the Ottawa Valley, where often no fewer than 4,000 decision cards[39] were accepted at one time: "we are able to certify that there is no abatement of interest that men and women of all ages are standing firm with no sign of backsliding; that there is no hysteria that there have been no subjects for the psychiatrists that all the churches have been quickened, and that there is a new note in the preaching of ministers who had contact with the Oxford Group."[40] The presence in Montreal of Leslie Pidgeon, a forceful preacher and the brother of George Pidgeon, the leading Canadian advocate of the Oxford Group's evangelism, ensured that the group expanded most rapidly throughout the Montreal-Ottawa corridor during 1932, but by 1933 its emphasis upon "personal relations with God" had made it a real force within evangelism throughout small-town Ontario and Western Canada. In 1933 the Rev. Walter Steven of Park Baptist Church, Brantford, was optimistic about the further growth of the movement because, from his experience, such intimate fellowship had gone far in "deepening the spiritual experience" of Canadians.[41]

It is not surprising that the Oxford Group was able to penetrate the already religiously conservative rural and small-town localities.[42] More remarkable was the fact that it quickly assumed the character of a national movement, spreading in 1934 from London westward to Vancouver and eastward to Halifax. The group was able to exert such an influence because, as George Pidgeon himself noted, its insistence upon the immediate and personal knowledge of God which circumvented even the local pastor[43] allowed ordinary Canadians to recover a modicum of control over their religious lives; as he stated, "[h]ere to desire is to receive." The key to its widespread popularity was the experience of feeling wholly possessed by the spirit, which harkened back to the folk culture of traditional evangelical piety.[44] In 1933 Alice S. Lewis expressed well the personalist and religiously traditional temper of the times when she confided to George Pidgeon: "I was so glad you mentioned the fact that the life of absolute surrender is only possible as we let the grace of God operate in our hearts through faith in our Lord Jesus Christ, not of works, lest any man should boast. Your Bible studies always encourage me to go back to the word of God to find out for myself whether these things are so & so your message sticks."[45] The very act of surrendering one's life entirely into God's hands removed the sense of personal failure which so haunted Canadians during the Depression. Unlike the progressive leadership, which had continually stressed that the responsibility for conversion ultimately lay with the individual, George Pidgeon, perhaps in response to people's frustrations at being unable to change their lives, defined the evangelical experience as one in which the whole conversion experience rested with the Almighty. Pidgeon outlined his optimistic and reassuring attitude to conversion: "So often we make the mistake of thinking of self-surrender as something we must do ourselves; in reality it is letting Him 'work in us to will and to do of His good pleasure.' Salvation is all of grace; that is, Christ gives and gives continually and we must be ready to receive."[46] Given the contemplative nature of the Oxford Group movement's evangelism, it is not surprising that the Rev. Allan Shatford remarked upon "the naturalness & joyousness of the Group – religion seems to have made them so radiant & so unaffected."[47]

In that definite moment of grace which conversion provided, those weary of the tedium of joblessness could find solace in renewal and a new beginning. Dorothy Newhold of Toronto was particularly touched by George Pidgeon's radio address, "Growth in Grace," and she was especially attracted to his method of "sharing" because it was so "definite."[48] More compelling still was the marvellous flexibility Pidgeon's evangelism offered, for as he told Miss Newhold, "the wonderful thing is how closely they [the resources of grace] apply to each person's peculiar circumstances."[49] In an era dominated by the arbitrariness of impersonal economic forces, evangelism returned to the individual a powerful sense of self-worth. Wrote one observer of the Oxford Group movement, "[t]ransformed lives are self-authenticating."[50] As King Gordon, a hostile critic of evangelism, averred, it "is very much easier to get the sense of release from the inner sins than from the great social sins under which we suffer."[51] Here lay the secret to the tremendous upsurge in the strength of evangelism after the Crash of 1929. Undoubtedly there was a clear and demonstrated interest among numerous Canadians for the emotional and spiritual awakening that only a conversion could provide. Although the Oxford Group's emphasis on public "sharing" was often criticized by officials in the United Church because of its potential salaciousness, public declaration was welcomed by ordinary Christians who saw it as the definitive method for individuals to renounce their sins and embark upon a new religious life.[52] Some historians have given undue weight to the protests of such church leaders as the fundamentalist Baptist T.T. Shields and those associated with the United Church publication, the *New Outlook*,[53] against the group's method of "sharing" one's personal sins. They have taken this criticism as the benchmark of church opinion and of the failure of personal evangelism in the 1930s. However, as the testimony of many rank-and-file believers clearly demonstrates, a distinction must be made between the opinions of some church officials and popular religious sentiment. By viewing the Oxford Group through the perspective of ordinary believers, it was a movement whose roots extended deeply into the subsoil of popular religious mores. The disjuncture between certain key church leaders and the populace was well articulated by Althea Dobie of Port Arthur, Ontario, when she informed Pidgeon in 1933 that "[a]lthough our ministers are divided in opinion, many, many people are anxious to hear for themselves the astonishing testimony of these Christians."[54]

The intense appeal of the Oxford Group movement throughout the evangelical community was commented upon by John Stevenson, a student at Queen's University. "After hearing both your sermon and your talk afterwards at Chalmers Church last night," he wrote George Pidgeon, "I should like to write you just a few lines in appreciation for what you have done. I have heard an awful lot of discussion upon it since you came, and I feel that apart from myself, sir, you helped a very large number of people last night very much, even though in this somewhat Presbyterian little Town they don't show it!"[55] Having taken hold of the popular desire for personal evangelism, the Oxford Group's impact extended far beyond its own rather evanescent institutional life in Canada. Rather than failing in 1934, as Marshall has concluded, it was overwhelmingly successful, for by that time it had inserted itself into the broad stream of evangelical worship in the mainline churches, which in fact had been the goal of its chief Canadian promoter, George Pidgeon. In reflecting upon the United Church's national campaign of evangelizing Canadian life, Pidgeon declared in 1933: "[t]he Movement here has grown far beyond the Oxford Group. From all parts of the city people are coming to ministers sympathetic to the Movement revealing the deepest moral and spiritual changes. The spirit has become atmospheric and is touching many who never attended the meetings. If anyone had told me a month ago that the changes I have seen and dealt with were possible I should have treated the idea as absurd."[56]

While the Oxford Group movement did not in itself instigate the United Church's change of direction towards evangelization, it did, nonetheless, through reviving the spiritual intensity of the old-fashioned class meeting by its fellowship meetings,[57] become an effective means for channelling the popular ground swell of traditional piety into the institutional churches. Thus, the importance of the movement was its ability to affect the upsurge in popular evangelism that characterized Canadian religious life in the 1930s. It was for this reason that D.N. McLachlan, secretary of the United Church's Board of Evangelism and Social Service, who was himself at the forefront among progressive clergymen in reinterpreting social evangelism so that the primacy of individual sin might be restored, hailed the arrival of the Oxford Group revivalists in 1932 as "Providential."[58]

Certainly George Pidgeon's dual role as leader of the Oxford Group and as chairman of the United Church's Committee on the Evangelization of Canadian Life demonstrated the all-pervasive character of popular evangelism and its ability to penetrate all facets of Protestant culture during the Depression. For over two decades Pidgeon stood near the centre of the Protestant progressive leadership, serving both on the Presbyterian Church Board of Social Service and Evangelism and the Social Service Council of Canada. By so forcefully throwing himself into the evangelistic cause in the early 1930s, he incarnated the transformed spirit of Canadian Protestantism during the Depression decade. Pidgeon explained this marvellous efflorescence of interest in conversion and revivalism in Canada to Frank Buchman, the American Oxford Group leader: "The interest in the Movement is both deepening and widening. Every Sunday some of those who have been changed are going out into the churches with their testimony and the requests for such services are so numerous that they are being almost overwhelmed."[59]

While the increasing popularity of inner piety among many Canadian Protestants in large part explains the resurgence of personal evangelism during the 1930s, church officials also embraced this spirituality precisely because it allowed them, in the politically charged cultural environment of the Depression, to circumvent the divisiveness of social Christianity. Traditional piety had always shaped the views of the church leadership, and during the 1920s it had been responsible for anchoring social Christianity to the tenets of individual religious experience. However, the cultural dominance of evangelicalism was even more evident during the 1930s, in large part because it converged with the views of the church leaders who were becoming wary of the political implications of social action. With the rise of clearly non-Christian political ideologies, such as materialistic socialism and Fascism, social evangelism had become much more politicized than it had been during the 1920s when social welfare policy and the movement towards increasing state intervention fell almost wholly under the aegis of the Protestant churches.

Significantly, until 1932–33, with the creation of the Co-operative Commonwealth Federation and its adoption of the Regina Manifesto calling for the eradication of capitalism and the extreme centralization of government control of the economy, the progressive equipoise between social reform and individual piety seemed to be holding firm within the United Church. During the early stages of the Depression, Protestant progressives, such as J.R. Mutchmor, were extremely optimistic over the capacity of practical Christianity to solve what was then considered a temporary economic downturn. Even in 1931 Mutchmor still privileged the social over the spiritual. "These are tragic times for all of us," he wrote to the Rev. R.B. Cochrane. "They would be almost overwhelming were it not for the growing spirit of brotherhood which I find all over the church. I believe myself that these days may bring the church, as no times of prosperity ever could, to see her responsibility and to make herself felt in bringing about a better day economically, socially, morally, and spiritually."[60] And in 1932, because key leaders of the churches still perceived the remedy for Depression in terms of immediate legislative solutions, the United Church's Commission on the Church and Industry recommended the creation of a national economic research and planning board, the institution of comprehensive social insurance, and the direct intervention of governments in order to palliate and humanize economic conditions.[61] This marked no new creative departure for the United Church, for it replicated the policy research perspective that had been carefully carved out by the Social Service Council of Canada during the 1920s.

By the early 1930s almost all United Church clergymen had gravitated to the more conservative pole of tenaciously defending the "inherent significance of the evangelical conscience" in order to avoid the perilous extremes of what Claris Silcox termed the "Scylla of radicalism and the Charybdis of reaction."[62] Whereas the United Church's Board of Evangelism and Social Service, in its 1931–32 annual report, commended the now well-established tradition of critiquing social inequalities, it was at the same time acutely aware that the church had to mobilize its forces to create a "distinctly Christian social order" so that it might unitedly "confront materialistic Communism."[63] When clergymen in the 1930s spoke of the threat of secular thought, they were not referring to all culture outside the institutional church, as some historians have concluded; rather, they were specifically referring to Communism and Fascism. What George Pidgeon called the "secular spirit" were those ideologies which "ignore[d] the spiritual altogether." And when the Anglican bishop of Montreal spoke about the "active propaganda for Materialism which is Godless," he was specifically identifying Communism as the chief enemy of Christianity.[64] The threat of Communism produced such alarm throughout Protestantism and caused such a conservative backlash against social Christianity that some loyal United Church members challenged W.B. Creighton's editorship of the *New Outlook* on the grounds that he had "taken a strong attitude in favour of the 'reds.'" Some even threatened to leave the United Church to become "good old Presbyterian[s]." As a result of this taint of Communism, in one week alone five or six old Methodists in Kingsville, Ontario, cancelled their subscriptions to the journal.[65]

Because of the serious spread of both nationalism (as Fascism was termed) and Communism throughout Europe, two ideologies which openly challenged the central assumption of social Christianity that all reforms, including those extending the power of the modern state, ultimately realized the Kingdom of God, Protestant leaders became far less complacent about the political implications of discussing contemporary social problems. Their new attitude was shared by conservative evangelicals and advocates of social Christianity because both constituencies accepted that even the modern interdependent social order was grounded upon the self-realization of the individual. It was for that very reason that ministers like the Rev. William B. William of Queen's Avenue United Church in New Westminster denounced equally the statism of the far right and the far left. "Wherever the new idea of Nationalism takes hold it will have to face the church," he told Dobson; "an idea which makes the state supreme over everything must inevitably come into conflict with a religion which bases its teachings upon the supreme worth of the individual."[66] Hugh Dobson's own championing of personal evangelism ahead of social service hinged upon the problem of the accession to power of these purely secular political ideologies. Thus, in 1934 Dobson apprised the Rev. W.H. Irwin that the church was under intense pressure to unite around the concept of the "totalitarianism of Christ" to fight the "totalitarianism of the state."[67] In a similar vein, the 1934 annual report of the United Church stated that in the cause of Christian unity the Department of Evangelism and Social Service must jettison its tradition of overt social criticism if it was to remain on the "cutting edge" of popular sentiment: "History shows that it is not necessary to preach untenable theories and doctrines in order to exercise a mighty evangelistic influence."[68]

By 1934 the outlook of the United Church had dramatically altered. The explanation for the church leadership's increasing deference to popular religious sentiment can be found in its recognition that the Depression was not a short-term phenomenon and that any solution lay well beyond mere reformist prescription. Witnessing daily the terrible psychological toll exacted by the Depression among members of their congregations, local Protestant clergymen were instrumental in formulating a new climate of opinion within the United Church, which now saw its primary role in terms of spiritual leadership.

This new realization of the poverty of faith among Canadians was responsible for a conservative reaction, even among some progressive clergymen, against what they saw as the futility of, and the ideological polarization aroused by, political solutions to the economic crisis. With an eye on the disruptive potential of the CCF, which many believed would only further inflame social tensions, George Pidgeon in 1934 expressed his wariness of social Christianity, which previously he had praised as the harbinger of order and social harmony: "The leaders of social reform seem to me to be so blind to the only power that can bring about the results they desire at times I almost despair of the church's influence in this direction." Pidgeon's exhortation that the church must take possession of "a victorious faith"[69] was shared by ministers from all across the political spectrum who wished to discover in these times of stress a new core of consensus within Protestantism. It was the increasing polarization between the social implications of religion and the notion of private spirituality[70] that impelled even the most socially radical, like Ernest Thomas, towards the non-political haven and emotional salve of traditional evangelical faith. There was no better statement evocative of the breakdown of the progressive consensus and of the consequent search for inner piety than Thomas's disillusioned observation concerning the "atmosphere of suspicion and lack of frank comradeship, if not definite mischief making" that now prevailed in the discussion of social questions.[71]

Even Hugh Dobson, who had so actively promoted social Christianity throughout the 1920s, began to question the verities of the progressive creed. Believing that the Depression had splintered Protestantism into a spectrum of belief extending from fundamentalism to extreme modernism, Dobson sought the recovery of "Christian brotherhood" in personal spiritual experience rather than social reform: "Beyond all doubt, the power of the Gospel does not lie in logic or research, useful as these are, but somehow in the Cross."[72] The decisive shift away from the practical application of Christian belief towards individual conversion as the quintessential benchmark of the Christian experience of God was shaped not by church officials but as a response by them to the changing patterns of popular piety in local congregations. The tendency of ordinary Canadians to withdraw from the acrimoniousness of political controversy into the emotionally healing quest for hope through personal salvation was powerfully expressed by the Rev. G.P. McLeod of Shaughnessy Heights United Church in Vancouver:

Some half-dozen people in my own congregation ... have "made their surrender" as they put it. I am tremendously anxious as, I feel that this experience should be preserved in fruitful ways. I can see the dangers ahead ...

I have made it my dominant aim in preaching to build up personal religious life through appeal both to the mind and will. I have not presumed to take sides in social and economic controversy from the pulpit ... For one thing, there are prominent business and professional people in the congregation who have had years of experience at these things & know far more about them than I do. For another thing it would be beginning at the wrong end. What I have said from the pulpit about the social and economic crisis, has, I fully believe, been so unmistakably implied in the teaching of Jesus his love for mankind, & his challenge to personal loyalty, as to be beyond serious controversy. There is plenty of moral realism in the Gospel so presented to challenge the standards both personal and social of our time ... "Reverence is not enough," unless it issues in a Christian social order.[73]

At heart, most clergymen were, in theory, morally outraged by the selfishness and greed of wealthy Canadians,[74] which they blamed in large part for the Depression, but as the churches began to face the real possibility of bankruptcy and the realization that they could no longer sustain social programs, they were forced by these exigencies to become extremely solicitous of the wealthy members of their congregations. Church officials were thus becoming exceedingly suspicious of any resolutions on social questions that appeared to be overly ideological in their tenor. Thus, R.B. Cochrane was outraged that in 1935 the United Church was once again discussing the economic and social situation of the country. That the churches had given A.E. Smith, the Communist leader, a hearing, Cochrane openly condemned as inflammatory. "I am not surprised," he told Pidgeon, "that such an action has caused unrest and questioning among a number of our laymen." For this atmosphere of confrontation within the church he blamed the secretaries of the Board of Evangelism and Social Service, namely Ernest Thomas and Hugh Dobson.[75] George Pidgeon was even more explicit as to why the United Church was rapidly moving away from advocacy of economic programs and towards more individualistic spiritual renewal. Writing to the moderator of the United Church, the Rev. Richard Roberts, who was then engaged in planning a massive cross-country evangelistic campaign led by a visiting team of British Methodist evangelists, Pidgeon was livid over the Toronto Conference's flirtation with socialism: "The Toronto Conference passed another absurd resolution on the social question and the feeling it aroused was such that one simply had not the *face* to approach any of our monied men on such a subject. William Birks, for example, wrote a hot letter to Dr. Laird over Line's utterances in Montreal and here the whole situation was made extremely difficult."[76]

In this atmosphere, in which the official commitment to the verities of the progressive creed of social evangelism was being challenged by the upsurge of popular evangelicalism, the United Church's Commission on Christianizing the Social Order was established in 1933 for the express purpose of reconstituting the dynamic between social action and individual piety. It was hoped that such a commission would quell the very real political tensions that existed within the church. Although the commission upheld the ideal of open and free discussion on social questions, the submissions of Sir Robert Falconer, Ernest Thomas, Richard Roberts, John Dow, John Line, Professor W.R. Taylor, E.J. Urwick, and Irene Biss clearly showed the commission's true agenda to be the reassertion of the primacy of Scripture and the devaluation of social service, to the point that the latter would remain only as a residuum of personal evangelism and it would be the responsibility of the individual Christian, and not of the pastor, to interpret the applicability of the social teachings of the Gospel to modern society.[77] The preaching of God's message was to be henceforth so contrived as to "transcend in importance all questions of social and political adjustment."

Whereas in the 1920s clergymen were instructed to read widely in the modern social sciences, the overriding desire in the 1930s to avoid political controversy dictated that only narrowly religious works were to be read in church.[78] This new conviction arose directly from the experience of local clergymen and was not simply a preoccupation of the United Church leadership. The sermons of the Rev. C.E. Bland, minister of Crescent United Church in Winnipeg from 1923 to 1934, have been preserved almost in their entirety and they represent the changing conventions of piety in those two decades. During the 1920s Bland upheld the tenets of social Christianity, but by 1931 he had become a champion of the Oxford Group movement, with its values of individual spiritual renewal, largely as an antidote to what he saw as the expanding anti-God movements of totalitarianism. On the one hand Bland despaired of that "old individualism" of selfishness among the wealthy, and yet at the same time he was extremely fearful of what he called the Russian experiment in Communism, which he equated with paganism. As a result he held firmly to the sound spiritualism contained in personal evangelism. "The Church is not an economic experiment," Bland stated in his sermon of 3 May 1931, "Economic Unrest and the Kingdom of God." "It is not a supporter of King-rule or noble-rule or bureaucracy or democracy – of Socialism or Communism or any other ism – theories devised to secure to every man his due in the world's economy ... As a pre-requisite for the working out of any theory, the heart must be free of covetousness." Like the majority of Protestant clergymen Bland had turned his back on the progressive emphasis on social renewal as the path to the Kingdom of God because he believed that all economic problems were moral in nature and thus could be solved only through personal repentance.[79]

While John Line's submission to the Commission on Christianizing the Social Order, "The Fundamental Unity of Spiritual and Social Religious Values," attempted to preserve the reconciliation of personal and social religion characteristic of the early twentieth century, his was clearly a minority perspective. Moreover, Irene Biss's recommendations for a thoroughgoing redistribution of wealth were rewritten many times until a more innocuous critique of wealth emerged, one which rested upon repentance of individual sins of avarice and selfishness.[80] In its final form, the submission of these social scientists accorded with D.N. McLachlan's estimation that the United Church had to emphasize the "ethical character of acts" rather than the economic sequence of events.[81] Believing that the responsibility for the redistribution of national wealth and income resided with governments, the majority view of the commission was that the church had to act merely as the conscience of the state, that it should be "the light rather than the engineer of the City of God."[82] Far from representing the failure of the church, this position was the fulfilment of the progressive Protestant ideal of increasing government intervention so that the church would be free to pursue its educational and evangelistic tasks as outlined by T. Albert Moore and Hugh Dobson in the early 1920s.

The analysis of The Gospels John Dow submitted to the commission in 1933 argued that Jesus was not a politician and that he was not primarily concerned with the creation of social policy regarding the redistribution of wealth. Similarly, the Rev. Richard Roberts could claim that the priority of the church must lie with the spiritual life of Christians and that the "Human Personality" was a reality supreme over the social polity. Although still sympathetic to the implementation of national programs for social security, Roberts believed that comprehensive social planning was but a palliative. Despite the claims of its promoter, the League for Social Reconstruction, that planning would work an immediate social transformation, Roberts maintained that any structural reform must by necessity be incremental and slow. Thus, his reflections on the power of personal evangelism rested upon the firm belief that the spiritual life of everyday experience must take precedence over social questions.[83]

The most compelling statement on the re-ordering of the balance between social service and individual piety which the commission proclaimed was issued by Sir Robert Falconer, the former president of the

University of Toronto and one of the principal architects of the alliance between social evangelism and the social sciences. Optimistic in his faith that the state had at last recognized its role in regulating the ways in which wealth was utilized and in protecting the insecure, Falconer articulated the consensus of church leaders that the church need no longer concern itself with the direct formulation and implementation of social welfare legislation because there now existed a critical mass of university-trained experts. In "The Church and the Social Order," Falconer argued that an informed political leadership must be founded upon expert knowledge, and that the church itself did not possess the kind of expertise suited to the direct management of the modern economy. However, he still insisted that because many evils in the social order touched on problems of morality, the church still had a function to fulfil as the moral conscience of the modern state: "If the evils of the social order are presented with insistence the members of the Church being in modern times also citizens of the State will use their intelligence and moral drive to have remedial action taken by the State." This was not a prescription for the complete disengagement of the church from the resolution of social problems; rather, it shifted responsibility from the institution of the church to Christian individuals, who could best help transform society by bringing to bear their personal ethical standards which had been inculcated in the churches through the experience of evangelical conversion. The church, Falconer contended, must merely arouse the conscience of her people, and refrain from confronting the economic system outright; the church should support the intentions of good people and not pronounce upon specific programs of social reform which must invariably be the creed of some political party.[84] In the final analysis the Commission for Christianizing the Social Order re-ordered the intellectual climate of the United Church and this led to the uncoupling of evangelism and social service; as one of the authors of its report, Ernest Thomas, commented, if Christian personal action formed the basis of all social justice, then Christian socialism must be a contradiction in terms.[85]

As a result, in 1936 the United Church reclaimed its Victorian evangelical inheritance when it rescinded the intellectual basis of Christian progressivism by announcing that social service was no longer the practical expression of one's inner spiritual commitment to Christ. Because of the changes in the expression of popular piety, the conversion experience was once again elevated as the sole measure of one's relationship to God. Christian action was no longer esteemed by church leaders as a substitute for personal conversion because it was no longer acceptable to ordinary Canadians, who had displaced it in favour of a reinstitution of the conversion experience as the mechanism for entry into a Christian life. The Christianization of the social order thus could no longer be placed under the rubric of evangelism. In 1936 the Board of Evangelism and Social Service issued the following redefinition of evangelism, which had its social component eviscerated: "We thus differentiate *Evangelism* on the one hand from that reorganization of life on a Christian basis which may properly be spoken of as *Christianization*, and on the other from that territorial expansion of the mission of the church which we have called *Evangelization*."[86]

Like the Protestant churches before 1900, the United Church of the late 1930s identified Christianity with personal conversion and missionary work and not with reform of the social order. The official sanctioning of the irrevocable severing of evangelism from social Christianity did not imply the failure of Protestantism, for, as clergymen in the 1930s themselves claimed, social Christianity was not the immutable standard of the vitality of the Christian message. "To do its work effectively the Church must at every stage of the world's life discover the mind of the Spirit and interpret that mind in relation to human need."[87] The external criterion of church attendance was no longer deemed sufficient evidence of Christian belief, and evangelistic campaigns were considered failures unless there were definite signs that actual conversion had taken place. Although muted during the 1920s because of the official promotion of social Christianity, conversion had never been wholly eradicated from the United Church, nor had it entirely ceased to be the essential definition of evangelism, for it rested upon an inward-looking popular piety.[88] Where social service had been the watchword of the 1920s, the idea that "the spiritual man" was "the measure of all things" was brought to the fore in the 1930s by the cataclysmic popular resurgence of traditional evangelicalism among ordinary Canadians searching for personal affirmation and spiritual solace in a world ruled by impersonal social forces.

What was significant about the experience of the United Church during the 1930s was not the reform of the social order but the evangelistic campaigns directed at the winning of new souls for Christ. Although the United Church established a Commission on Economic and Social Research in 1937–38 to frame the church's submission to the Rowell-Sirois Royal Commission on Dominion-Provincial Relations, this body did not have the backing of influential church conservatives, though social scientists, financiers, and industrialists comprised the majority of its membership. More revealing of the changed relationship in the United Church and of the priority given to individual evangelization over the investigation of social questions, the church commission initiated no new departures in social welfare policy but merely offered a somewhat vague and tepid endorsement of the principle of social security laid down by both R.B. Bennett's New Deal and Mackenzie King's National Employment Commission.[89]

The immense influence of personal evangelism within the United Church was clearly demonstrated when even the "radical" Commission on Economic and Social Research declared that the primary responsibility of the Protestant churches was to maintain "the inherent worth of personality."[90] With the eclipse of the external expression of Christian commitment in social action, the church did not simply collapse into indecision and futile hand wringing in the face of social adversity. Nor did it meekly surrender its core of evangelical faith to the secular zeal of political protest. Ministering to the religious experience of ordinary Canadians absorbed the real energy of the church, which fostered a popular spiritual renewal through a series of immensely successful revival campaigns. It was during the 1935 Services of Witness at Maple Leaf Gardens in Toronto and the Montreal Forum, those temples of modern popular culture, and at events replicated in local arenas and theatres all across Canada, that thousands of people in attendance celebrated the centrality of Christ, his Incarnation, Atonement, and redemption.[91] Here, and not in left-wing political protest movements such as the CCF, was to be found the popular Protestant response to the Great Depression.

Conclusion
Encompassing the Modern Age

J.S. Woodsworth's passionate conviction that there was no distinction between the secular and the sacred, and that, in fact, all manner of social and cultural existence was penetrated by Christian feeling and purpose, was a powerful testament to the impressive authority of Protestantism in Canadian public life. It evoked the belief shared by a large majority of Canadians that all facets of everyday living fell under the guiding superintendence of God's grace. Like so many other clergymen who responded to the increasing social distress and conflict of the early twentieth century by calling for the revitalization of evangelicalism so that it might transcend the traditionally restrictive class confines of Protestantism, Woodsworth sought to eradicate what he called the "withered ecclesiasticism" and doctrinal rigidity of his faith.

Woodsworth favoured an egalitarian spirituality that, through its emphasis upon a direct emotional apprehension of God and a pragmatic insistence upon the priority of everyday human experience, would make religion accessible and inclusive of ordinary Canadians. His view, that the theoretical disputation of doctrinal minutiae, so characteristic of the Victorian church colleges, was an outmoded encumbrance shackling the church by severing it from the broader social problems of the community, was shared by an increasing number of clergymen after 1900. By so thoroughly expunging the wider social reality from its purview, theology, according to Woodsworth and his fellow progressive clergymen, was in truth ensnaring Protestantism in the coils of a more "wretched secularism." It was in this revulsion against the élitism and spiritual sterility of the Victorian clergyman-professor that the modern Protestant churches underwent a dramatic transformation after 1900. By accepting social evangelism, or what they termed a "full-orbed Christianity," as their central axiom, progressive Protestant church leaders not only set out to bridge class divisions by building a consensual Christian community, but, also, in so doing, they sought to expand greatly the power of the Methodist and Presbyterian churches, which then became the chief instruments through which modern values and sensibilities were translated to the wider Canadian society.

Between 1900 and 1940 the new evangelism, which placed greater priority on social action than on inner piety as the barometer of Christian commitment, thus inextricably linked private and public morality. Social evangelism was the creation of a new generation of middle-class clergymen who wished to bind Christianity more firmly to the wider contemporary world. Although progressive clergymen, after years of persistent education and promotion of the necessity of social service for the continued vitality of Protestantism, succeeded in making social evangelism the official creed of both the Methodist and Presbyterian churches, it did not represent the totality of the evangelical experience. For, unlike its social gospel counterpart in the United States, the appeal of social service in Canada was powerful because it responded to a popular spirituality that characterized the religious experience of the majority of Canadian Protestants. Because this enduring stream of popular piety, with its requirement of personal conversion and atonement for sin, remained a dominant stream within Canadian evangelicalism, progressive clergymen were compelled to refashion their social creed in terms of the enduring individualism of traditional piety. Far from simply imposing their own middle-class assumptions of social redemption upon the masses, the church progressives, in their ideas and methods, were themselves consistently shaped by the forces of localism, and consequently the old-fashioned revival meeting became the primary forum for the inculcation of what they deemed to be more modern principles of social evangelism.

Social evangelism won its greatest number of adherents among middle-class Canadians, who shared the broad progressive impulse for a social reconstruction that would mediate the social tensions spawned by the warfare between capital and labour. That the great majority of early twentieth-century movements of social reform cohered around the leadership of the Protestant churches was a direct function of social evangelism's marvellous ability to absorb the multifarious transatlantic intellectual currents of modern liberal collectivism which were then beginning to animate the sciences of sociology, psychology, and the new political economy. Social evangelism provided the crucial theoretical framework for social action in Canada because it enclosed within a

Christian matrix many of the key insights that had become integral to the new liberal and progressive thinkers in Britain and the United States. Social evangelism was intellectually rigorous and on the leading edge of current debate concerning the causes and nature of social change because the new modern minister had turned to the social sciences and critiques of industrial capitalism to find the intellectual justification for Christian social action. In his more modern guise, the local clergyman kept abreast of recent debates concerning ideas of social evolution, the causes of social conflict, theories of social control and assimilation, and integrated socialist arguments for social cooperation based upon the moral ideal of social service – an ideal that meshed precisely with the tenets of social evangelism. As a result, the Protestant churches accumulated even greater public authority when they secured the unchallenged recognition from other reform groups that they were the vanguards of reform and the progenitors of modern social welfare policy.

In contrast to the 1890s, when social reform activism was largely sponsored by secular bodies operating outside the confines of the churches, in the decades following World War I the tremendous facility of social evangelism to incorporate a wide spectrum of reform impulses within its Christian aegis brought Protestantism and secular organizations into ever closer affinity. Far from drifting apart, as the secularization thesis posits, the churches and the reformist constituency were actually more closely bound between 1900 and 1935 than they had ever been. In the aftermath of World War I, when experimentation in state policies of reconstruction and urban reform collapsed, the Protestant churches became the fulcrum for the creation of protectionist social policies. Unlike the fate of progressive reform in the United States, which after World War I became increasingly divorced from Christian endeavour, in Canada the increasing specialization in the social sciences, the creation of such new professions as social work, and the growing dependence of government upon expert scientific knowledge – the hallmark of modern social policy creation – occurred under the governance of the Protestant churches. Whereas in the United States the reformer Jane Addams could openly proclaim her loss of Christian faith and the social scientist Robert Park could confidently announce that no moral man could become a sociologist, in Canada Charlotte Whitton, Carl Dawson, and E.J. Urwick all articulated an ideal of professional social work which was encompassed within Christian social service, and as late as 1940 the sociologist Harry Cassidy believed that the modern social order must rest upon the twin pillars of government and church.

What this book has clearly demonstrated is that the Protestant churches did not simply accommodate Christianity to modern thought; rather, they were the central means by which modern values and institutions were introduced into the Canadian social landscape. Whereas in other Western democracies the universities, business corporations, and trade unions led the way in promoting the development of modern social policy, in Canada this role was occupied by the Protestant churches. Under the banner of social evangelism, clergymen introduced the technologies of mass popular entertainment and advertising, evolved a system of national bureaucratic organization, founded the modern profession of social work, and became the chief vehicles for the importation of American methods of social investigation and reform. Most importantly, they were the first to articulate the need for scientific social planning and to supply the key benchmark of the modern state, the application of systematically gathered social facts to the formulation of social legislation.

Until recently, contemporary Canadian historians have mirrored the main currents of American scholarship in suggesting that business interests formed the major impetus behind social reform and that the largely urban movement for reform petered out after 1918. By focusing on the activities of the Protestant churches in the realm of social welfare, this book reorients both the periodization and the locus of reform in Canada during the first four decades of the twentieth century. The central pillar supporting the creation in Canada of social policy prior to World War II was a reform network dominated by the Protestant churches. That they provided the funding, personnel, and organizational structure for social reform was a critical factor in defining the contours of the modern welfare state as it developed in the decades following World War I. Because the Methodist and Presbyterian churches had decentralized structures and rested upon local congregations, small-town and rural reform organizations constituted the life-blood of the movement for social evangelism, and until the 1930s they nourished the strength of national reform networks, in particular that of the church-sponsored Social Service Council of Canada. The influence of the various women's temperance societies, institutes, and farm organizations was particularly acute at the local and provincial levels. This, combined with the prominence of the Protestant churches in reform organizations, ensured that issues of concern to maternal feminists, such as the reconstruction of rural life, child welfare, mothers' pensions, the minimum wage, temperance, and public health, informed much of the early social welfare legislation which contributed to the expansion of the modern state in Canada. This symbiotic relationship between the churches and womens' reform organizations contributed to the longevity of a climate of unspecialized, non-technocratic attitudes towards social security. It was not until the mid-1930s that the expertise of university-trained social scientists made its impact upon federal legislation, but even then the conduit for this revolution in government policymaking was controlled by the churches through the Social Service Council of Canada. Again, the interposition of the churches into the field of social policy determined the rate of state expansion and the interplay between the university and the state. As this book makes abundantly clear, however, the outlines of social welfare legislation emerged from the liberal collectivist ideals of social evangelism, not from the influence of the Protestant churches on the democratic socialism of the Co-operative Commonwealth Federation. Moreover, the outstanding role the churches played in insisting that sociology and social work gain footholds within the academy ensured that these social sciences remained closely entwined with the goals of social reform and thus impervious to the blandishments of the scientistic objectivity that had become fashionable during the 1920s in the United States.

Like progressivism itself, the impetus for social evangelism waned. In the nadir of the Great Depression, when the majority of ordinary Canadians felt particularly overwhelmed by the caprices of impersonal economic forces, the desire to recapture a direct and personal relationship with God that only traditional evangelicalism could provide resulted in the rescinding of many of the tenets of social service. Ever attuned to the inner search for spiritual fulfilment among their congregations, even the most committed progressive clergymen heeded the popular call to jettison social Christianity in favour of a more private religion based upon the emotional experience of conversion and repentance. While modern defenders of the secularization thesis have pointed to the declension of social evangelism as synonymous with the growth of a secular culture, early twentieth-century progressive clergymen did not view social evangelism as an eternally valid theology. Rather, they conceived it as a contingent phenomenon, one explicitly designed to awaken the conscience of both the public and the state to the need for identifying, studying, and resolving contemporary social problems. The educational goals of social evangelism were immensely successful, for by the mid-1930s progressive clergymen had achieved their aim of converting provincial and federal governments to the principle of providing social security. Having accomplished this aim, progressive clergymen were sanguine about the increasing influence exerted by university social scientists and secular reformers in the realm of social policy. Indeed, Protestant ministers were the major exponents of a government-funded national economic and social research council. The Protestant churches then enthusiastically re-embraced what they viewed as the core of evangelicalism itself, the personal conversion experience.

Far from acting as the unwitting accomplices in their own secularization, as many historians have argued, progressive clergymen had always promoted social evangelism only as the outward manifestation of inner piety. If they were capable of viewing social Christianity as a conditioned response to the social disruptions of the early twentieth century, surely modern historians should be able to do likewise. What this book has demonstrated is that instead of a linear decline into secularization after 1890, evangelicalism was fed by two powerful streams, inner piety and social evangelism, whose fortunes rose and fell in a cyclical manner. The 1920s saw the efflorescence of social service, while the new social realities of the 1930s called forth the more pietistic and private aspect of evangelicalism. What is crucial to our understanding of the character of Canadian Protestantism, however, is the enduring persistence of the popular fountain of traditional piety, which has continued to feed the larger stream of evangelicalism.

In the 1940s the concern of church leaders that middle-class Canadians were for the first time failing to attend church services *twice* on Sundays,[1] led to a resurgence of demands among clergymen for a campaign to reinterpret the limits of evangelicalism by insisting that it must once again transcend its institutional confines and permeate the wider culture. If mass culture was making incursions upon the authority of Christianity, the awareness of this among clergymen and conscientious Christians was beginning to occur only in the late 1940s when the majority of Canadians had sufficient wealth to consume the new diversions and when the flood-tide of American popular culture had for the first time begun to encroach upon the borders of Canada. The lament of Norman Mackenzie, the president of the University of British Columbia, that the granting of the freedom of the city of Vancouver to Bing Crosby signalled a decisive shift in public values, elicited from the Rev. William Creighton Graham, principal of United College, Winnipeg, the observation that while young middle-class Canadians displayed little interest in attending the institutional church they were, nevertheless, extremely religious. In response to this upsurge in interest in religion, as distinguished from church doctrine, Graham exactly replicated the progressive Protestant critique of the Victorian church. As he told Mackenzie in March 1948, the church must endeavour to escape the politics of its own inner machinery and make Christianity the matrix of modern culture by clothing it in visible and tangible social forms which would make it a living force among all Canadians. "In an important sense," Graham declared, "religion is more than a part of culture. A vital religious faith permeates every cultural good and influences every aspect of life."[2]

Here Graham was attempting, as had Hugh Dobson and T. Albert Moore two decades earlier, to ensure that Protestantism and religious belief would act as the central principles around which modern culture would cohere. Unfortunately his plea went forth into a much-changed culture. Even though evangelicalism continued to form the backbone of the mainline Protestant churches, these denominations found themselves in ever increasing competition with a proliferation of conservative evangelical groups, largely because the United Church, especially in urban Canada, had failed to preserve that delicate equipoise between its search for middle-class respectability and its desire to be the religion of the common man. By the late 1950s these new populist evangelical churches, with their overt rejection of modern culture, had effectively siphoned off much of the constituency of the Protestant core,[3] reducing the United Church of Canada to an almost wholly middle-class institution. Ironically, while the success of these new evangelical denominations appeared to rejuvenate Protestantism in Canada, they nevertheless stood for a type of Christianity that most middle-class Canadians perceived to be unsophisticated and anti-intellectual, and so, irrelevant to the needs of a modern, consumer-oriented society. Thus, if historians wish to seek out the origins of secularization in Canada, when Protestantism seemingly lost its identification with the cultural mainstream, these might be located in the increasing diversity of spiritual choice and the consequent fragmentation of the evangelical experience in the decades following World War II.

Notes

ABBREVIATIONS

AO	Archives of Ontario
DESS	Department of Evangelism and Social Service
GGG	*Grain Growers' Guide*
MUA	McGill University Archives
NA	National Archives of Canada
PAM	Provincial Archives of Manitoba
SAB	Saskatchewan Archives Board
SW	*Social Welfare*
UBCA	University of British Columbia Archives
UCA	United Church Archives (at Victoria University, Toronto)
UCA/UW	United Church Archives (at the University of Winnipeg)
UMA	University of Manitoba Archives
UTA	University of Toronto Archives

INTRODUCTION

1 The discontinuous chronology of 20th-century social reform in Canada has been most forcefully articulated by Doug Owram, *The Government Generation: Canadian Intellectuals and the State, 1900–1945* (Toronto: University of Toronto Press, 1986), xii–xiii. It also undergirds influential studies of more specific aspects of social policy and Canadian society. See, for example, Michiel Horn, *The League for Social Reconstruction: Intellectual Origins of the Democratic Left in Canada, 1930–1942* (Toronto: University

of Toronto Press, 1980); James Struthers, *No Fault of their Own: Unemployment and the Canadian Welfare State, 1914–1941* (Toronto: University of Toronto Press, 1983); Veronica Strong-Boag, *The New Day Recalled: Lives of Girls and Women in English Canada, 1919–1939* (Toronto: Copp Clark Pitman, 1988); Tom Traves, *The State and Enterprise: Canadian Manufacturers and the Federal Government, 1917–1931* (Toronto: University of Toronto Press, 1979). The view of social reform simply disappearing in the 1920s is so pervasive that it informs a recent synthetic treatment of the interwar years in Canada. See John Herd Thompson with Allen Seager, *Canada 1922–1939: Decades of Discord* (Toronto: McClelland and Stewart, 1986).

2 This social and cultural approach to secularization has been most recently advanced by David B. Marshall, *Secularizing the Faith: Canadian Protestant Clergy and the Crisis of Belief, 1850–1940* (Toronto: University of Toronto Press, 1992), 7. Marshall argues that secularization consists of the replacement of religious explanations of the world with scientific ones and, more importantly, of the "laicization" of social institutions, whereby churches lose their monopoly position in education and social welfare and are thrust into competition with secular institutions. Thus, religious values and clerical control "are superseded by concerns about good citizenship and the imposition of bureaucratic and state control."

Ramsay Cook's earlier study, *The Regenerators: Social Criticism in Late Victorian Canada* (Toronto: University of Toronto Press, 1985), 196–227, sought to demonstrate, through examination of the careers of J.S. Woodsworth and Mackenzie King, that the political ideologies of both modern liberalism and democratic socialism were forged by individuals who rejected the Protestant churches for the "secular" calling of politics.

3 See Marshall, *Secularizing the Faith*, 145–55; Cook, *The Regenerators*, 228–32.

4 For this theological definition of religious vitality, in which any departure from religious "orthodoxy" is viewed as secularization, see Marshall, *Secularizing the Faith*, 49–98; Cook, *The Regenerators*, 7–25. For the relationship between the cultural authority of the Victorian clergy and a dogmatic, Bible-centred theology, see Michael Gauvreau, *The Evangelical Century: College and Creed in English Canada from the Great Revival to the Great Depression* (Montreal and Kingston: McGill-Queen's University Press, 1991).

5 Owram has argued that by 1919 there existed two groups of reformers: one, based upon a "radical social gospel" and characterized by "ideological idealism" and by what he pejoratively terms "a degree of naivete," concentrated on specifically "moral issues" such as Sabbatarianism, censorship, and prohibition; the other, an "urban middle-class progressivism," sought a more social scientific basis of reform. See *The Government*

Generation, 107–14. Mariana Valverde's *The Age of Light, Soap, and Water: Moral Reform in English Canada, 1885–1914* (Toronto: McClelland and Stewart, 1991), identifies the Protestant churches primarily with a conservative fear-driven campaign to promote social purity.

6 Richard Allen, *The Social Passion: Religion and Social Reform in Canada, 1914–28* (Toronto: University of Toronto Press, 1973), introduction.

7 Aspects of this transatlantic redefinition of liberalism have been treated in Stefan Collini, *Liberalism and Sociology: L.T. Hobhouse and Political Argument in England, 1880–1914* (Cambridge: Cambridge University Press, 1979), 13–50; Michael Freeden, *The New Liberalism* (Oxford: Oxford University Press, 1978); James T. Kloppenberg, *Uncertain Victory: Social Democracy and Progressivism in European and American Thought, 1870–1920* (New York and Oxford: Oxford University Press, 1986).

8 Here we revise the view advanced by Phyllis Airhart in *Serving the Present Age: Revivalism, Progressivism, and the Methodist Tradition in Canada* (Montreal and Kingston: McGill-Queen's University Press, 1992), who argues that the most important response of the Methodist Church to modernity was an intellectual redefinition of the individual in terms of social experience. While not discounting the importance of this transformation, we argue that it represents at best a partial view and only the first stage in a larger transformation by which the Protestant churches expanded into all facets of Canadian social and cultural life.

9 For the presence of liberal collectivist ideas in Canadian universities prior to 1930, see Barry Ferguson, *Remaking Liberalism: The Intellectual Legacy of Adam Shortt, O.D. Skelton, W.C. Clark and W.A. Mackintosh, 1890–1925* (Montreal and Kingston: McGill-Queen's University Press, 1993); Owram, *The Government Generation*, 50–79, 107–34. Owram's argument, however, is premised upon the view that prior to 1935 university social scientists were unable to carve out an independent relationship with the federal government.

10 For this interpretation in the American context, see Robert Wiebe, *The Search for Order, 1877–1920* (New York: Hill and Wang, 1967); Samuel Haber, *Efficiency and Uplift: Scientific Management in the Progressive Era, 1890–1920* (Chicago: University of Chicago Press, 1964); Thomas L. Haskell, *The Emergence of Professional Social Science: The American Social Science Association and the Nineteenth Century Crisis of Authority* (Urbana, Ill.: University of Illinois Press, 1977); Martin J. Sklar, *The Corporate Reconstruction of American Capitalism* (Cambridge: Cambridge University Press, 1988). On the importance of voluntary charity in state welfare formation, see Jane Lewis, *The Voluntary Sector, the State and Social Work in Britain* (Aldershot, Hants: E. Elgar, 1995).

11 The importation of the models of progressivism developed with reference to the United States is most evident in Owram, *The Government*

Generation. See also H.V. Nelles, *The Politics of Development: Forests, Mines, and Hydro-Electric Power in Ontario, 1850–1940* (Toronto: Macmillan and Co., 1974); Christopher Armstrong and H.V. Nelles, *Monopoly's Moment: The Organization and Regulation of Canadian Utilities, 1830–1930* (Philadelphia: Temple University Press, 1986); Ken Cruikshank, *Close Ties* (Montreal and Kingston: McGill-Queen's University Press, 1992); Paul Craven, *'An Impartial Umpire': Industrial Relations and the Canadian State, 1900–1911* (Toronto: University of Toronto Press, 1980); James Naylor, *The New Democracy* (Toronto: University of Toronto Press, 1992); Paul Rutherford, "Tomorrow's Metropolis," in G.A. Stelter and Allan Artibise, eds., *The Canadian City* (Toronto: McClelland and Stewart, 1977).

CHAPTER ONE

1 UCA, Hugh Dobson Papers, box A5, file C2, Dobson to Mrs R. Casselman, 2 Feb. 1920. This was the title of one of the many pamphlets issued by the new Department of Evangelism and Social Service.
2 Alice A. Chown, *The Stairway* (Toronto: University of Toronto Press, 1988), introduction by Diana Chown, xxxv.
3 The Methodist Department of Evangelism and Social Service was founded under the title Department of Temperance and Moral Reform in 1902. For the sake of consistency we will call it by its later designation.
4 UCA, Dobson Papers, box A5, file C2, Dobson to Dear Brother, 28 June 1919. For the convergence of individual conversion and social service, see the seminal work by Phyllis Airhart, *Serving the Present Age: Revivalism, Progressivism, and the Methodist Tradition in Canada* (Montreal and Kingston: McGill-Queen's University Press, 1992).
5 UCA, Dobson Papers, box A5, file R, Dobson to the Rev. William Sparling, 30 Jan. 1920.
6 In the Canadian context this interpretation has been advanced most forcefully by Richard Allen, *The Social Passion: Religion and Social Reform in Canada, 1914–28* (Toronto: University of Toronto Press, 1973). See also A.B. McKillop, *A Disciplined Intelligence: Critical Enquiry and Canadian Thought in the Victorian Era* (Montreal and Kingston: McGill-Queen's University Press, 1979); Ramsay Cook, *The Regenerators: Social Criticism in Late Victorian Canada* (Toronto: University of Toronto Press, 1985). For the relationship in the Methodist Church between a persistent individualist temper and social service, see Airhart, *Serving the Present Age*.
7 UCA, Biographical Files, "Ernest Thomas."
8 Cook, *The Regenerators*; David B. Marshall, *Secularizing the Faith: Canadian Protestant Clergy and the Crisis of Belief, 1850–1940* (Toronto: University of Toronto Press, 1992).

9 UCA, Samuel Dwight Chown Papers, box 6, file 146, "Bear ye one another's burdens and so fulfil the law of Christ," sermon, n.d. Criticism of the élitism and hypocrisy of the Victorian church was fairly widespread among younger ministers. See, for example, NA, Woodsworth Papers, MG 27 III C7, vol. 2, N. Lashley Hall to Woodsworth, 15 July 1918: "Meantime I am at one with you as regards the crisis for organized Christianity. The blindness that has befallen leaders when it comes to any real application of the ethics of Jesus, or rather applied Christianity, is appalling." See also, UCA, Dobson Papers, box 5A, file S, J. Wesley Smiley, Rolla, B.C., to Dobson, 10 April 1920; Ibid., box 4A, file D, Dobson to the Rev. Manson Doyle, 14 Nov. 1919.

10 UMA, C.W. Gordon Papers, MSS. 56, box 30, file 9, untitled sermon, n.d.

11 UCA, Dobson Papers, box A4, file F, the Rev. J.W. Flatt to Dobson, 13 Feb. 1920. Flatt was one of the most vociferous opponents of labour during the Winnipeg General Strike.

12 Marshall, *Secularizing the Faith*, chapters 5–7.

13 UCA, Dobson Papers, box A4, file D, E.A. Davis, Oxbow, Sask., to Dobson, 18 March 1912.

14 For the interdependence of the church colleges and Victorian Protestantism, see Michael Gauvreau, *The Evangelical Century: College and Creed in English Canada from the Great Revival to the Great Depression* (Montreal and Kingston: McGill-Queen's University Press, 1991), 236–42. The evangelical theology of Burwash has been superbly treated in Marguerite Van Die, *An Evangelical Mind: Nathanael Burwash and the Methodist Tradition in Canada, 1839–1918* (Montreal and Kingston: McGill-Queen's University Press, 1989).

15 UCA, Chown Papers, box 13, file 377, "The Sociological Man," n.d.; Ibid., box 13, file 378, "The Preacher's Study of Sociology," n.d.

16 Ibid., box 13, file 378, "The Preacher's Study of Sociology," n.d.; Ibid., Box 11, file 295, "Address. The Present Need, Jan. 1912."

17 UMA, Gordon Papers, box 30, file 9, untitled sermon; Ibid., box 29, folder 2, "The Spirituality of Religion," n.d.

18 UCA/UW, John A. Cormie Papers, PP6, folder F, "Some Problems of Rural Life in Canada," n.d.

19 See Jackson Lears, "From Salvation to Self-Realization: Advertising and the Therapeutic Roots of the Consumer Culture, 1880–1930," in R.W. Fox and T.J. Jackson Lears, eds., *The Culture of Consumption: Critical Essays in American History, 1880–1980* (New York: Pantheon Books, 1983), 1–38, for the view that Christianity uncritically adopted modern consumerism. For a similar interpretation, see Susan Curtis, *A Consuming Faith: The Social Gospel and Modern American Culture* (Baltimore and London: The Johns Hopkins University Press, 1991).

20 UCA, Dobson Papers, box As, file G, W.H. Smith, *The Ministry and Spiritual Leadership, May 7, 1920* [DESS pamphlet], 6–19. For a critique of the commercialized church, see NA, J.S. Woodsworth Papers, MG 27 III C7, box 15, file 1, H.R. Magee to Woodsworth, 29 Dec. 1916.

21 UCA, DESS, box 7, file 141, Moore to Dear Brother, 18 Sept. 1922.

22 NA, Woodsworth Papers, vol. 2, Woodsworth to James Mills, Board of Railway Commissioners, 14 Feb. 1913; Ibid., vol. 15, file 1, clipping, "J.S. Woodsworth Resigns Ministry." Throughout his career Woodsworth demonstrated a complete inability to be a team player, even within his own political party, the Co-operative Commonwealth Federation. See Michiel Horn, *The League for Social Reconstruction*, 47.

23 NA, C.B. Sissons Papers, MG 27 III F3, vol. 5, Woodsworth to Sissons, 13 June 1907; Woodsworth Papers, vol. 2, Woodsworth to My Brothers of the Manitoba Conference, June 1902; UCA, J.R. Mutchmor Papers, 86.252, box 16, "Autobiography," chapter 5, 11–12.

24 NA, Woodsworth Papers, vol. 15, file 1, clipping, "J.S. Woodsworth Resigns from Ministry."

25 UCA, Nathanael Burwash Papers, 92.002, box 2, file 21, Woodsworth to Burwash, 5 March 1906.

26 NA, Sissons Papers, Woodsworth to Sissons, 17 June 1902; Ibid., Woodsworth to Sissons, 27 March 1902, 10 April 1902, 26 May 1902. On Woodsworth's ambition to teach theology at the University of Toronto or the University of British Columbia, see Ibid., Woodsworth to Sissons, 25 April, 1912.

27 Ibid., Woodsworth to Sissons, 25 April 1912, in which Woodsworth notes that he told Henry Frederick Cope, general secretary of the Religious Educational Association of the United States that in Canada "really we are very conservative."

28 NA, Woodsworth Papers, vol. 2, T. Albert Moore to Woodsworth, 15 Feb. 1913, 6 March 1913.

29 Ibid., vol. 2, Woodsworth to James Mills, 14 Feb. 1914.

30 Ibid., vol. 2, Woodsworth to James Mills, 14 Feb. 1913; Ibid., vol. 11, file 6, sermons and addresses, "Pure Religion Undefiled," n.d.

31 NA, Sissons Papers, vol. 5, Woodsworth to Sissons, 2 March 1900.

32 NA, Woodsworth Papers, vol. 11, file 6, sermons and addresses, "Be Strong and of Good Courage," 31 Dec. 1906.

33 J.S. Woodsworth, "The Community: The Social Gospel," *GGG*, 23 Feb. 1916, 41.

34 NA, Sissons Papers, Woodsworth to Sissons, 17 Feb. 1902.

35 NA, Woodsworth Papers, vol. 11, file 6, sermons and addresses, "The Wider Evangel," n.d.

36 This was Woodsworth's own assessment in his autobiography, *Following the Gleam*, published in 1926. See Airhart, *Serving the Present Age*, 113.

37 NA, Woodsworth Papers, vol. 11, file 3, Diary, 10 Aug. 1896, 13 Aug. 1896.

38 Ibid., vol. 11, file 3, Diary, 1 Sept. 1897, 30 May 1898.

39 Ibid., vol. 11, file 3, Diary, 29 April 1897. As late as 1914 Woodsworth was protesting against the "old heathen spirit" of a certain Rev. Puttenham. See Ibid., vol. 15, file 1, W.B. Creighton, editor of the *Christian Guardian*, to Woodsworth, 16 Jan. 1914. For portrayals of Woodsworth as a crypto-secularist, see Allen Mills, *Fool for Christ: The Political Thought of J.S. Woodsworth* (Toronto: University of Toronto Press, 1991), 21, 30, 38; Ramsay Cook, *The Regenerators*, 196–227.

40 SAB, Violet McNaughton Papers, J.S. Woodsworth to Violet McNaughton, 16 Jan. 1925.

41 NA, Sissons Papers, vol. 5, Woodsworth to Sissons, 17 Feb. 1902. For Woodsworth's attitude to King, see Mills, *Fool for Christ*, 10.

42 UCA, Nathanael Burwash Papers, 92.002, box 1, file 14, Woodsworth to Burwash, 14 Jan. 1902.

43 NA, Sissons Papers, vol. 5, Woodsworth to Sissons, 22 Dec. 1905.

44 NA, Woodsworth Papers, vol. 2, Woodsworth to A.E. Smith, 8 June 1918; Ibid., Woodsworth to My Brothers of the Manitoba Conference, June 1902.

45 UCA, Dobson Papers, box A2, file G, *What Delays the Revival?* [DESS special evangelism leaflet, no. VII], n.d., n.p.

46 UMA, Gordon Papers, James D. Orr to Gordon, 16 Oct. 1909.

47 UCA, Dobson Papers, box A5, file S2, Dobson to J.G. Shearer, 23 Dec. 1919.

48 Ibid., box A5, file W, the Rev. H. Whitely to Dobson, 16 Feb. 1920.

49 Ibid., box A2, file G, *Evangelism* [DESS pamphlet]. For the existence of the "prophetic-millennial" view of history at the core of the nineteenth-century evangelical creed, see Gauvreau, *The Evangelical Century*, chapter 3.

50 Marshall, *Secularizing the Faith*, chapter 5.

51 NA, Sissons Papers, vol. 5, Woodsworth to Sissons, 21 Dec. 1901.

52 UCA, Dobson Papers, box A10, file McL, Dobson to D.N. McLachlan, 4 Jan. 1926.

53 For the international currency of these reform liberal attitudes, see James T. Kloppenberg, *Uncertain Victory: Social Democracy and Progressivism in European and American Thought, 1870–1920* (New York and Oxford: Oxford University Press, 1986).

54 UCA, Chown Papers, box 3, file 66, "Ordination Sermon, Bay of Quinte Conference," Peterborough, 5 June 1904; Ibid., box 13, file 378, "The Preacher's Study of Sociology."

55 UCA, United Church, General Committee on the Tenth Anniversary of Church Union, 82.027. Ernest Thomas, "Ten Years of Evangelism and

Social Service," in *United Church of Canada: Ten Years of Union, 1925–1935*, 12.

56 J.S. Woodsworth, *My Neighbor* (Toronto: University of Toronto Press, 1972; introduction by Richard Allen), 14, 50–2.

57 UCA, Burwash Papers, box 2, file 21, Dr A. Kirschmann, professor of philosophy, University of Toronto, to Burwash, 23 Feb. 1906.

58 UCA, James Robertson Memorial Lectures, 87.022C, box 2, D.N. McLachlan, "Factors in Canada to be Molded into a Christian Unity," 7–8.

59 UCA, DESS, box 3, file 60, "Report of Beatrice Brigden," 1916–17; Ibid., box 3, file 61, "Our Worker Among Girls and Women – Report," 1918.

60 UCA, Presbyterian Church, Minutes of the Board of Moral and Social Reform, 6 Sept. 1920; UCA/UW, Cormie Papers, PP8, folder 13, "Notebook, Rural Life and the Church," n.d.

61 UCA, James Robertson Memorial Lectures, box 2, file 6, D.N. McLachlan, "The Minister of To-Day," 1–2.

62 UCA, Dobson Papers, box A2, file G, T. Albert Moore, "The Christian Hope: Redemption by Revolution, Millenium or Economic Determinism," n.d.; UCA, DESS, box 7, file 134, T. Albert Moore, "The Methodist Social Program: An Antidote for Bolshevism," n.d.

63 UMA, Gordon Papers, box 16, file 14, "Report on Moral and Social Reform," n.d.; UCA, Dobson Papers, box A4 file S, the Rev. J.M. Singleton to Dobson, 2 Jan. 1919.

64 UCA, Chown Papers, box 13, file 370, Conference Address, "Industrial Unrest," n.d.

65 UCA, Biographical Files, Ernest Thomas, "The Clash in the Social Order," *Winnipeg Free Press Evening Bulletin*, 1 Nov. 1920; Thomas, "Co-operation the Only Road," *Winnipeg Free Press*, 3 June 1919; Thomas, "Says Democracy Helps Morality," *Toronto Mail*, 5 April 1920.

66 NA, Woodsworth Papers, vol. 11, file 6, Ernest Thomas to Woodsworth, 18 Feb. 1920.

67 For this interpretation, see Allen, *The Social Passion*.

68 UCA, Dobson Papers, box A5, file K, William Keal to Dobson, 6 Feb. 1919; Ibid., box A5, file Moore, S.D. Chown to Dear Sir, 12 May 1920.

69 UCA, James Robertson Memorial Lectures, box 2, file 6, D.N. McLachlan, "Factors in Canada to be Molded into a Christian Unity," 1920, 3.

70 UCA, Chown Papers, box 11, file 293, "Address for the Moral and Social Reform Conference, The Social Teaching of Jesus," 19 Sept. 1910. See also UCA, Presbyterian Church, Board of Moral and Social Reform, W.C. Good, "For the Committee on Direct Legislation," for an broader definition of social democracy. See also UCA, Dobson Papers, box A5, file Andrews, "Report of the Committee on Evangelism and Social Service," Saskatchewan Conference, 10 June 1919.

71 UCA, Chown Papers, box 6, file 165, "The Enthronement of Christ in the Industrial Life of the Nation," n.d. Moore opposed the Winnipeg General Strike because it selfishly addressed the rights of only one class within the larger community. UCA, DESS, Moore to C.F. Hamilton, 3 Aug. 1921.

72 University of Toronto, Thomas Fisher Rare Book Library, Robert S. Kenny Collection, MS 179, box 32, A.E. Smith Notebooks, "Lecture 5 – The Beginning of the Social Prophets," n.d.; Ibid., "Two Schools of Prophets," n.d.

73 Ibid., box 32, "The Work of Jesus," n.d. For the role of "communion" in eighteenth- and nineteenth-century popular Christian experience, see Leigh Eric Schmidt, *Holy Fairs: Scottish Communions and American Revivals in the Early Modern Period* (Princeton: Princeton University Press, 1989).

74 Ibid., box 32, "Book 2, Brandon Election Records, 1920."

75 Ibid., box 32, "Lecture 5 – The Beginning of the Social Prophets."

76 Ibid., box 32, "Lectures on the Sociological Study of the Bible," n.d.; "Brandon Election Records, 1920."

77 Quoted in Vera Fast, "The Labor Church in Winnipeg," in Dennis L. Butcher, et al., eds., *Prairie Spirit: Perspectives on the Heritage of the United Church of Canada in the West* (Winnipeg: University of Manitoba Press, 1985), 249.

78 University of Toronto, Thomas Fisher Rare Book Library, Robert S. Kenny Collection, box 33, William Ivens to A.E. Smith, 31 March 1920.

79 For the centrality of the ideal of moral collectivism to reform liberalism, see Stefan Collini, *Liberalism and Sociology: L.T. Hobhouse and Political Argument in England, 1880–1914* (Cambridge: Cambridge University Press, 1979), 42–3.

80 UCA, James Robertson Memorial Lectures, box 2, file 6, McLachlan, "Factors in Canada to be Molded into a Christian Unity," 12.

81 UCA, Dobson Papers, box A7, file Mo, Dobson to Moore, 28 May 1923; Ibid., Dobson to Moore, 26 June 1923.

82 UCA, DESS, box 7, file 127, Moore to C.E. Crowell, president of the Nova Scotia Conference, 23 Dec. 1921; Ibid., Moore to Frank Yeigh, 26 Jan. 1921. See also UCA, Chown Papers, box 1, file 1, Chown to the Rev. Eber Crummy, 7 Jan. 1907; Ibid., J.A. Wilson, secretary of Hamilton Ministerial Association, to Chown, 29 Nov. 1907, referring to Chown's address, "The Social Crisis and How to Meet It."

83 University of Toronto, Thomas Fisher Rare Book Library, Robert S. Kenny Collection, box 33, Billie Hill to Smith, Peoples Church, Brandon, 16 Feb. 1924; Ibid., box 37, folder 51, "Lectures delivered at the Labor Temple, Toronto, 1923," "Love conquers greed," "Service conquers greed." Smith and his associates also continued to insist on a Christian code of personal morality, frequently castigating workers for smoking,

playing pool, and drinking. See Ibid., box 33, Billie Hill to Smith, 16 Feb. 1924; A.E. Smith to chairman, Board of Evangelism and Social Service, 14 Dec. 1946, in which, writing as a hard-line Communist ideologue, he urged support for a campaign of prohibition.

84 Ibid., box 33, A.E. Smith to Billie Hill, 28 Nov. 1924; A.E. Smith to the Rev. Dr E.C. Laker, Trenton, Ont., 15 Nov. 1924. For a similar interpretation of Smith's adherence to Communism, see Tom Mitchell, "From the Social Gospel to 'the Plain Bread of Leninism': A.E. Smith's Journey to the Left in the Epoch of Reaction after World War I," *Labour/Le travail*, 33 (spring 1994), 125–51.

85 For an account of what Smith termed his three "conversion" experiences, see Ibid., box 37, folder 13, "My Religion," n.d. According to one recent scholar, "Smith's decision to become a Communist seems more a strategic political and professional decision than one based in any profound intellectual transformation." See Tom Mitchell, "From the Social Gospel to 'the Plain Bread of Leninism': A.E. Smith's Journey to the Left in the Epoch of Reaction After World War I," *Labour/Le Travail*, 33 (spring 1994), 148.

86 University of Toronto, Thomas Fisher Rare Book Library, Robert S. Kenny Collection, box 33, A.E. Smith to Dear Sir, 3 May 1946.

87 Ibid., box 33, A.E. Smith to Mrs Mary Birchard, 5 Jan. 1947; Smith to Dear Sir, *ca.* Jan. 1944; Ernest Hunter, Knox Church, Winnipeg, to Smith, 20 Aug. 1946.

88 UCA, DESS, box 3, file 53, Brigden to Moore, 23 Oct. 1917; Ibid., box 3, file 52, Brigden to Moore, 16 Jan. 1917. From Brigden's observation that she was "socialist enough to dislike the exploitation of my labors" when she discovered that the local church was intending to purloin funds designated for the DESS, historians have claimed that she was a political socialist. Ibid., box 3, file 49, Brigden to Moore, 9 Oct. 1916. See, for example, Mariana Valverde, *The Age of Light, Soap and Water: Moral Reform in English Canada 1885–1914* (Toronto: McClelland and Stewart, 1991); and Joan Sangster, *Dreams of Equality* (Toronto: McClelland and Stewart, 1989).

89 UCA, DESS, box 3, file 49, Brigden to Moore, 1 Feb. 1916.

90 UCA, Dobson Papers, box A2, file G, *Applying Christian Principles to Industrial Unrest* [DESS, leaflet #59], n.d., n.p.

91 UMA, Gordon Papers, box 16, file 1, "Minutes of the Board of Moral and Social Reform", 9 Sept. 1908. For a more extended treatment of the social service outlook of the Presbyterian church, see Brian Fraser, *The Social Uplifters: Presbyterian Progressives and the Social Gospel in Canada, 1875–1915* (Waterloo: Wilfrid Laurier University Press, 1988).

92 UMA, Gordon Papers, box 17, file 7, Gordon to Shearer, 2 May 1914; Ibid., box 23, file 2, C.W. Gordon, "The Attitude of the Church to

Labor in Industry," n.d. For an analysis of labour relations in Winnipeg prior to the World War I, see David Bercuson, *Confrontation at Winnipeg* (Montreal and Kingston: McGill-Queen's University Press, 1974), and for the varieties of radical sentiment, see A. Ross McCormack, *Reformers, Rebels, Revolutionaries* (Toronto: University of Toronto Press, 1977).

93 NA, Woodsworth Papers, box 11, file 6, A. Vernon Thomas to Woodsworth, 28 June 1917.

94 UCA, Chown Papers, box 6, file 165, "The Enthronement of Christ in the Industrial Life of the Nation," n.d.

95 UCA, Methodist Church, DESS, box 2, file 33a, "Memorandum, Moral and Social Reform Council of Canada, Historical Statement by Dr. Chown," 14 Dec. 1908.

96 Albert Carman has been almost universally castigated by historians as a "conservative" because of his opposition to the higher criticism in the church colleges. See Margaret Prang, *Newton Wesley Rowell: Ontario Nationalist* (Toronto: University of Toronto Press, 1975); Gauvreau, *The Evangelical Century*, chapter 6.

97 UMA, Gordon Papers, box 17, folder 4, G.M. Macdonnell to Gordon, 26 Aug. 1910; UCA, Bliss Carman Papers, box 26, file 148, Chown to Carman, 6 Feb. 1908, 29 April 1908.

98 UCA, Presbyterian Church, Board of Moral and Social Reform, William J. Knox to Shearer, 3 Sept. 1909.

99 NA, Woodsworth Papers, vol. 2, Moore to Woodsworth, 6 March 1913.

100 UCA, United Church, DESS, *Annual Report*, 1937, 5. So powerful had this department become by 1937 that even under the financial constraints of the Depression it was able to forestall yet another motion by the Department of Missions to absorb it. See also UCA, Dobson Papers, box A10, file Mo, Dobson to Moore, 26 Nov. 1925.

101 UCA, Presbyterian Church, "Minutes of the Board of Moral and Social Reform," 16 Nov. 1910, 6 Sept. 1910; UCA, Methodist Church, DESS, box 7, file 141, "Department of Temperance and Moral Reform," 22 Oct. 1910; Ibid., "Social Service and Evangelism," 14 Sept. 1916; NA, Woodsworth Papers, vol. 2, Moore to Woodsworth, 27 March 1913; UCA, Presbyterian Church, "Minutes of Board of Moral and Social Reform," 27 Jan. 1911; Ibid., J.G. Shearer to President Westbrook, University of British Columbia, 2 Oct. 1916; UCA, Dobson Papers, box A5 file Moore, Moore to Dobson, 26 Nov., 1920; UMA, Gordon Papers, box 17, file 5, Shearer to Gordon, 20 Sept. 1909. For Brigden, see UCA, DESS, box 3, file 46, Moore to Brigden, 10 June 1914; Ibid., box 1, file 146, clipping, "A Convention of Business Girls," for Brigden's training in psychology and sociology. See also UCA, Dobson Papers, box A5, file B2, Moore to Dobson, 24 Jan. 1920.

102 UCA, Dobson Papers, box A5, file C2, Dobson to district secretaries of evangelism and social service, 31 July 1919.

103 UMA, Gordon Papers, box 17, file 3, R.H. Lowry to Gordon, 28 Sept. 1910.

104 UCA, Dobson Papers, box A4, file C, Dobson to Brother Cairns, 27 Dec. 1918.

105 Ibid., box A5, file S, David Simpson to Dobson, 13 Jan. 1920.

106 Ibid., box A5, file A, Dobson to John B. Andrews, 14 Nov. 1919.

107 Ibid., box A5, file R, Dobson to J. Wesley Smiley, 9 Feb. 1920.

108 See Airhart, *Serving the Present Age*, 92, for Thomas's observations.

109 UCA, Dobson Papers, box A5, file C2, Dobson to Dear Brother, 23 Oct. 1917.

110 UCA, Methodist Church, DESS, box 3, file 50, Moore to Brigden, 2 June 1915. Brigden was paid approximately $30 to $40 per week. Although many people were less responsive to her because of her sex, Brigden was more readily employed than her male counterpart William Clark because he was more expensive.

111 See Sangster, *Dreams of Equality*; Valverde, *The Age of Light, Soap and Water*, 73. The letter quoted by Valverde is taken out of context and should be read as a response to Moore's query as to what specialist work she would like to do. It should be noted that Brigden soon saw the limitations on speaking just to women and proposed that she address groups that included both men and women.

112 UCA, Methodist Church, DESS, box 3, file 49, Brigden to Moore, 29 Nov. 1915.

113 Ibid., box 3, file 47, Brigden to Moore, 30 Jan. 1915.

114 Ibid., box 3, file 54, Moore to Brigden, n.d.

115 Ibid., box 3, file 48, Brigden to Moore, 31 Aug. 1915; Ibid., box 3, file 49, Brigden to Moore, 20 Nov. 1915, "I have always maintained all work was religious."

116 Ibid., box 3, file 48, Brigden to Moore, 22 May 1915.

117 Ibid., box 3, file 47, Brigden to Moore, 6 Feb. 1915.

118 Ibid., box 3, file 49, Brigden to Moore, 29 Nov. 1915.

119 Ibid., box 3, file 46, Moore to Brigden, 10 June 1914; Ibid., box 3, file 50, Moore to Brigden, 2 June 1915; Ibid., box 3, file 48, Moore to Brigden, 12 July 1915.

120 Ibid., box 3, file 48, Brigden to Moore, 15 April, 1915.

121 Ibid., box 3, file 54, Brigden to Moore, 19 Feb. 1918, 12 March 1918.

122 Ibid., box 3, file 47, Brigden to Moore, 22 Aug. 1914, and *passim*.

123 Ibid., box 3, file 50, Moore to Brigden, 2 June 1915.

124 UMA, Gordon Papers, box 17, file 3, the Rev. R.H. Lowry to Gordon, 28 Sept. 1910.

125 UCA, Methdodist Church, DESS, box 3, file 47, Brigden to Moore, 6 March 1915.

126 Ibid., box 3, file 46, Brigden to Moore, 2 June 1914.
127 Ibid., box 3, file 49, Brigden to Moore, 20 Nov. 1915.
128 Ibid., Brigden to Moore, file 46, 2 June 1914.
129 Ibid., box 3, file 46, Brigden to Moore, 12 June 1914, 10 June 1914.
130 See George Rawlyk, *Ravished by the Spirit* (Montreal and Kingston: McGill-Queen's University Press, 1985); and Rawlyk, *Wrapped Up in God: A Study of Several Canadian Revivals and Revivalists* (Burlington, Ont.: Welch Academic Publications, 1988).
131 For the belief that Western Canada gave a monolithic allegiance to the social gospel, see Allen, *The Social Passion*; Gerald Friesen, *The Canadian Prairies: A History* (Toronto: University of Toronto Press, 1984); Butcher, ed., *Prairie Spirit*.
132 UCA, Methodist Church, DESS, box 3, file 47, Brigden to Moore, May 1915.
133 Ibid., box 3, file 48, Moore to Brigden, 12 May 1915.
134 Ibid., box 3, file 49, Brigden to Moore, 27 Oct. 1915.
135 Ibid., Moore to Brigden, 29 Oct. 1915, Brigden to Moore, 8 Nov. 1915, 11 Nov. 1915; Moore to Brigden, 12 Nov. 1915.
136 Ibid., Brigden to Moore, 29 Nov. 1915, 11 Nov. 1915.
137 Ibid., Brigden to Moore, 6 Dec. 1915.
138 Ibid., box 3, file 48, Brigden to Moore, 18 May 1915; Ibid., box 3, file 49, Brigden to Moore, 1 Feb. 1916.
139 Ibid., box 3 file 48, Brigden to Moore, 21 June 1915.
140 Ibid., box 3, file 50, Brigden to Moore, 11 May 1916.
141 Ibid., box 3, file 49, Brigden to Moore, 7 Feb. 1916, 31 March 1916.
142 UCA, Dobson Papers, box A2, file G, "Report of Committee on Social Service and Evangelism," Manitoba Conference, June 1917. Smith was the president and M.C. Flett was the representative for North Winnipeg.
143 UCA, Methodist Church, DESS, box 3, file 55, Brigden to Moore, 26 July 1919, 19 May 1919; Ibid., Moore to Brigden, 18 July 1919. For Brigden's early friendship with Smith, see Ibid., box 3, file 45, Brigden to Moore, 13 Jan. 1914.
144 Ibid., box 3, file 56, Brigden to Moore, 27 April 1920.
145 Ibid., box 3, file 55, Brigden to Moore, 26 July 1919.
146 Ibid., box 7, file 122, Hamilton to Moore, 12 July 1920, 17 July 1920, 29 July 1921, 25 April 1922; Hamilton, "Notes on the Labor Churches," n.d. These letter reflect Hamilton's views more than those of Moore.
147 Ibid., box 3, file 56, Brigden to Moore, 14 Jan. 1920.
148 Ibid., box 3, file 55, Moore to Brigden, 31 July 1919.
149 For the view that there were intellectual differences between conservatives, progressives, and radicals, see Allen, *The Social Passion*.
150 UCA, Dobson Papers, box A5, file Moore, Dobson to Moore, 3 March 1920.

151 NA, Sissons Papers, vol. 5, Woodsworth to Sissons, 9 Aug. 1905.

152 UCA, Dobson Papers, box A5, file A, Dobson to John B. Andrews, 14 Nov. 1919.

153 Ibid., box A4, file C, Dobson to William T. Cross, general secretary, National Conference of Social Work, 11 Oct. 1917; Ibid., box A4, file A, Dobson to John B. Andrews, 21 May 1918; Ibid., box A5, file Andrews, "Committee on Evangelism and Social Service, Manitoba Conference, 1920."

154 UCA, Chown Papers, box 1, file 1, "Extract from the Annual Report of the Department of Temperance and Moral Reform of the Methodist Church, 1908"; UCA, Methodist Church, DESS, box 7, file 141, "Circular from Moore and Chown," 22 Oct. 1910.

155 UMA, Gordon Papers, box 16, file 1, "Minutes of Board of Moral and Social Reform," 9 Sept. 1908; Ibid., box 17, file 5, J.G. Shearer to Gordon, 9 May 1913.

156 NA, Canadian Council of Churches, box 29, "Report of the Executive of the Social Service Council of Canada for the Year 1925," 8; UCA, Dobson Papers, box A5, file Andrews, W.W. Andrews to Moore, 14 Dec. 1916; Ibid., box A5, file Moore, "Memo of Conference of Field Secretaries," 3 Aug. 1920, Dobson to Moore, 29 June 1921; Ibid., box A5, file E, Dobson to the Rev. Samuel East, Osago, Sask., 21 Sept. 1920; Ibid., box A4, file B, Dobson to the Rev. Charles Burnes, 14 Nov. 1919; UCA, Methodist Church, DESS, box 2, file 37, Moore to the Rev. W.W. Andrews, 19 Dec. 1913; UMA, Gordon Papers, box 16, folder 1, "Minutes of Joint Executives of Moral and Social Reform and Evangelism," 23 March 1911. *"...that IS getting down to business*, Methodist National Campaign Pamphlet, n.d., contains a photograph of T. Albert Moore and the office staff of the DESS. The photograph conveys the image of a smooth-running, efficient organization.

157 UCA, Dobson Papers, box A4, file F, Dobson to the Rev. S.W. Fallis, book steward, Methodist Book and Publishing House, 16 Aug. 1919.

158 UCA, Methodist Church, DESS, box 3, file 55, Brigden to Moore, 26 July 1919.

CHAPTER TWO

1 UMA, Gordon Papers, box 50, file 4, E. de B. Ramsay to Gordon, 14 Jan. 1912.

2 UMA, Gordon Papers, box 49, file 7, Frederick S. Hartman to Gordon, 8 March 1907; Ibid., box 49, file 6, Alfred Fitzpatrick to Gordon, 20 Jan. 1904.

3 UMA, Gordon Papers, box 49, folder 7, 10 Jan. 1907.

4 David B. Marshall, *Secularizing the Faith: Canadian Protestant Clergy and the Crisis of Belief 1840–1940* (Toronto: University of Toronto Press, 1992), 139–45.

5 Nathan O. Hatch, *The Democratization of American Christianity* (New Haven and London: Yale University Press, 1989); William McLoughlin, *Revivals, Awakenings and Reform: An Essay on Religion and Social Change in America, 1607–1977* (Chicago: University of Chicago Press, 1978); Timothy L. Smith, *Revivalism and Social Reform in Mid-Nineteenth-Century America* (New York: Abingdon Press, 1957); James Gilbert, *Perfect Cities: Chicago's Utopias of 1893* (Chicago: University of Chicago Press, 1991).

6 For the importance of revivalism in Canada, see George Rawlyk, *Ravished by the Spirit* (Montreal and Kingston: McGill-Queen's University Press, 1985), *Wrapped up in God: A Study of Several Canadian Revivals and Revivalists* (Burlington: Welch Publishing Company, 1988). For the connection between evangelicalism and democratic popular culture in the eighteenth century, see Nancy J. Christie, "'In These Times of Democratic Rage and Delusion': Popular Religion and the Challenge to the Established Order, 1760–1815," in G.A. Rawlyk, ed., *The Canadian Protestant Experience* (Burlington: Welch Publishing, 1991), 9–47. For a recent statement on a similar theme, see Rawlyk, "'A Total Revolution in Religious and Civil Government': The Maritimes, New England and the Evolving Evangelical Ethos, 1776–1812," in Mark Noll, et al., eds., *Evangelicalism* (New York: Oxford University Press, 1994), 137–55.

7 See Christie, "'In These Times of Democratic Rage and Delusion,'" and, for the weakening of English Methodism's influence through class fragmentation, see Hatch, *The Democratization of American Christianity*, 91–3.

8 For the deliberate downplaying of revivalism among Methodists between 1830 and 1870, see William Westfall, *Two Worlds* (Montreal and Kingston: McGill-Queen's University Press, 1989), chapter 3. For a case study of the "genteel" and sanitized revivalism acceptable to the Victorian middle classes, see Neil Semple, "The Quest for the Kingdom: Aspects of Protestant Revivalism in Nineteenth-Century Ontario," in David Keane and Colin Read, eds., *Old Ontario: Essays in Honour of J.M.S. Careless* (Toronto: Dundurn Press, 1990), 95–117. For the Baptist desire to create a "respectable" religion, see Rawlyk, *Ravished by the Spirit*. For the evangelical alliance with middle-class élites and the process of institution-building, see Gauvreau, "Personal Piety and the Evangelical Social Vision," in Rawlyk, ed., *The Canadian Protestant Experience*, 48–98.

9 David Gagan, *Hopeful Travellers* (Toronto: University of Toronto Press, 1978).

10 To date the best analysis of the divisions between old Canadian and immigrant farmers and between owner-operators and farm labourers is R. W. Murchie, *Unused Lands of Manitoba* (Winnipeg: n.p., 1926).

11 For divisions of status within the middle classes, see Nancy J. Christie, "Psychology, Sociology and the Secular Moment: the Ontario Educational

Association's Quest for Authority, 1880–1900," *Journal of Canadian Studies*, 25:2 (Summer 1990), 119–43.

12 See UCA, Biographical Files; UCA, Dobson Papers, box A11, file P.

13 In the American context, historians of modern revivalism have made much of this split in the evangelical consensus between social reform "liberals" and conservative revivalist "fundamentalists." See, for example, Bernard A. Weisberger, *They Gathered at the River: The Story of the Great Revivalists and their Impact on Religion in America* (Boston and Toronto: Little, Brown & Co., 1958), 177–8; William McLoughlin, *Modern Revivalism: Charles Grandison Finney to Billy Graham* (New York: Ronald Press, 1959), 347–99; George Marsden, *Fundamentalism and American Culture: The Shaping of Twentieth-Century Evangelicalism, 1870–1925* (New York: Oxford University Press, 1980), 91; McLoughlin, *Revivals, Awakenings, and Reform.*

14 Phyllis Airhart, *Serving the Present Age: Revivalism, Progressivism, and the Methodist Tradition in Canada* (Montreal and Kingston: McGill-Queen's University Press, 1992), 108–9.

15 UCA, Dobson Papers, box 5A, file Andrews, the Rev. Harball to Dobson, 27 Nov. 1918.

16 UCA, Presbyterian Church, box 1, file 3, "Annual Meeting of Department of Evangelism and Social Service," 15–17 Sept. 1915.

17 UCA, Methodist Church, DESS, box 3, file 48, Brigden to Moore, 3 May 1915. The lack of advertising material was a constant complaint throughout Brigden's correspondence with Moore.

18 UCA, Dobson Papers, box A5, file Mo, Moore to Dobson, 15 May 1920; Ibid., file L, Dobson to Mr J. Levine, Allen Theatre, Regina, 8 Nov. 1919; Ibid., box A4, file A, W.W. Abbott to Dobson, 28 March 1918.

19 UCA, Dobson Papers, box A5, file B1, Moore to the Rev. John Pate, Rouleau, Sask., 21 Sept. 1920.

20 Ibid., box A4, file S, Dobson to the Rev. James Smith, Biggar, Sask., 27 May 1918. That these exhibits reached thousands of people was Dobson's own observation.

21 For the prominent role child conversion played in both British and American revivalism, see John Kent, *Holding the Fort* (London: Epworth Press, 1978), 90–4.

22 UCA, Dobson Papers, box A4, file C, A.W. Coone, general secretary, Alberta Social Service League, to Dobson, 24 Oct. 1917.

23 Ibid., box A5, file Mo, Dobson to Moore, 6 Sept. 1920.

24 For this interpretation, see Marshall, *Secularizing the Faith*, 127–55; and, for the view that "mass culture" weakened the few existing bonds of working-class unity, see Bryan D. Palmer, *Working-Class Experience: The Rise and Reconstitution of Canadian Labour, 1800–1980* (Toronto: Butterworth Press, 1983), 190–5.

25 UMA, Gordon Papers, "Minutes of the Joint Executives of the Board of Moral and Social Reform and Evangelism," 23 March 1911; UCA, Methodist Church, DESS, box 3, file 48, Brigden to Moore, 31 Aug. 1915; Ibid., box 7, file 146, "Rev. Dr. Moore's Visit," clipping, *Western Methodist Recorder*, n.d.; AO, Ontario Welfare Council, F837, series 3, box 14, file 1928, "Annual Report of the General Secretary of the Social Service Council of Ontario," 17 May 1928. The latter reported that until the late 1920s, there were few vaudeville houses in Ontario, but that these had mushroomed so that by 1928 there existed approximately 300, with one third being in Toronto.

26 William Leach, *Land of Desire: Merchants, Power, and the Rise of a New American Culture* (New York: Pantheon Books, 1993), 6–15.

27 James Gilbert defines mass culture as "those signs, symbols, language, institutions, and behavior by which one defines oneself and interacts with others that are translated through and communicated by the commercial media." See *Perfect Cities*, 262, n.74. Because of the weakness of commercial media in the more localized and rural Canadian society of the early twentieth century, according to this definition mass culture was correspondingly less strong than in the United States.

28 R.C. Brown and Ramsay Cook, *Canada 1896–1921: A Nation Transformed* (Toronto: McClelland and Stewart, 1974). For most working-class Canadians, consumerist amusements and "mass culture" remained economically out of reach. See Terry Copp, *The Anatomy of Poverty* (Toronto: McClelland and Stewart, 1974).

29 This point is implicitly made in J.H. Thompson with Allen Seager, *Canada 1922–1939: Decades of Discord* (Toronto: McClelland and Stewart, 1985), 3–4.

30 Thompson and Seager, *Decades of Discord*, 181.

31 Paul Litt, *The Muses, the Masses, and the Massey Commission* (Toronto: University of Toronto Press, 1992).

32 Russell Johnston, "The Early Trials of Protestant Radio, 1922–38," *Canadian Historical Review*, 75:3 (September 1994), 376–402.

33 UMA, Gordon Papers, box 17, folder 5, Shearer to Gordon, 30 Jan. 1902.

34 Ibid., box 48, folder 4, the Rev. J. Burrow, Te Aroha, Auckland, New Zealand, to Gordon, 22 Nov. 1906.

35 Ibid., box 48, file 4, E.A. Hardy to Gordon, 19 May 1908; Ibid., box 17, folder 5, Trotter to Gordon, 30 Jan. 1902.

36 Ibid., box 50, folder 2, John Moffatt to Gordon, 12 Dec. 1932; Ibid., box 48, folder 4, J.W. Graves, Carnduff, Sask., to Gordon, 6 Aug. 1906; Ibid., box 17, folder 4, James D. Orr to Gordon, 5 Aug. 1909.

37 NA, Sissons Papers, vol. 5, Woodsworth to Sissons, 16 June 1902.

38 For the theme of usefulness suffusing the social gospel in the United States, see Susan Curtis, *A Consuming Faith: The Social Gospel and*

Modern American Culture (Baltimore and London: Johns Hopkins University Press, 1991).

39 For the breakdown of the connection between the church college and the local congregation, see Michael Gauvreau, *The Evangelical Century: College and Creed in English Canada from the Great Revival to the Great Depression* (Montreal & Kingston: McGill-Queen's University Press, 1991), chapter 6.

40 UMA, Gordon Papers, box 17, folder 5, Shearer to Gordon, 22 Nov. 1909. According to Brian Fraser, the insistence upon the importance of the "person" of Christ was a hallmark of progressive piety among leading Presbyterian clergymen, who were strongly influenced by the revivalism of Dwight Moody. See Brian Fraser, *The Social Uplifters: Presbyterian Progressives and the Social Gospel in Canada, 1875–1915* (Waterloo: Wilfrid Laurier University Press, 1988), 1–17.

41 UCA, Methodist Church, DESS, box 3, file 51, "Report to Dept. of Temperance and Moral Reform," 1916; Ibid., box 3, file 52, Brigden to Moore, 17 July 1917, clipping from Lloydminster *Gazette* noting Brigden's "clear vision of social redemption and her whole-hearted belief in the expression of the Christ spirit in all phases of life."

42 UCA, Methodist Church, DESS, box 3, file 48, Brigden to Moore, n.d.

43 UCA, Dobson Papers, box A5, file B2, Joseph B. Francis, Camrose Methodist Church to Dobson, 9 June 1920.

44 UCA, Methodist Church, DESS, box 3, file 48, Brigden to Moore, 18 May 1915.

45 UMA, Gordon Papers, box 16, folder 1, "Minutes of the Board of Social Service and Evangelism," Sept. 5–7, 1911; UCA, Methodist Church, DESS, box 7, file 146, "Rev. Dr. Moore's Visit," *Western Methodist Recorder*, n.d., where he advocated the establishment of social clubs to compete with saloons.

46 UMA, Gordon Papers, box 17, folder 2, the Rev. R.J. Koffend to Gordon, 12 Nov. 1914.

47 UCA/UW, All People's Mission Papers, box B, "Interdenominational Advisory Council," n.d.

48 UCA/UW, All People's Mission Papers, box B, E. Chambers, "Burrows Avenue – The Polish Work," n.d.; Ibid., W. Wyman, "Maple Street," n.d.; Ibid., Walter H. Pavy, "Sutherland Avenue Institute," n.d.

49 UCA/UW, All People's Mission Papers, box B, J.S. Woodsworth, "Grand Theatre Meetings," n.d.

50 NA, Woodsworth Papers, vol. 15, file 7, "Methodist Social Service in Winnipeg," program for the People's Forum, 1916–17. For the view that the People's Forum promoted an incipient radicalism, see Ramsay Cook, "Francis Marion Beynon and the Crisis of Christian Reformism," in Carl Berger and Ramsay Cook, eds., *The West and the Nation:*

Essays in Honour of W.L. Morton (Toronto: McClelland and Stewart, 1976).

51 Quoted in J.S. Woodsworth, *My Neighbor* (Toronto: University of Toronto Press, 1972), introduction by Richard Allen, 201.

52 UCA, Methodist Church, DESS, box 3, file 54, Brigden to Moore, 12 March 1918.

53 UCA, Dobson Papers, box A4, file C, the Rev. R.O. Armstrong to Dobson, 17 May 1918.

54 For the appeal of the new culture of consumer capitalism, see Leach, *Land of Desire*.

55 UMA, Gordon Papers, box 17, folder 5, Shearer to Gordon, 11 Dec. 1908.

56 UCA, Methodist Church, DESS, box 7, file 175, "Report of Department of Evangelism and Social Service," 1918.

57 UCA, Dobson Papers, box A2, file G, *Five Thousand Canadians Gathered to Hear Dr. Oliver deliver His Famous Lecture: "The Lake of Fire"* (pamphlet, n.d.).

58 Ibid., box A7, file Mo, Moore to Mr H.H. Hull, general secretary, Alberta Social Service Council, 14 May, 1923; Ibid., box A2, file G, *Applying Christian Principles to Industrial Unrest – How a Methodist Minister Did It* (pamphlet no. 59, DESS, n.d.)

59 Ibid., box A2, file G, the Rev. Charles W. Gordon, *The Simultaneous Evangelistic Mission in Minnedosa Presbytery* (pamphlet, n.d.), 7–11.

60 UCA, Methodist Church, DESS, box 3, file 52, William MacNiven to Moore, 7 Feb. 1917.

61 Ibid., box 3, file 47, Brigden to Moore, 30 Jan. 1915; Ibid., box 3, file 49, Brigden to Moore, 7 Feb. 1916.

62 Ibid., box 3, file 59, Brigden to Moore, 22 Oct. 1915; Ibid., box 3, file 56, Brigden to Moore, May 1920.

63 UMA, Gordon Papers, box 17, folder 5, Shearer to Gordon, 24 Nov. 1910.

64 UCA, Methodist Church, DESS, box 3, file 49, Brigden to Moore, 20 Nov. 1915.

65 Ibid., box 3, file 49, Brigden to Moore, 20 Dec. 1915.

66 Ibid., box 3, file 48, Brigden to Moore, 18 May 1915.

67 Ibid., box 3, file 48, Brigden to Moore, 29 May 1915; Ibid., box 3, file 49, Brigden to Moore, 7 Feb. 1916.

68 UCA, Dobson Papers, box A5, file B2, Moore to Dobson, 10 March 1920.

69 UCA, Methodist Church, DESS, box 3, file 49, Brigden to Moore, 18 April 1916.

70 Ibid., box 3, file 51, Brigden to Moore, 15 May 1916.

71 Ibid., box 3, file 49, Brigden to Moore, 7 Feb. 1916.

72 Ibid., box 3, file 51, Brigden to Moore, 21 Aug. 1916.

73 Ibid., box 3, file 52, Brigden to Moore, 24 Feb. 1917; Ibid., Box 3, file 49, Brigden to Moore, 18 Jan. 1916.

74 Ibid., box 3, file 49, Brigden to Moore, 7 Feb. 1916.
75 UCA, Dobson Papers, box A4, file C, Dobson to Clarke, 6 Sept. 1919; UCA, Methodist Church, DESS, box 3, file 48, Brigden to Moore, 22 May 1915.
76 UCA, Dobson Papers, box A4, file B, the Rev. Bentley to Dobson, 22 Feb. 1919.
77 Ibid., box A4, file B, the Rev. E.D. Braden to Dobson, 18 Aug. 1919.
78 UMA, Gordon Papers, box 17, folder 7, Gordon to the Rev. A. Macmillan, 27 July 1909.
79 PAM, MG 14 C58, Charles W. Gordon Papers, Dave to my dear wife, 23 April, 1905. The tradition of Scottish popular evangelism has been well treated in Leigh Eric Schmidt, *Holy Fairs* (Princeton: Princeton University Press, 1989).
80 UMA, Charles W. Gordon Papers, box 16, folder 7, the Rev. Francis Hall to Gordon, 28 Dec. 1909.
81 Ibid., box 17, folder 4, the Rev. W. McNally to Gordon, 15 April 1909.
82 Rawlyk, *Wrapped Up in God*, 88.
83 UMA, Charles W. Gordon Papers, box 30, folder 10, "Social Service and Evangelism," n.d.
84 Ibid., box 16, folder 6, the Rev. Anderson Rogers to Gordon, 8 May 1909.
85 See Bryan D. Palmer, *A Culture in Conflict* (Montreal and Kingston: McGill-Queen's University Press, 1979); Gregory S. Kealey, *Toronto Workers Respond to Industrial Capitalism, 1867–1892* (Toronto: University of Toronto Press, 1980).
86 UMA, Charles W. Gordon Papers, box 17, folder 5, Shearer to Gordon, 27 Nov. 1909.
87 For a longer discussion of this pattern of working-class religious conservatism in Winnipeg, see Nancy Christie and Michael Gauvreau, "'The World of the Common Man Is Filled with Religious Fervour': The Labouring People of Winnipeg and the Persistence of Revivalism, 1914–1925," paper delivered to Aspects of the Canadian Evangelical Experience Conference, 10–14 May 1995, Kingston, Ont.
88 Thomas Fisher Rare Books Library, Robert S. Kenny Collection, box 37, folder 2, A.E. Smith, "The Passing Shadow," incomplete and unpublished typescript, n.d., chapter 1, "The Revival Passion," 2–7; chapter 2, "The Industrial Crucible," 3.
89 UCA, John Maclean Papers, box 11, file 16, "Diary," entry for 26 Nov. 1919. For Ivens's typical sermons during this period, see "Church News," *Winnipeg Free Press*, 3 May 1919, when he spoke on "The Significance of the One Big Union," and 18 May 1918, when he addressed his congregation on "The Right to Strike."
90 Christie and Gauvreau, "'The World of the Common People Is Filled with Religious Fervour.'"

91 On Pentecostalism in Winnipeg, see Edith L. Blumhofer, *Aimee Semple McPherson: Everybody's Sister* (Grand Rapids: William B. Eerdman's Company, 1993), 150–1. On the appeal of conservative evangelicalism to workers in Vancouver, see Robert K. Burkinshaw, *Pilgrims in Lotus Land: Conservative Protestantism in British Columbia, 1917–81* (Montreal and Kingston: McGill-Queen's University Press, 1995), 101–8.

92 Billy Graham Center Archives, Wheaton College, Wheaton, Ill., J. Wilbur Chapman Papers, collection 77, box 3, folder 5, scrapbook 15, "Evangelistic Campaign Inaugurated in Toronto," *World*, 6 Jan. 1911.

93 Ibid., "Toronto Revival Starts in Earnest," *World*, 6 Jan. 1911; "Evangelists Sway Audience of Men," *Globe*, 9 Jan. 1911.

94 The venues included Massey Hall, where Chapman and Alexander held mass meetings, College Street Baptist, Cooke's Presbyterian, Wesley Methodist, Westmoreland Methodist, Zion Methodist, Dunn Avenue Presbyterian, Euclid Avenue Methodist, Central Methodist Church, East Toronto Baptist, Simpson Avenue Methodist, and Walmer Road Baptist churches, as well as a women's meeting at Metropolitan Methodist Church. See *Telegram*, 9 Jan. 1911.

95 Billy Graham Center Archives, Chapman Papers, box 3, folder 5, "Hold a Service in Railway Car," *Globe*, 12 Jan. 1911; Ibid., "Attendances on Monday," *Telegram*, 10 Jan. 1911.

96 Ibid., box 3, folder 5, "A Great Meeting at Taylor Works," *Star*, 6 Jan. 1911. During his services Chapman often stated that industrial unrest could be reconciled through the extension of spiritual concern in industrial life. See "Crowds Increase as Revival Spreads," *World*, 11 Jan. 1911.

97 Ibid., Professor Joseph Gilmour, "Put Finishing Touches on the Preliminary Part of Campaign," *Star*, 13 Jan. 1911; Ibid., "Noted Evangelists Receiving Daily Many Pathetic Requests for Prayer," *Globe*, 6 Jan. 1911.

98 Airhart, *Serving the Present Age*, 3–11.

99 Marsden, *Fundamentalism and American Culture*.

100 Billy Sunday was a disciple of J. Wilbur Chapman and began his evangelistic career as an advance man for Chapman. For the importance of Sunday's legacy for conservative fundamentalism, see Lyle W. Dorset, *Billy Sunday and the Redemption of Urban America* (Grand Rapids, Mich.: William B. Eerdmann's, 1991); Roger A. Bruns, *Preacher: Billy Sunday and Big Time American Evangelism* (New York: W. W. Norton and Co., 1992). For Chapman's Canadian campaigns and their importance in promoting social service, see Airhart, *Serving the Present Age*, 86, 129.

101 NA, Canadian Council of Churches, T. Albert Moore, "The Challenge of Social Service to the Christian Church," Conference on Social Welfare, 26–29 Jan. 1927, 89.

102 UMA, Gordon Papers, box 17, folder 5, Shearer to Gordon, 28 May 1914.

103 Ibid., box 17, folder 5, Shearer to Gordon, 25 Jan. 1909.

104 Numerous clergymen from all across Canada reported to C.W. Gordon on the immense popularity of Chapman's revivalistic campaigns of 1908–9. See UMA, Gordon Papers, box 17, folder 1, the Rev. W.A. Brown, convenor of home missions, to Gordon, 14 Sept. 1909; Ibid., box 16, folder 3, "Minutes General Assembly's Committee on Evangelism," 1909; Ibid., box 17, folder 5, Shearer to Gordon, 19 June 1908; UCA, Dobson Papers, box A2, file G, *The Sin that We Are Afraid to Mention, the Confessions of a Businessman* (pamphlet, 1913), 3.

105 UCA, Methodist Church, DESS, box 7, file 140, *Hamilton Herald*, clipping, n.d.

106 UMA, Gordon Papers, box 16, folder 13, "Truro Campaign," n.d.

107 Ibid., box 17, folder 4, the Rev. H. Fern MacKay to Gordon, 30 Nov., 1908; Ibid., box 17, folder 6, R.A. Torrey to Gordon, 28 May 1906; Ibid., box 17, folder 2, the Rev. John H. Elliott to Gordon, 27 Oct. 1909.

108 UCA, Dobson Papers, box A2, file G, "Union Tabernacle Campaign, Sault Ste. Marie, Ontario, conducted by Rev. H.L. Stephens and Party," n.d.

109 UCA, Methodist Church Army and Navy Board, 78.801C, box 28, file 619, T. Albert Moore to Brother, 17 July 1919.

110 UCA, Dobson Papers, box A8, file Mo, Moore to Dobson, 20 Jan. 1924.

111 Ibid., box A7, file Mo, Moore to Dobson, 5 May 1923.

112 UCA, Methodist Church, DESS, box 7, file 136, T. Albert Moore, "The Revival in Progress," n.d., 5–7; UCA, Mutchmor Papers, box 16, "Autobiography MS.," 31.

113 UCA, Dobson Papers, box A2, file G, E.I. Hart, *The Challenge of Montreal* (pamphlet, n.d.), 1–5.

114 UMA, Gordon Papers, box 16, folder 6, "Report on Evangelism, Central Section," 11 May 1909.

115 Ibid. Despite his desire to attract a new working-class audience, Gordon's real sympathies lay with the traditional constituency of middle-class church-goers, who he said were embittered against the emotional excesses associated with revivalism; UCA, Dobson Papers, box A2, file G, *H. Arthur Barton, Special Preacher* (pamphlet, n.d.), n.p.

116 Ibid., *H. Arthur Barton, Special Preacher*; UCA, Mutchmor Papers, box 16, "Autobiography, MS.," 32.

117 UMA, Gordon Papers, box 16, folder 7, the Rev. John W. Little to Gordon, 24 Dec. 1909.

118 UMA, Gordon Papers, box 7, folder 4, the Rev. H. Fern McKay to Gordon, 30 Nov. 1908.

119 For Nicholson, see Horn, *The League for Social Reconstruction*, 63.

120 UMA, Gordon Papers, box 17, folder 4, the Rev. J.W.A. Nicholson to Gordon, 6 April 1909; Ibid., box 17, folder 1, George H. Doran to Gordon, 18 May 1906.

121 Ibid., box 18, folder 2, Gordon to Presbytery of Minnedosa, 2 Dec. 1908; UCA, Methodist Church, DESS, box 7, file 133, T. Albert Moore, "Human Brotherhood," n.d., 7; Ibid., box 7, file 136, Moore, "The Revival in Progress," n.d., 5–7.

122 Ibid., box 7, file 133, Moore "Human Brotherhood," 9. A more practical and real-life form of preaching was directed particularly to converting recent European immigrants. See UCA, Dobson papers, box A2, file A, "Manitoba Conference Report of Commission on Work Among Non-English-speaking People," n.d. J.S. Woodsworth, W.A. Cook, W.W. Adamson, and A.O Rose were the ministers who conducted this initial social survey among Ruthenians in Western Canada.

123 UCA, Methodist Church, DESS, box 7, file 136, Moore, "The Revival in Progress," n.d., 5–7; Ibid., box 7, file 133, Moore, "Human Brotherhood," 18.

124 UCA, Presbyterian Church, Board of Moral and Social Reform, "Confidential Suggestions to Pastors, Missioners and Directors of Song," 1911, 5; UMA, Gordon Papers, box 18, folder 2, Gordon to Presbytery of Minnedosa, 2 Dec. 1908.

125 UCA, Methodist Church, DESS, box 7, file 133, Moore, "Human Brotherhood," 9–10; Ibid., box 7, file 136, Moore, "The Revival in Progress," 5–7; UMA, Gordon Papers, box 16, folder 13, "Extracts from Letters of Missioners," the Rev. R.J. Wilson to Gordon, n.d; UCA, Presbyterian Church, Board of Moral and Social Reform, "Confidential Suggestions to Pastors, Missioners and Directors of Song," 1911, 4.

126 UCA, James Robertson Memorial Lectures, box 2, file 6, D.N. McLachlan, "The Minister of To-Day," n.d.

127 Wiebe, *The Search for Order*; for the conflict between "moral" and "scientistic" emphases in American Progressivism, see David B. Danbom, *"The World of Hope": Progressives and the Struggle for an Ethical Public Life* (Philadelphia: Temple University Press, 1987).

128 UCA, Methodist Church, DESS, box 2, file 34, "Minutes and Correspondence of Manitoba Conference, Evangelistic Committee, 1913"; UMA, Gordon Papers, box 16, folder 7, the Rev. A.M. Churchill to Gordon, 22 Dec. 1909; Ibid., box 16, folder 6, John A. McDonald, secretary of the Evangelism Committee, Ottawa, to the Rev. D. McTavish, 15 May 1909.

129 UMA, Gordon Papers, box 16, folder 17, "The Conduct of a Simultaneous Mission of Evangelism," n.d., 1–3; Ibid., box 16, folder 6, "Preparation for Revival."

130 UCA, Methodist Church, DESS, box 7, file 133, Moore, "Human Brothhood," n.d., 15; UCA, Dobson Papers, box A5, file For, *The Methodist National Campaign* (pamphlet, #19), n.d., 4–7; Ibid., *The Methodist National Campaign* (pamphlet, #6), n.d., 7.

131 Ibid., 5–7.

132 Ibid., box A7, file Mo, Dobson to Moore, 13 Dec. 1922. For the important role of advertising, see UCA, Methodist Church, DESS, box 3, file 48, Brigden to Moore, 15 April 1915.

133 UMA, Gordon Papers, box 16, folder 6, "Preparation for Revival," n.d., 4. The Presbyterian Church defended its desire to stay on the cutting-edge of modern methods by asking "what religious movement is not advertised these days." See Ibid., box 17, folder 4, the Rev. H. Fern McKay to Gordon, 3 Nov. 1908.

134 UMA, Gordon Papers, box 16, folder 13, "Confidential Report, Fort Frances Mission," n.d.

135 Ibid., box 16, folder 7, J.A. Coldwell, Pilot Mound, Sask., to Gordon, 28 Dec. 1909.

136 See Airhart, *Serving the Present Age*, 95–9.

137 UMA, Gordon Papers, box 16, folder 7, Alexander J. McIntosh to Gordon, 31 Dec. 1909; Ibid., J.A. Coldwell to Gordon, 28 Dec. 1909. On this point, see Airhart, *Serving the Present Age*, 6–9, 107; Airhart, "Christian Socialism and the Legacy of Revivalism in the 1930's," in Harold Wells and Roger Hutchison, eds., *A Long and Faithful March* (Toronto: United Church Publishing House, 1989), 35.

138 UCA, Methodist Church, DESS, box 7, file 145, "Evangelism and Social Service," General Conference of 1918; Ibid., box 7, file 128, "Toronto Confence Annual Report, Evangelism and Social Service, 1919," 2; UCA, Dobson Papers, box A8, file Mo, Moore to Dobson, 19 May 1924. That this new evangelism multiplied and diversified the activities of the church was attested to by the Hamilton Methodist Conference. See UCA, Methodist Church, DESS, box 7, file 128, "Hamilton Conference Annual Report of Evangelism and Social Service, 1919." For the Presbyterian belief that testifying for Christ involved both private and public piety, see UCA, Presbyterian Church, "Minutes of the General Assembly's Committee on Evangelism, 9 Sept. 1909." David B. Danbom has argued that American Progressivism was based on the reconciliation between private and public morality. See *The World of Hope*, viii.

139 UMA, Gordon Papers, box 16, folder 7, McIntosh to Gordon, 31 Dec. 1909.

140 J.S. Woodsworth, *My Neighbor*, 55.

141 UCA, Chown Papers, box 3, file 66, "Ordination Sermon, Bay of Quinte Conference, Peterborough, 5 June 1904." On this same point, see Airhart, *Serving the Present Age*, 82, 96. David Marshall interprets this quotation as evidence of secularization. See Marshall, *Secularizing the Faith*, 149–50. Rather than repudiating the transcendence of nineteenth-century revivalism, Chown is arguing against the more spontaneous and flamboyant, yet less enduring, methods of revivalism fashionable in the nineteenth century. Like Moore and Dobson, Chown preferred to see

professional-led mass revivals give way to ongoing evangelistic practices within each local congregation.

142 UCA, Dobson Papers, box A5, file Mo, Moore to Dobson, 17 Feb. 1920; Ibid., Methodist Church, DESS, box 6, file 113, "Memorandum Social Service and Evangelism," 21 Sept. 1916; UCA, Mutchmor Papers, box 16, "Autobiography MS," 31–2.

143 UCA, Dobson Papers, box A7, file Mo, Moore to Dobson, 31 July 1922. Progressive clergymen placed a new emphasis upon developing a "better conscience" rather than church membership, and this implied that their program of evangelism and social service could be undertaken within a wide range of professions and institutions in modern society.

144 UMA, Gordon Papers, box 16, folder 14, "Report of the Committee on Social Service and Evangelism," n.d.

145 Ibid., box 17, file 5, Shearer to Gordon, 20 Jan. 1911; Ibid., box 17, file 7, Gordon to Shearer, 12 April 1913.

146 Ibid., box 17, folder 7, Gordon to Shearer, 2 May 1914.

147 UCA, Methodist Church, DESS, box 7, file 40, "Great Crowds Hear Conference Men, June 22, Lunenburg, Nova Scotia," newspaper clipping, n.d.; UMA, Gordon Papers, box 16, file 13, "West Fort William Mission," n.d.; UCA, Dobson Papers, box 19, file Dobson, Dobson to Dr Switzer, 22 Feb. 1925.

148 UCA, Dobson Papers, box A2, file G, *The Church, the War and Patriotism* (pamphlet, Army and Navy Board, Methodist Church, n.d.), 2; Ibid., box A5, file Forward Movement, *The Next Phase* (pamphlet, n.d.), 2, 6; UCA, James Robertson Memorial Lectures, box 2, file 6, D.N. McLachlan, "Factors in Canada to be Molded into a Christian Unity," 1–2. In 1919 the pamphlet *The Church, the War and Patriotism* was mailed along with *Evangelism and Social Service* to all families in each Western Canadian Methodist circuit. See UCA, Dobson Papers, box A4, file E, Dobson to the Rev. W.P. Ewing, Penticton, B.C., 5 June 1919. For the notion of sacrifice as a prominent theme in the religious thought of the 1920s, see Gauvreau, *The Evangelical Century*, chapter 7. Canadian religious leaders were successful in elevating the idea of sacrificial service to the status of the official ideology of government and society by 1917. See John English, *The Decline of Politics: The Conservatives and the Party System, 1901–1920* (Toronto: University of Toronto Press, 1977). For these reasons, World War I was the catalyst in the reinvigoration of progressivism rather than, as Doug Owram has argued, the graveyard of social reform. For the collapse of social reform following the war, see Doug Owram, *The Government Generation: Canadian Intellectuals and the State, 1900–1945* (Toronto: University of Toronto Press, 1986), 80–106.

149 UCA, Methodist Church, DESS, box 1, file 3, "Annual Meeting, Department of Social Service and Evangelism, Sept. 15–17, 1915." This well-

known spiritualist's pronouncements on evangelism belie the easy equation between spiritualism and disbelief set forward by Ramsay Cook in *The Regenerators: Social Criticism in Late Victorian Canada* (Toronto: University of Toronto Press, 1985), 67–85.

150 UCA, Dobson Papers, box A5, file Andrews, Dobson to Dear Brother, 13 Nov. 1918.

151 UCA, Chown Papers, box 11, file 290, "Address to the International Epworth League Convention, Denver, Colorado, Manhood and Citizenship," 8 July 1905; Ibid., Methodist Church, DESS, box 6, file 114, "Social Congress Opens," *Daily News*, 10 Oct. 1917. Here, Moore is quoted as saying that "The real heart of Social Service is Evangelism, the hands of Evangelism are Social Service. Brotherhood is the great word. It is Social Service in a word." See also UCA, Mutchmor Papers, box 14, file 190, "Evangelism and Social Service – The United Church of Canada," n.d., 6. Mutchmor echoed Chown when he wrote that "evangelism gives the authentic notes and moral and social witness make it relevant and compelling."

152 UCA, Dobson Papers, box A4, file C, Dobson to the Rev. Fred Chapman, Bowsman River, Man., 2 Sept. 1919. There was still a resounding popular allegiance to individual conversion. See Ibid., box A4, file C, Chapman to Dobson, 27 Aug. 1919, in which he claimed that personal conversion must still precede the introduction of "community welfare schemes."

153 Ibid., box A2, file G, *What Delays the Revival* (pamphlet, #8), 1918; Ibid., box A4, file T, Dobson to Aubrey S. Tuttle, MA, president of Conference, Edmonton, 30 Oct. 1918; UMA, Gordon Papers, box 23, folder 2, "Circular for the General Assembly's Forward Movement Committee," 1921"; Ibid., box 17, folder 5, Shearer to Gordon, 26 April 1910. In this letter Shearer subscribes to T.B. Kilpatrick's view that New Testament evangelism was the instrument of both revival and the Kingdom of God on earth.

154 UCA, Methodist Church, DESS, box 7, file 128, "Annual Report of Evangelism and Social Service, British Columbia Conference, 1919."

155 UCA, Dobson Papers, box A5, file W, Dobson to the Rev. H. Whitely, 29 Jan. 1920. Many local ministers reminded Dobson that their congregations demanded personal evangelism should precede social Christianity. See Ibid., box A5, file A, the Rev. William Arnett, Elstow, Sask., to Dobson, 16 April 1921. In fact, the Rev. Salem Bland was popular all across Canada only because his practical Christianity was enveloped in an overtly evangelistic message and thereby appealed to "the man on the street." See Ibid., box A5, file C, the Rev. Cairns to Dobson, 19 Dec. 1918; box A8, file Mo, Moore to Brother, 19 Dec. 1923.

156 Ibid., box A5, file W, the Rev. H. Whitely to Dobson, 16 Feb. 1920. See also UCA, Chown Papers, box 3, file 66, "Ordination Sermon, Bay of Quinte Conference"; UCA, Dobson Papers, box A2, file G, *Evangelism in the Local Church* (pamphlet #57, n.d.), 1–2; Ibid., box A5, file Moore, Dobson to Moore, 19 April 1920. The balance between individual and social Christianity was still being enunciated as late as 1925. See Ibid., box A10, file Mo, Dobson to Moore, 29 Dec. 1925. As Dobson wrote: "The change in the temper of the people due to the mighty upheavals as well as culminating movements of the past century which came to a culmination at the close of the war may mean changes and adjustments in the nature of the work that the Church is doing. Never before have we needed the emphasis on the social aspects of Christianity as we need it at present ... To my mind we should guard ourselves very carefully against the fads, emphasise greatly individual responsibility, and concentrate ourselves with fresh determination to emphasis from the social outlook and the responsibility of individuals to see and fulfil the Christian life in its application to social, national, and international matters." For the persistent union between an individualist spirit and social evangelism, see Airhart, *Serving the Present Age.*

CHAPTER THREE

1 UCA, Chown Papers, box 13, file 378, "The Preacher's Study of Sociology," n.d.

2 The impact of the idea of "planning" on both social scientists and federal politics in Canada has been described by Doug Owram, *The Government Generation: Canadian Intellectuals and the State, 1900–1945* (Toronto: University of Toronto Press, 1986), chapters 7 and 8; and Michiel Horn, *The League for Social Reconstruction: Intellectual Origins of the Democratic Left in Canada, 1930–1942* (Toronto: University of Toronto Press, 1980).

3 See Ramsay Cook, "Francis Marion Beynon and the Crisis of Christian Reformism," in Carl Berger and Ramsay Cook, eds., *The West and the Nation: Essays in Honour of W.L. Morton* (Toronto: McClelland and Stewart, 1976), 203–4.

4 For a negative estimate of "maternal feminism," see Carol Bacchi, *Liberation Deferred? The Ideas of the English Canadian Suffragists, 1877–1918* (Toronto: University of Toronto Press, 1983); Wayne Roberts, "'Rocking the Cradle for the World': The New Woman and Maternal Feminism, Toronto, 1877–1914," in Linda Kealey, ed., *A Not Unreasonable Claim: Women and Reform in Canada, 1880s-1920s* (Toronto: The Women's Educational Press, 1979), 15–45; Terry Crowley, "Madonnas

before Magdalenes: Adelaide Hoodless and the Making of the Canadian Gibson Girl," *Canadian Historical Review*, 67:4 (Dec. 1986).

5 For this interpretation, see Joan Sangster, *Dreams of Equality* (Toronto: McClelland and Stewart, 1989); Veronica Strong-Boag, *The Parliament of Women: The National Council of Women of Canada, 1893–1929* (Ottawa: National Museums, 1976); Strong-Boag, *The New Day Recalled: Lives of Girls and Women in English Canada, 1919–1939* (Toronto: Copp Clark, 1988).

6 On the resistance to female ordination, see Valerie J. Korinek, "No Women Need Apply: The Ordination of Women in the United Church, 1918–65," *Canadian Historical Review*, 74:4 (Dec. 1993), which notes the convergence of the "Social Gospel" with masculinity, but fails to examine the alliance between these male progressives and women's groups.

7 Recently American historians have argued the need to study women's social movements in conjunction with arguments relating to the growth of the welfare state. See Sonya Michel and Seth Koven, "Womanly Duties: Maternalist Politics and the Origins of Welfare States in France, Germany, Great Britain and the United States, 1880–1920," *American Historical Review*, 95:4 (Oct. 1990), 1077. This excellent article has reaffirmed the importance of maternal feminism over equal-rights feminism in initiating modern social legislation. Historians of progressivism have also called for the need to examine the connections between reform groups. See Daniel T. Rodgers, "In Search of Progressivism," *Reviews in American History*, 10:4 (Dec. 1982), 117.

8 See Michael Gauvreau, *The Evangelical Century: College and Creed in English Canada from the Great Revival to the Great Depression* (Montreal and Kingston: McGill-Queen's University Press), 284–91.

9 Nancy J. Christie, "'Prophecy and the Principles of Social Life': Historical Writing and the Making of New Societies in Canada and Australia, 1880–1920," PH.D. thesis, University of Sydney, 1987; Christie, "Psychology, Sociology and the Secular Moment."

10 James T. Kloppenberg, *Uncertain Victory: Social Democracy in European and American Thought, 1870–1920* (New York and Oxford: Oxford University Press, 1986), 26, 140; Robert B. Westbrook, *John Dewey and American Democracy* (Ithaca and London: Cornell University Press, 1991), 11–21. For the importance of Spencer in American social scientific thought, see Robert C. Bannister, *Social Darwinism: Science and Myth in Anglo-American Social Thought* (Philadelphia: Temple University Press, 1979); Dorothy Ross, *The Origins of American Social Science* (Cambridge: Cambridge University Press, 1991).

11 For the popularity of neo-Lamarckism in the early twentieth century, see Peter J. Bowler, *Evolution: The History of an Idea* (Berkeley: University of California Press, 1984), 243–53; Bannister, *Social Darwinism*, 137–42;

James R. Moore, *The Post-Darwinian Controversies: A Study of the Protestant Struggle to Come to Terms with Darwin in Great Britain and America, 1870–1900*, 217–51; David N. Livingstone, *Darwin's Forgotten Defenders: The Encounter Between Evangelical Theology and Evolutionary Thought* (Grand Rapids, Mich.: William B. Eerdmans, 1987); Robert J. Richards, *Darwin and the Emergence of Evolutionary Theories of Mind and Behavior* (Chicago: University of Chicago Press, 1987). For the blending of Lamarckian and Darwinian ideas in anthropology and geography, see Nancy J. Christie, "Environment and Race: Geography's Search for a Darwinian Synthesis," in Roy MacLeod and P.F. Rehbock, eds., *Darwin and the Pacific* (Honolulu: University of Hawaii Press, 1994).

12 UCA, Dobson Papers, box A2, file G, the Rev. A.E. Cooke, *Evolution and Religion* (pamphlet, n.d.), 1–8. Drummond's leading Canadian disciple, C.W. Gordon, also espoused the harmony of science and ethical ideas. See UMA, Gordon Papers, box 30, folder 16, "The Motives for the Christian Worker," n.d., n.p. For the Methodist defence of the natural sciences, see NA, Canadian Council of Churches, box 29, D.N. McLachlan, "Destructive and Constructive Forces in Society," Conference on Social Welfare, 26–29 Jan. 1927, 5; Richard Roberts, "The Social Ministry of the Church," *SW*, IX:11 (Aug. 1927), 485–92. The Anglican and Baptist churches also supported the introduction of modern scientific methods to social investigation. See C.W. Vernon, "The Story of the Council for Social Service for the Church of England in Canada," *SW*, IX:7 (April 1927), 400; "Baptist Social Service, 1925–26," *SW*, IX:2 (Nov. 1926), 299.

13 UCA, Dobson Papers, box A2, file G, *Five Thousand Canadians Gathered to Hear Dr. Oliver Deliver His Famous Lecture* (pamphlet, n.d.), n.p. For the growing conflict in America over the cultural role of evolutionary ideas, see Marsden, *Fundamentalism and American Culture*.

14 UCA, Dobson Papers, box A2, file G, W.A. Douglas, *The Church and Social Relations* (pamphlet, DESS, #36), n.d., n.p.

15 Ibid., W.W. Andrews, *Nature and Self-Sacrifice: A Study* (pamphlet, June 1913), 3–9.

16 Ibid., box A6, file C, "National Social Efficiency," presidential address, Canadian Conference on Public Welfare, 25 Sept. 1917, Ottawa, 4–9.

17 NA, Canadian Council of Churches, box 29, Hugh Dobson, "The Trend of Family Life and Marriage in Our Times," Report of the Committee on the Maintenance of the Integrity of the Family, Social Service Council, 1930, 7, 21.

18 UCA, Presbyterian Church, Board of Moral and Social Reform, "Minutes of the Meeting of the Executive," 16 Nov. 1910; Ibid., 9 Sept. 1908.

19 UCA, Chown Papers, box 11, file 294, "Address to the Ecumenical Conference, Toronto, The Adaptation of the Church to the Needs of Modern

Life," 10 Oct. 1911; Ibid., box 1, file 1, "Extract from the Annual Report of the Department of Temperance and Moral Reform of the Methodist Church, 1908." According to David Hollinger, although the "social gospel" of Christian social reform and the "intellectual gospel" of applying modern science to industrial and social problems were rivals for cultural authority, in fact they dovetailed in the early twentieth century, the former providing religious sanction for reform and the latter considering the production of the new knowledge as a "religious mission." See Hollinger, "Justification by Verification: The Scientific Challenge to the Moral Authority of Christianity in Modern America," in Michael J. Lacey, ed., *Religion and Twentieth Century American Intellectual Life* (Cambridge: Cambridge University Press, 1989), 116–35.

20 UCA, Dobson Papers, box A4, file G, Mrs Alberta Gieser, Moose Jaw, to Dobson, 15 July 1918. Dobson's reply stressed that only when joined with larger social Christianity would single-tax secure "recognition and consciousness of a living God." Ibid., Dobson to Mrs Gieser, 31 July 1918. Dobson saw no conflict between science and religion and later fully defended the contributions which biology and physics made to theology. See Ibid., box 19, Dobson to Willan, 5 Feb. 1935.

21 University of Toronto, Thomas Fisher Rare Book Library, James Mavor Papers, MSS Collection 119, box 3A, Burwash to Mavor, 30 March 1898; Ibid., box 28B, "Caird Lecture, XXII," 4 Dec. 1874; Ibid., box 28A, "Logic Class Session 1869–70, John Veitch," lecture XI, 5 Nov. 1869, Lecture XXII, 14 Jan. 1870.

22 UCA, Chown Papers, box 1, file 1, "Extract from the Annual Report of the Department of Temperance and Moral Reform of the Methodist Church, 1908"; UCA, United Church Commission on Courses of Study Records, 1926–28, 82.008, box 1, file 3, the Rev. Trevor Davies to William Creighton Graham, 16 Feb. 1927; Ibid., box 1, file 3, A.E. Hewell, Department of Extension, University of Alberta, to Graham, 8 March 1927.

23 Ashley was a strong advocate of the application of economics to public policy. See British Library of Political and Economic Science, Edwin Cannan Papers, Alfred Marshall to Cannan, 22 Sept. 1902. Ashley was one of the early British promoters of economics as a tool for the solution of social problems and at Oxford was closely associated with such collectivist social philosophers as L.T. Hobhouse, D.G. Ritchie, M.E Sadler, and W.A.S. Hewins, later director of the London School of Economics. See Oxford University, Bodleian Library, Oxford University Economic Papers, 1886–91, Edwin Cannan minute-book. The society was founded in Ashley's college rooms on 20 Oct. 1886. For Ashley's links with Arnold Toynbee, see Alon Kadish, *The Oxford Economists in the Late Nineteenth Century* (Oxford: Clarendon Press, 1982), 42–50.

24 NA, Woodsworth Papers, vol. 2, "Report of the Hon. Secretary-Treasurer to the Board of Management of the Winnipeg Training Class in Social Work," 28 Sept. 1914. This alliance between Christianity and social investigation became the matrix of Woodsworth's later work for the Bureau of Social Research. See Ibid., vol. 15, file 7, "Bureau of Social Research, Governments of Manitoba, Saskatchewan and Alberta, Report of First Year's Work," 6 Dec. 1916. Following Ramsay Cook, Allen Mills has portrayed this period in Woodsworth's life as his transition to secular social philosophy. Mills, *Fool for Christ: The Political Thought of J.S. Woodsworth* (Toronto: University of Toronto Press, 1991), 38–43.

25 UTA, Department of Graduate Records, A73/0026/292(51), Biographical Files, John Walker Macmillan, "Heard in College Halls," *Toronto Telegram*, 13 May 1919; "Death of Professor J.W. Macmillan," *Social Welfare*, XIV:7 (April–May, 1932), 123. Macmillan, born on 26 Sept. 1868, later served as chaplain to the 66th Halifax Rifles at Fort Halifax and died on 18 March 1932.

26 J.W. Macmillan, "Standards of Wages," *SW*, III:5 (Feb. 1921), 138; "Profit, Competition and Service," *SW*, II:11 (Aug. 1920), 311–12.

27 O.G.S, "Rev. John Walker Macmillan," *New Outlook*, 21 Dec. 1932.

28 J.W. Macmillan, *Happiness and Goodwill and Other Essays on Christian Living* (Toronto: McClelland and Stewart, 1922), 11, 15–16, 69, 154.

29 J.W. Macmillan, "Unemployment and Its Causes," *New Outlook*, 12 Nov. 1930; *Happiness and Goodwill*, 99.

30 A.L. McCrimmon, "Christianity and the Social Claim," *SW*, VII:5 (Feb. 1925), 87–90. On McCrimmon, see G.A. Rawlyk, "A.L. McCrimmon, H.P. Whidden, T.T. Shields, Christian Education, and McMaster University," in Rawlyk, ed., *Canadian Baptists and Christian Higher Education* (Montreal and Kingston: McGill-Queen's University Press, 1988), 31–62.

31 A.L. McCrimmon, "Christianity and the Social Claim," 87. On McCrimmon's combining of sociology with practical theology, see C.M. Johnston, *McMaster University, Vol. 1: The Toronto Years* (Toronto: University of Toronto Press, 1976), 123–4. This Baptist tendency to link social science with Christian thought also animated Acadia University. See UCA, Dobson Papers, box A8, file So, the Rev. F.W. Patterson, president, Acadia University, "The Church and Social Science," Seventeenth Annual Convention of the Social Service Council of Canada, Saint John, N.B., 28–31 Jan. 1924. Another Baptist minister-cum-social scientist, C.A. Dawson of the Department of Social Science and School for Social Workers at McGill University, also exemplified this alliance between Protestantism and social science, and he spoke on "Waste and Welfare."

32 Ross, *The Origins of American Social Science*, 18–19.

33 UCA, Chown Papers, box 11, file 195, "Address: The Present Need," Jan. 1912.

34 Ibid.

35 Ibid., box 3, file 66, "Ordination Sermon, Bay of Quinte Conference," Peterborough, 5 June 1904.

36 Ibid., box 13, file 378, "The Preacher's Study of Sociology," n.d.; Ibid., box 11, file 295, "Address: The Present Need"; Ibid., box 13, file 365, "The Church Member's Responsibility for Social Conditions," n.d.; Ibid., box 6, file 146, "Bear ye one another's burdens and so fulfil the law of Christ," n.d.; Ibid., box 11, file 300, "Socialism and the Social Teachings of Jesus," address, Vancouver, 14 Feb. 1914. For the perception of Alfred Marshall's concern with poverty as a new evocation of godliness, see British Library of Political and Economic Science, Edwin Cannan Papers, "Marshall's Political Economy," 14 Oct 1891. For a different view, see David B. Marshall, *Secularizing the Faith: Canadian Protestant Clergy and the Crisis of Belief, 1850–1940* (Toronto: University of Toronto Press, 1992), 149.

37 Hugh Dobson, "The Christian Way of Life and the Labor Movement," *SW*, VII:11 (Aug.-Sept. 1925), 211–12.

38 Robert Connell, "Economics in Light of Christianity," *SW*, II:11 (Aug. 1920), 299–300.

39 Ramsay Cook, *The Regenerators: Social Criticism in Late Victorian Canada* (Toronto: University of Toronto Press, 1985), 5.

40 For this shift away from reform social science during the 1920s, see Ross, *The Origins of American Social Science*, 322; Cecil E. Greek, *The Religious Roots of American Sociology* (New York and London: Garland Publishing, 1992), 208; Bannister, *Sociology and Scientism*, 3–11. The notion that scientism had captured the allegiance of the majority of American social scientists by the 1920s has been recently challenged by William McGuire King, "The Reform Establishment and the Ambiguities of Influence," in William R. Hutchison, ed., *The Travail of the Protestant Establishment in America, 1900–1960* (Cambridge and New York: Cambridge University Press, 1989), 122–3, and by Kloppenberg, *Uncertain Victory*, 359, who has argued against drawing rigid distinctions between reformist social science and scientific social control.

41 University of Waterloo, Department of Special Collections, Elizabeth Smith Shortt Papers, box 20, file 810, Adam Shortt to Elizabeth Smith, 14 Aug. 1883.

42 For this view of Adam Shortt and the "Queen's tradition" of political economy, see Barry Ferguson, *Remaking Liberalism: The Intellectual Legacy of Adam Shortt, O.D. Skelton, W.C. Clark, and W.A. Mackintosh, 1890–1925* (Montreal and Kingston: McGill-Queen's University Press, 1993), xv, 9–21.

43 Allen, "Introduction," in Woodsworth, *My Neighbor* (Toronto: University of Toronto Press, 1972), introduction by Richard Allen, xv.

44 NA, Woodsworth Papers, vol. 11, file 5, "Lecture Notes, Oxford, 1899." For the influence of the idealist philosopher Edward Caird, see NA, Sissons Papers, vol. 5, Woodsworth to Sissons, 29 Oct. 1899.

45 NA, Sissons Papers, vol. 5, Woodsworth to Sissons, 25 April 1912; Ibid., 20 May 1912; Ibid., Woodsworth to James Mills, Board of Railway Commissioners, 14 Feb. 1913.

46 UCA, Dobson Papers, box A5, file G, Dobson to H.A. Goodwin, 4 Jan. 1920; Ibid., box A5, file B2, Dobson to Edward S. Bishop, editor of the *Searchlight*, Social Service Council of Alberta, 2 April 1920; Ibid., box A7, file H, Dobson to the Rev. George G. Hacker, Prince Rupert, B.C., 25 Oct. 1921; Ibid., box A4, file D, Dobson to the Rev. A.E. Doan, 6 Feb. 1918; Ibid., box A6, file B, Shirley Jackson Case, *The Millennial Hope: A Phase of War-Time Thinking*, pamphlet in Dobson's files. For the early influences of progressive reform upon Canadian social critics, see Carl Berger, *The Sense of Power* (Toronto: University of Toronto Press, 1970), 190–1.

47 NA, Canadian Council of Churches, "Minutes of Moral and Social Reform Council of Canada," 23 Sept. 1910; UCA, Presbyterian Church, "Minutes of the Literature Committee of the Board of Moral and Social Reform," 3 Dec. 1909.

48 Charles Harvey Arnold, *Near the Edge of Battle: A Short History of the Divinity School and the "Chicago School of Theology," 1866–1966* (Chicago: Divinity School Association, 1966), 39; William McGuire King, "An Enthusiasm for Humanity: The Social Emphasis in Religion and Its Accommodation in Protestant Theology," in Lacey, ed., *Religion and Twentieth-Century American Intellectual Life*, 76; King, "The Reform Establishment," 234–7; Greek, *The Religious Roots of American Sociology*, ix; Susan E. Henking, "Protestant Religious Experience and the Rise of American Sociology: Evidence from the Bernard Papers," *Journal of the History of the Behavioral Sciences*, 28 (Oct. 1992), 328–31. For the influence of religion upon the thought of Mead and Cooley, see Martin E. Marty, *Modern American Religion, Vol. 1: The Irony of It All, 1893–1919* (Chicago and London: University of Chicago Press, 1986), 78–81. For a dissenting view, see George M. Marsden, "Evangelicals and the Scientific Culture: An Overview," in Lacey, ed., *Religion and Twentieth-Century American Intellectual Life*, 42.

49 A.L. McCrimmon, *The Spiritual Basis of the Social Character of the Christian Religion* (pamphlet, Board of Social Service of the Baptist Convention of Ontario and Quebec, 1931), 10. For the close alignment of religion with social science, see "Labour Day Sunday," *SW*, I:11 (1 Aug. 1919), 255, 263; UCA, Dobson Papers, box A4, file C, "The Religious Education Association." Robert Falconer, president of the University of Toronto, derived his inspiration for the social sciences from his early

associations with Mathews and Peabody in the American Religious Education Association. See also Allen F. Davis, *Spearheads for Reform: The Social Settlements and the Progressive Movement, 1890–1914* (New York and Oxford: Oxford University Press, 1967), 392–3.

50 UCA, Presbyterian Church, Minutes of Board of Moral and Social Reform, 9 Sept. 1908; Ibid., 6 Sept. 1910; NA, Canadian Council of Churches, "Minutes of Moral and Social Reform Council of Canada," 26 Sept. 1911. Although less well known than the other social scientists, Robert Magill had a distinguished career in university and government. Born in Ireland, he was educated at Queen's College, Belfast, the Royal University of Ireland, and the University of Jena, Germany. In 1903 he came to Canada as a professor at Pine Hill Theological College and was principal of that institution in 1907–8. He accepted an appointment as professor of political economy at Dalhousie, which he held from 1908 to 1912 when he was appointed chairman of the Board of Grain Commissioners. See "An Observer," "Robert Magill, M.A., PH.D.," *GGG*, 2 Jan. 1918, 24. Titles recommended were: Stephen Leacock, *Elements of Political Science*; Woodrow Wilson, *The State*; Richard Ely, *Outlines of Economics*; Alfred Marshall, *Principles of Economics*; William Cunningham, *Growth of English Industry and Commerce*; E.R.A. Seligman, *The Economic Interpretation of History*; Sidney and Beatrice Webb, *Industrial Democracy*; John R. Commons, *Trade Unionism and Labor Problems*; Richard Ely, *Socialism and Social Reform*; Robert Flint, *Socialism*; O.D. Skelton, *Socialism*; John Spargo, *Socialism*; Francis Peabody, *Jesus Christ and the Social Question*; Walter Rauschenbusch, *Christianity and the Social Crisis*; Jane Addams, *Democracy and Social Ethics*; Charles Ellwood, *Sociology*; Helen Bosanquet, *The Family*; J.A. Hobson, *Evolution of Capitalism*; C.R. Henderson, *Social Settlements*; Charles Zeublin, *Municipal Progress*; E.A. Ross, *Social Control* and *Social Psychology*; Albion Small and George Vincent, *An Introduction to the Science of Society*; and Franklin Giddings, *The Principles of Sociology.*

51 UMA, Gordon Papers, box 17, folder 2, Alfred Gandier, principal, Knox College, to Gordon, 3 Sept. 1912; Ibid., box 17, folder 7, 2 May 1914; UCA, Dobson Papers, box A4, file B, J.F. Bentley to Dobson, 6 Aug. 1919.

52 UCA, United Church of Canada, Commission on Courses of Study, box 1, file 2, "Required Lecture Hours in Four Colleges of the United Church"; Ibid., box 1, file 1, "Matriculation Courses as Prescribed by McGill University"; Ibid., "Knox-Victoria, the Curriculum in Divinity"; UCA, Dobson Papers, box A7, file We, "The Report of the Department of Theology, April 1923."

53 UCA, Commission on Courses of Study, box 1, file 2, "Methodist Church, Department of Education, by J.W. Graham."

54 UMA, Gordon Papers, box 16, folder 1, "Minutes of the Board of Moral and Social Reform and Evangelism," 5–7 Sept. 1911; Ibid., box 17, folder 7, Gordon to Shearer, 2 May 1914; UCA, Presbyterian Church, Minutes of Board of Moral and Social Reform, 6 Sept. 1910.

55 UCA, Dobson Papers, box A5, file C2, Dobson to Dear Brother, n.d.; Ibid., box A4, file C, Dobson to the Rev. Fred Chapman, Bowsman River, Man., 2 Sept. 1919. See especially Dobson Papers, box A5, file C2, "Report of Committee on Social Service and Evangelism, 1918"; Ibid., box A4, file B, the Rev. J.M. Baird to Dobson, 2 Nov. 1918.

56 For Dobson's reading course, see UCA, Dobson Papers, box A4, file T, "A Recommended List of Books for Yorkton District Reading Course," n.d.; Ibid., box A4, file B, Dobson to J.M. Baird, Alma College, 8 Nov. 1918; Ibid., box A5, file G, Dobson to H.A. Goodwin, 4 Jan. 1920; Ibid., box A5, file F, Dobson to John Fitzpatrick, Tompkin, Sask., 21 Oct. 1920; Ibid., box A5, file H, Dobson to the Rev. J.W.A. Henderson, Carnduff, Sask., 13 July 1920.

57 John Maloney, *Marshall, Orthodoxy, and the Professionalisation of Economics* (Cambridge: Cambridge University Press, 1985); Reba N. Soffer, *Ethics and Society in England: The Revolution in the Social Sciences, 1870–1914* (Berkeley and London: University of California Press, 1978), 2–4. The works of Marshall, Hobson, and J.N. Keynes were read at McMaster University prior to World War I. See *McMaster University Calendar, 1912–13*, 73; see also the description of the contents of the Social Service Council Library, *SW*, XI:4 (Jan. 1929).

58 UMA, Gordon Papers, box 16, folder 1, "Board of Moral and Social Reform," 16 Nov. 1910.

59 Quoted in Michael Freeden, *The New Liberalism* (Oxford: Oxford University Press, 1978), 104.

60 On new liberalism and its intersection with collectivist social reform, see Freeden, *The New Liberalism*; Freeden, "The New Liberalism and Its Aftermath," in Richard Bellamy, ed., *Victorian Liberalism: Nineteenth-Century Political Thought and Practice* (London and New York: Routledge, 1990), 178; Stefan Collini, *Liberalism and Sociology: L.T. Hobhouse and Political Argument in England, 1880–1914* (Cambridge: Cambridge University Press, 1979); Peter Clarke, *Liberals and Social Democrats* (Cambridge: Cambridge University Press, 1978); Martin J. Wiener, *Between Two Worlds: The Political Thought of Graham Wallas* (Oxford: Oxford University Press, 1971); Philip Abrams, *The Origins of British Sociology, 1834–1914* (Chicago and London: University of Chicago Press, 1968); Soffer, *Ethics and Society in England*; J.A. Hobson and Morris Ginsberg, *L.T. Hobhouse, His Life and Work* (London: Allen and Unwin, 1931). For the moral content in the thought of Beatrice

Webb, see Deborah Epstein Nord, *The Apprenticeship of Beatrice Webb* (London: Macmillan, 1985) and Norman and Jeanne Mackenzie, eds., *The Diary of Beatrice Webb, Vol. 1: 1873–1892* (Cambridge, Mass.: Harvard University Press, 1982), 165. For the transatlantic context for progressivism, see Kloppenberg, *Uncertain Victory*; Kenneth O. Morgan, "The Future at Work: Anglo-American Progressivism, 1890–1917," in H.C. Allen and Roger Thompson, eds., *Contrast and Connection: Bicentennial Essays in Anglo-American History* (London: G. Bell and Sons, 1976), 245–71.

61 Stephen Leacock, *The Unsolved Riddle of Social Justice* (Toronto: University of Toronto Press, 1973; first edition, 1920), 136–45.

62 UTA, Robert Falconer Papers, A67–0007, box 65, MacIver to Falconer, 27 Jan. 1921.

63 UCA, Methodist Church, DESS, box 7, file 132, T. Albert Moore, "Democracy and Law Observance," n.d.

64 For the ongoing affinity between American social science and American liberal exceptionalism, see Ross, *The Origins of American Social Science*, xiii–xv.

65 Greek, *The Religious Roots of American Sociology*, vii–viii.

66 See especially Martin Bulmer, *The Chicago School of Sociology: Institutionalization, Diversity, and the Rise of Sociological Research* (Chicago: University of Chicago Press, 1984), and for a similarly secularist interpretation of the rise of sociology in Canada, see Marlene G. Shore, *The Science of Social Redemption: McGill, the Chicago School, and the Origins of Social Research in Canada* (Toronto: University of Toronto Press, 1987). The recently published study by A.B. McKillop, *Matters of Mind: The University in Ontario, 1791–1951* (Toronto: University of Toronto Press, 1994), 483–520, asserts that the social sciences rejected the American path of objectivism and behaviourism characteristic of the Chicago School. However, he rests content with the conventional assumption that by 1920 the social sciences in the university were carried on with little reference to religion.

67 Ross, *The Origins of American Social Science*, 103, 187–8, 192.

68 See Leon Fink, "'Intellectuals' versus 'Workers': Academic Requirements and the Creation of Labor History," *American Historical Review* 96:2 (April 1991), 403.

69 Ibid., 203–4.

70 Greek, *Religious Roots of American Sociology*, 122–39; Ross, *The Origins of American Social Science*, 125–31, 222–6. See also Jean B. Quandt, "Religion and Social Thought: The Secularization of Postmillennialism," *American Quarterly*, 34:4 (Oct. 1973), 402.

71 For this alternate tradition, see Steven R. Cohen, "From Industrial Democracy to Professional Adjustment: The Development of Industrial

Sociology in the United States, 1900–1955," *Theory and Society*, 2:1 (Jan. 1983), 55–6.

72 See E.A. Ross to Lester Ward, 2 Feb. 1896, "The Ward-Ross Correspondence, 1891–1896," Bernhard J. Stern, ed., *American Sociological Review*, 3:3 (June 1938), 391. Like Canadian clergymen, Ross was also a follower of the Lamarckian naturalist Joseph LeConte.

73 Ross, *The Origins of American Social Science*, 231–3, 238–51; R. Jackson Wilson, *In Quest of Community: Social Philosophy in the United States, 1860–1920* (New York: Oxford University Press, 1968), 88–107.

74 For Ross's rejection of theological disputation, see Ross to Ward, 13 Dec. 1891, in "The Ross-Ward Correspondence," 364.

75 UMA, Gordon Papers, box 17, folder 3, the Rev. R.H. Lowry to Gordon, 28 Sept. 1910; Ibid., box 16, folder 7, Alexander J. McIntosh to Gordon, 31 Dec. 1909, who anguished that thus far evangelism had resulted merely in "a quickening of influence" among the "holy women of the congregations."

76 Ibid., box 17, folder 4, James D. Orr to Gordon, 16 Oct. 1909.

77 Ibid., box 16, folder 7, the Rev. F.J. Hartley to Gordon, 21 Jan. 1910.

78 Ibid., box 17, folder 7, Gordon to the Rev. A. Macmillan, 27 July 1909; Ibid., box 17, folder 4, James D. Orr to Gordon, 5 Aug. 1909.

79 UCA, Methodist Church, DESS, box 3, file 55, Brigden to Moore, 26 July 1919; Ibid., box 3, file 49, Brigden to Moore, 2 Oct. 1915, in which Brigden requested that future advertising for her lectures be aimed more prominently at men. This campaign to enlist men to shore up the reform activities of the Methodist Church persisted well into the 1920s. See UCA, Dobson Papers, box A10, file McL, Dobson to D.N. McLachlan, 20 March 1929.

80 UCA, Gordon Papers, box 16, folder 14, "Report on Moral and Social Reform," n.d.; Ibid., box 17, folder 4, the Rev. R.A. Walton, Association of Evangelistic Missions, to Gordon, 2 July 1909. This concern over male participation was also prevalent in the Methodist Church: see UCA, Dobson Papers, box A5, file C2, Dobson to Dear Brother, 31 Dec. 1920; UCA, Methodist Church, DESS, box 7, file 146, *Western Methodist Recorder*, "Rev. Dr. Moore's Visit," clipping, n.d.

81 UCA, Dobson Papers, box A5, file H, Thomas Howell, director and general secretary of the Canadian Brotherhood Federation, to Dobson, 27 Sept. 1920; Ibid., box A5, file Moore, Dobson to Moore, 26 Aug. 1920; Moore to Dobson, 20 Oct. 1920.

82 UCA, Methodist Church, DESS, box 6, file 113, "Memorandum for Use at Executive Meeting," 21 Sept. 1916; UCA, Presbyterian Church, Minutes of the Executive of the Board of Moral and Social Reform, 24 March 1910; Ibid., 6 Sept. 1920; UCA, Dobson Papers, box A5, file J, Dobson to the Rev. A.B. Johnston, Heward, Sask., 30 Jan. 1920. In 1920 the Methodist

Church placed the Army and Navy Board under the supervision of the Department of Evangelism and Social Service, and with it the responsibility of rehabilitating 400 probationers who went overseas.

83 UCA, Dobson Papers, box A5, file Bi, "World Brotherhood," 1920.

84 UCA, Presbyterian Church, Minutes of the Board of Social Service and Evangelism, 19 Aug. 1911; UCA, Dobson Papers, box A2, file G, "Evangelism and Social Service," flyer introducing Sister Margaret Saunders, August 1924.

85 UMA, Gordon Papers, box 16, folder 14, "Report of the Conference Committee on Social Service and Evangelization, re: the Christianizing of Industry," n.d.; UCA, Methodist Church, DESS, box 1, file 8, "Annual Meeting of the Department of Evangelism and Social Service – Report on Brotherhoods," 8 Nov. 1921; UCA, Biographical Files, "Ernest Thomas," clipping: Hilda Ridley, "Canadian Brotherhood Urges Everyone to Awaken to Our Social Problems," *Toronto Star*, 8 Jan. 1921, which focused on the connection between the Canadian Brotherhoods and American social reformers in studying industrial problems.

86 UCA, Methodist Church, DESS, box 1, file 1, "Minutes of Annual Meetings of General Board, 1910–12"; UCA, Dobson Papers, box A7, file Mo, Moore to Dobson, 26 Feb. 1923.

87 UCA, Dobson Papers, box A4, file D, Dobson to the Rev. E.A. Davis, Oxbow, Sask., 23 Oct. 1917.

88 UCA, Presbyterian Church, Minutes of the Board of Moral and Social Reform, 30 Oct. 1907; UMA, Gordon Papers, box 16, folder 1, "Minutes of the Board of Moral and Social Reform," 30 Sept. 1908 For the connection between the study of sociology and male-centred reform, see Ibid., box 17, folder 7, Gordon to Shearer, 7 Sept. 1913; Ibid., box 16, folder 1, "Minutes of Board of Moral and Social Reform," 9 Sept. 1908; UCA, Carman Papers, box 20, file 134, "Department of Temperance and Moral Reform of the Methodist Church," 22 Sept. 1910; UCA, Dobson Papers, box A5, file I, Dobson to the Rev. H.A. Ireland, Kamloops, B.C., 23 June 1919.

89 UCA, United Church of Canada, Recruits for the Ministry, 82.012, "Report, 1930." See also UCA, Methodist Church, DESS, box 7, file 128, "Nova Scotia Conference, Annual Report of Evangelism and Social Service," n.d., for the need to attract men to the ministry.

90 UCA, Chown Papers, box 6, file 165, "The Enthronement of Christ in the Industrial Life of the Nation," n.d.

91 UCA, James Robertson Memorial Lectures, box 2, file 6, D.N. McLachlan, "The Minister of To-Day," n.d., 3.

92 See UCA, Methodist Church, DESS, box 7, file 133, T. Albert Moore, "Brotherhood Evangelism," n.d., in which Moore connected the rejection of the "abstract truths" of theology with a revitalized, manly, and relevant Christianity that attacked urban social problems much as the military

campaigns of World War I. See also UMA, Gordon Papers, box 16, folder 14, "Report of Conference Committee on Church Life and Work," n.d., in which Gordon saw the commitment of male preachers to social reform as an "outflanking movement" around "fat and self-centred materialism"; UCA, Dobson Papers, box A5, file "Forward Movement, 1919," in which Dobson recommended turning the traditional class meeting into a "council of war" by turning it into a discussion group of modern social problems.

93 UCA, Chown Papers, box 3, file 66, "Ordination Sermon, Bay of Quinte Conference," 5 June 1904.

94 Ibid., box 13, file 378, "The Preacher's Study of Sociology," n.d.

95 Ibid.

96 UCA/UW, John A. Cormie Papers, PP6, folder F, "Some Problems of Rural Life in Canada," n.d., 18, 26–27.

97 NA, Sissons Papers, vol. 5, Woodsworth to Sissons, 16 June 1902.

98 NA, Woodsworth Papers, vol. 11, file 37, "Social Conditions in Rural Communities," n.d., 22, 48, 58.

99 "Dr. Macmillan is Inducted to Chair," *Winnipeg Free Press*, 9 Oct. 1915, 5. See also "Needed: Canadian Training Schools for Social Workers," by Horace Westwood, Canadian Welfare League Bulletin, *Winnipeg Free Press*, 1 April 1914.

100 UCA, Dobson Papers, box A5, file C2, T. Albert Moore to Dear Brother, 11 May, 1918; UCA, A.E. Smith Papers,"Autobiography," 222; UMA, Gordon Papers, box 29, folder 2, "The Inner Side of Christian Life and Service," sermon, n.d.; Ibid., box 29, folder 2, "Religion Essential to Permanent Industrial Peace," sermon, n.d.; Ibid., box 17, folder 5, Shearer to Gordon, 17 Oct. 1914.

101 T. Albert Moore, "The Challenge of Social Service to the Christian Church," *SW*, IX:6 (March 1927), 376.

102 NA, Woodsworth Papers, box 11, file 29, "Theological Students' Course in Community Problems," n.d.

103 Richard Roberts, "The Social Ministry of the Church," *SW*, IX:11 (Aug. 1927), 484–5.

104 NA, Woodsworth Papers, vol. 11, file 6, "The Wider Evangel," n.d. Woodsworth believed that there was no secular. See *My Neighbor*, 177; NA, Sissons Papers, vol. 5, Woodsworth to Sissons, 14 Feb. 1902.

105 NA, Sissons Papers, vol. 5, Woodsworth to Sissons, 14 Feb. 1902; NA, Woodsworth Papers, vol. 11, file 6, "Be Strong and of Good Courage," sermon, 31 Dec. 1906. The notion that the minister must also contribute to the polity was echoed in W.R. Taylor, "The Social Teachings of the Old Testament," 4, in UCA, United Church of Canada, Commission on Christianizing the Social Order, 82.018C. The idea that one could serve God in a secular calling was a long-held attitude. See Berger, *The Sense of Power*, 221.

106 Quoted in Joan Sangster, "The Making of a Socialist-Feminist: The Early Career of Beatrice Brigden, 1888–1941," *Atlantis*, 13:1 (fall 1987), 21. For the complex reasons for Brigden's departure from the Methodist Church, see UCA, Dobson Papers, box A5, file Moore, Moore to Dobson, 15 March 1920; Ibid., box A5, file F, Dobson to the Rev. Flatt, 12 April 1920; UCA, Methodist Church, DESS, box 3, file 52, Brigden to Moore, 6 June 1917, in which Brigden notes her desire to have her own church. See also Ibid., box 3, file 55, Brigden to Moore, 21 Aug. 1919; Ibid., box 3, file 55, Brigden to Moore, 26 July 1919; Ibid., box 3, file 56, Brigden to Moore, 12 July 1920.

107 C.A. Dawson, "Social Work as a National Institution," presidential address at the Canadian Conference on Social Work, Montreal, 24–27 April 1928, *SW*, X:10 (July 1928), 225–6. For a similar view, see UCA, Chown Papers, box 13, file 377, "The Sociological Man," n.d.

108 Quoted in Robert T. Handy, *A History of Union Theological Seminary in New York* (New York: Columbia University Press, 1987), 139.

109 UCA, Mutchmor Papers, "Autobiography."

110 "News of the Council," *SW*, XV:5 (Dec. 1934); UTA, Department of Political Economy Papers, box 1, C.E. Silcox to E.J. Urwick, 20 March 1935. In this letter Silcox commented on the lack of university instruction in sociology prior to World War I in Canada. For Lester Ward's social evolutionism, see Bannister, *Social Darwinism*, 126–31.

111 UCA, Claris Edwin Silcox Papers, box 20, file 1, "Appointment Book, 1912–13," entries for 1 Oct., 10 Nov 1912, and 23 May, 25 May 1913; Ibid., box 20, file 2, "Diary, 1913," entries for 5 Jan., 8 Jan., 19 Jan.; Ibid., box 20, file 3, "Diary 1918," entries for 10 Feb., 9 June, 20 Feb.; Ibid., box 20, file 4, "Diary 1919," entries for 30 Jan., 29 June.

112 See Mark Van Stempvoort, "Search for Social Unity: The Career of C.E. Silcox, 1888–1940," unpublished M.A. paper, York University, 1982, 35.

113 UCA, Dobson Papers, box A4, file B, J.F. Bentley to Dobson, 11 Jan. 1919, 22 Feb. 1919; Dobson to Bentley, 18 Feb. 1919.

114 Henry Wise Wood, "U.F.A. President's Address," *GGG*, 31 Jan. 1917, 7.

115 UCA, Dobson Papers, box A4, file H, the Rev. W.J. Haggith to Dobson, 25 Feb. 1918.

116 Ibid., box A4, file H, Dobson to Haggith, 14 March 1918.

117 Ibid., box A5, file B2, Edward S. Bishop to Dobson, 30 March 1920, 24 Feb. 1920; Ibid., Dobson to Bishop, 13 May 1919, 17 Feb. 1920.

118 For the recognition among Canadian clergymen that social service in the United States was practised apart from a religious impulse, see "The National Conference on Social Work," *SW*, III:9 (1 June 1920), 233. Robert Crunden, *Ministers of Reform: The Progressives' Achievement in American Civilization, 1889–1920* (New York: Basic Books, 1982), 13, while attesting to the importance of religion in American reform, argues

that the central role of religion in shaping social reform occurred prior to 1920. See also Donald K. Gorrell, *The Age of Social Responsibility: The Social Gospel in the Progressive Era, 1900–1920* (Macon, Ga: Mercer University Press, 1988).

119 UCA, Dobson Papers, box A2, file G, W.H. Smith, "The Ministry and Spiritual Leadership," lecture delivered at St John's Presbyterian Church, 7 May 1920, 5.

120 Ibid., box A11, file G, Moore to Dobson, 19 June 1913; Ibid., box A5, file "Forward Movement," *Reconstruction* (pamphlet, DESS, n.d), 1–7. Dobson had previously taught biology and human relations at Regina College but later recounted that he had found his "real life work" when made field secretary in 1913. See Ibid., box A11, file P, Autobiographical Sketch.

121 UCA, Presbyterian Church, Minutes of the Executive of the Board of Moral and Social Reform, 16 Nov. 1910; UMA, Gordon Papers, box 16, folder 1, Dr Macmillan, "Christianity in Relation to Present Social Problems," 2–3, in "Minutes of Joint Executives," 23 March 1911. For the continued insistence on the Christian character of social settlements, see UCA, Mutchmor Papers, box 1, file 1, the Rev. William Simons, superintendent of missions, to Mutchmor, 9 Feb. 1921; Ibid., box 1, file 1, the Rev. D.N. McLachlan, field secretary, Presbyterian Board of Home Missions and Social Service, 13 May 1922; Ibid., box 1, file 3, Mutchmor to the Rev. D.B. Smith, 20 Jan. 1938. St Christopher House, which opened on 15 June 1912, remained under Presbyterian control until it was challenged by the Rev. R. B. Cochrane in 1930 largely because of a lack of funds, and it was then placed under the Federation for Community Service. See UCA, United Church, Board of Home Missions, box 14, file 91, the Rev. R.B. Cochrane to James Woods, 6 Feb. 1930; Ibid., box 14, file 109, "St. Christopher House," memo J.G. Shearer, 21 Sept. 1931.

122 UCA, Methodist Church, DESS, box 2, file 37, Moore to the Rev. M.M. Bennett, Regina, 18 Feb. 1914.

123 Ibid., Moore to Bennett, 18 Feb. 1914.

124 UCA, Dobson Papers, box A4, file B, Dobson to the Rev. G.H. Bennes, Rouleau, Sask., 24 Jan. 1919. See also UCA, Carman Papers, box 20, file 134, "Minutes of the Executive of the Dept. of Temperance and Moral Reform," 10 June 1914. During the financial constraints of wartime the church was able, by providing funding, to extend its control over urban social agencies.

125 UCA, Dobson Papers, box A4, file Mac, Dobson to Miss Ada G. McLean, 1 June 1921; Ibid., box A4, file B, *Child Welfare Activities in Canada* (pamphlet, n.d.). Cynthia Comacchio, *Nations Are Built of Babies: Saving Ontario's Mothers and Children, 1900–1940* (Montreal and Kingston: McGill-Queen's University Press, 1993), emphasizes the role of the

medical profession in promoting government action on child welfare but neglects the central role of the churches and of women's organizations.

126 UCA, Dobson Papers, box A4, file S, A.E. Smith to Dobson, 28 Dec. 1917.

127 O.D. Skelton, "The Problem of the City," in W.R. McIntosh, ed., *Social Service* (Toronto: R. Douglas Fraser, 1912), 42. For Skelton's involvement with the Presbyterian Board of Social Service and Evangelism, see Fraser, *The Social Uplifters*, 81–3. Skelton's role as the progenitor of the modern secular bureaucratic state has been addressed in J.L. Granatstein, *The Ottawa Men* (Toronto: University of Toronto Press, 1982); Owram, *The Government Generation*; and Barry Ferguson, *Remaking Liberalism* (Montreal and Kingston: McGill-Queen's University Press, 1993).

128 UCA, Dobson Papers, box A6, file F, *Conservation of Life*, 1:1 (Aug. 1914), Sir Clifford Sifton, "Forward," 7. For the view that the Commission of Conservation constituted a "secular" vehicle for reform because of its focus on issues of science and health, see Owram, *The Government Generation*, 57–8.

129 UCA, Dobson Papers, box A3, file F, Professor T.R. Robinson, "Report on Industrial Relations," Annual Meeting, Canadian Conference on Public Welfare, 10–11 May 1920, Hamilton, Ont.

130 Quoted in Woodsworth, *My Neighbor*, 194.

131 UCA, Carman Papers, box 20, file 137, Carman to Brother Campbell, 11 Jan. 1906.

132 Owram, *The Government Generation*, 98.

133 UCA, Dobson Papers, box A5, file W, Dobson to the Rev. J.W. Wilson, 10 Jan. 1919.

134 UMA, Gordon Papers, Box 16, folder 4, "Minutes of Moral and Social Reform Council of Manitoba," 21 Jan. 1913.

135 NA, Woodsworth Papers, vol. 2, Moore to Woodsworth, 27 March 1913.

136 NA, Canadian Council of Churches, box 29, "Second Meeting of the Programme Committee of the 15th Annual Conference of Charities and Corrections, 9 April 1914."

137 NA, Woodsworth Papers, box 11, file 7, "All People's Reports and Papers, 1908–9"; Ibid., box 15, file 5, *Organized Helpfulness*, n.d., 11; UCA/UW, All People's Mission Papers, box B, "Practical Christianity 1910–11 Reports."

138 UCA, Dobson Papers, box A4, file Sb, J.G. Shearer to Dobson, 30 Nov. 1918; NA, Canadian Council of Churches, box 29, Dr Ernest Thomas, "Creative Community Spirit," Conference on Social Welfare, 3–4 May, Halifax, 1928, 36.

139 *SW*, I:6 (1 March 1919), 98.

140 UCA, Dobson Papers, box A5, file Moore, Dobson to Moore, 23 March 1920; Ibid., box A5, file C1, Dobson to the Rev. William T. Cleaver,

Unity, Sask., 5 May 1920; Ibid., box A5, file G, Dobson to Mr L.J. Gullivan, Vantage, Sask., 14 Feb. 1920.

141 Ibid., box A5, file H, Dobson to D.B. Harkness, the Baptist secretary of the Social Service Council of Manitoba, 30 April 1920; Ibid., box A4, file W, Charlotte Whitton to Dobson, 25 Feb. 1919; Ibid., Dobson to Whitton, 7 March 1919;

142 *SW*, IX:11 (Aug. 1927), 493; UCA, Dobson Papers, box A6, file F, *What Is 'The Ward' Going to do with Toronto?* (pamphlet, Bureau of Municipal Research, 1918).

143 UCA, Dobson Papers, box A5, file H, Dobson to Mr C.A. Hodgetts, 5 March 1920. For the connection between the Baptist Church and local government welfare councils, see Carl C. Farmer, "Social Service within the Baptist Convention of Ontario and Quebec," *SW*, XI:8 (May 1927).

144 SAB, Violet McNaughton Papers, Arthur Wilson to Violet McNaughton, 12 April 1917. For the pivotal role of church progressives and agrarian women's organizations in pressing for this important health legislation, see "Medical and Nursing Care: Saskatchewan," *GGG*, 19 Jan. 1916, 12; "The Women's Convention," *GGG*, 23 Feb. 1916, 18, 29; "Saskatchewan's New Laws," *GGG*, 5 April 1916, 7.

145 UCA, Dobson Papers, box A5, file H, Dobson to Methodist ministers, 23 April 1920; Ibid., D.B. Harkness to Dobson, 17 April 1920; Ibid., Dobson to Harkness, 30 April 1920.

146 "Four Churches and the Social Order," *SW*, I:8 (1 May 1919), 187–8; Edward Pulker, *We Stand on their Shoulders: The Growth of the Social Concern in Canadian Anglicanism* (Toronto: Anglican Book Centre, 1986).

147 UCA, Dobson Papers, box A4, file F, Dobson to Glenn Frank, 11 Sept. 1919.

148 For a discussion of the AALL see Theda Skocpol, *Protecting Soldiers and Mothers: The Political Origins of Social Policy in the United States* (Cambridge, Mass.: The Belknap Press, 1992), 176–89.

149 When he was minister of labour, Mackenzie King frequently turned to such Presbyterian clergymen as C.W. Gordon to head the ad hoc boards of investigation and conciliation appointed under the Industrial Disputes Investigation Act. See Paul Craven, *"An Impartial Umpire": Industrial Relations and the Canadian State, 1900–1911* (Toronto: University of Toronto Press, 1980), 296; UMA, Gordon Papers, box 13, folder 7, William Lyon Mackenzie King to Gordon, 20 May 1911; Ibid., Gordon to King, 7 July 1911.

150 Richard Allen, *The Social Passion: Religion and Social Reform in Canada, 1914–28* (Toronto: University of Toronto Press, 1973).

151 Craven, *"An Impartial Umpire"*, 138–42, 189–96.

152 James Naylor, *The New Democracy* (Toronto: University of Toronto Press, 1992), 216

153 For the failure of business reform in the 1920s to develop a "corporate liberal" strategy, see Tom Traves, *The State and Enterprise* (Toronto: University of Toronto Press, 1977); and for the marginal role of university social scientists in influencing the state, see Owram, *The Government Generation*, chapter 5.

154 James Struthers, *No Fault of their Own* (Toronto: University of Toronto Press, 1983), chapters 1 and 2. For the weakness of labour's role in forging the modern welfare state in the United States, see Kathryn Kish Sklar, "The Historical Foundation of Women's Power in the Creation of the American Welfare State, 1830–1930," in Seth Koven and Sonya Michel, eds., *Mothers of a New World: Maternalist Politics and the Origin of Welfare States* (New York and London: Routledge, 1993), 54–7; Mary O. Furner, "The Republican Tradition and the New Liberalism: Social Investigation, State Building, and Social Learning in the Gilded Age," in Michael J. Lacey and Mary O. Furner, eds., *The State and Social Investigation in Britain and the United States* (Princeton and Cambridge: Woodrow Wilson Center Press, Cambridge University Press, 1993), 202–4.

155 For this interpretation, see Bryan D. Palmer, *A Culture in Conflict* (Montreal and Kingston: McGill-Queen's University Press, 1979); Gregory S. Kealey, *Toronto Workers Respond to Industrial Capitalism, 1867–1892* (Toronto: University of Toronto Press, 1980); Bryan Palmer and Gregory Kealey, *Dreaming of What Might Be: The Knights of Labor in Ontario* (Cambridge: Cambridge University Press, 1982). For the persistence of this male craft culture into the twentieth century, see Craig Heron, *Working in Steel* (Toronto: McClelland and Stewart), 1988.

156 Koven and Michel, "Womanly Duties," *American Historical Review*, 95:4, 1084–94. See also, Skocpol, *Protecting Soldiers and Mothers*, introduction, 488; Sklar, "The Historical Foundations of Women's Power in the Creation of the American Welfare State," 43–93.

157 Ruth A. Frager, *Sweatshop Strife: Class, Ethnicity, and Gender in the Jewish Labour Movement of Toronto, 1910–1939* (Toronto: University of Toronto Press, 1992), 213–14.

158 Margaret McCallum, "Keeping Women in their Place: The Minimum Wage in Canada, 1910–25," *Labour/Le travail*, 17 (spring 1986), 21–39.

159 AO, F837, series 3, box 14, "Report of the Committee on Industrial Life," *Fifth Annual Meeting and Congress of the Social Service Council of Ontario*, 1923.

160 UCA, Dobson Papers, box A3, file F, Robinson, "Report on Industrial Relations," n.d., 59.

161 Richard Allen has noted the simultaneous rise of a "new evangelism" promoted by Salem Bland and Ernest Thomas, without drawing any explicit links between this phenomenon and the waning interest in labour reform legislation.

162 Struthers, *No Fault of their Own*, has noted the decreasing interest of the federal government after 1922 in strengthening the wartime experiment with a national unemployment policy. For the erosion of social insurance schemes for veterans, see Desmond Morton and Glenn Wright, *Winning the Second Battle: Canadian Veterans and the Return to Civilian Life, 1915–1930* (Toronto: University of Toronto Press, 1987).

163 UCA, Methodist Church, DESS, box 1, file 2, "Annual Meeting of General Board, Department of Temperance, Prohibition, and Moral Reform," 22 Oct. 1913; UCA, Dobson Papers, box A5, file Pb, Dobson to W.M. Martin, premier of Saskatchewan, 24 Nov. 1917.

164 For this tradition of maternal feminist activism, see Linda Gordon, "The New Feminist Scholarship and the Welfare State", in Linda Gordon, ed., *Women, the State, and Welfare* (Madison: University of Wisconsin Press, 1990), 17.

165 UCA, Dobson Papers, box A5, file C2, annual report of field secretary, 1 Aug. 1920; Ibid., box A4, file A, Dobson to the Rev. A.E. Allin, 12 May 1919, in which Dobson instructed the minister to read his pamphlets on mothers' allowances and minimum wages for women.

166 UCA, Dobson Papers, box A8, file Mo, Moore, annual conference report, 6 May 1924; Professor Keirstead, "Mothers Allowances in Canadian Provinces," *SW*, VII:9 (June 1925), 175–80. The Methodist Church's platform replicated that of the National Council of Women. See Veronica Strong-Boag, *"The Parliament of Women": The National Council of Women of Canada, 1893–1929* (Ottawa: National Museums of Canada, 1976), 296–7, 367–9; N.E.S. Griffiths, *The Splendid Vision: Centennial History of the National Council of Women of Canada, 1893–1993* (Ottawa: Carleton University Press, 1993), 103, 114–17, 140–2, 171–5; Strong-Boag, in "Mothers Allowances and the Beginnings of Social Security in Canada," *Journal of Canadian Studies*, 14:1 (spring 1979), 25, has noted the influence of the churches' Social Service Council of Canada in pressing for mothers' allowances.

167 Sangster, *Dreams of Equality*; Strong-Boag, *The New Day Recalled*. For the view that during the 1920s and 1930s women were only concerned with the "non-political" issues of the private sphere, see Pauline Rankin, "The Politicization of Ontario Farm Women," in Linda Kealey and Joan Sangster, eds., *Beyond the Vote: Canadian Women and Politics* (Toronto: University of Toronto Press, 1989), 318.

168 On the largest and most powerful of these women's organizations, see Sharon Cook, *"Through Sunshine and Shadow": The Woman's Christian Temperance Union, Evangelicalism, and Reform in Ontario, 1874–1930* (Montreal and Kingston: McGill-Queen's University Press, 1995).

169 SAB, Saskatchewan Grain Growers' Association, B2, file III, Women's Section of Saskatchewan Grain Growers' Association, "Minutes of Execu-

tive Meeting," 28 July 1916. The SGGA formed a research bureau within the organization, mainly to investigate social policies such as free hospitals and social insurance, which had been sponsored by its women's section.

170 Cheryl Jahn, "Class, Gender and Agrarian Socialism: the United Farm Women of Saskatchewan, 1926–1931," *Prairie Forum*, 19:2 (fall 1994), 189–206.

171 SAB, McNaughton Papers, Mrs Walter McBain to McNaughton, 17 Feb. 1919.

172 SAB, Violet McNaughton Papers, A1, file 4, McNaughton to Mary Elliott Campbell, 29 Sept. 1949; Ibid., McNaughton to Agnes Macphail, 14 March 1922; Ibid., file 48, McNaughton to Margaret McWilliams, 31 March 1943. Alison Prentice, et al., *Canadian Women: A History* (Toronto: Harcourt, Brace, Jovanovich, 1988), 210–11; Wendy Mitchinson, "Early Women's Organizations and Social Reform: Prelude to the Welfare State," in Allan Moscovitch and Jim Albert, eds., *The "Benevolent" State: The Growth of Welfare in Canada* (Toronto: Garamond Press, 1987), 77–94; Nancy M. Sheehan, "The W.C.T.U. on the Prairies, 1888–1930: An Alberta-Saskatchewan Comparison," *Prairie Forum*, 6:1 (1981). For the American context, see Nancy F. Cott, *The Grounding of Modern Feminism* (New Haven and London: Yale University Press, 1987), 88–91; Robyn Muncy, *Creating a Female Dominion in American Reform, 1890–1935* (New York and Oxford: Oxford University Press, 1991); Skocpol, *Protecting Soldiers and Mothers*, 327. Even in the United States, where middle-class women were clearly dominant in social reform movements, women entered mainstream politics through alliances with male reformers. See Kathryn Kish Sklar, "Hull House in the 1890's, a Community of Women Reformers," *Signs*, 10:4 (summer 1985), 676–7.

173 SAB, McNaughton, file E7, Jean S. Robson to McNaughton, 16 May 1919; Ibid., Mary McCallum to McNaughton, 10 Dec. 1921; McCallum stated that the time was ripe for a women's branch in the federal Department of Agriculture while Mackenzie King was in the process of reorganizing the cabinet.

174 SAB, McNaughton Papers, file 54, Parlby to McNaughton, 14 March 1916, 10 May 1916, 2 Oct 1916.

175 W.L. Morton, *The Progressive Party in Canada* (Toronto: University of Toronto Press, 1950). A recent reassessment of western populism does not move beyond a narrowly "political" agenda. See David Laycock, *Populism and Social Democratic Thought in the Canadian Prairies, 1910 to 1945* (Toronto: University of Toronto Press, 1990).

176 For this program of rural reconstruction, see UCA, Dobson papers, Box A6, file C, "Rural Problems: Suggested Outline for Lantern Lecture," n.d.

177 *Winnipeg Free Press*, 13 April 1918.

178 SAB, McNaughton Papers, Shearer to McNaughton, 1 Feb. 1918; Ibid., "Saskatchewan Social Service Council, Annual Meeting, 26 Nov. 1916." At this same meeting Violet McNaughton also spoke on "Women in Political Life."

179 UCA, Methodist Church, DESS, box 3, file 45, Brigden to Miss Wiggins, 14 May 1914; UCA, Dobson Papers, box A5, file B2, Brigden to Dobson, 13 Feb. 1920.

180 UCA, Dobson Papers, box A4, file T, Dobson to Miss Twiss, Normal School, Regina, 9 Nov. 1917; Ibid., box A4, file D, Dobson to Brother Howard, 30 Feb. 1919.

181 SAB, McNaughton Papers, J.S. Woodsworth to McNaughton, 23 March 1914, 2 May 1914, 4 May 1914, 8 July 1916; Ibid., Woodsworth, "The Advent of Women," n.d. For this moral emphasis of maternalist politics, see Paula Baker, "The Domestication of Politics: Women and American Political Society, 1780–1920," in L. Gordon, *Women, the State, and Welfare* (Madison: University of Wisconsin Press, 1990), 55–91.

182 SAB, McNaughton Papers, file 48, McNaughton to Margaret McWilliams, 7 July 1932.

183 Ibid., file E81, "United Farmers of Ontario," May Wallace to McNaughton, n.d. McNaughton herself avidly read the *New Outlook* published by the United Church; Irene Parlby read Salem Bland's *The New Christianity* and the works of the American social gospeller Walter Rauschenbusch. See Ibid., file 48, McNaughton to Anna Martinson, 23 May 1938; Ibid., file 54, Parlby to McNaughton, n.d., 14 April 1920. For the ideal of closer ties between farm women and the churches, see Ibid., file 48, Martinson to McNaughton, 15 Dec. 1923.

184 Ibid., file 1, Mrs Alice B. Richardson to McNaughton, 10 March 1916.

185 "Johnson Explains Minimum Wage," *Winnipeg Free Press*, 19 April 1918.

186 "Dr. Riddell Chairman on Minimum Wage," *Winnipeg Free Press*, 13 Feb. 1918.

187 "Women in Mass Meeting Seek Many Changes in Laws," *Winnipeg Free Press*, 22 Jan. 1918; "Act on Minimum Wage for Women," *Ibid.*, 5 Feb. 1918; "Ministers Endorse a Minimum Wage," Ibid., 5 Feb. 1918; "Dr. Riddell Chairman on Minimum Wage," Ibid., 13 Feb. 1918. It is noteworthy that the minimum wage campaign in Ontario was publicized by a clergyman, the Rev. Peter Bryce. See "Minimum Wage Law Gaining Advocates," *Winnipeg Free Press*, 7 June 1919.

188 "Strong Plea for Minimum Wage," *Winnipeg Free Press*, 8 Feb. 1918.

189 "Minimum Wage Everyone's Right," *Winnipeg Free Press*, 14 Jan. 1918; "Minimum Wage for Working Girls," Ibid., 16 Jan. 1918, in which Edward McGrath, secretary of the Labor Bureau, lent his support based upon the natural right of workers to a fair wage.

190 Alison Craig, "Over the Tea Cups," *Winnipeg Free Press*, 2 Feb. 1918.

191 J.A. Stevenson, "Reconstruction in Canada and the Social and Economic Forces which Will Condition It," *Survey*, 4 Jan. 1919, 442.

192 "Manitoba's Legislative Program," GGG, 29 March 1916, 7; and on the record of the United Farmers of Manitoba after 1922, see John Kendle, *John Bracken: A Political Biography* (Toronto: University of Toronto Press, 1976). The weakness of historical discussions of "social reform" and "progressivism" in Canada centres around lack of attention given to the actual content of legislation and to the interests that supported and opposed particular reforms.

193 On Drury, see C.M. Johnston, *E.C. Drury: Agrarian Idealist* (Toronto: University of Toronto Press, 1986), 150–7.

194 For recent examples of this interpretation, see Comacchio, *Nations are Built of Babies*, 3–4; Veronica Strong-Boag, "Intruders in the Nursery: Childcare Professionals Reshape the Years one to Five," in Joy Parr, ed., *Childhood and Family in Canadian History* (Toronto: McClelland and Stewart, 1982), 160–78; Strong-Boag, *The New Day Recalled*, 145–77.

195 UTA, Falconer Papers, box 32, Emily F. Guest to Falconer, 18 March 1914, and enclosure: "Social Service – Women's Institute Problems."

196 SAB, McNaughton Papers, Shearer to McNaughton, 9 Jan. 1920.

197 Ibid., Peter Bryce and Charlotte Whitton, Social Service Council of Canada to McNaughton, 5 March 1920.

198 Ibid., Women's Grain Grower's petition to Prime Minister Borden, moved by Minnie J.B. Campbell of Winnipeg, seconded by Miss Hanna, Port Arthur, Ont.; SAB, J.B. Musselman Papers, W.P. Reekie to Fellow Workers, "On the Need for Intensive and Province-Wide Programs for the Welfare of Little Children," 17 March 1925; UTA, Falconer Papers, box 32, Guest to Falconer, 18 March 1914, enclosure: "Social Service." Guest also believed that the government should take the lead in training fathers in financial responsibility.

199 AO, F837, series 3, Ontario Welfare Council Papers, box 14, *Annual Meeting and Conference of the Social Service Council of Ontario*, Charlotte Whitton, "Child Welfare as the Approach to the Community," 19.

200 UCA, Dobson Papers, box A4, file C, Hugh Dobson, "Child Welfare Activities in Canada," n.d.

201 Ibid., box A4, file A, Carl Kelsey, American Academy of Political and Social Science, to Dobson, 13 March 1919; Ibid., box A5, file K, Carl Kelsey to Dobson, 12 Nov. 1920, in which it is stated that J.G. Shearer nominated Dobson for membership in the academy.

202 Ibid., box A5, file B1, Dobson to Allen T. Burns, 17 Sept. 1919.

203 Ibid., box A6, file B; Ibid., box A6, file C, for a list of journals and pamphlets which Dobson collected from the Chicago School of Civics and Philanthropy. It was mainly from these that he learned how to mount his social reform exhibits.

204 Ibid., box A4, file B, Dobson to the Rev. Edward S. Bishop, 13 May 1919; Ibid., box A5, file K, Dobson to the Rev. H.H. Kerley, Mossbank, Sask., 8 Nov. 1919; Ibid., box A4, file F, Dobson to J.H.T. Falk, secretary, Social Welfare Commission of Winnipeg, 26 April 1918; Ibid., box A7, file K, Dobson to Robert W. Kelso, 5 Nov. 1921; NA, Woodsworth Papers, box 11, file 6, A. Vernon Thomas to Woodsworth, 1 Aug. 1920; UCA/UW, All People's Mission Papers, box B, Graham Taylor to the Rev. Arthur O. Rose, Stella Avenue Institute, 3 Oct. 1916. Beatrice Brigden had also visited Addams. See UCA, Methodist Church, DESS, Box 3, file 45, Brigden to Moore, 28 Jan. 1914. For the importance of women in shaping the Chicago reform network, see Louise C. Wade, *Graham Taylor: Pioneer for Social Justice, 1851–1938* (Chicago and London: University of Chicago Press, 1964), 23, 82, 95; Lela B. Costin, *Two Sisters for Social Justice: A Biography of Grace and Edith Abbott* (Urbana and Chicago: University of Illinois Press, 1983), 184–93; Kathryn Kish Sklar, *Florence Kelley and the Nation's Work* (New Haven: Yale University Press, 1994); Muncy, *Creating a Female Dominion*, 31, 66–71; Daniel Levine, *Poverty and Society: The Growth of the American Welfare State in International Comparison* (New Brunswick and London: Rutgers University Press, 1988), 29–35; Donna L. Franklin, "Mary Richmond and Jane Addams: From Moral Certainty to Rational Inquiry in Social Work Practice," *Social Service Review*, 60:4 (Dec. 1986), 508–16.

205 UCA, Dobson Papers, box A5, file Sub, Paul Kellogg, editor the *Survey*, to Dobson, 2 Oct. 1919. Dobson had all his clergymen read the *Survey*, which became the model for *Social Welfare*, the sole Canadian journal devoted to social policy. For example, see Ibid., box A5, file H, Dobson to the Rev. H.E. Horton, Cloverdale, Sask., 19 Jan. 1920.

206 Ibid., box A5, file W, Dobson to Whitton, 9 Feb. 1920; Whitton to Dobson, 11 Feb. 1920. Dobson had pressed for the creation of a children's bureau with a broad agenda of social reform based on the American model and was disappointed with the federal government's decision to narrow the focus of children's welfare to public health by placing it as a branch of the Department of Health. He and Whitton also regretted that Helen McMurchy rather than their own choice, Helen Reid, was placed at the head of this new organization. For the American example, see Jacqueline K. Parker and Edward M. Carpenter, "Julia Lathrop and the Children's Bureau: The Emergence of an Institution," *Social Service Review*, 55:1 (March 1981), 61–73; Molly Ladd-Taylor, "Federal Help for Mothers: The Rise and Fall of the Sheppard-Towner Act in the 1920's," in Dorothy O. Helly and Susan M. Reverby, eds., *Gendered Domains: Rethinking Public and Private in Women's History* (Ithaca and London: Cornell University Press, 1992), 221–3; Muncy, *Creating a Female Dominion*, 39–51, 86–9; Linda Gordon, *Heroes of Their Own Lives: The*

Politics and History of Family Violence, Boston, 1880–1960 (New York: Viking Press, 1988), vi–viii; Skocpol, *Protecting Soldiers and Mothers*, 483–524. All these authors argue that by the 1930s the upsurge in women's influence on social policy-making, both at the state and the national levels, was in decline.

207 UCA, Dobson Papers, box A4, file C, "Child Welfare Activities in Canada."

208 Ibid., box A4, file Sc, Dobson to W.J. Stark, 26 Jan. 1918; Ibid., box A5, file S2, Dobson, "Suggestions on a Child Welfare Week for Canada," memorandum to J.G. Shearer, 13 Jan. 1919.

209 Ibid., Dobson to W.J. Stark, 26 Jan. 1918. For a Marxist-feminist interpretation, which assumes that the state was all-powerful in imposing a strategy of child welfare upon working-class women, see Comacchio, *Nations are Built of Babies.*

210 UCA, Dobson Papers, box A4, file B, the Rev. Edward S. Bishop, secretary of child welfare, Alberta Social Service League, to Dobson, 15 April 1918, 30 July 1918; Ibid., box A4, file F, Dobson to Mrs M.G. Ferguson, secretary, Local Council of Women, Dauphin, Man., 15 March 1918. On Blatz's career, see Jocelyn Motyer Raymond, *The Nursery World of Dr. Blatz* (Toronto: University of Toronto Press, 1991).

211 SAB, McNaughton Papers, Peter Bryce and Charlotte Whitton to McNaughton, 5 March 1920.

212 UCA, Dobson Papers, box A5, file W2, Dobson to Whitton, 23 March 1920.

213 Ibid., box A4, file E, Mrs S. Szapko to Dobson, 8 Aug. 1918.

214 Molly Ladd-Taylor, *Raising a Baby the Government Way: Mothers' Letters to the Children's Bureau, 1915–32* (New Brunswick and London: Rutgers University Press, 1986), 5, 32, 44. See also, Muncy, *Creating a Female Dominion*, who estimates that 125,000 letters per year were received from women of all classes, 55–7.

215 See, for example, "The Canadian Mother," *SW*, V:8 (1923), 160.

216 UCA, Dobson Papers, box A4, file F, Dobson to C.D. Fischer, secretary, Fair Board, Saskatoon, 15 March 1919.

217 Ibid., box A3, file H, pamphlets penned by McMurchy between 1913 and 1921.

218 Ibid., box A4, file Sc, Dobson to W.J. Stark, 26 Jan. 1918; Ibid., box A3, file K, *Our Exhibits* (pamphlet, DESS), n.d.

219 Ibid., box A4, file D, Dobson to the Rev. Manson Doyle, 14 Nov. 1919.

220 Ibid., box A4, file B, Dobson to the Rev. E.D. Brayden, Kelowna, B.C., 18 Aug. 1919.

221 Ibid., box A4, file D, Dobson to Doyle, 14 Nov. 1919.

222 Ibid., box A4, file B, Dobson to Bryce, 23 Sept. 1918. For Bryce, see UCA, Biographical Files, "Peter Bryce."

CHAPTER FOUR

1 Edward Johns Urwick, *A Philosophy of Social Progress* (London: Methuen, 1912), 179.

2 Richard Allen, *The Social Passion: Religion and Social Reform in Canada, 1914–28* (Toronto: University of Toronto Press, 1973), 240–1, 284, 294–5.

3 For an interpretation that accepts Allen's orthodox view of the conflict between science and religion, see Marlene Shore, *The Science of Social Redemption: McGill, the Chicago School, and the Origins of Social Research in Canada* (Toronto: University of Toronto Press, 1987). The view that there was a disjunction between moral reform on the one hand and scientific sociology and social work on the other has been most forcefully argued by sociologists like Martin Bulmer who are concerned with the scientific and professional identity of their own discipline. See Martin Bulmer, *The Chicago School of Sociology: Institutionalization, Diversity, and the Rise of Sociological Research* (Chicago: University of Chicago Press, 1984). Historians have begun to drastically revise this view. See, for example, Eileen Janes Yeo, "The Social Survey in Social Perspective, 1830–1930," in Martin Bulmer, et al., eds., *The Social Survey in Historical Perspective, 1880–1940* (Cambridge: Cambridge University Press, 1991), 55–6.

4 "Howard Falk is Named," *Montreal Gazette*, 31 Oct. 1935. Falk began his social work career in Liverpool and served at Christadora House in New York from 1906 until 1908 when he moved to Winnipeg to organize the city charities.

5 UMA, Gordon Papers, box 17, folder 7, Gordon to Shearer, 9 July 1912; Ibid., Gordon to Falk, 9 July 1912; UCA, Dobson Papers, box A4, file F, Dobson to Falk, 13 May 1918.

6 See J. Howard Falk, "Social Work and Industrial Efficiency," *SW*, VI:10 (July 1924), 229.

7 UCA, Dobson Papers, box A4, file F, Dobson to Falk, 13 May 1918.

8 "Social Service and Theological Training," *SW*, I:11 (Aug. 1919), 272.

9 UTA, B90–0029, S.D. Clark Papers, box 18, "McGill Department of Social Service Advisory Committee," 9 March 1921.

10 MUA, ACC. 1563–1, Minutes of the Board of Governors, 30 Sept. 1920; McGill University, *Annual Calendar for Session, 1918–1919*, "Department of Social Study and Training"; "Report on McGill Social Service," *Montreal Gazette*, 3 June 1922; "Special Courses in Social Service," *Montreal Star*, 4 Jan. 1922. For the close links between social Christianity and social work at McGill, see Principal James Smyth, "The Message and Mission of Christianity," *SW*, VI:6 (March 1924), 106. This theological model for social work was replicated at the University of Western

Ontario as late as the 1930s when courses in sociology were taught by the Rev. Arthur Waring. See Principal Cameron Walker, "What Huron College is Doing," *SW*, XVI:5 (Dec. 1936), 156.

11 See McGill University, "Annual Report of the Corporation 1918–1919," 15.

12 "Report on McGill Social Service," *Montreal Gazette*, 3 June 1922; UTA, Clark Papers, "McGill Department of Social Service – Advisory Committee," 9 Oct. 1918, 7 Nov. 1918, 13 Feb. 1919.

13 UTA, Clark Papers, "McGill Department of Social Service – Advisory Committee," 2 Oct. 1919.

14 For Leacock's views, see "Usefulness not the Aim of Education: Stephen Leacock Scores Utilitarian Idea in Addressing Students," *Montreal Gazette*, 26 April 1924. In *The Science of Social Redemption*, xii–xiii, Marlene Shore has argued that McGill was dominated by a "utilitarian philosophy" which imbued the university with "a strong sense of service to the community," particularly in the years after World War I. The fact that Leacock's anti-utilitarian pronouncements were so readily listened to by the administration and Board of Governors would suggest the need to qualify strongly Shore's argument in the direction of greater influence for the ideal of liberal education.

15 MUA, RG2 C62, file 1060, President's Papers, Stephen Leacock, "A Memorandum on a Department of Sociology and Social Service," 13 Feb. 1922, 1–4.

16 UTA, Clark Papers, "McGill University, Department of Social Service, Committee of Management," 19 April 1922, 2.

17 Ibid., 20 Feb. 1922.

18 Ibid., 24 June 1919, 19 April 1922.

19 MUA, President's Papers, file 1060, Gordon Laing to President Currie, 29 March 1922.

20 UTA, Clark Papers, "Minutes of Committee of Management," 11 July 1922.

21 MUA, President's Papers, Arthur Currie to Dean Gordon Laing, 10 March 1922; UTA, James Mavor Papers, box 3B, Sedley Cudmore to Mavor, 26 May 1922.

22 UTA, James Mavor Papers, box 3B, Cudmore to Mavor, 14 June 1922.

23 On Dawson's early career, see Watson Kirkconnell, *The Acadia Record, 1838–1953*; MUA, President's Papers, file 1061, Dawson to Currie, 24 Feb. 1921.

24 Shore, *The Science of Social Redemption*, 70–1.

25 For Small and Henderson, see our discussion in Chapter 3. Before obtaining his PH.D. in psychology in 1914, Ellsworth Faris had served as a missionary in the Belgian Congo. See Bulmer, *The Chicago School of Sociology*, 249, n. 3.

26 MUA, President's Papers, file 1061, Dawson to Currie, 24 Feb. 1921. Dawson's letters of reference show a decided bias towards his Baptist theological culture. Besides letters from the Chicago sociologists Albion Small, Ellsworth Faris, Robert Park, and Ernest Burgess, he requested testimonials from such leading theologians as Dean Shailer Mathews, Professor Bedford, who taught rural sociology in the Chicago Divinity School, Professor John T. McNeil of Queen's University, President Waring of the Baptist Woodstock College, and Professor Thomas Dadson of Wesley College, Winnipeg.

27 UTA, Mavor Papers, box 3A, William Caldwell to Mavor, 9 June 1922; MUA, President's Papers, file 1060, Currie to Laing, 10 March 1922.

28 MUA, President's Papers, file 1060, Laing to Currie, 29 March 1922.

29 UTA, Clark Papers, "Minutes of Committee of Management," 28 April 1925; McGill University, *Annual Calendar for the Session, 1922–23*, "Department of Social Science," 413.

30 For this view of Dawson, see Shore, *The Science of Social Redemption*, 65, 121.

31 "University and Social Service," *Montreal Star*, 1 March 1922.

32 "Social Workers' Extension Course," *Montreal Star*, 28 Jan. 1924; "Family Life Given Greater Attention," *Montreal Gazette*, 14 Jan. 1931. This series of ten lectures was given by Dawson to the Westmount YMCA. See also "Would Ban Union of Human Unfit," *Montreal Star*, 21 Feb. 1923. His colleague and co-author, W.E. Gettys, was also a promoter of the union between sociology and social reform. See Dr W.E. Gettys, "Progress in Education and Recreation," *SW*, VIII:2 (Nov. 1925), 32–37.

33 Carl Dawson, "Research and Social Action," *SW*, V:5 (Feb. 1923), 93; "Vocational Guidance," *Montreal Star*, 20 Feb. 1924, in which Dawson linked the scientific study of character with "important problems of the day."

34 Carl Dawson, "Social Research in Canada," *SW*, IX:10 (July 1927), 471. Dawson's plea for empirical university research on social problems must be seen in light of the Canadian context where even by the late 1920s the collection of social data remained largely in the hands of untrained female charity workers, a situation that paralleled that of American progressives in the 1890s.

35 Dawson, "Research and Social Action," 94–5.

36 "Visit C.N.R. Shops," *Montreal Gazette*, 28 Jan. 1925; "Social Science is Theme of Address," *Montreal Gazette*, 13 March 1931. In this lecture to the Lions' Club, Dawson spoke on the connection between social science, business efficiency, and the formation of "leaders of vision." For Dawson's views on immigration restriction, see "Opposed to Immigration," *Winnipeg Free Press*, 20 March 1936; "Peculiar Groups Slowly Changing," *Montreal Star*, 11 April 1936; "Philanthropy not Immigrants

Needed," *Montreal Gazette*, June 1937. As these articles demonstrate, Dawson's incentive for investigating immigrant communities was anything but "objective."

37 Bulmer, *The Chicago School of Sociology*, xiv–xv.

38 Quoted in Mary Jo Deegan, *Jane Addams and the Men of the Chicago School, 1892–1918* (New Brunswick, N.J.: Transaction Books, 1988), 153.

39 The conflicting approaches of historians and sociologists is most evident in the collection of essays edited by Martin Bulmer, Kevin Bales, and Kathryn Kish Sklar, *The Social Survey in Historical Perspective, 1880–1940* (Cambridge: Cambridge University Press, 1991). For articles critical of Bulmer, see Stephen P. Turner, "The World of the Academic Quantifiers: the Columbia University Family and its Connections"; Kathryn Kish Sklar, "Hull-House Maps and Papers: Social Science as Women's Work in the 1890's"; Steven R. Cohen, "The Pittsburgh Survey and the Social Survey Movement: A Sociological road not taken."

40 See Turner, "The World of the Academic Quanitifiers," in Bulmer, Bales, and Sklar, 281.

41 See Bulmer, "The Decline of the Social Survey Movement and the Rise of American Empirical Sociology," in Bulmer, Bales, and Sklar, 301.

42 Lewis Mumford, "Review of Park and Burgess, *An Introduction to the Science of Sociology*," *Sociological Review*, 14:3 (July 1922), 234–5. The later development of Park's ecological views is confirmed by Marlene Shore, whose documentary evidence, drawn from Dawson's writings of the late 1930s, disputes, however, the main thrust of her argument. See *The Science of Social Redemption*, 292n93.

43 See Deegan, *Jane Addams and the Men of the Chicago School*, 146–8. Graham Taylor also attributed Park's ecological urban sociology to the earlier survey studies of Hull House. See Graham Taylor, *Chicago Commons Through Forty Years* (Chicago: Chicago Commons Association, 1936), 235.

44 See Steven J. Diner, "Department and Discipline: The Department of Sociology at the University of Chicago, 1892–1920," *Minerva*, 13:4 (winter 1975), 524. In *A City and its Universities: Public Policy in Chicago, 1892–1919* (Chapel Hill: University of North Carolina Press, 1980), Diner has underscored the strong connections between the teaching of sociology and urban reform. This is an important but frequently overlooked account of early sociology at the University of Chicago.

45 See Deegan, *Jane Addams and the Men of the Chicago School*, 146–8.

46 See E.W. Burgess, "The Social Survey," *American Journal of Sociology*, 21 (1915–16), 492–500; Burgess, "The Interdependence of Sociology and Social Work," *Journal of Social Forces*, 1:4 (May 1923), 367–9.

47 On Mead, see Dorothy Ross, *The Origins of American Social Science*, 169.

48 See University of Chicago Library, *Annual Register, 1913–14*, 315–41; *Annual Register, 1914–15*, 317–41.

49 McGill University, *Calendar, 1922–23*, "Department of Social Science," 409.

50 Dawson, "Social Work as a National Institution," *SW*, X:10 (July 1928), 225.

51 NA, Canadian Council of Churches, box 29, "Annual Meeting of the Social Service Council," 23 April 1928. See also Muriel McCall, "The Academic Equipment of the Social Worker," *SW*, XIII:1 (Oct. 1930), 129. For May Reid, see J. Brian Scott, "Brandon College and Social Christianity," in Jarold K. Zeman, ed., *Costly Vision: The Baptist Pilgrimage in Canada* (Burlington: Welch, 1988), 157.

52 See, for example, "Divorce Increase Due to Previously Existing Causes," *Montreal Herald*, 30 Jan. 1928; "Social Workers' Annual Meeting," *Montreal Star*, 9 May 1923; "Social Workers Meet in Toronto," *Montreal Gazette*, 25 June 1924; "Family Life Given Greater Attention," *Montreal Gazette*, 14 Jan. 1931. Even when Dawson recommended the establishment of a Prisoners' Aid and Welfare Association in 1944, he recommended that the Rev. Burgoyne be its president. Dawson often invited clergymen such as the Rev. Peter Bryce to speak on child welfare to the Department of Social Science; see "Dawson to Give Lectures on Social Problems of Daily Life," *Montreal Star*, 9 Feb. 1923.

53 Carl Dawson, "The Social Nature of Knowledge," PH.D. thesis, University of Chicago, 1922; on Dawson's gardening interests, see Shore, *The Science of Social Redemption*, 71. Apropos his rural roots Dawson earned the sobriquet "Spud" while at Acadia University. See *Acadia Athenaeum*, June 1912, 463.

54 For a view of Park that portrays him as a conservative rather than as a liberal progressive, see Jean B. Quandt, *From the Small Town to the Great Community* (New Brunswick, N.J.: Rutgers University Press, 1970), 4, 57.

55 NA, MG 28 I, 10, Canadian Council on Social Development, vol. 30, file 157, "Canadian Association of Social Workers, 1927," C.A. Dawson, "Why a Canadian National Conference of Social Work?" memorandum, n.d.

56 Carl Dawson, "The Human Side of the Problem," in the symposium, "The Christian Industrial Order," *SW*, V:11 (Aug. 1923), 221.

57 "Science Spoiled Christian Faith," *Montreal Star*, 25 Oct. 1922.

58 Ibid.

59 "Social Workers and Work Can Co-operate," *Montreal Star*, 8 April 1924.

60 UTA, Clark Papers, box 18, "Minutes of Committee of Management," 30 Nov. 1926, 22 May 1928.

61 Ibid., 11 May 1927.

62 C.A Dawson, "School for Social Workers," McGill University, *Annual Report of the Corporation, 1930–31*, which demonstrates that much of the financial support for the school came from the Montreal Women's Club and the Rotary Club, along with the James Ogilvy family. On the increased pressure from women for more practical training, see Malca Friedman, who wrote to *SW*, XIII:9 (June 1931), 192, calling for greater emphasis on fieldwork at McGill.

63 "Social Workers Courses Begin," *Montreal Star*, 3 Oct. 1924.

64 On the withdrawal of the church college funding, see UTA, Clark Papers, "Statement from the Principal on the Closing of the School for Social Workers at McGill University," 4 Aug. 1931. On Dawson's veering to vocationalism, see McGill University, *Annual Report of the Corporation, 1930–31*, 17–18; Esther W. Kerry, "Early Professional Development in Montreal," *Social Worker*, 29:3 (June 1961), 36–8. Kerry's recollections of the politics surrounding the closing of the McGill Department of Social Science are reaffirmed in Miss Dorothy King, "Trends in Schools of Social Work," *Social Worker*, 15:5 (Feb. 1947), 2.

65 MUA, RG 2, container 60, file 957, "Economics and Political Science," Stephen Leacock, "Memorandum on the Organisation of Research," 13 April 1932.

66 NA, MG 28 I, 10, Canadian Council on Social Development, vol. 6, file 150, "Canadian Association of Social Workers, 1929–31," Charlotte Whitton to Canon Cody, chair, Board of Governors, University of Toronto, 23 Nov. 1931 (confidential). Whitton stated that "Contrary to the advice of all the most powerful social agencies in Montreal and the East, McGill some years ago appointed a sociologist as head of their School of Social Work. The result has been three years of most unsatisfactory relations and practically forced the closing of the McGill School ... largely because the social agencies did not get the material which they needed from the School and were forced to send their workers elsewhere for training."

67 MUA, RG 2, container 58, file 872, "Survey: Arts 1931"; "Minutes of Meeting, March 27, 1931"; Ibid., "Minutes of Meeting, March 6, 1931."

68 See Kerry, "Early Professional Development in Montreal," 41–2. On the Social Science Research Project, see McGill University, *Annual Report of the Corporation, 1930–31*, 17–18. Dawson was not in accord with the principles of this project. See Allan Irving, "Leonard Marsh and the McGill Social Science Research Project," *Journal of Canadian Studies*, 21:2 (summer 1986), 13. On the budget crisis, see Sir Arthur Currie, "The Position of McGill To-Day", *McGill News*, XII:4 (Sept. 1931), 10. For Dawson's belated conversion to social scientific research in social work, see C.A. Dawson, "Social Workers in the Making," *SW*, XIII:2 (Nov. 1930), 27–8.

69 "Inaugural Address of President Falconer," *University of Toronto Monthly*, 1:1 (1907–8), 12. Whereas James Greenlee, in *Sir Robert Falconer: A Biography* (Toronto: University of Toronto Press, 1988), has argued that Falconer's ideal of service was in essence a form of secular moralism, Michael Gauvreau has recently interpreted Falconer in terms of his enduring Presbyterian convictions, which continued to lend a Christian cast to the secular activities of the University of Toronto. See "Presbyterianism, Liberal Education and the Research Ideal: Sir Robert Falconer and the University of Toronto, 1907–1932," in William Klempa, ed., *The Burning Bush and a Few Acres of Snow: The Presbyterian Contribution to Canadian Life and Culture* (Ottawa: Carleton University Press, 1994).

70 UTA, Falconer Papers, box 32, "Proposed School of Social Service," n.d.

71 Ibid., file "Social Service," Gaylord G. White to Falconer, 22 May 1914; Falconer to Graham Taylor, 23 May 1914; Falconer to C.R. Henderson, 28 May 1914; Ibid., box 112, "Memo Regarding Social Service Department," 1917–28. Women prominent in social reform were also instrumental in pressuring for the creation of a School of Social Service. Adelaide Plumptre, a member of the Social Service Council of Ontario and of the National Council of Women, served as the spokeswoman for the Social Workers' Club of Toronto, which was largely comprised of female reformers and charity workers. See *Training for Social Work in the Department of Social Science at the University of Toronto, 1914–40* (Toronto: University of Toronto Press, 1940), 12.

72 For Brett, see Michael Gauvreau, "Philosophy, Psychology, and History: George Sidney Brett and the Quest for a Social Science at the University of Toronto, 1910–1940," Canadian Historical Association, *Historical Papers*, 1988, 209–36.

73 UTA, Falconer Papers, box 70B, J.A. Dale to Falconer, 23 Dec. 1921; *Training for Social Work*, 14. The School of Social Service at the University of Toronto also conducted special bible classes in practical Christianity for the YMCA. See "Training Course for Social Work," *SW*, 1:11 (1 Aug. 1919), 271; "The Y.M.C.A. in Social Work," *SW*, II:9 (1 June 1920), 233.

74 See Andrew Seth, *Hegelianism and Personality* (New York: Burt Franklin, 1971), 4, 27, 58; John Passmore, *A Hundred Years of Philosophy* (London: Pelican Books, 1957), 58, 73; James T. Kloppenberg, *Uncertain Victory: Social Democracy and Progressivism in European and American Thought, 1870–1920* (New York and Oxford: Oxford University Press, 1986), 149. On MacIver's rejection of Hegel, see MacIver, "Society and 'The Individual,'" *Sociological Review*, 8:1 (Jan. 1915), 60–4; UTA, James Mavor Papers, MacIver to Mavor, 24 Aug. 1918. For the encounter between Seth and Robert Falconer in the 1880s and the former's con-

tribution to defining Falconer's educational philosophy, see Gauvreau, "Presbyterianism, Liberal Education, and the Research Ideal."

75 MacIver, "Personality and the Supernatural," *Philosophical Review*, 24:5 (Sept. 1915), 514; MacIver, "What is Social Psychology?" *Sociological Review*, 6:2 (April 1913), 149–54.

76 MacIver, "Sociology," in Dixon Ryan Fox, ed., *A Quarter Century of Learning, 1904–29* (New York: Columbia University Press, 1931), 222–34; MacIver, "Ethics and History," in MacIver, *Politics & Society* (New York: Atherton Press, 1969), 75.

77 "Is World Approaching a Fixed Population," *Toronto Star Weekly*, 13 March 1926.

78 MacIver, "Ethics and History," 75.

79 MacIver, *The Elements of Social Science* (London: Methuen, 1921), 158.

80 Ibid., 164.

81 MacIver, "Society and the Individual," 60–4.

82 See A.R.M. Lower, "Origins of Government Found in the Family: Review of MacIver's *The Web of Government*," *Globe and Mail*, 14 May 1947.

83 MacIver, *The Contribution of Sociology to Social Work* (The Forbes Lectures of the New York School of Social Work) (New York: Columbia University Press, 1931), 3–6, 10–15, 47, 75–6.

84 "Many Chance to Give Help," *Globe*, 31 Jan. 1919, which reported on the Women's Vocational Conference where MacIver spoke.

85 UTA, Department of Graduate Records, "Robert MacIver," "The Department of Social Service as a Branch of the University," n.d., 100–1.

86 Ibid., "James A. Dale," Sir Michael Sadler, "J.A. Dale: A Character Sketch," n.d.; Barbara M. Finlayson, "Professor Dale," *SW*, IX:3 (Dec. 1926), 325.

87 UTA, Department of Graduate Records, "James A. Dale."

88 Professor J.A. Dale, "Social Service in the University," *McGill News*, VII:2 (March 1926), 17–18.

89 "Scoutmaster's Training," *Presbyterian Witness*, 27 Jan. 1912.

90 Dale, "Social Service in the University," 18; "Likens State to Lava Crust," *Globe*, 28 March 1921; "Professor Dale Gives Varsity Students a New Viewpoint," *Star Weekly*, n.d.

91 "Engineers are Told of Social Service," *Globe*, 2 Dec. 1921.

92 "Basic Cure is Education," *Globe*, 6 Jan. 1922; "Need of Education in Social Work," *Toronto Mail*, 27 April 1921; "Professor Dale Inaugurated," *Varsity*, 6 Oct. 1920.

93 For Premier Drury's membership on the Social Service Council of Ontario and his role in fostering closer ties between the provincial government and the council during his term of office, see AO, RG 3, Drury Correspondence, 03–04–0–083, Gilbert Agar, secretary, Social Service

Council of Ontario, to Drury, 14 July 1920; Ibid., 15 July 1920; AO, E.C. Drury Papers, MU 950, box 1, "Correspondence 1932–1948," J.W. Graham, Frank Langford, secretaries, United Church of Canada, Board of Christian Education, to Drury, 12 Nov. 1932.

94 Professor J.A. Dale, "The Training of Social Workers," *SW*, VI:10 (July 1924), 202; "Prof. Dale Delivers Fine Address to Neighborhood Workers," *Globe*, 15 April 1921. The Baptist Rev. M.C. McLean presided over the meeting, where Dale stated that all social workers should share his view: "Let me live my life from day to day, with forward-looking face and unreluctant soul."

95 "Health Department Undergoes Shake-up," *Mail*, 30 May 1923; "Labor Men Want Prof. Dale to Direct Social Service," *Mail*, 20 April 1923; "Action of Prof. Dale Backed by I.L.P. Head," *Star*, 23 April 1923; "Conscientious Objectors to Views of Scott Nearing and His Crowd," *Toronto Telegram*, 23 April 1923.

96 "Forgets Catholic Martyrs Late Victims of Soviet," *Toronto Telegram*, 30 May 1923; "Fair Play for Dale Asks Big Deputation," *Toronto Star*, 23 May 1923; "Clergy Uphold Appointment of Prof. Dale," *Toronto Star*, 23 April 1923; "Dale is No Bolshevik Says Michael Sadler," *Toronto Star*, 4 April 1923.

97 "Failure to Appoint Prof. Dale Protested," *Toronto Star*, 14 April 1923.

98 For a very different view, that assertions of academic freedom were largely defensive struggles against attempts by the provincial government to expand its control of the university, see McKillop, *Matters of Mind*, 362–401.

99 On this enduring opposition, see Greenlee, *Sir Robert Falconer*, 284.

100 For the interpretation of Ontario political culture as hegemonically conservative, see Peter N. Oliver, "The Ontario Liberal Party in the 1920s: A Study in Political Collapse," in Oliver, *Private and Public Persons* (Toronto: Clarke, Irwin & Co., 1975), 126–55. On Hepburn's close links with the Druryite progressives, see J.T. Saywell, *"Just Call Me Mitch": The Life of Mitchell F. Hepburn* (Toronto: University of Toronto Press, 1992), 12.

101 UTA, Falconer Papers, box 104, Falconer to Urwick, 25 April 1927. Urwick replaced R.M. MacIver who had departed to the chair of sociology at Columbia University.

102 Urwick, *A Philosophy of Social Progress*, 229.

103 Urwick, *The Values of Life* (Toronto: University of Toronto Press, 1948), 166; *A Philosophy of Social Progress*, 227.

104 H.A.I. [Harold Innis], "Edward Johns Urwick," *Canadian Journal of Economics and Political Science*, XI (May 1945), 265.

105 Urwick, *Studies of Boy Life in Our Cities* (London: Dent, 1904), 311. For Urwick's contributions to the sociology of child labour and urban

delinquency, see Harry Hendrick, *Images of Youth: Age, Class, and the Male Youth Problem, 1880–1920* (Oxford: Clarendon Press, 1990), 140, 187–8.

106 Canon Barnett, "Personal Service," *Toynbee Record*, XIII:1 (Oct. 1900), 3. On Barnett and Toynbee Hall, see Chris Waters, *British Socialists and the Politics of Popular Culture, 1884–1914* (California: Stanford University Press, 1990), 68; Norman and Jeanne Mackenzie, eds., *The Diary of Beatrice Webb, Vol. I, 1873–92* (Cambridge, Mass.: Harvard University Press, 1982), 171; J.A.R. Pimlott, *Toynbee Hall: Fifty Years of Social Progress, 1884–1934* (London: J.M. Dent & Sons, 1934); Gertrude Himmelfarb, *Poverty and Compassion: The Moral Imagination of the Late Victorians* (New York: Alfred A. Knopf, 1991), 241.

107 For Beveridge's career, see Jose Harris, *William Beveridge: A Biography* (Oxford: Clarendon Press, 1977).

108 Charles Loch Mowat, *The Charity Organisation Society, 1869–1913: Its Ideas and Work* (London: Methuen & Co., 1961), 71.

109 Jose Harris, "The Webbs, the Charity Organisation Society, and the Ratan Tata Foundation: Social Policy from the Perspective of 1912," in Martin Bulmer, Jane Lewis, and David Piachaud, eds., *The Goals of Social Policy* (London and Boston: Unwin Hyman, 1989), 35–6; Martha Vicinus, *Independent Women: Work and Community for Single Women, 1850–1920* (Chicago: University of Chicago Press, 1985), 231; Mowat, *The Charity Organisation Society*, 72, 107. The Cambridge economist Alfred Marshall had also been a consistent advocate of the training of social workers. For the important role of women, especially Helen Bosanquet, in the professionalization of British social work, see Noel Parry and Jose Parry, "Social Work, Professionalism, and the State," in Noel Parry, Michael Rustin, and Carole Satyamurti, eds., *Social Work, Welfare and the State* (Beverly Hills: Sage Publications, 1979), 22–5; Enid Harrison, "The Changing Meaning of Social Work," in A.H. Halsey, ed., *Traditions of Social Policy: Essays in Honour of Violet Butler* (London: Basil Blackwell, 1976), 90–1.

110 Harris, "The Webbs, the Charity Organisation Society, and the Ratan Tata Foundation," 41–3.

111 For biographical details of Urwick, see Innis, "Edward Johns Urwick," 265; H.A. Innis, ed., *Essays in Political Economy* (Toronto: University of Toronto Press, 1938); Urwick, *The Values of Life*, introduction by John Irving, xi–xvi. Jose Harris has recently assigned Urwick a prominent role among new liberal social thinkers in Britain. See Harris, "The Webbs, the Charity Organisation Society, and the Ratan Tata Foundation," 51–4.

112 In 1919 Urwick, Hobhouse, and the Webbs wrote a report evaluating the welfare facilities of Tata Steel in India. See Ibid., 48.

113 John W. Mason, "Political Economy and the Response to Socialism in Britain, 1870–1914," *Historical Journal*, 23:3 (1980), 568.

114 On Barnett's break with the Charity Organisation Society, see Gareth Stedman Jones, *Outcast London* (Harmondsworth: Penguin Books, 1971), 1, 303. Much of Urwick's thought retained the early impress with the society. See Urwick, "Underfed Children," *Toynbee Record*, 14:2 (Nov. 1901), 24.

115 Urwick, "The Future of Voluntary Social Work," *Clare Market Review* [student magazine of the London School of Economics and Political Science], 9:2 (Feb. 1914), 48.

116 For the traditional critique of the Charity Organisation Society, see Jones, *Outcast London*, 254. The social control hypothesis of Jones has recently been critiqued by Jose Harris and Jane Lewis, who have argued that the social policy ideas of the Bosanquets were not nearly as antediluvian as Jones has estimated and that they had more in common with those of the Webbs than has been previously assumed. See Jose Harris, "The Webbs, the Charity Organisation Society and Ratan Tata," 31–4; Jane Lewis, "The Place of Social Investigation, Social Theory and Social Work in the Approach to Late Victorian and Edwardian Social Problems: The Case of Beatrice Webb and Helen Bosanquet," in Bulmer, Bales, and Sklar, *The Social Survey in Historical Perspective*, 158–9. For an older work that advances a similar argument about the interpenetration between Fabians and liberals, see Peter Clarke, *Liberals and Social Democrats* (Cambridge: Cambridge University Press, 1978).

117 See Urwick, "The Future of Voluntary Social Work," 41, 49.

118 On this quarrel among English social thinkers, see Stefan Collini, "Political Theory and the 'Science of Society' in Victorian Britain," *Historical Journal*, 23:1 (1980), 203–31. Collini's interpretation has been more fully elaborated in Stefan Collini, Donald Winch, and John Burrow, *That Noble Science of Politics: A study in nineteenth-century intellectual history* (Cambridge: Cambridge University Press, 1983). For the curriculum at Urwick's School of Sociology and Economics, see Seth Kovan, "Surveying the Social Survey," in Bulmer, Bales, and Sklar, *The Social Survey in Historical Perspective*, 374. See also Helen Bosanquet, *Social Work in London* (London: John Murray, 1914), 405.

119 See *Toynbee Record*, June 1890, Aug. 1890, Nov. 1890.

120 Reba N. Soffer, *Ethics and Society in England: The Revolution in the Social Sciences, 1870–1914* (Berkeley and London: University of California Press, 1978), 58; I.D. McKillop, *The British Ethical Societies* (Cambridge: Cambridge University Press, 1986), 83–97.

121 Along with W.H. Beveridge, Hobson, Hobhouse, James Bryce, Beatrice Webb, and Canon Barnett, Urwick directed the social survey of West Ham in 1907 which reported on rents, wages, poor rates, and the spiral

of economic dependence caused by casual labour. See Soffer, *Ethics and Society*, 151.

122 The Sociological Society again reflected the wide spectrum of political and disciplinary interests that promoted organic notions of social change. It was founded by Hobson, Hobhouse, Urwick, Bernard Bosanquet, the Scottish town planner Patrick Geddes, Robert Flint, professor of divinity at Edinburgh, Andrew Seth, professor of logic and metaphysics at Edinburgh, the sociologist Edward Westermarck, and the eugenicist Francis Galton. See *Sociological Papers*, vol. 1 (1901), xi. James Bryce, "The Use and Purpose of the Sociological Society," ibid., 18 April 1904, xiv–xviii; Stefan Collini, *Liberalism and Sociology: L.T. Hobhouse and Political Argument in England, 1880–1914* (Cambridge: Cambridge University Press, 1979), 203; Soffer, *Ethics and Society*, 111–12; Reba Soffer, "The Revolution in English Social Thought, 1880–1914," *American Historical Review*, LXXV (1970), 1938–64. Lawrence Goldman has denigrated the reformist tradition in British sociology as methodologically naïve and moralistic compared to the American and French. See "A Peculiarity of the English? The Social Science Association and the Absence of Sociology in Nineteenth-century Britain," *Past and Present*, 114 (Feb. 1987), 133–71. For a more positive assessment of the contributions of British reform social science to modern social policy, see Jose Harris, *Private Lives, Public Spirit: A Social History of Britain, 1870–1914* (Oxford: Oxford University Press, 1993), 221–2.

123 On Hobhouse's harmonization of empiricism and idealism, see Stefan Collini, *Liberalism and Sociology*; Collini, "Hobhouse, Bosanquet and the State: Philosophical Idealism and Political Argument in England, 1880–1918," *Past and Present*, 72 (Aug. 1976), 86–111; Morris Ginsberg and J.A. Hobson, *L.T. Hobhouse: His Life and Work* (London: Allen and Unwin, 1931). On Wallas, see Martin J. Wiener, *Between Two Worlds: The Political Thought of Graham Wallas* (Oxford: Clarendon Press, 1971).

124 Urwick, *A Philosophy of Social Progress*, 70, 91.

125 Urwick, *The Social Good* (London: Methuen, 1927), 70. For the misconception which historians have had regarding Spencer as the advocate of the concept of the survival of the fittest, see Stefan Collini, "Political Theory and the 'Science of Society,'" 209.

126 For the most important discussion of Huxley's lecture, see James Paradis and George C. Williams, eds., *Evolution and Ethics: T.H. Huxley's Evolution and Ethics with New Essays on Its Victorian and Sociobiological Context* (Princeton: Princeton University Press, 1989).

127 Urwick, "Review of *Work and Wealth* by J.A. Hobson," *Sociological Review*, VIII:1 (Jan. 1915), 57.

128 Urwick, *Spending in Wartime* (Oxford: Oxford University Press, 1915), 15–16.

129 Urwick, *A Philosophy of Social Progress*, IX; Urwick, "Review of *Individualism and After* by Benjamin Kidd," *Sociological Review*, II (Jan. 1909), 89–90. On Benjamin Kidd, see D.P. Crook, *Benjamin Kidd: Portrait of a Social Darwinist* (Cambridge: Cambridge University Press, 1984).

130 UTA, A73/0026/482, Department of Graduate Records, Urwick Biographical File, "Questionnaire Found Limited," *Globe and Mail*, 4 Feb. 1936.

131 Urwick, *A Philosophy of Social Progress*, 7.

132 Urwick, *The Social Good*, 39, 68; *A Philosophy of Social Progress*, 14.

133 The Department of Social Service changed its name to the Department of Social Science in 1929–30.

134 University of Toronto, *Calendar, 1925–26*, "Department of Social Service," 758–9; *Training for Social Work*, 7–8.

135 UTA, Harry Cassidy Papers, B72–0022/014, Urwick to Cassidy, 24 Jan. 1929, in which Urwick sharply informed Cassidy that at the University of Toronto social work was taught on British lines which studied "the problems of society – not merely in the limited sense of relief or family case-work, but in the wider sense which includes problems of labour adjustment, social reorganization, governmental assistance and so on." Innis briefly welcomed Cassidy's appointment to head the Department of Social Science but he vociferously opposed him during the 1940s. See UTA, Cassidy Papers, box 16, Innis to Cassidy, 8 Nov. 1939.

136 UTA, Falconer Papers, box 123, Urwick to Falconer, 4 Oct. 1929, "The Education of Social Workers." For a similar assessment of the importance of the moral dimension in social work, see "T.R. Robinson, Professor of Social Ethics, University of Toronto, Lectures in Social Service Department," *SW*, VIII:4 (1926), 73.

137 UTA, Falconer Papers, box 117, Urwick to Falconer, 22 May 1929.

138 Ernest Thomas, "Social Service Work in the United Church of Canada," *SW*, IX:9 (June 1927), 445–6.

139 For this view, see Roy Lubove, *The Professional Altruist: The Emergence of Social Work as a Career, 1880–1930* (Cambridge, Mass.: Harvard University Press, 1965).

140 For recent critics of the view that moralism was antithetical to professionalization, see Eileen Janes Yeo, "The Social Survey in Social Perspective, 1830–1930," in Bulmer, Bales, and Sklar, eds., *The Social Survey in Historical Perspective*, 55–6; Daniel J. Walkowitz, "The Making of a Feminine Professional Identity: Social Workers in the 1920's," *American Historical Review*, 95:4 (Oct. 1990), 1051–75; John H. Ehrenreich, *The Altruistic Imagination: A History of Social Work and Social Policy in the United States* (Ithaca: Cornell University Press, 1985), 79, who argues that well into the 1930s, despite outward signs of professional status, the professional remained racked by internal divisions between the older moral philanthropy and the advocates of objective science.

141 All social workers in settlement houses, orphanages, and juvenile homes were appointed directly by the churches. See UCA, United Church Board of Home Missions, box 17, file 175, "College Street Church and St. Christopher House," 16 June 1933; UCA, Methodist Church, DESS, box 1, file 7, "Annual Meeting of the General Board," 26–27 Aug. 1919; Ibid., box 1, file 11, "Minutes of Executive Committee of the General Board," 24 April 1913; Ibid., box 2, file 43, T. Albert Moore to the Rev. R.W. Armstrong, 15 July 1920.

142 NA, Canadian Council of Churches, box 29, "Third Meeting of Program Committee of the Fifteenth Annual Conference of Charities and Corrections," 22 April 1914, 3. This body had invited Dr E.T. Devine, professor of social work at Columbia, to speak on "The Training of Social Workers." For Falconer's and Pidgeon's links with American social work, see "Social Work in the Life of To-Day: A Better America," *Journal of Social Forces*, 1:3 (March 1923). Hugh Dobson, another prominent Methodist progressive clergyman, also regularly attended these American conferences.

143 SAB, McNaughton Papers, Woodsworth to McNaughton, 23 Feb. 1914.

144 Principal James Smyth, "The Approach to Social Work," *SW*, II:3 (Jan. 1920), 46.

145 F.N. Stapleford, "The Church as a Social Agency," *SW*, II:7 (April 1920), 180–3; Stapleford, "Social Work and Social Progress," *SW*, III:9 (June 1921), 230, 255; Stapleford, "The Contribution of Social Work to Social Progress," *SW*, VIII:8 (June–July 1926), 190.

146 "Neighbourhood Workers' Association Toronto Meets," *SW*, IX:9 (June 1927), 450.

147 Carl Dawson, "A Canadian Conference of Social and Health Work," *SW*, VI:10 (July 1924), 189.

148 NA, Canadian Council of Churches, box 29, "Annual Meeting of the Canadian Conference on Public Welfare," 11 May 1920; Falk, "Volunteer Workers and Social Records," *SW*, 11 Aug. 1927, 501.

149 Dawson, "Social Research in Canada," *SW*, IX:10 (July 1927), 470; "51st Annual Meeting of National Conference of Social Workers," *SW*, VI:7 (April 1924), 118, at which Dawson spoke on how scientific thought could make social welfare more efficient; Dawson, "The Canadian Conference of Social Work," *SW*, X:5 (Feb. 1928), 101.

150 NA, Canadian Council of Churches, box 29, "Annual Meeting," 26–28 Jan. 1927.

151 NA, MG 28 I, 441, Canadian Association of Social Workers, vol. 1, file 19, "Minutes of Meeting, 18 June 1926."

152 Ibid., vol. 3, file 15, "Organization, General Correspondence 1926–27," R.W. Hopper to J.H. McMenemy, City Relief Department, Hamilton, Ont., 23 Oct. 1926; Ibid., vol. 3, file 14, "Organization, General Corre-

spondence, 1926–27," A. Maude Riley, president, Calgary Council on Child Welfare, to R.W. Hopper, 30 July 1926; Ibid., vol. 3, file 15, "Organization, Correspondence, Provisional Chairman and Provisional Secretary, 1926–28," R.W. Hopper to G.B. Clarke, president, Canadian Association of Social Workers, 26 Nov. 1926, in which Hopper stated that he believed J.S. Woodsworth was qualified for full membership because he had been "professionally engaged for the necessary period as a Minister. I suppose Ministers would be professional social workers."

153 NA, MG 28 I, 10, Canadian Council on Social Development, vol. 6, file 150, Jane Wisdom to Charlotte Whitton, 18 April 1931. For similar views, see NA, MG 28 I, 441, Canadian Association of Social Workers, vol. 3, file 12, "Correspondence with Provisional Executive, 1922–1928," Ernest H. Blois to the R.W. Hopper, 5 April 1927; Ibid., vol. 3, file 13, G.B. Clarke to Miss Cecilia Calder, secretary, Winnipeg Children's Aid Society, 2 June 1925.

154 UCA, John Maclean Papers, box 2, file 51, S.A. Maclean, Cliffee Woodworth, W.C. Searle, J.R. Van Norman, on behalf of Bethel Mission Congregation, to Miss Maud Dickinson, Bethel Mission deaconess, n.d. It should come as no surprise that J.S. Woodsworth's autobiography, published in 1926, was entitled *Following the Gleam.*

155 AO, F837, series 3, Ontario Welfare Council Papers, box 14, the Rev. Peter Bryce, "Recent Constructive Developments in Child Welfare," in *Annual Meeting and Conference of the Social Service Council of Ontario: May 10–11 Convention Hall, Royal Connaught Hotel, Hamilton, Ontario, 1920*, 32.

156 On the personnel of the executive of the Canadian Association of Social Workers, see "Canadian Association of Social Workers," *SW*, IX:1 (Oct. 1926), 284; NA, Canadian Council of Churches, box 29, Judge Helen Gregory MacGill to Harkness, 5 Dec. 1927; G.B. Clarke to Harkness, 26 Nov. 1927; the Rev. Peter Bryce to Harkness, 23 Nov. 1927 (Bryce agreed to support Dawson's initiative to establish a professional organization for Canadian social workers). See also "The Canadian Conference on Social Work and the Future," *SW*, X:8 (May 1928), 176–7. Interestingly, the annual meeting of the Montreal Branch of the association, in which Dawson was a leading member, was held in the church parlour of St James's United Church. See *SW*, XI:6 (March 1929), 42. For a contrary interpretation, which stresses the presence of the churches in the administration of public welfare, see B.L. Vigod, "Ideology and Institutions in Quebec: The Public Charities Controversy, 1921–1926," *Histoire Sociale/Social History*, 11:2 (May 1978), 167–82.

157 NA, Canadian Council of Churches, box 32, "Minutes, Committee on Future Policy," 7 Feb. 1929; Ibid., box 29, "Report of the Executive of SSCC for Year 1928," 4.

158 AO, Ontario Welfare Council Papers, box 14, file 1929, "Report of the Executive Secretary," 18 April 1929.

159 NA, Canadian Council of Churches, box 29, "Supplement to the Report of the Executive of the SSC for Year 1925."

160 J.R. Mutchmor, "Is Social Work Inspiration Declining?," *SW*, XI:2 (Nov. 1928), 44.

161 See P.T. Rooke and R.L. Schnell, "Making the Way More Comfortable," *Journal of Canadian Studies*, 17:4 (winter 1982–83), 37. It is significant that in 1932 Whitton became a public welfare consultant for R.B. Bennett's Conservative government, and that she recommended the centralized direction of relief under the administration of professional social workers. See James Struthers, *No Fault of their Own* (Toronto: University of Toronto Press, 1983), 75–8.

162 Grace B. Cole, "Inter-Relations Between the Professional Agency and the Church," *SW*, XII:5 (Feb. 1930), 117; E. Phyllis Pettit, "The Professional Agency and the Church," *SW*, XII:6 (March 1930), 138.

163 A. Ethel Parker, "Stengthening Bulwarks in Toronto," *SW*, XIII:7 (April 1931), 137–8. For the negative impact of the Depression on women's work, see Margaret Hobbs, "Rethinking Antifeminism in the 1930's: Gender Crisis or Workplace Justice? A Response to Alice Kessler-Harris," *Gender and History*, 5:1 (spring 1993). For the rapid decline in the number of women social workers during the Depression in the United States, see Cott, *The Grounding of Modern Feminism*, 218–25, and, for the Canadian situation, James Struthers, "A Profession in Crisis: Charlotte Whitton and Canadian Social Work in the 1930s," *Canadian Historical Review*, June 1981, 169–85; Struthers, "'Lord Give Us Men': Women and Social Work in English Canada 1918–1953," Canadian Historical Association, *Historical Papers*, 1983.

164 See F.N. Stapleford, "Social Work as a Vocation," *SW*, XIV:8 (Sept. 1932), 159.

165 NA, Canadian Council of Churches, box 29, "Executive Meeting of SSC," 8 Sept. 1931, 2; Ibid, 21 June 1932, 2; "New of Social Workers and Agencies," *SW*, XIII:8 (May 1931), 175, which announced that social work employment was dominated by church-based charities; D.N. McLachlan, "The United Church Relief Work, 1930–31," *SW*, XIII:6 (March 1931); Canon C.W. Vernon, "The Anglican Church and Unemployment," *SW*, XIII:6 (March 1931); the Rev. J.R. Mutchmor, "That the City May be Saved," *SW*, XIV:4 (Jan. 1932); Prof. J.W. Macmillan, "Unemployment and Its Causes," *New Outlook*, 12 Nov. 1930.

166 See Gilbert Agar, "A Minister of Public Welfare," *SW*, XIII:1 (Oct. 1930), 5; UCA, Mutchmor Papers, box 1, file 1, H.G. Dawson, president of the Central Council of Social Agencies of Manitoba to Mutchmor, 11 Dec. 1939; Ibid., Mutchmor to Dawson, 14 Dec. 1939.

167 Richard Allen, *The Social Passion*, 287–301. Significantly, the Canadian Association of Social Workers did not establish its own journal until 1935.
168 For the dominance of this conservative strand of economic thinking during the period 1930–34, see Struthers, *No Fault of their Own*, 95.
169 Hugh Dobson, "Unemployment and the Unemployed: A Religious as Well as an Economic Problem," SW, XIII:7 (April 1931), 148; C.W. Vernon, "The Mother and the Warrior," SW, XIII:8 (May 1931), 155–6.
170 Mutchmor, "That the City May be Saved," SW, XIV:4 (Jan. 1932), 65.
171 This coincided with the increasing financial difficulties of *Social Welfare* because of a decreasing circulation during the Depression. See UCA, Silcox Papers, box 8, "Report on the Publication of *Social Welfare*," 1935.
172 "Church Conference of Social Work in Montreal," SW, XV:6 (March 1935).
173 UCA, Dobson Papers, box 19, "The Canadian Association of Social Workers, Constitution and Directory of Members, 1928"; Ibid., "Third Canadian Conference on Social Work, June 6–9 1932"; Ibid., box 16, J.R. Mutchmor to Dobson, 8 Dec. 1937, in which Mutchmor promised to give a series of lectures on the church and social work at Manitoba College.
174 NA, Canadian Council of Churches, box 29, "Report of the Executive Committee of SSC for the Year 1930," 20; Canon Shatford, "The Minister and the Social Worker," SW, XIV:8 (Sept. 1932), 148–9.
175 "Church Social Service Board Reviews Canadian Welfare Problems," *Canadian Welfare*, XIV:3 (Sept. 1938), 3–4.
176 W.E. Taylor, "The Church and Society," SW, XVI:2 (March 1936), 51. See also UCA/UW, Cormie Papers, folder G, "The General Council's Commission on Urban Problems: Questionnaire," 1938.
177 William Creighton Graham, "The Responsibility of the Church for Social Work," *Canadian Welfare*, XIV:6 (March 1939), 14–20. Graham studied at the University of Chicago under Shailer Mathews and later taught there in the Divinity School from 1926 to 1938. See Phyllis Airhart, *Serving the Present Age: Revivalism, Progressivism, and the Methodist Tradition in Canada* (Montreal and Kingston: McGill-Queen's University Press, 1992), 114–16.
178 UCA, Silcox Papers, box 5, file 8, "Opening Vesper Address," Church Conference of Social Work, Montreal, 9 June 1935, 2–10. On the Oxford Group movement during the 1930s, see David Marshall, *Secularizing the Faith: Canadian Protestant Clergy and the Crisis of Belief, 1850–1940* (Toronto: University of Toronto Press, 1992), 213–9.
179 UCA, Silcox Papers, article, SW, XVIII:2 (winter 1939), 34–5; Ibid., box 5, file 6, "Unoccupied Areas of Social Work," 10 May 1935, 2.
180 See Marshall, *Secularizing the Faith*, 249.
181 R.M. MacIver, "Education and Life," SW, X:2 (Nov. 1927), 24.

182 UTA, Cassidy Papers, box 35, file 49, J. Howard Falk, executive director, Vancouver Council of Social Agencies, "An Address to the Representatives of its Institutional Membership," 29 Dec. 1931. For Falk's career as director of the Vancouver Council of Social Agencies, see F. Ivor Jackson, "Profiles 4: Howard Falk", *Canadian Welfare*, 41:6 (Nov.–Dec. 1965), 266–73.
183 "E.J. Urwick", "Urwick Foresees Feeble-Minded Society," *Varsity*, 20 Nov. 1935.
184 Urwick, "The Training of Social Workers," SW, XII:8 (May 1930), 176.
185 UTA, Innis Papers, B72–0025, box 11, file 15, Urwick to Innis, 30 Dec. 1942, 24 Sept. 1940. On the Quakers, see Urwick, *Training for Social Work*, 54.
186 Urwick, "Review of Rev. J.C. Pringle, *The Social Work of the London Churches*," SW, XVII:6 (June 1938), 112. In "Study Closer Civic Politics," *Toronto Telegram*, 20 Sept. 1938, Urwick deplored the decline in voluntary social service agencies.
187 Urwick, "The Building of the Community," SW, XV:6 (Sept. 1936), 104–7; Urwick, "Student Training for Widening Fields," *The Social Worker*, 3:5 (Feb. 1935); UTA, Cassidy Papers, box 14, Urwick to Cassidy, 6 Dec. 1934, on Urwick's support for a closer relationship with the provincial Liberal minister of welfare, David Croll. For Urwick's views of Whitton, see UTA, Innis Papers, box 11, file 15, Urwick to Innis, 7 March 1944, 15 Sept. 1942.
188 On Mutchmor's resignation, see Rooke and Schnell, "'Making the Way More Comfortable,'" 37. See also Patricia T. Rooke and R.L. Schnell, "Charlotte Whitton Meets 'The Last Best West': The Politics of Child Welfare in Alberta, 1929–49," *Prairie Forum*, 6:2 (fall 1981), 144–6, who argue that Whitton was forced out of the council because she opposed the proposals of Harry Cassidy. On the connection between the feminization of social work and opposition to state social planning, see Urwick, "Student Training for Widening Fields."
189 Irving, "Canadian Fabians."
190 UTA, Cassidy Papers, "Religion and Social Work," University of Chicago lecture, fall 1940, n.p.
191 Urwick, "Review of Harold A. Phelps, *Contemporary Social Problems*," SW, XVIII:2 (winter 1939), 55.

CHAPTER FIVE

1 J.W. Macmillan, "The Country Town: Its Relation to the City and to the Surrounding Country District," GGG, 17 April 1918, 62.
2 J.A. Stevenson, "Reconstruction in Canada and the Social and Economic Forces which will Condition It," *Survey*, 4 Jan. 1919, 442.

3 For a review of the main currents in Canadian historical writing since 1970, see Carl Berger, "Writings in Canadian History," in W.H. New, et al., eds., *Literary History of Canada: Canadian Literature in English, Second Edition* (Toronto: University of Toronto Press, 1990), IV:293–333.

4 See, for example, H.V. Nelles, *The Politics of Development* (Toronto: Macmillan, 1974); Christopher Armstrong, *The Politics of Federalism* (Toronto: University of Toronto Press, 1981); Nelles and Armstrong, *Monopoly's Moment* (Philadelphia: Temple University Press, 1986); Tom Traves, *The State and Enterprise* (Toronto: University of Toronto Press, 1977); Ken Cruikshank, *Close Ties* (Montreal and Kingston: McGill-Queen's University Press, 1992).

5 Although some American progressives were concerned with reform of the countryside, such efforts constituted but a minor strand in an overwhelmingly urban movement. See, for example, Clayton S. Ellsworth, "Theodore Roosevelt's Country Life Commission," *Agricultural History Review*, 34 (1960), 155–72; David B. Danbom, "Rural Education Reform and the Country Life Movement 1900–1920," *Agricultural History Review*, 53 (1979), 462–73; William L. Bowers, *The Country Life Movement* (Port Washington, N.Y.: Kennikat Press, 1974).

6 James Struthers, *No Fault of Their Own: Unemployment and the Canadian Welfare State, 1914–1941* (Toronto: University of Toronto Press, 1983), 8–9, 43.

7 John Kendle, *John Bracken* (Toronto: University of Toronto Press, 1976), 15–25.

8 R.W. Murchie, *Unused Lands of Manitoba* (Winnipeg: Department of Agriculture and Colonization, 1926); R.W. Murchie, W.H. Carter, and F.J. Dixon, *Seasonal Unemployment in Manitoba: A Report*, 1 Feb. 1928.

9 R.G. MacBeth, "Problems of the Country and the City," in W.R. McIntosh, *Canadian Problems* (Toronto: R. Douglas Fraser, 1910), 29.

10 See George Emery, "Methodism on the Canadian Prairies, 1896–1914: The Dynamics of an Institution in a New Environment," PH.D. thesis, University of British Columbia, 1970.

11 On creating conferences specifically addressing the decline of the rural church, see UCA, Dobson Papers, box A4, file S, Dobson to the Rev. J.M. Singleton, Outlook, Sask., 3 May 1919. Dobson instructed all ministers to read the American rural sociologist John Gillette's *Constructive Rural Sociology* and K.L. Butterfield's *The Country Church and the Rural Problem*, and he personally persuaded ministers on the need for community social reform through his lantern-slide presentation devoted to the depletion of rural life. See UCA, Dobson Papers, box A6, file C, "Rural Problems: Suggested Outline for Lantern Lecture"; box A4, file D, Dobson to Brother Dixon, Neville, Sask., 6 Feb. 1918; Ibid., Dobson to Miss Joslyn, 9 Feb. 1918.

12 AO, Ontario Welfare Council Papers, series 3, box 14, Alex McLaren, "Annual Report of the Community Centres Committee of the Social Service Council of Ontario," 1922–23.

13 NA, Canadian Council of Churches, box 29, "Meeting of the Programme Committee of the First Conference of Charities and Corrections," 20 July 1914, 3; John MacDougall, *Rural Life in Canada* (Toronto: University of Toronto Press, 1973; introduction by Robert Craig Brown; first published 1913). See also Edmund de S. Brunner, "The Country Church," *SW*, 3:9 (June 1921), 231–3. In 1916 the Social Service Council of Saskatchewan instituted a conference "On the Religious Problem in the Rural Community." See SAB, McNaughton Papers, memorandum by J.B. Musselman, 21 Nov. 1916.

14 On the Country Life Movement in the United States, see Clayton S. Ellsworth, "Theodore Roosevelt's Country Life Commission," *Agricultural History Review*, 34 (1960), 155–72; James H. Madison, "Reformers and the Rural Church, 1900–1950," *Journal of American History*, 73:4 (Dec. 1986), 645–68. Methodist ministers read a foremost American supporter of the Country Life Movement, Professor Ross L. Finney's *Solving the Country Church Problem*: UCA, Dobson Papers, box A6, file B. See also "Country Life," *GGG*, 24 July 1918, 5–6. For the connections of Canadian university social scientists with the American Country Life Movement, see University of Toronto, Thomas Fisher Library, James Mavor Papers, box 3B, T.N. Carver, secretary of the American Economic Association to Mavor, 4 Jan. 1910, in which Carver commented on Mavor's remarks made at a meeting of the Association on the Problems of Country Life. Canadian clergymen also followed the activities of rural reformers in Australia. See UCA/UW, Rev. J.A. Cormie Papers, PP8, folder D, Annie Osborn, "Their Problems Resemble Ours: Australia Can't Keep Young Men on Farm – Fails to Secure Right Kind of Population," *Maclean's Magazine*, 15 May 1929.

15 AO, Ontario Welfare Council Papers, box 14, "Minutes of the Social Service Council of Ontario Meetings, 1918," 8 Jan. 1918; Ibid., "Annual Meeting of the Social Service Council of Ontario," 8–10 May 1921.

16 C.W. Vernon, "A Pilgrimage to the Country Life Association Conference at Richmond, Virginia," *SW*, 8:4 (Jan. 1926), 77–9.

17 UCA, James Robertson Memorial Lectures, box 3, file 21, the Rev. John R. Watts, "The Rural Problem in Canada in Relation to Church Life," 1932, 5–6; Judge Ethel McLachlan, "Rural Delinquency – Juvenile Delinquents and for Reasons Distinctly Rural," *GGG*, 14 April 1920, 46–8; "Housing Rural Peoples," *SW*, 1:12 (Sept. 1919), 287.

18 J.S. Woodsworth, "The Community: The Rail Fence as a Factor in Public Life and its Prairie Substitute," *GGG*, 10 May 1916, 46. For

Woodsworth's comments regarding the feminine basis of community life, see "Rural Leadership: Farm Women's Clubs," GGG, 6 Sept. 1916, 23.

19 On Sifton's role in the Commission of Conservation and the place of that organization in the Canadian progressive movement, see Doug Owram, *The Government Generation: Canadian Intellectuals and the State, 1900–1945* (Toronto: University of Toronto Press, 1986), 57–8; D.J. Hall, *Clifford Sifton: The Lonely Eminence 1901–1929* (Toronto: University of Toronto Press, 1985), chapter 11.

20 *Conservation*, 1:7 (Nov. 1912); "Timely Hints for Farmers," *Conservation*, 2:1 (Feb. 1913), 3; F.C.N., "Backyard Environment: Untidiness of Home Surroundings the Cause of Many Children Leaving the Farm," *Conservation*, Jan. 1916, 3.

21 "Farm Home Conveniences," *Conservation*, July 1916, 26.

22 Leona R. Barritt, "The Protection of the Woman in Agriculture," SW, IV:11 (Aug. 1922), 234.

23 AO, Ontario Welfare Council Papers, box 14, *Fifth Annual Meeting and Congress of the Social Service Council of Ontario, 1923*, "Second Annual Conference on Country Life."

24 J.A. Cormie, "Trends in Canadian Rural Life – IX: Revivifying the Country Home," SW, XI:1 (Oct. 1928), 7–10; "A Constructive Programme for Rural Communities, II," SW, IV:8 (May 1922), 181–2.

25 Rev. Father Boyle, "Education and Its Relation to Social Problems," SW, 7:1 (Oct. 1924), 271.

26 "H.W. Wood's Address," GGG, 24 Jan. 1923, 8. J.B. Reynolds, a prominent leader in agricultural education, shared these evolutionary views in the application of science to improve the rural environment. See University of Guelph Archives, RE1, OAC A0101, President J.B. Reynolds Papers, "Addresses and Writings," "The Challenge to the Educated," an address in the OAC Chapel, Sunday, 2 Oct. 1921.

27 Watts, "The Rural Problem in Canada in Relation to Church Life," 11, 65.

28 Salem Bland, "The Deeper Life – The Divinely Ordained Occupation of Farming," GGG, 20 Nov. 1918, 39; J.S. Woodsworth, *Studies in Rural Citizenship* (pamphlet, 1913), preface. In 1916 Woodsworth argued that the independence of the farmer must give way to interdependence, and he was especially critical of the proliferation of denominational churches and fraternal societies, which only divided rural people. See "The Women's Convention," GGG, 23 Feb. 1916, 98. On the reconciliation of town and country interests, see O.D. Skelton, "The Problem of the City," in W.R. McIntosh, ed., *Social Service: A Book for Young Canadians* (Toronto: R. Douglas Fraser, 1911), 35; J.B. Reynolds, "The Mission of the Agricultural College," *Ontario Agricultural College Review*, 33:9 (May 1921), 398.

29 Watts, "The Rural Problem in Canada in Relation to Church Life," 9.
30 Ibid., 73.
31 NA, Canadian Council of Churches, box 32, *The Community Survey: A Basis for Social Action*, 1920, 13.
32 What progressive clergymen actually feared was the spread of religious fundamentalism in the countryside. See UCA/UW, J.A. Cormie Papers, PP8, folder D, "Does the Farmer Go to Church? Survey is Made," *Tribune*, 13 Oct. 1928.
33 AO, Ontario Welfare Council Papers, box 14, Dr Lorne Pierce, "Mobilizing the Community for Results," 1923, 133–4.
34 J.R. Donaldson, "What Agriculture Expects of the Church," *New Outlook*, 2 April 1930.
35 Lorne Pierce, "A Rural Survey," *SW*, IV:5 (Feb. 1922), 106.
36 Pierce, "A Social Survey," 106; F.C.N., "Preaching the Gospel of Good Farming," *Conservation*, 2:1 (Feb. 1913), 4; J.A. Cormie, "Some Trends of Country Life – VI: The Weakness of the Country Church," *SW*, X:10 (July 1928), 232.
37 F.C.N., "An Opportunity for the Rural Minister," *Conservation*, II:2 (March 1913), 3.
38 Watts, "The Rural Problem in Canada in Relation to Church Life," 43.
39 AO, Ontario Welfare Council Papers, box 14, "Report of the Committee on Community Centres," n.d.
40 J.A. Cormie, "The Country Church," *SW*, VI:5 (Feb. 1924), 98.
41 Woodsworth, *Studies in Rural Citizenship*, "Study 9 – The Socialization of Rural Communities," 51–4.
42 UCA, Dobson Papers, box A5, file C2, Moore to Dear Brother, 1 May 1918. See also R.A. Robinson, "The Rural Church as a Community Institute," *SW*, 2:8 (May 1920), 213–16.
43 Woodsworth, *Studies in Rural Citizenship*, "Study 3 – Proposed Solutions: A – The Better Farming Movement," 20–8.
44 A.D. "Training Rural Leaders," *Conservation*, Jan. 1919, 5; "The Country Preacher's Training," *Conservation*, 2:7 (Aug. 1913), 1; J.A. Cormie, "Some Trends in Rural Life – X: Revitalizing the Country Church," *SW*, XI:2 (Nov. 1928), 31–3; J.S. Woodsworth, "The Community: The University and 'the foreigner,'" *GGG*, 1 March 1916, 34, in which he recommended that all ministers take courses in agriculture.
45 This was the view expressed by Hugh Dobson, who in 1919 noted to an American correspondent the real possibility of the fall of the Union Government and the emergence of the farmers as the most powerful national political force. See UCA, Dobson Papers, box A5, file T, Dobson to Mr A.M. Todd, president, Public Ownership League of America, 19 Dec. 1919. In a much neglected article, Richard Allen has noted the convergence between the ideas and personnel of Protestant social Christianity

and the agrarian revolt in Western Canada. See Allen, "The Social Gospel as the Religion of the Agrarian Revolt," in Berger and Cook, *The West and the Nation*, 174–86.

46 UCA, United Church of Canada Commission on Courses of Study, Records, 1926–28, file 3, A.D. Miller to William Creighton Graham, 1 Feb. 1927.

47 "Rural Leadership Conference," *GGG*, 23 Aug. 1916; "Rural Citizenship," *GGG*, 25 Dec. 1918, 47. See also "Manitoba Farmers' Platform," *GGG*, 15 Jan. 1919, 11, for a report of a speech by J.B. Reynolds, who was then principal of Manitoba Agricultural College, on the subject of reconstruction.

48 See J.H.T. Falk, "Land Settlement and After-War Employment Problems," appendix E in Thomas Adams, *Rural Planning and Development: A Study of Rural Conditions and Problems in Canada* (Ottawa: Commission of Conservation, 1917), 268; Robert S. Rayson, "Health Conditions in Ontario's 'Back Counties,'" *SW*, I:5 (1 Feb. 1919), 99–100; R.T. Ely, "Settlement of Sub-Marginal Lands," *Conservation*, April 1919, 17.

49 NA, Canadian Council of Churches, box 29, "A Meeting of the Executive of the Canadian Conference of Charities and Corrections," 2 Feb. 1917.

50 Thomas Adams, *Rural Planning and Development*, 1, 11, 61, 112. For a similar attack on unplanned settlement which focused upon the lumbering frontier, see C.L. "Non-Agricultural Lands Should be Reserved," *Conservation*, March 1914, 10; O.M., "Conservation and Rural Depopulation," *Conservation*, August 1914, 35.

51 UCA, Dobson Papers, 1918–19, *passim*; J.W. Macmillan, "The Country Town: Its Relation to the City and the Surrounding Country District," *GGG*, 17 April 1918, 8, 62. Macmillan wrote a synthesis of Adams's book *Rural Planning* for Western farmers. See Macmillan, "Rural Planning and Development," *GGG*, 16 Oct. 1918, 36–7; Macmillan, "The Country Town: Its Relation to the City and to the Surrounding Country District," *GGG*, 17 April 1918, 8, 62; AO, Ontario Welfare Council Papers, box 14, S.B. McCready, "Community Associations for Towns and Villages," 1923, 134–8. Protestant clergymen were opponents of the back-to-the-land movement because it replicated the problem of unregulated agricultural development. See D.M. Solandt, "Rural Librairies and Social Centres," *GGG*, 9 Feb. 1916, 26–7; UCA, Board of Home Missions, box 18, file 178, R.B. Cochrane, "Report on Conditions of 'Back-to-land' Settlers in Northern Ontario," n.d.

52 "Preventing Waste of Human Efficiency," *Conservation*, Nov. 1918, 41; "Duty of Government is to Classify Land," *Conservation*, Nov. 1917, 41.

53 F.C.N., "Social Conditions on the Farm: Rural Church Can Largely Assist in Keeping Young People on the Farm," *Conservation*, Feb. 1916, 7.

54 There has been a persistent view among historians that the social reform experiments of the Union Government were a "road not taken" in

Canadian history. See, for example, Struthers, *No Fault of Their Own*, chapter 1; Traves, *The State and Enterprise*; Owram, *The Government Generation*, chapter 4. It is clear, however, that the leadership of this government subscribed to a clearly voluntarist philosophy based upon a limited idea of state intervention in partnership with such organizations as the Protestant churches. Sir Robert Borden was a prominent member of the Social Service Council of Nova Scotia, and his colleague Newton Wesley Rowell was prominent in Methodist social reform organizations. See Robert Craig Brown, *Sir Robert Borden* (Toronto: Macmillan, 1976); Margaret Prang, *Newton Wesley Rowell: Ontario Nationalist* (Toronto: University of Toronto Press, 1975). John English, in *The Decline of Politics: The Conservatives and the Party System, 1901–1920* (Toronto: University of Toronto Press, 1977), has argued that Borden and the Liberal Unionists adhered to a view of government in which the state would be a partner enlisting the energies of voluntary agencies, such as churches and middle-class social reform organizations, premised upon an idea of "service" derived from the tenets of social Christianity.

55 Owram, *The Government Generation*, 108–14.

56 For the survey tradition in the United States, see Martin Bulmer, "The Decline of the Social Survey Movement and the Rise of American Empirical Sociology," and Stephen P. Turner, "The World of the Academic Quantifiers: The Columbia University Family and its Connections," both in Bulmer, Bales, and Sklar, eds., *The Social Survey in Historical Perspective*. See also Jean M. Converse, *Survey Research in the United States: Roots and Emergence, 1890–1960* (Berkeley: University of California Press, 1987), 22–9. On Warren Wilson's career as a social investigator into the problem of the country church, see Madison, "Reformers and the Rural Church, 1900–1950."

57 UCA, Albert Carman Papers, box 20, file 157, "Social Service Bureau and Exhibits," n.d.

58 On the influence of the Pittsburgh Survey, see Walter A. Riddell, "The Value of the Social Survey," 56–7; *Vancouver, British Columbia: The Report by the Board of Temperance and Moral Reform of the Methodist Church and the Board of Social Service and Evangelism of the Presbyterian Church, 1914* (n.p., n.d.), introduction; Gordon Dickie, "A New Canadian Sociologist Author," *SW*, III:5 (1 Feb. 1921), in which he called for investigations like those conducted by the Rockefeller and Russell Sage foundations, 134. See also Steven R. Cohen, "The Pittsburgh Survey and the Social Survey Movement: A Sociological Road not Taken," in Bulmer, Bales, and Sklar, eds., *The Social Survey in Historical Perspective*, 248; Jeffrey M. Taylor, "Dominant and Popular Ideologies in the Making of Rural Manitobans, 1890–1925," PH.D. thesis, University of Manitoba, 1988, 139–41.

59 Greek, *The Religious Origins of American Sociology* (New York and London: Garland Publishing, 1992), 74.

60 University of British Columbia Archives, N.A.M. Mackenzie Papers, S.D. Clark and B.S. Keirstead, "The Social Sciences in Canada." Written as a background paper for the Massey Commission, this study asserted that, as late as 1947, sociology and psychology were woefully weak in Canadian university departments and only Toronto and McGill possessed either the numbers of faculty or the resources to carry on social research. Clark and Keirstead also reported that only traditional forms of political economy were well developed in Canadian universities. Even if one allows for some exaggeration because of the authors' quest for government assistance for the social sciences, the existence of this document compels historians to rethink the development of modern university social science in Canada and to place it in the context of the late 1950s and the 1960s.

61 UCA, Dobson Papers, box A3, file K, "Social Surveys and Exhibits," n.d. On Dobson's role in ensuring the entrenchment of the survey idea in the Methodist Church, see UCA, Dobson Papers, box A11, file G, Moore to Dobson, 19 June 1913; Ibid., box A4, file A, Dobson to the Hon. J.A. Calder, minister of immigration and colonization, 29 Oct. 1917; Ibid., box A4, file E, Dobson to Brother Egan, 19 Feb. 1919; Ibid., box A5, file E, Dobson to the Rev. Samuel East, 28 June 1920; UCA, Methodist Church, DESS, box 7, file 146, "Rev. Dr. Moore's Visit," *Western Methodist Recorder*, n.d.

62 NA, Canadian Council of Churches, box 32, *The Community Survey: A Basis for Social Action*, 1920, 1–2. See also "Do You Know Your Own Community," *SW*, II:9 (1 June 1920), 252.

63 UCA, Methodist Church, DESS, box 2, file 36, Moore to D.H. Williamson, Community Council of Hamilton, 13 Jan. 1914, on the distribution of these questionnaires; SAB, Violet McNaughton Papers, J.S. Woodsworth to Violet McNaughton, 10 May 1916; NA, Canadian Council of Churches, "Social Service Council of Canada, Minutes of Annual Meeting, 1918," 7; UCA, Dobson Papers, box A7, file A, Dobson to Dr J.T.M. Anderson, director of education among New Canadians, 24 Oct. 1921, regarding a church survey of immigration in Toronto, the best "laboratory" for the melting-pot problem; "Housing Immigrant Workers," *Conservation*, Feb. 1914, 6; Anna E. Wells, acting superintendent, Manitoba Public Health Nurses, "Attacking Maternal and Infant Mortality in Rural Areas," *SW*, V:2 (1 Nov. 1922), 35; E.R. Fitch, "The Church in a Rural Community," MA thesis, McMaster University, n.d. On the farm survey, see Kinnear, "'Do You Want Your Daughter to Marry a Farmer?'" *Canadian Papers in Rural History*, 138–9.

64 UMA, Gordon Papers, box 19, folder 1, "Social Service and Evangelism, Questionnaires for Kirk Sessions 1909." By 1912 these surveys had been transformed into broader social surveys. See Ibid., box 17, folder 2, J.

Howard Falk to Gordon, 3 July 1912; Ibid., box 17, folder 5, Shearer to Gordon, 23 April 1913.

65 *Vancouver, British Columbia: The Report by Board of Temperance and Moral Reform of the Methodist Church and the Board of Social Service and Evangelism of the Presbyterian Church* (n.p., n.d.), preface.

66 UCA, Dobson Papers, box A4, file C, Dobson to the Rev. Fred Chapman, 2 Sept. 1919; Ibid., "The Methodist Church of Canada – Social Survey Outline," n.d.

67 UCA, Dobson Papers, box A2, file A, "Methodist Church of Canada – Social Survey Outline," n.d.; Ibid., box A4, file E, Dobson to Brother Egan, 19 Feb. 1919.

68 *The Pictou Survey, July–August 1915 – Report on a Limited Survey of Both Rural and Urban Conditions*, 1915, 37–47.

69 *The London Survey, Oct.-Dec. 1913*, 1913, 45.

70 *Report of a Preliminary and General Social Survey of Regina, Sept. 1913* (n.p., n.d.), 4, 42–3.

71 *Rural Survey, Turtle Mountain District, Manitoba June–July 1914*, 25.

72 *Report of a Preliminary and General Social Survey of Regina*, 35.

73 *Report of a Preliminary and General Social Survey of Regina*, 26–8.

74 *Rural Survey, Turtle Mountain District, Manitoba, 1914*, 12, 24.

75 Ibid., 72–3.

76 *The London Survey*, 47.

77 *Report of a Preliminary and General Social Survey of Port Arthur, March 1913*, 6. See similar conclusions in *County of Huron, Ontario, Report on a Rural Survey of the Agricultural, Educational, Social and Religious Life, Dec.–Jan. 1913–14*, 19. For Stewart's later career as the "father" of the modern system of unemployment insurance, see Struthers, *No Fault of Their Own*.

78 *Report of a Preliminary and General Social Survey of Regina, Sept. 1913*, 4–28.

79 John MacDougall, *Rural Life in Canada*, 148, 164, 170.

80 NA, Canadian Council of Churches, box 29, "Meeting of the Executive Committee of the Canadian Conference of Charities and Corrections," 4 Feb. 1914.

81 *Sydney, Nova Scotia, the Report*, n.d., 29; Walter A. Riddell, "The Value of the Social Survey," *Social Service Congress, Ottawa 1914, Report of Addresses and Proceedings* (Toronto: Social Service Council of Canada, 1914), 59; UCA, Methodist Church, DESS, box 1, file 2, "Annual Meeting of General Board," 22 Oct. 1913; *Report of the Social Survey Commission, Toronto* (Toronto: The Carswell Company, 1915). Although not originally commissioned by the churches, the report was drafted by Presbyterian minister and University of Toronto professor T. Rutherford Robinson, in

association with the Rev. Andrew S. Grant, general superintendent of Home Missions for the Presbyterian Church.

82 UCA, Methodist Church, DESS, box 7, file 146, "The Truth About Ontario," *London Free Press*, 12 June 1922.

83 UCA, Dobson Papers, box A4, file C, Dobson to Mr T. McDordon, secretary of Regina Board of Trade, 31 July 1918; Ibid., Dobson to Mr C.A. Cooke, secretary, Board of Trade, Weyburn, Sask., 31 July 1918; Ibid., box A5, file W2, Dobson to Charlotte Whitton, 15 May 1920; Ibid., box A5, file Pb, W.M. Martin, premier of Saskatchewan, to Dobson, 16 April 1920, Dobson to Martin, 12 April 1920, Dobson to Martin, 5 Feb. 1918; Ibid., box A5, file W2, R. Bows, medical health officer, Saskatchewan, to Dobson, 16 June 1921, Whitton to Dobson, 27 May 1921; Ibid., box A5, file M, R.W. Murchie, Manitoba Agricultural College, to Dobson, 16 Sept. 1920, Dobson to Murchie, 21 Sept. 1920; Ibid., box A4, file A, Dobson to Dr Archer, 18 Dec. 1917.

84 UCA, Dobson Papers, box A5, file C2, Dobson to Shearer, 31 Aug. 1920; Lorne Pierce, "A Rural Survey," *SW*, Feb. 1922, 105–6; David B. Harkness, educational secretary, Social Service Council of Ontario, *SW*, X:1 (Oct. 1927), 14–15.

85 On the supersession of the earlier social surveys by the Social Service Council, see UCA, Methodist Church, DESS, box 6, file 13, "Memorandum from Presbyterian Board of Evangelism and Social Service for use at Executive Meeting," 21 Sept. 1916, at which church surveys were discontinued but would be resumed under the direction of the Social Service Council. See also NA, Canadian Council of Churches, box 32, "Minutes of Child Welfare Committee," 5 March 1924, 20 March 1924; Ibid., box 29, the Rev. Peter Bryce to Harkness, 23 Nov. 1927.

86 SAB, McNaughton Papers, Woodsworth to McNaughton, 8 July 1916.

87 NA, Woodsworth Papers, vol. 11, file 37, "Social Conditions in Rural Communities," 3; Ibid., vol. 15, file 7, "Bureau of Social Research, Governments of Manitoba, Saskatchewan, and Alberta: Report of First Year's Work," 6 Dec. 1916, 1.

88 In addition, Professor A.S. Morton of the University of Saskatchewan, himself a Presbyterian clergyman, presented a sketch of Ukrainian history, and Mr Ivan Petruschevitch contributed an outline of contemporary Ukrainian life.

89 NA, Woodsworth Papers, vol. 18, "Ukrainian Rural Communities, Report by Bureau of Social Research, 1917," 13, 15; NA, Woodsworth Papers, vol. 15, file 7, "Bureau of Social Research," 3–7.

90 NA, Woodsworth Papers, vol. 18, "Ukrainian Rural Communities," 157; Woodsworth Papers, vol. 11, file 37, "Social Conditions in Rural Communities," 20.

91 UCA, Dobson Papers, box A4, file D, Dobson to Brother Howard, 3 Feb. 1919.

92 A number of surveys were taken of immigrant life by the churches, many of which were conducted at the parish level by the resident clergyman. One of the most extensive was initiated by J.G. Shearer of the Social Council of Canada and was interpreted by Hugh Dobson. See UCA, Dobson Papers, box A4, file Sb, Shearer to Dobson, 5 June 1917, Dobson to Shearer, 23 Nov. 1917, R.E. Spence to Dobson, 6 July 1917, J.K. Smith to Dobson, 25 Dec. 1917, G.R. Lang, Vegreville, Alta, to Dobson, 10 July 1917. See also Ibid., the Rev. Richard C.T. Othen to Dobson, 12 Jan. 1918, the Rev. N. McPhedran to Dobson, 29 June 1917; UCA/UW, Cormie Papers, "Outline of a Possible Survey of Work among New Canadians Limited to Three Provinces, Manitoba, Saskatchewan, and Alberta," n.d.; UCA, George Dorey Papers, box 1, file 6, "Outline of a Possible Survey of Work among the New Canadians, Limited to Three Provinces, Manitoba, Saskatchewan and Alberta," n.d.

93 As a devotee of the views of Thomas Adams of the Commission of Conservation, Dobson more than any other progressive clergyman illustrated the convergence in attitude between the Protestant churches and the federal government on the immigration issue. See UCA, Dobson Papers, box A4, file D, Dobson to Brother Doyle, 19 Dec. 1917.

94 For this critique of the social control thesis, see Roger Davidson, "The state and social investigation in Britain, 1880–1914," in Lacey and Furner, eds., *The State and Social Investigation in Britain and the United States* (Cambridge: Cambridge University Press, 1993), 243.

95 Mariana Valverde, *The Age of Light, Soap, and Water: Moral Reform in English Canada, 1885–1914* (Toronto: McClelland and Stewart, 1991), 15, 112, 123–8. Recent scholarship on the subject of early twentieth-century Canadian attitudes to immigrants proceeds from the premise that fear and "racism" were the underlying assumptions, and that the Protestant churches played a prominent role in the promotion of these opinions. Donald Avery's *Dangerous Foreigners* (Toronto: McClelland and Stewart, 1976), associates the entire spectrum of Protestant opinion with the cause of immigration restriction, and especially with the ideas of the Anglican bishop of Saskatchewan George Exton Lloyd, an extremist by any standard. See also Howard Palmer, *Patterns of Prejudice: Nativism in Alberta* (Toronto: McClelland and Stewart, 1982); Martin Robin, *Shades of Right: Nativist and Fascist Politics in Canada, 1920–1940* (Toronto: University of Toronto Press, 1992), 45–86.

96 UCA, James Robertson Memorial Lectures, box 2, file 6, D.N. McLachlan, "Factors in Canada to be Molded into a Christian Unity," n.d., 4–7; Woodsworth, *Strangers Within Our Gates*.

97 UCA, George Dorey Papers, box 2, file 12, A.J. Hunter, "Reflection on the Ukrainian Situation," n.d.

98 UCA, Dobson Papers, box A4, file D, Patience Day, National Council of Women, to Dobson, 21 Dec. 1919; J. Russell Harris, "'Canadians All,'" *SW*, I:12 (1 Sept. 1919), 286.

99 UCA, Chown Papers, box 12, file 320, "Star Radio Concert," 22 May 1922, "The Immigration Policy of Canada"; UCA, Dobson Papers, box A2, file A, S.D. Chown, "The New Canadian in the West," St. Catharines *Standard*, 6 April 1922; "Shudders to Think of Future of West Unless Standard of Living is Greatly Altered," *Ibid.*, 6 April 1922.

100 UCA, Dobson Papers, box A2, file A, Dobson, "The Immigration Policy of Canada," memorandum, n.d., 3–13. Similar views were advanced by the Methodist Church's General Board of Missions. See Ibid., box A2, file A, "General Board of Missions of the Methodist Church, Oct. 1917, Report of the Committee on Work among European Foreigners in Canada."

101 Adelaide M. Plumptre, "The Social Consequences of Immigration," *SW*, VI:10 (July 1924), 190–3; "Immigration of British Women to Canada," *SW*, I:1 (Oct. 1918), 18–19; "The Outlook for Immigration," *SW*, I:3 (1 Dec. 1918), 52.

102 UCA, Dobson Papers, box A2, file A1, Dobson, "The Task of Canadianization with Special Reports on Ruthenian and Doukhobor Settlements," 1917, 1918; Ibid., box A2, file A, "Communities in Saskatchewan," 1915.

103 NA, Canadian Council of Churches, box 29, "Annual Meeting of the Social Service Council, 1925," 28 Jan. 1926; Ibid., box 32, "Committee on Immigration and Colonization," 9 March 1923, 20 April 1923; Ibid., box 32, "Minutes of Committee on Industrial Life and Immigration," 12 March 1919, 17 Sept. 1919, 17 Oct. 1919; UCA, Dobson Papers, box A6, file C, Dobson, "The Community Centre and the School as an Instrument of Canadianization," n.d. Criticisms of Whitton's study focused not on its recommendations for restriction of agricultural labour, but on its arguments on the need for higher wages to prevent immigrant labour from drifting into urban centres. See UCA, Dobson Papers, box A7, file Wh, M.N. Staples to Miss Elizabeth P. MacCallum, 13 April 1925.

104 UCA, Dobson Papers, box A2, file A, *The Problem of the Melting Pot*, 1917, n.p.; Ibid., box A5, file L, the Rev. Frank Langford to Dobson, 2 April 1921; Ibid., box A5, file B1, Dobson to Allen T. Burns, 17 Sept. 1919; Dobson, "Canadianization and Our Immigrants," *SW*, II:4 (1 Jan. 1920), 95–7.

105 H.D. Ranns, "Religion and Life – An Ideal for Canada," *GGG*, 14 April 1920, 48.

106 H.G. Forster, "Non-Anglo-Saxons in Canada," *SW*, XIV:4 (Jan. 1932), 69.

107 R.H. MacDonald, "Rural Education," *GGG*, 29 Sept. 1920, 48–9.

108 Mary Irish Jennison, "Canadianization – An Experiment in Friendship," *SW*, XIII:4 (Jan. 1930), 87–9; Corday MacKay, "Democracy and Ethnic Fusion," MA thesis, McMaster University, 1921, 31.

109 H.E. Wright, "Immigration and the Cultural Development of Canada," MA thesis, McMaster University, Jan. 1931, 11, 47. On the origins of the pioneer fringe concept, see Nancy J. Christie, "'Pioneering for a Civilized World': Griffith Taylor and the Ecology of Geography," in Richard Jarrell and Roy MacLeod, eds., *Dominions Apart: Comparative Studies in the History of Science in Canada and Australia* (Toronto: Scientia Press, 1994). Such attempts to create harmony among old and new Canadians also underwrote the efforts in the 1930s of the prominent Baptist educator Watson Kirkconnell to collect and translate literary classics from European languages into English. For Kirkconnell, see J.R.C. Perkin, "'There Were Giants in the Earth in Those Days': An Assessment of Watson Kirkconnell," in Rawlyk, ed., *Canadian Baptists and Christian Higher Education*, 89–110.

110 Charlotte E. Whitton, *Some Aspects of the Immigration Problem* (pamphlet, Social Service Council of Canada, 1922), 2. It should be pointed out that Whitton also advocated strict medical inspection and regulation to accompany the open-door policy. See Ibid., 19–21.

111 NA, Canadian Council of Churches, box 29, J.A. Cormie, "Canadianization of the Foreign Born," n.d., 2.

112 J.A. Cormie, "A Plea for the Open Country," *SW*, Dec. 1923, 46.

113 Cormie, "The Church and the European Immigrant," *SW*, XII:1 (Oct. 1929), 10; UCA/UW, Cormie Papers, PP8, folder B, "Notebook, Rural Life and the Church," n.d.; Ibid., Cormie Papers, folder G, "The Changing Countryside," radio address, n.d.

114 Cormie, "Some Trends of Country Life – VI. The Weakness of the Country Church," *SW*, July 1928, 232; NA, Canadian Council of Churches, box 29, Cormie, "Some Problems of Rural Life in Canada," 10; A.J. Hunter and Eugene Forsey, "The Immigration Question," *SW*, XVII:1 (March 1937), 7.

115 Cormie, "Some Trends in Rural Life – IV. The Strain on the Country Home," *SW*, May 1928, 187. See also Cormie, "The Country Church," 96–7. The central issue remained that the vast majority of male farm labourers were immigrants. See UCA, United Church of Canada, Board of Home Missions, box 14, file 94, "Statement from Commission on Rural Work," 4 Nov. 1930.

116 J.S. Woodsworth, "The Community – Prairie Breezes," *GGG*, 9 Feb. 1916, 35. The concept of the "marginal man" has been attributed to Robert Park's sociology of the late 1920s, however, it appeared frequently in the work of both Woodsworth and Cormie much earlier.

117 J.S. Woodsworth, "The Community: Standards of Living for the Hired Man," *GGG*, 14 March 1917, 17.

118 UCA/UW, All People's Mission Papers, box A, Mrs R.K. Baker, Portage La Prairie, Man., to Woodsworth, 11 Jan. 1909; Emma Noble, Boissevain, Man., to Woodsworth, 16 Aug. 1909.

119 J.S. Woodsworth, "Study 6 – The Rural Home – Yesterday and Tomorrow," in *Studies in Rural Citizenship*, 37. J.B. Reynolds, later president of the Ontario Agricultural College, saw the hired man, with his "coarse and obscene language," as the major contributor to the moral degradation of rural youth, especially young women. See J.B. Reynolds, "Standards of Country Life," *Ontario Agricultural College Review*, 21:9 (June 1909), 521–4.

120 Woodsworth, *Studies in Rural Citizenship*, "Study I – Changed Conditions Demand a new Programme," 9, 11. Woodsworth feared that government policy was allowing immigrants to remain "insoluble lumps in our Canadian Commonwealth," UCA/UW, All People's Mission Papers, box A, Woodsworth, "Work among Foreigners in Canada," n.d.

121 UCA/UW, All People's Mission Papers, box B, Woodsworth to Miss Mason, n.d.

122 For the continued prominence of the church-led social survey, see UCA, Dobson Papers, box 19, "Tentative Draft of Program for Conference on the Church and Rural Welfare," 10 Dec. 1934, where the president of the University of British Columbia, Dr L.S. Klink, spoke on "The Church in Rural Life," the Rev. William Deans on rural health, the Rev. Hugh Rae on crime prevention, and the Rev. J.A. Leslie on rural leisure, and Dobson led a round table discussion on achieving a balanced rural and urban economy. See also UCA, United Church, Board of Home Missions, box 14, file 94, "Minutes of Rural Commission," 10 April 1931, which called for surveys of Cumberland County, N.S., Abernathy, Sask., and an unspecified county in Ontario; Ibid., box 15, file 108, "Surveys: Their Use and Method," n.d.; AO, Ontario Welfare Council Papers, F837, series 3, box 14, "Minutes of the Annual Meeting of the Community Welfare Council," 28 April 1930, regarding five surveys of Ontario cities. Only by the late 1930s did the focus of these social surveys shift to urban concerns. See, for example, UCA/UW, Cormie Papers, folder G, "The General Council's Commission on Urban Problems: Questionnaire 1938."

123 NA, Canadian Council of Churches, box 29, "Report of Executive for the Year 1929, presented 1 May 1930," 11.

124 For Murchie's career, see UCA, Biographical Files, "R.W. Murchie, 1883–1937"; "News, Notes and Announcements," *Rural Sociology*, 2:1 (March 1937), 246; R.W. Murchie, with William Allen and J.F. Booth, *Agricultural Progress on the Prairie Frontier* (Toronto: Macmillan, 1936), 1–5;

UMA, Faculty of Agriculture, Rural Sociology Department, 1927–28, UA 21, Box 2, file 40, R.W. Murchie to Dean McKillican, 21 Sept. 1927, R.W. Murchie, "Special Report on Research," 21 Sept. 1927, H.C. Grant, "Department of Economics and Sociology Appropriation"; PAM, Valentine Winkler Papers, MG 14 B45, box 1, Winkler to Murchie, 24 Sept. 1915, in which it is noted that when he was an active clergyman Murchie taught at the Ruthenian Training School in Brandon; Taylor, "Dominant and Popular Ideologies in the Making of Rural Manitobans," 141. Other publications by Murchie are *Unused Lands of Manitoba* (Winnipeg: Department of Agriculture and Colonization, 1926), 54; *Land Settlement as a Relief Measure* (Minneapolis: University of Minnesota Press, 1933); and, with C.R. Wasson, *Beltrami Island, Minnesota: Resettlement Project* (Minneapolis: University of Minnesota Press, 1938).

125 R.W. Murchie, "The Home of the Husbandman: In Professionalizing and Making Agriculture Permanent Good Homes are Needed," *GGG*, 9 July 1919, 10, 29.

126 See Marlene Shore, *The Science of Social Redemption: McGill, The Chicago School, and the Origins of Social Research in Canada* (Toronto: University of Toronto Press, 1987), chapter 5, in which she attributes the Frontiers of Settlement Series to the influence of Robert Park's social ecology on C.A. Dawson and W.A. Mackintosh. What appears more likely is that Dawson derived his ideas concerning zones of contact of rural communities from the American rural sociologist Charles Galpin, whose work was widely known among Canadian progressive clergymen. See UCA, Dobson Papers, box A6, file C, "Rural Social Work," n.d. Barry Ferguson, *Remaking Liberalism: The Intellectual Legacy of Adam Shortt, O.D. Skelton, W.C. Clark and W.A. Mackintosh* (Montreal and Kingston: McGill-Queen's University Press, 1993), chapter 8, 186–209, argues that the Frontiers of Settlement Series can be traced to the interest of Queen's political economists in the rural problem after 1918, and he is apparently unaware to the connections between Mackintosh's ideas of cooperation and the long-standing interest of the churches in rural economic cooperation.

127 Dawson and Murchie, *The Settlement of the Peace River Country*, Canadian Frontiers of Settlement, vol. VI (Toronto: Macmillan Co., 1934), 1, 184–5, 248–9; foreword by W.A. Mackintosh, ix. For reviews of this work, see the hostile comment by J.A. Cormie, "Immigration, No Remedy!" *SW*, XVII:3 (Sept. 1936), 97–100, and the more favourable assessment by George Dorey, "Problems of Western Settlement," *SW*, XVII: 4–5 (Dec. 1937-March 1938), 83–7.

128 UCA/UW, Cormie Papers, folder D, J.R. Mutchmor to Cormie, 20 July 1942.

CHAPTER SIX

1 NA, Canadian Council of Churches, box 29, Dean Tucker, "Report of Executive of the Social Service Council of Canada for 1929," 1 May 1930.

2 Doug Owram, *The Government Generation: Canadian Intellectuals and the State, 1900–1945* (Toronto: University of Toronto Press, 1986), chapters 7–11.

3 Quoted in Michael J. Lacey and Mary O. Furner, "Social Investigation, Social Knowledge and the State: An Introduction," in Lacey and Furner, eds., *The State and Social Investigation in Britain and the United States* (Cambridge: Cambridge University Press, 1993), 10.

4 The dominant current of historical writing since the 1960s has been to underscore the role of academic social scientists in formulating social welfare policy. This perspective is fundamentally flawed because it has ignored the important role the churches in the field of social investigation. On the link between universities and the modern state, see Michiel Horn, *The League for Social Reconstruction: The Intellectual Origins of the Democratic Left in Canada, 1930–1942* (Toronto: University of Toronto Press, 1980); Barry Ferguson, *Remaking Liberalism: The Intellectual Legacy of Adam Shortt, O.D. Skelton, W.C. Clark, and W.A. Mackintosh, 1890–1925* (Montreal and Kingston: McGill-Queen's University Press, 1993); Jack Granatstein, *The Ottawa Men* (Toronto: University of Toronto Press, 1982); Marlene Shore, *The Science of Social Redemption: McGill, the Chicago School, and the Origins of Social Research in Canada* (Toronto: University of Toronto Press, 1987); Doug Owram, *The Government Generation.*

5 Lacey and Furner, "Social Investigation, Social Knowledge and the State," 40. On the importance of Hoover's Commission in Canada, see UCA, Dobson Papers, box 19, Dobson to the Rev. Clarence Halliday, 11 May 1935; Mossie May Kirkwood, *Duty and Happiness in a Changed World* (Toronto: Macmillan Co., 1933), 196. Kirkwood wrote for the Social Service Council's Machine Age Series, published in the mid-1930s.

6 UCA, Methodist Church, DESS, box 7, file 129, Ernest Thomas, "Muddling Through? Policy of Britain," 15 Feb. 1921; UM, Gordon Papers, box 30, folder 9, "What Does Jesus Mean to Me?" n.d., 4–5.

7 O.D. Skelton, "The Problem of the City," in W.R. McIntosh, ed., *Social Service* (Toronto: R. Douglas Fraser, 1913), 42.

8 UCA, Methodist Church, DESS, box 7, file 129, "Muddling Through?"

9 UMA, Gordon Papers, box 16, folder 16, "The Social Service Council – Its Function in Canada," n.d.; Ibid., box 18, folder 2, "A Moral and Social Reform Council of Manitoba," circular, n.d.

10 UCA, Dobson Papers, box A5, file C2, "Annual Report of the Field Secretary," 1 Aug. 1920.

11 UMA, Gordon Papers, box 28, folder 7, "One Life, One Directing Mind, One Vitalizing Power," n.d.; Ibid., box 30, folder 4, "Church and Civilization," n.d. Archibald B. Clark, professor of political economy at the University of Manitoba, disagreed with Gordon's notion of the inherent rights of such groups as labour, which Clark believed evinced too much the ideas of French socialists like Charles Fourier, a Utopian socialist thinker and opponent of Marxism. See Ibid., box 50, folder 2, Clark to Gordon, 29 Nov. 1931.

12 UMA, Gordon Papers, box 30, file 4, "The New Spirit in Industry," n.d.

13 Skelton, "The Problem of the City," 42. On the importance of Skelton's Christianity in defining his ideas of liberal reform, see Brian Fraser, *The Social Uplifters: Presbyterian Progressives and the Social Gospel in Canada* (Waterloo: Wilfrid Laurier University Press, 1988), 82–3. The crucial role played by social Christianity in redefining liberalism in Canada has been consciously ignored by Barry Ferguson who, in *Remaking Liberalism*, sees the thought of Skelton as motivated by a current of ideas explicitly divorced from Christian social reformism.

14 C.W. Gordon, "The New State and the New Church," *Social Service Congress, 1914*, 192–3.

15 UCA, Methodist Church, DESS, box 6, file 114, "Distinguished Preachers at the Churches," *Daily News*, St John's, Nfld, 8 Oct. 1917.

16 UCA, Chown Papers, box 11, file 300, "Socialism and the Social Teachings of Jesus," 14 Feb. 1914; Ibid., box 13, file 365, "The Church Member's Responsibility for Social Conditions," n.d.; box 11, file 289, "Address to London Conference Assessing Work of the Department of Temperance and Moral Reform and the Political Situation in Ontario," 2 June 1904; Ibid., box 9, file 218, "Righteousness Exalteth a Nation," sermon, n.d.; Ibid., box 10, file 258, "The Gospel Sieve," n.d.; Ibid., box 11, file 293, "The Social Teaching of Jesus," 19 Sept. 1910; Ibid., box 6, file 165, "The Enthronement of Christ in the Industrial Life of the Nation," n.d.

17 Ibid., box 13, file 365, "The Church Member's Responsibility for Social Conditions," n.d. Chown was an admirer of John Spargo, the American socialist who penned *The Bitter Cry of the Children*. Chown believed that the Gospels of Jesus formed "the foundation stones of a permanent social state" and that the function of the state was to create legislation in accordance with Christian ideals.

18 Like social Christianity, new liberalism was based upon the conjunction between the social responsibility of individuals and a collective good. Moreover, as Stefan Collini has argued, the new liberal acceptance of collectivism owed much to an ethical vision of the social order and did not imply political socialism. See Stefan Collini, *Liberalism and Sociology: L.T. Hobhouse and Political Argument in England, 1880–1914* (Cambridge: Cambridge University Press, 1979), 43–4; Morris Ginzburg and

John Hobson, *L.T. Hobhouse: His Life and Work* (London: Allen & Unwin, 1931), 127, 144, 194; Michael Freeden, "The New Liberalism and Its Aftermath," in Richard Bellamy, ed., *Victorian Liberalism: Nineteenth-Century Political Thought and Practice* (London and New York: Routledge, 1990), 178; Martin J. Wiener, *Between Two Worlds: The Political Thought of Graham Wallas* (Cambridge: Cambridge University Press, 1976), 17; Peter Clarke, *Liberals and Social Democrats* (Cambridge: Cambridge University Press, 1978), 160–1; James T. Kloppenberg, *Uncertain Victory: Social Democracy and Progressivism in European and American Thought, 1870–1920* (New York and Oxford: Oxford University Press, 1986), 330, 357, 400.

19 Quoted in Phyllis Airhart, *Serving the Present Age: Revivalism, Progressivism, and the Methodist Tradition in Canada* (Montreal and Kingston: McGill-Queen's University Press, 1992), 92. Thomas was an adamant opponent of state socialism. See UCA, Biographical Files, "Ernest Thomas," "Says Democracy Helps Morality," *Toronto Mail*, 5 April 1920. Likewise, T. Albert Moore situated his brand of social reform in the tradition of Bright, Macaulay, and Gladstone. See UCA, Methodist Church, DESS, box 7, file 137, Moore, "Sermon on Behalf of the Lord's Day Alliance"; Ibid., box 7, file 140, Moore, "The Uplift of Citizenship," Feb. 1916.

20 UCA, Chown Papers, box 1, file 1, "Circular: Associated Charities of Toronto," 1907.

21 UCA, Dobson Papers, box A4, file D, Dobson to the Rev. J.A. Doyle, 19 Dec. 1917. For the longevity of the wartime climate of national efficiency, see UCA, Dobson Papers, box A8, file So, C.A. Dawson, "Waste and Welfare," 17th annual convention of the Social Service Council of Canada, Saint John, N.B., 28–31 Jan. 1924. For the "ideology of service" which underlay the formation of the Unionist coalition, see John English, *The Decline of Politics: The Conservatives and the Party System, 1901–20* (Toronto: University of Toronto Press, 1977).

22 UCA, Dobson Papers, box A4, file D, Dobson to the Rev. J.A. Doyle, 14 Nov. 1919. Like Chown, Dobson was an admirer of John Spargo.

23 R.L. Schnell, "'A Children's Bureau for Canada': The Origins of the Canadian Council on Child Welfare, 1913–21," in Allan Moscovitch and Jim Albert, *The "Benevolent" State: The Growth of Welfare in Canada* (Toronto: Garamond Press, 1987), 95–110. On the quasi-public nature of the Canadian Council on Child Welfare, see Rooke and Schnell, "Child Welfare in English Canada, 1920–48," *Social Service Review*, Sept. 1981, 484–506.

24 UCA, Dobson Papers, box A5, file W2, Dobson to Whitton, 23 May 1920; Ibid., box A5, file S2, Dobson, "Suggestions on a Child Welfare Week for Canada," which notes the alliance between the social service councils

and the National Council of Women regarding the creation of a federal children's bureau within the Department of Health.

25 UCA, Dobson Papers, box A3, file K, quoted by Dobson in his "Social Surveys and Exhibits," n.d.

26 Ibid., Edward S. Bishop to Dobson, 30 March 1920.

27 Ibid., box A5, file B2, Bishop to Dobson, 25 Feb. 1920.

28 Ibid., box A5, file S2, Shearer to Dobson, 7 Oct. 1919.

29 UMA, Gordon Papers, box 30, folder 4, "Government," n.d. One should also note that this statement was made prior to church union, which he saw as redressing the balance between church and state.

30 UCA, Dobson Papers, box A7, file Mo, Moore to Dobson, 20 Dec. 1922, 8 March 1922; UCA, Methodist Church, DESS, box 2, file 37, Moore and Shearer to the Hon. W.F.A. Turgeon, attorney-general of Saskatchewan, 5 Jan. 1917.

31 See David Marshall, *Secularizing the Faith: Canadian Protestant Clergy and the Crisis of Belief, 1850–1940* (Toronto: University of Toronto Press, 1992), 249.

32 UCA, Dobson Papers, Box A5, file T, Dobson to Thomas, 26 April 1920.

33 Ibid., box A5, file Moore, Dobson to Moore, 21 May 1920; Ibid., box A5, file Mac, Dobson to the Rev. R.J. McDonald, 6 April 1920.

34 Ibid., box A4, file F, Dobson to Falk, 26 April 1918, Falk to Dobson, 29 April 1918.

35 AO, Ontario Welfare Council Papers, box 14, file 1928, "Annual Report of the General Secretary," 1928.

36 AO, Ontario Welfare Council Papers, box 14, "Minutes of the Social Service Council of Ontario," 1919; UCA, Dobson Papers, box A5, file W2, Whitton to Percy Paget, Public Welfare Commission, Winnipeg, Whitton to Dobson, 14 Sept. 1920. In 1907 the Board of Moral and Social Reform of the Presbyterian Church noted that J.A. Macdonald, editor of the *Globe*, sat on the Press Committee to ensure that the social reform issues of the church be kept before the public in the secular, religious, and labour press. See UCA, Presbyterian Church, Board of Moral and Social Reform, "Minutes of Meeting," 30 Oct. 1907. For the wide circulation of the Machine Age Series, see NA, Canadian Council of Churches, box 29, "Report of the General Secretary to the Annual Meeting of the Social Service Council of Canada," 2 Dec. 1937, 8.

37 SAB, Violet McNaughton Papers, W.J. Stewart, "Memorandum: The Social Service Council of Saskatchewan," report of Service Committee, 18 Feb. 1918.

38 UCA, Dobson Papers, box A5, file C2, "Report of the Field Secretary," 1 Aug. 1920.

39 Ibid., box A5, file F, Dobson to Falk, 21 Oct. 1920; Ibid., box A4, file H, Dobson to the Rev. D.B. Harkness, secretary, Social Service Council of

Manitoba, 15 March 1918; Ibid., box A4, file H, Dobson to F.A.E. Hamilton, 11 Dec. 1918.

40 Ibid., box A4, file H, Dobson to Harkness, 15 March 1918.

41 Ibid., box A4, file E, Dobson to Brother Egan, 19 Feb. 1919; Ibid., box A4, file C, Dobson to Mrs J.S. Chalmers, 10 May 1919.

42 Ibid., box A7, file Wh, Whitton to Dobson, 9 March 1922; Ibid., "Minutes of Child Welfare Committee," 15 Dec. 1922.

43 Ibid., box A5, file H, Dobson to Harkness, 30 April 1920; Ibid., box A5, file B, Dobson to Bishop, 29 April 1921; UCA, Methodist Church, DESS, box 2, file 38, 23 Jan. 1923.

44 UCA, Dobson Papers, box A7, file Mo, Moore to Dobson, 22 April 1922. There was a long tradition of church leaders lobbying Mackenzie King, whom they viewed as a kindred spirit. See UCA, Methodist Church, DESS, box 2, file 33b, Chown to King, 26 Sept. 1908, who celebrated King's election, stating that the churches needed a voice in Parliament that "will ring true and courageously upon the great moral issues we are seeking in common to promote." See also UCA, Dobson Papers, box A5, file Andrews, the Rev. W.W. Andrews to King, 30 Oct. 1919, in which Andrews advocates government ownership of railways and, regarding electoral purity, declared: "If a reign of terror can be established and a strong campaign of education carried out, Idealism can win hands down."

45 For King's early desire to be a Christian minister, see R. MacGregor Dawson, *William Lyon Mackenzie King, 1874–1923* (Toronto: University of Toronto Press, 1958), 42–57, 86–8. For King's views on the role of the state in labour relations, see Craven *"An Impartial Umpire": Industrial Relations and the Canadian State, 1900–1911* (Toronto: University of Toronto Press, 1980).

46 Dawson, *William Lyon Mackenzie King*, 86.

47 UCA, Presbyterian Church, Board of Moral and Social Reform, 9 Sept. 1908.

48 Ibid.

49 UMA, Gordon Papers, box 5, folder 7, W.L.M. King to Gordon, 12 July 1929.

50 Ibid. For King's use of clergymen while minister of labour on boards of industrial conciliation, see UMA, Gordon Papers, box 13, folder 7, King to Gordon, 20 May 1911, in which Gordon was asked to arbitrate the dispute between the Western Coal Operators Association and District 18 of the United Mine Workers.

51 NA, Canadian Council of Churches, box 29, "Annual Meeting of the Social Service Council of Canada," 23 April 1928, 1; UCA, Methodist Church, DESS, S.D. Chown to Albert Carman, 1 Oct. 1908.

52 For this assessment of the Social Service Council, see UCA, George Campbell Pidgeon Papers, 86.243, box 60, file 3211, "St. Christopher

House," n.d. According to Pidgeon, the founding of the council brought J.G. Shearer back into active church work. See Ibid., box 61, file 3224, "Autobiographical Notes," n.d. We have listed the churches in the order of their financial contribution to the Social Service Council of Canada. See NA, Canadian Council of Churches, box 29, "Minutes of the Moral and Social Reform Council," 23 Sept. 1910; Ibid., box 29, "Moral and Social Reform Council of Canada, Constitution," n.d.

53 NA, Canadian Council of Churches, box 29, "Moral and Social Reform Council of Canada, Constitution."

54 Ibid., "Minutes of the Moral and Social Reform Council," 26 Sept. 1911, 19–21.

55 Ibid., box 29, "Minutes of the Moral and Social Reform Council," 6 Sept. 1912.

56 UCA, Carman Papers, box 20, file 137, James Crisp, president of the Methodist Conference of New Brunswick and Prince Edward Island to Carman, 13 Feb. 1908.

57 Ibid., box 20, file 137, Chown to Carman, 22 Jan. 1908.

58 UCA, Methodist Church, DESS, Chown to Carman, 1 Oct. 1908.

59 For this debate within the Methodist Church, see UCA, Methodist Church, DESS, box 2, file 33a, "Memorandum, Moral and Social Reform Council of Canada, Historical Statement by Dr. Chown," 14 Dec. 1908, 2–10; UCA, Carman Papers, box 20, file 134, B.H. Spence, Dominion Alliance, to T. Albert Moore, 28 April 1911; Ibid., box 26, file 148, Chown to Carman, 6 Feb. 1908, 29 April 1908, 21 Oct. 1908; Ibid., box 20, file 137, Shearer to the Executive of the Temperance and Moral Reform Committee of the Methodist Church, 12 Feb. 1908, in which he agreed that each unit would retain its individuality.

60 UCA, Dobson Papers, box A8, file So, Shearer to Dobson, 7 Feb. 1924; Ibid., box A8, file Mo, Dobson to Moore, 5 Dec. 1923; Ibid., box A8, file Prov. SSC, "Notice of Meeting," 20 Feb. 1924. Shearer was well-known for his high-handedness and lack of consultation with provincial bodies. See Ibid., box A5, file Moore, Moore to Dobson, 9 Nov. 1920. There was also dissension between the Methodist Church and the Social Service Council of Ontario when Lady Eaton tempted the Rev. Peter Bryce to take up the position of secretary of the Child Welfare Department within the Social Service Council rather than becoming a field secretary for the Department of Evangelism and Social Service by personally paying him a salary of $4,000 per annum. Ibid., box A5, file Moore, Moore to Dobson, 15 March 1920.

61 See Ibid., box A5, file Moore, "Extract from Minutes of the Executive of the Board of Evangelism and Social Service," March 1921, which advocated that a lump-sum grant be given by the churches to the provincial social service councils, Moore to Dobson, 16 Nov. 1920.

62 For the Christian outlook of the Social Service Council of Saskatchewan, see SAB, J.B. Musselman Papers, W.P. Reekie to Dear Fellow Worker, 27 Sept. 1924; Ibid., "On the Need of an Intensive and Province-wide Program for the Welfare of Little Children," memorandum, 17 March 1925; Ibid., "Digest Report of Meeting of the Executive of the Social Service Council in the YMCA Building, Regina," 8 Sept. 1922. The Social Service Council of Saskatchewan had standing committees on the family, child welfare, social health, and prison reform. See also UCA, Dobson Papers, Box A6, file B, "Annual Meeting of the Social Service Council of Saskatchewan, in St. Andrews Presbyterian Church, Moose Jaw, Sask.," 25–26 Feb. 1919, where C.M. Hincks spoke on "Mental Defectiveness in Canada" and the Rev. J.M. Telford addressed the problem of "The Child, the Nation's Care and Hope." See also Ibid., box A5, file Moore, "Short Statement of the Activities of the Social Service Council of Manitoba for the Past Year," June 1921, where child welfare featured prominently. Under the influence of the Rev. Edward Bishop, the Alberta Social Service League had made the issue of child protection its centrepiece. See UCA, Dobson Papers, box A4, file B, Bishop to Dobson, 30 July 1918. The Social Service Council of Ontario was heavily influenced by the National Council of Women, the YMCA, and the Women's Christian Temperance Union, and the Women's Institutes, and for this reason child welfare, education, and rural reform were central issues. See AO, Ontario Welfare Council Papers, box 14, "Minutes of Meeting," 12 Dec. 1916, 2 March 1917.

63 UCA, Dobson Papers, box A8, file So, Shearer to Dobson, 7 Feb. 1924.

64 Ibid., box A8, file Mo, Moore to Dobson, 18 March 1924; Ibid., box A4, file D, Dobson to Brother Dorey, 10 Jan. 1919. When the Social Service Council of Saskatchewan finally joined the national body, the Rev. J.M. Singleton informed Dobson that he had safeguarded the interests of the church. Ibid., box A4, file S, Singleton to Dobson, 2 Jan. 1919.

65 Ibid., box A8, file Mo, Moore to Dobson, 15 Feb. 1924; Ibid., box A9, file SoS, W.P. Reekie, "Executive Meeting," 6 Feb. 1925. The first city social service committees were established in Hamilton, London, Toronto, and Ottawa in 1918. For this decentralized aspect of the activities of the Social Service Council, see Ibid., box A4, file C, "Child Welfare Activities in Canada," n.d.

66 UCA, Presbyterian Church, "Minutes of the Board of Moral and Social Reform," 13 April 1908, 9 Sept. 1908.

67 NA, Canadian Council of Churches, box 32, "Minutes of Committee on Industrial Life and Immigration," 14 Dec. 1921; Ibid., R.M. MacIver, "The National Guilds, Syndicalism, the Soviet," 1919.

68 Ibid., box 29, "Second Meeting of the Program Committee of the Fifteenth Annual Conference of Charities and Correction," 9 April 1914, 22

April 1914, 20 July 1914; Ibid., "A Meeting of the Executive of the Canadian Conference of Charities and Correction," 2 Feb. 1917, 13 Jan. 1918; Ibid., box 32, "Recommendations re Unemployment," 1918, in which the Social Service Council of Canada proposed unemployment insurance.

69 Ibid., box 29, "Minutes of the Meeting of the Committee of Arrangements of the Canadian Conference on Public Welfare," 19 Nov. 1918; Ibid., "Minutes of a Meeting of the Executive of the Canadian Conference on Public Welfare," 14 Jan. 1919.

70 Robinson was in fact an admirer of Beveridge's work. See NA, Canadian Council of Churches, box 32, "Annual Report of the Committee on Industrial Life," Jan. 1924, 2. For Beveridge's ideas on the subject of contributory pensions, see E.P. Hennock, *British Social Reform and German Precedents: The Case of Social Insurance, 1880–1914* (Oxford: Oxford University Press, 1987), 136.

71 AO, Ontario Welfare Council Papers, box 14, "Report of the Committee on Industrial Life," 8–10 May, 1923. Robinson's approach to unemployment insurance within the broader context of state responsibility for social welfare closely resembled that of that more "secular" social scientist and fellow disciple of William Beveridge, Bryce Stewart, whose early social research had been conducted under church auspices and who is credited by James Struthers as the most far-sighted architect of social policy in the interwar period. For Stewart, see *No Fault of Their Own*, 19.

72 NA, Canadian Council of Churches, box 29, "Supplement to the Report of the Executive of the Social Service Council of Canada for the Year 1925", 2–3.

73 For the churches' discussion of the need for increased specialization in social service research, see NA, Canadian Council of Churches, box 29, "Annual Meeting," 26 Jan. 1925, 2; Ibid., "Supplement to the Report of the Executive of the Social Service Council of Canada for the Year 1925," 2–3.

74 AO, Ontario Welfare Council Papers, box 14, "Report of General Secretary," 1 April 1919. The Ontario Council had committees on Industrial life and reconstruction, public health, child welfare, patronage, and law enforcement. See also Ibid., "Annual Meeting," 18 April 1929. Brian McKillop believes that E.A. Bott's psychology replicated American-style behaviourism and ignored morality and the soul in favour of objective measurement. In the 1930s E.A. Bott and Helen Bott were active participants in the Oxford Group movement, which was devoted to personal conversion and intense spirituality. This, together with Bott's participation in the church-based Social Service Council of Ontario, which sustained the unity of morality and science, calls into serious question McKillop's conclusion that Bott's appointment marked the dismissal of

metaphysics from Canadian psychology. See A.B. McKillop, *Matters of Mind: The University in Ontario, 1791–1951* (Toronto: University of Toronto Press, 1994), 493. For the participation of the Botts in the Oxford Group, see UCA, George Campbell Pidgeon Papers, box 23, file 408, the Rev. John Bick to Helen Bott, 26 April 1934.

75 SAB, Violet McNaughton Papers, W.P. Reekie and W.J. Stewart, "Memorandum Regarding Legislation," 7 Oct. 1919.

76 NA, Canadian Council of Churches, box 32, "Minutes of Committee on Industrial Life and Immigration," 14 Dec. 1921, 3, 6 Oct. 1922, 21 March 1924.

77 NA, Canadian Council of Churches, box 32, "Minutes of the Industrial Life and Immigration Committee," 1919–22. As usual, Charlotte Whitton saw fit to produce a dissenting report and spoke out against unemployment insurance and family allowances. See NA, Canadian Council of Churches, box 29, "Report of the Executive for 1929," 1 May 1930, 4–5.

78 NA, Canadian Council of Churches, box 32, "Minutes of Criminology Committee," 26 Oct. 1933.

79 NA, Canadian Council of Churches, box 32, "Minutes of Committee on Industrial Life," 9 April 1925, 11 Dec. 1925, 18 May 1926, 12 Nov. 1926. T.R. Robinson also wrote "The Jobless Man," Jan. 1926, in which he interviewed 200 unemployed men, while J.W. Macmillan wrote *Out of Work* in 1926, which stressed the problem of seasonal unemployment, and "The Man out of Work," 1927, which called for unemployment insurance.

80 Ibid., box 32, "Minutes of Rural Life Committee," "Agriculture and Immigration," Jan. 1925.

81 Ibid., box 32, "Minutes of Child Welfare Committee," 13 Feb. 1922, 15 Dec. 1922, and 2 Oct. 1923, in which New Zealand's maternity welfare legislation was debated; Ibid., box 29, Hugh Dobson, "The Trend of Family Life and Marriage in Our Times," 1930, 19–23.

82 Ibid., box 29, "Supplement to the Report ... for the Year 1925," 3.

83 Ibid., box 29, "Annual Meeting," 26–28 Jan. 1927, 2–6.

84 Ibid., box 29, the Rev. J.R. Mutchmor, "Urban Unemployment," Conference on Social Welfare, Knox Church, Regina, 26–29 Jan. 1927.

85 Ibid., box 32, "Minutes of Committee on Industrial Life," 4 May 1927, 20 May 1927, 20 Feb. 1928; Ibid., "Preliminary Report on Old Age Pensions," April 1928.

86 UTA, Department of Political Economy Papers, box 14, Innis to Cassidy, 23 Oct. 1939. For the Social Service Council's sponsorship of old-age pensions, see NA, Canadian Council of Churches, box 29, "Annual Meeting," 23 April 1928.

87 Innis and Urwick both rejected Harry Cassidy's proposal for the creation of a research institute at the University of Toronto dedicated to

social policy study. See UTA, Department of Political Economy Papers, box 14, Innis to Cassidy, 4 April 1937; Ibid., box 1, H.M. Cassidy, "A Canadian Institute of Social-Economic Research: A Preliminary Plan," 25 Sept. 1936. It was only in 1931 that McGill University secured Rockefeller funding for its Social Science Research Project. See Marlene Shore, *The Science of Social Redemption: McGill, the Chicago School, and the Origins of Social Research in Canada* (Toronto: University of Toronto Press, 1987), 196–223.

88 NA, Canadian Council of Churches, box 29, "Report of the Executive for the Year 1928"; Ibid., "Annual Meeting," 23 April 1928.

89 Ibid.

90 Ibid., box 29, "Annual Convention of the Social Service Council of Canada," 29 April–2 May 1930; UTA, Department of Political Economy Papers, box 1, Urwick to George Sidney Brett, 3 Dec. 1929.

91 NA, Canadian Council of Churches, box 29, "Report of Executive for 1930," 2; Ibid., "Report of Executive for 1931," 6. Marlene Shore gives the date 1932 for Heaton's MA degree, which leaves the impression that the research was inspired by Leonard Marsh's McGill Social Science Research Project. Shore, *The Science of Social Redemption*, 227–8.

92 NA, Canadian Council of Churches, box 29, "Report of the Executive Committee 1930," 5–7; Ibid., "Executive Meeting of the Social Service Council," 21 Jan. 1932, 2; L. Norman Tucker, "Presidential Address," *SW*, XI:9 (June 1929), 199. The idea of creating the new council had been canvassed in 1917 by the Social Service Council of Manitoba, which recommended that the national council open a permanent office in Ottawa and constitute itself as a Bureau of Social Research for Canada. See UCA, Dobson Papers, box A6, file B, *The Statesman, a Journal of Public Welfare*, Nov. 1917.

93 UCA, Dobson Papers, box 19, file B770, "Memorandum re Social Service Council of Canada," n.d.

94 AO, Ontario Welfare Council Papers, box 1, "Minutes of Executive," 23 March 1931.

95 NA, Canadian Council of Churches, box 29, "Meeting of Executive," 24 June 1931.

96 Ibid., box 32, "Minutes of the Committee on the Unemployed," 24 June 1931, 2. The increasing turn of the Social Service Council towards sustaining individual morale can be discerned in the proceedings of the council's 1933 meeting, where C.E. Silcox presented a paper on "Constructive Social Work in its Bearing on Unemployment," and D.N. McLachlan spoke on "Personal Care of the Underprivileged." See Ibid., box 29, "Annual Meeting, Social Service Council of Canada 1933," held at Temple Baptist Church, Windsor, 15 June 1933. At the same meeting, Chancellor H.P. Whidden of McMaster University spoke on "Are We

Slipping or Progressing Socially in Canada Today?" On the increasing preoccupation of the churches with the administration of local relief, see UCA, Dobson Papers, box 19, "Minutes of the Canadian Association of Social Workers at the Sunshine Camp," 24–25 Sept. 1932; Ibid., Dobson to D.N. McLachlan, 14 Jan. 1929; "Some Canadian Churches in Service," *SW*, XV:5 (Dec. 1934), 77.

97 NA, Canadian Council of Churches, box 29, "Meeting of Executive for Year 1930"; Ibid., box 29, "Meeting of Executive of Social Service Council," 24 June 1931, 3; AO, Ontario Welfare Council Papers, box 1, "Resolutions Passed by the Community Welfare Council of Ontario in Annual Meeting Bearing on Unemployment, Direct Relief and Public Works," 1931. *Social Planning for Canada* (Toronto: University of Toronto Press, 1975; first edition, 1935), of which Cassidy was a principal author, frequently averred to the need to make family assistance dependent upon individual merit.

98 NA, Canadian Council of Churches, box 29, "Report of Executive for 1930," 3.

99 *Social Planning for Canada*, 257.

100 I.M. Biss, *The Industrial Revolution in Canada* (The Machine Age Series, Social Service Council of Canada, pamphlet 1), foreword, 13.

101 Ibid., 16.

102 D.C. MacGregor, *The Canadian Wage Earner in the Machine Age* (Toronto: Social Service Council of Canada, 1934), 16.

103 D.L. Ritchie, *Youth and the Machine Age* (Toronto: Social Service Council of Canada, 1934), 6–7.

104 W.M. Drummond, *The Canadian Farmer and the Machine Age* (Toronto: Social Service Council of Canada, 1934), 2–6; G.E. Britnell, *The Western Farmer* (Toronto: Social Service Council of Canada), 1.

105 Britnell, *The Western Farmer*, 2, 15.

106 E.A. Forsey, *Unemployment in the Machine Age: Its Causes* (Toronto: Social Service Council of Canada, n.d.), 13.

107 See Britnell, *The Western Farmer*; W.M. Drummond, *The Canadian Farmer and the Machine Age* (Toronto: Social Service Council of Canada, n.d.).

108 Britnell, *The Wheat Economy*, 7.

109 Britnell, *The Western Farmer*, 12, MacGregor, *The Canadian Wage Earner*, 15–16.

110 UCA, United Church of Canada, Commission on Christianizing the Social Order, 82.018C, Irene Biss, "The Essential Conditions of the Good Society," 1.

111 Biss, *The Industrial Revolution in Canada*, 14; Ritchie, *Youth and the Machine Age*, 15. Biss's perspective was echoed by another prominent member of the League for Social Reconstruction, Graham Spry, who wrote "The ideal of the socialist is no less libertarian, no less 'liberal' than

that of the liberal philosopher. What the socialist seeks is not a narrowing of liberty but an enlargement of it." Graham Spry, "Socialism in Our Time," *SW*, XVI:5 (Dec. 1936), 133. The nebulous boundaries between new liberals and socialists in the 1930s have not been appreciated by the historian of the League for Social Reconstruction, who argues for the monolithic "socialist" character of the group. See Michiel Horn, *The League for Social Reconstruction: Intellectual Origins of the Democratic Left in Canada, 1930–42* (Toronto: University of Toronto Press, 1980).

112 M.M. Kirkwood, *Duty and Happiness in a Changed World* (Toronto: Macmillan Co., 1933), 37.

113 M.M. Kirkwood, *Women and the Machine Age* (Toronto: Social Service Council of Canada, n.d.), 7.

114 UBCA, N.A.M. Mackenzie Papers, box 11, folder 3, "Minutes, Canadian Institute on Economics and Politics, Planning and Promotion Committee," 21 May 1934. There was also unanimous approval for a whole course devoted to church proposals for social reconstruction throughout the world. See Ibid., "Minutes, 16 Jan. 1934." N.A.M. Mackenzie, then in the Department of Political Economy at the University of Toronto and later president of the University of New Brunswick and then of the University of British Columbia, also sat on this committee and wrote that "Social Security suggests to me the security of the individual and of the family unit in the community or society ..." See Ibid., box 96, folder 1/3, "Social Security in Democracy," n.d.

115 NA, Canadian Council of Churches, box 29, "Report of the General Secretary to the Annual Meeting of the Social Service Council of Canada," 2 Dec. 1937, 8.

116 UCA, Dobson Papers, box 19, Dobson to the Rev. Hugh Rae, 31 March 1936. The article appeared in the 11 March issue of *New Outlook*.

117 For Silcox's appointment, see NA, Canadian Council of Churches, box 29, "Executive Meeting of Social Service Council," 22 Oct. 1934; "Comments from Church Leaders and the United States," *SW*, XV:5 (Dec. 1934), 84–5.

118 UCA, Claris Edwin Silcox Papers, box 5, file 4, "The Study of Church Union in Canada," enclosed letter from Edwin de S. Brunner to E.W. Burgess, 20 Feb. 1931. This important study had been commended by Chicago sociologist E.W. Burgess, who gave Silcox an entrée into the American Sociological Society. For Jones's tenure of office, see UCA, Dobson Papers, box 19, Dobson to Jones, 24 March 1934.

119 NA, Canadian Council of Churches, Box 29, "Report of the General Secretary," 2 Dec. 1937.

120 While Silcox continued to press for housing and prison reform legislation, largely at the behest of E.J. Urwick of the University of Toronto, and paid lip-service to unity of evangelism and social service, he progressively posited a disjuncture between the spiritual and the secular. See

NA, Canadian Council of Churches, box 29, "Facts and Considerations Regarding the Work of the Social Service Council of Canada," 1935, 1–2. For Silcox's extremely conservative views regarding the social control of the working poor, see "Extract of letter of Silcox to J.R. Mutchmor, 26 Mar. 1935," in UTA, Department of Political Economy Papers, box 1; Ibid., Urwick to Silcox, 1 April 1936. On Urwick's influence, see NA, Canadian Council of Churches, box 29, "Executive Meeting," 9 Jan. 1935.

121 NA, Canadian Council of Churches, box 29, "Annual Meeting," 1935, 9.

122 UCA, George Pidgeon Papers, box 9, file 180, "A Conference on the Church Facing the Social Crisis," 10–11 Dec. 1934, at which Silcox presented a paper on "The Church and the Protection of Public Morals."

123 NA, Canadian Council of Churches, box 29, "Executive Meeting," 12 Nov. 1934.

124 On Silcox's attempt to usurp the church's prosecution of the temperance campaign, see UCA, Dobson Papers, box 16, Dobson to McLachlan, 11 Feb. 1935; Ibid., box 16, Dobson to Mutchmor, 18 Nov. 1937.

125 UCA, Dobson Papers, box 16, D.N. McLachlan to Dobson, 11 May 1937.

126 AO, Ontario Welfare Council Papers, box 1, "Minutes, 8 Sept. 1931." For example, the Committee on Employment and Unemployment struck a new body called the Unemployment Research Committee of Ontario in which which Professor Cassidy was both the secretary and director of research.

127 UCA, Dobson Papers, box 16, Dobson to McLachlan, 11 Feb. 1935.

128 NA, Canadian Council of Churches, box 29, "Facts and Considerations Regarding the Work of the Social Service Council of Canada," 1. For Silcox's resignation, see Ibid., "The Christian Social Council of Canada, Minutes of Annual Meeting," 10 April 1940, 13.

129 Mutchmor and Silcox disagreed heartily over whether the council should lobby federal or provincial governments, and thus fell out over what line their submissions should take for the Rowell-Sirois Commission. See NA, Canadian Council of Churches, box 29, "Annual Meeting, 1937," 6, 14 March 1938, 4. See also Ibid., "The Christian Social Welfare Council of Canada," meeting of special sub-committee, 14 Dec. 1939; Ibid., "Annual Meeting," 10 April 1940; Ibid., box 32, "Minutes, Committee on Future Policy," 19 June 1925, in which some clergymen expressed the fear that their connection with other reform organizations would imperil the Christian tenor of their work. On Mutchmor's attitudes to social security, see Mutchmor Papers, "Autobiography," chapter XII, 21.

CHAPTER SEVEN

1 UCA, George Pidgeon Papers, box 9, file 182, leaflet, Joint Committee for the Evangelization of Canadian Life, 1935.

2 For Gilbert Jackson's interpretation of the Depression in terms of faith, see Jackson, *An Economist's Confession of Faith* (Toronto: Macmillan, 1935), 28–9, 151–2. In 1933 he stated: "The root causes of the depression lie in no fault of the economic mechanism by which we live, but in ourselves ... Perhaps – and here I tread upon the threshold of theology – perhaps the depression ought to last, until we recognize that it is due to the faults in ourselves." Quoted in David Marshall, *Secularizing the Faith: Canadian Protestant Clergy and the Crisis of Belief, 1850–1940* (Toronto: University of Toronto Press, 1992), 212.

3 UCA, Dobson Papers, box 19, "Evangelism and Social Service," n.d.; UCA, United Church, Board of Home Missions, box 7, file 108, "Minutes of Regina Conference," 5 Jan. 1931.

4 McCord Museum of Canadian History, Canadian Patriotic Fund, Montreal Branch, "File Philanthropy," T. Albert Moore to Dr J.W. Ross, 16 Feb. 1933.

5 *Annual Report of the Board of Evangelism and Social Service*, 1933, enclosed memorandum, 4 May 1934.

6 UCA, Dobson Papers, box 19, Dobson to D.N. McLachlan, "Report," 1931; Ibid., Dobson to Ernest Thomas, 18 June 1936.

7 Marshall, *Secularizing the Faith*, 248.

8 UCA, United Church, DESS, box 64, file 321, Thomas to Nicholson, 19 April 1932. See also United Church, General Council Committee on the Tenth Anniversary of Church Union, "Ten Years of Evangelism and Social Service," in *Ten Years of Union, 1925–35*, 12.

9 UCA, Pidgeon Papers, box 20, file 339, W.H. Smith, honorary principal, Union College, British Columbia, to Pidgeon, 24 Jan. 1928; Ibid., Pidgeon to the Rev. Bruce G. Gray, 12 Dec. 1929.

10 UCA, Dobson Papers, box 19, the Rev. Charles Daniel to Brother, 6 May 1935.

11 UCA, Pidgeon Papers, box 23, file 407, Bailey to Pidgeon, 13 Dec. 1933.

12 Ibid., box 23, file 401, Milne to the Rev. A.E. Armstrong, secretary, United Church Board of Foreign Missions, 17 Feb. 1933. Significantly, Armstrong presented his copy of Gilbert Jackson's *An Economist's Confession of Faith* to the University of Toronto Library.

13 Ibid., box 23, file 403, McLeod to Pidgeon, 1 May 1933.

14 Ibid., box 20, file 340, Pidgeon to the Rev. E.W. Chadwick, general secretary, YMCA, St Joseph, Missouri, 1930.

15 Ibid., box 20, file 342, Pidgeon to the Rev. W.G. Wilson, Vancouver, 9 May 1930; Ibid., box 20, file 343, Clarence Mackinnon, principal, Pine Hill Divinity Hall, to Pidgeon, 11 June 1930. For the persistence of interest in revival campaigns at the local level, see G.A. Rawlyk, "J.J. Sidey and the Soul Winner's Revival of the 1920s," in George Rawlyk, *Wrapped Up in God: A Study of Several Canadian Revivals and Revivalists* (Burlington: Welch Publishing, 1988), 120–34.

16 UCA, Pidgeon Papers, box 23, file 401, McLachlan to Pidgeon, 3 Jan. 1933.

17 Ibid., box 23, file 393, "Mass Meetings for Oxford Group," *Woodstock Sentinel*, 8 Jan. 1934. For the Oxford Group Movement in Canada, see R.G. Stewart, "Radiant Smiles in the Dirty Thirties: History and Ideology of the Oxford Group Movement in Canada, 1932–1936," M.Div. thesis, Vancouver School of Theology, 1979; Robert Wright, "The Canadian Protestant Experience, 1914–1945," in Rawlyk, ed., *The Canadian Protestant Experience* (Burlington: Welch Academic Press, 1990).

18 UCA, Pidgeon Papers, box 23, file 398, "The Oxford Group Movement: The Movement's Real Significance," *Era* (Newmarket, Ont.), 20 Dec. 1933.

19 UCA, Pidgeon Papers, box 23, file 398, "Group House Party Not Merely Series of Meetings," *Winnipeg Tribune*, 13 Jan. 1934.

20 UCA, Pidgeon Papers, box 23, file 403, the Rev. J.W.H. Milne to Pidgeon, 31 March 1933. For the appeal of the Oxford Group to women, see Ibid., box 23, file 406, the Rev. J.W. Clarke, Knox United Church, Winnipeg, to Pidgeon, 18 Sept. 1933.

21 UCA, Dobson Papers, box 19, D.N. McLachlan to Brethren, 4 May 1934; UCA, Pidgeon Papers, box 9, file 173, "Report of the Proposed Simultaneous Movement for the Evangelization of Canadian Life," 1932.

22 UCA, DESS, *Annual Report*, 1931, 15; UCA, Pidgeon Papers, box 9, file 173, "Joint Committee on the Evangelization of Canadian Life," 2 Nov. 1932.

23 UCA, Pidgeon Papers, box 23, file 407, the Rev. Leslie Pidgeon to the Rev. Richard O. Flinn, 5 Dec. 1933.

24 Ibid., box 23, file 403, "The Oxford Group Message and Methods," n.d.; Ibid., box 9, file 179, Pidgeon to the Rev. J.W.H. Milne, 8 Nov. 1934, in which he saw Roberts's support as crucial for enlisting the support of United Church ministers. See also Ibid., box 9, file 173, Pidgeon to Mr W.H. Goodwin, 17 Nov. 1932; Ibid., box 23, file 406, the Rev. J.W. Clarke to Pidgeon, 18 Sept. 1933. Leading Anglican social reformers, such as Canon Vernon, head of the Social Service Council of Canada, warmly endorsed the Oxford Group. Vernon was particularly enthusiastic about the "quiet hour" idea but was less enamoured of public confession. See Ibid., box 9, file 173, Pidgeon to Vernon, 17 Nov. 1932, Vernon to Pidgeon, 6 Nov. 1932.

25 UCA, Pidgeon Papers, box 23, file 400, T. Albert Moore to Pidgeon, 5 Nov. 1932.

26 Ibid., box 23, file 400, Moore to Pidgeon, 7 Nov. 1932.

27 See, for example, Ibid., box 23, file 403, the Rev. John Mackay, Manitoba College, to Pidgeon, 5 June 1933. This type of criticism was also frequently mooted within the Oxford Group movement itself.

28 Ibid., box 23, file 398, "Theological Students Held Annual Dinner," *Kingston Whig-Standard*, 16 Jan. 1934.

29 Ibid., box 23, file 400, the Rev. Albert E. Jones to Pidgeon, 22 Dec. 1932.
30 For W.B. Creighton's ostracism, see the telling memoir by his son, historian Donald Creighton, "My Father and the United Church," in Donald Creighton, *The Passionate Observer: Selected Writings* (Toronto: McClelland and Stewart, 1980), 99.
31 UCA, Pidgeon Papers, box 23, file 401, McLachlan to Pidgeon, 3 Jan. 1933.
32 Ibid., box 9, file 176, "Committee on Evangelism and Social Service," n.d.
33 Ibid., "The Evangelization of Canadian Life," which observed that the spirit among Canadians was ripe for a country-wide movement. In 1935 four spiritual leaders were brought by Richard Roberts from England to lead these campaigns.
34 Ibid., box 23, file 406, the Rev. J.W. Clarke to Pidgeon, 18 Sept. 1933.
35 Marshall, *Secularizing the Faith*, 218, 248.
36 UCA, Pidgeon Papers, box 23, file 400, L.A. Dixon, secretary, Student Christian Association of the University of Toronto to Pidgeon, 22 Nov. 1933.
37 Ibid., box 23, file 406, the Rev. J.W. Clarke to Pidgeon, 18 Sept. 1933.
38 Ibid., box 23, file 400, Mr and Mrs J.C. Fletcher to Pidgeon, 19 Dec. 1932.
39 Ibid., box 23, file 403, Milne to Pidgeon, 27 March 1933.
40 Ibid., box 23, file 401, Milne to A.E. Armstrong, 5 Feb. 1933.
41 Ibid., box 23, file 407, Pidgeon to the Rev. Walter Steven, 8 Dec. 1933; Ibid., box 9, file 173, Pidgeon to the Rev. Harold Ackert, Allenford, Ont., 23 Nov. 1932.
42 Ibid., box 23, file 407, Frank Schofield to Pidgeon, 15 Nov. 1933.
43 Ibid., box 23, file 398, "The Oxford Group Movement: The Movement's Real Significance," *Era*, Newmarket, Ont., 20 Dec. 1933.
44 Ibid., box 23, file 408, Pidgeon to the Rev. Hallen Viney, London, 19 Jan. 1934. The Oxford Group movement also had fellowship groups in the middle-class holiday resorts of the Muskokas, and in addition its brand of evangelicalism brought into its fold such social scientists as E.A. Bott and Helen Bott of the Institute of Child Study at the University of Toronto. See Ibid., the Rev. John Bick, Whitevale, Ont., to Mrs Bott, 26 April 1934, Charles Shaw to Pidgeon, 3 May 1934, regarding introducing the group to the Bigwin Inn, Lake of Bays, Muskoka.
45 Ibid., box 23, file 401, Alice S. Lewis to Pidgeon, 13 Jan. 1933.
46 Ibid., box 23, file 407, Pidgeon to Mr John Stevenson, 22 Dec. 1933.
47 Ibid., box 23, file 400, the Rev. Allan Shatford to Pidgeon, 1 Nov. 1932.
48 Ibid., box 23, file 408, Dorothy Newhold, Toronto, to Pidgeon, 22 Jan. 1934.
49 Ibid., Pidgeon to Miss Newhold, 25 Jan. 1934.
50 Ibid., box 23, file 398, "The Oxford Group Movement," *Era*, 20 Dec. 1933.

51 Ibid., box 23, file 408, Russell Harris to Pidgeon, 24 Jan. 1934.
52 Ibid., box 23, file 408, the Rev. Clayton Munro, Hamilton, Bermuda, 24 Jan. 1934.
53 Ibid., box 23, file 408, Clayton Munro to Pidgeon, 12 Jan. 1934. For an example of this historical approach, see the analysis in Marshall, *Secularizing the Faith*, which relies too heavily upon the comments of the Toronto Protestant leadership. See chapter 8, "Why No Revival?"
54 Ibid., box 23, file 401, Althea Dobie to Pidgeon, 24 Jan. 1933.
55 Ibid., box 23, file 407, John Stevenson, Kingston, to Pidgeon, 11 Dec. 1933.
56 Ibid., box 23, file 400, Pidgeon to the Rev. George Shepherd, Presbyterian Theological Seminary, Chicago, 20 Jan. 1933.
57 Ibid., box 23, file 400, S.E.H., "The Oxford Movement: A First-Century Christian Fellowship," n.d.
58 Ibid., box 23, file 400, McLachlan to Pidgeon, 1 Dec. 1932. Apart from the United Church's criticisms of public confession, there existed a widespread consensus favourable to the Oxford Group's emphasis on the revival of individual spirituality. For the overlap in their views, see Ibid., box 23, file 399, R.W. Armstrong, "The Twin Challenges of the Kingdom: Professor Harry F. Ward and the Oxford Group," *New Outlook*, 23 Nov. 1932.
59 UCA, Pidgeon Papers, box 23, file 401, Pidgeon to Frank Buchman, 17 Feb. 1933. For Pidgeon's career in the inner circle of social Christian leadership, see Ibid, box 61, file 3224; UCA, George Campbell Pidgeon Papers, 92.185C, box 1, file 1.
60 UCA, Mutchmor Papers, box 1, file 1, Mutchmor to R.B. Cochrane, 7 Oct. 1931.
61 UCA, Pidgeon Papers, box 9, file 173, "Commission on the Church and Industry," 30 April 1932.
62 NA, Canadian Council of Churches, box 29, "Annual Meeting of the Social Service Council of Canada," 1935, 6.
63 United Church, Board of Evangelism and Social Service, *Annual Report, 1931–32*, 14.
64 UCA, Pidgeon Papers, box 9, file 179, John Montreal to the Rev. A. Lloyd Smith, Westmount, 12 Oct. 1934; Ibid., box 20, file 339c, Pidgeon to Mr Charles J. Stephens, 23 Dec. 1929; UCA, Dobson Papers, box 19, Dobson to W.A. Carrothers, 5 Sept. 1934; Ibid., Dobson to the Rev. Albert Larke, 4 May 1935, in which Dobson described his personal opposition to the protests within work camps because he believed the men were being manipulated by Communist agitators.
65 UCA, Pidgeon Papers, box 23, file 401, Manly F. Miner, Jack Miner Migratory Bird Foundation, Kingsville, Ont., to Pidgeon, 25 Jan. 1933, D.H. Dobbin to Pidgeon, 10 Feb. 1933.

66 UCA, Dobson Papers, box 19, William to Dobson, 26 Jan. 1935. See also Ibid., the Rev. Albert Larke to Dobson, 11 July 1935, on the threat of economic determinism.

67 Ibid., box 19, Dobson to the Rev. W.H. Irwin, 16 Nov. 1934.

68 United Church, *Annual Report*, 4 May 1934, 6–7.

69 UCA, Pidgeon Papers, box 23, file 408, Pidgeon to Russell Harris, 2 Feb. 1934.

70 Ibid., box 23, file 408, Russell Harris to Pidgeon, 24 Jan. 1934.

71 UCA, Dobson Papers, box 19, Ernest Thomas to Dobson, 14 May 1935.

72 Ibid., box 19, annual report of the field secretary, 1931–32, 16.

73 UCA, Pidgeon Papers, box 23, file 403, McLeod to Pidgeon, 1 May 1933.

74 Canadian Baptists had experienced serious divisions in the 1920s over the social implications of wealth, and these spilled over into rival definitions of Christian education. On this question, see George Rawlyk, "A.L. McCrimmon, H.P. Whidden, T.T. Shields, Christian Education, and McMaster University," in Rawlyk, ed., *Canadian Baptists and Christian Higher Education* (Montreal and Kingston: McGill-Queen's University Press, 1988).

75 UCA, Pidgeon Papers, box 9, file 183, R.B. Cochrane to Pidgeon, 17 June 1935. As head of the Board of Home Missions, Cochrane held conservative attitudes that were distinctly shaped by his anxiety over church funding. See, for example, UCA, Mutchmor Papers, box 1, file 1, Mutchmor to Cochrane, 7 Oct. 1931, 24 Feb. 1932, Cochrane to Mutchmor, 25 May 1932.

76 UCA, Pidgeon Papers, Pidgeon to Roberts, 2 July 1935; Ibid., box 23, file 403, Pidgeon to J.W.H. Milne, 20 June 1933: "Our Toronto Conference has won such unenviable notoriety over its economic programme that I am glad to report a real move forward over the spiritual side."

77 UCA, Pidgeon Papers, box 9, file 179, "Agenda on Evangelism," 1934.

78 Ibid., box 9, file 173, "Suggestions for Conference Committees," n.d.

79 UCA, Dobson Papers, box A1, file Q, "Sermons of Rev. C.E. Bland," "Economic Unrest and the Kingdom of God," 3 May 1931; "Canada's Thanksgiving," 11 Oct. 1931; "Religion in Everyday Life: *In Hard Times*," 11 Oct. 1931, evening service, Crescent United Church, Fort Rouge; "The Oxford Group: Its Value to Us," Crescent United Church, 21 May 1933. For Bland's views during the 1920s, see "The Joy of the Lord," 19 Aug. 1923; "Labor Day Sermon," 2 Sept. 1933.

80 UCA, United Church, Commission on Christianizing the Social Order, 82.018C, John Line, "The Fundamental Unity of Spiritual and Social Religious Values," 3–5; *Supplement to Christianizing the Social Order*, E.J. Urwick and Irene Biss, "Modern Industry," 23–4.

81 UCA, Commission on Christianizing the Social Order, McLachlan to members of the commission, 28 May 1934.

82 *Christianizing the Social Order*, 14; United Church, *Annual Report*, 4 May 1934, 12. This statement on the different roles of church and state was issued by James Semple and Ernest Thomas.

83 UCA, Commission on Christianizing the Social Order, "A Statement by Rev. Richard Roberts," 1–3.

84 Ibid., Robert Falconer, "The Church and the Social Order," 3–6. See also Ibid., W.R. Taylor, "The Social Teachings of the Old Testament," 17 Feb. 1933. On the indirect role of the Church regarding social issues, see UCA, Mutchmor Papers, box 14, file 190, "Evangelism and Social Service in the United Church of Canada," n.d., 5; UCA, Dobson Papers, box 19, W.A. Carrothers to Dobson, 7 Sept. 1934, who commented that because of clashing "individual interests" the church could not move ahead on social issues.

85 Ibid., Ernest Thomas, "Christian Churches and Economic Conditions," 11.

86 Ibid., box 19, Department of Evangelism and Social Service, *Annual Report*, 38.

87 UCA, Commission on Christianizing the Social Order, "Christian Standards and Teaching," 2.

88 UCA, Pidgeon Papers, box 9, file 173, John Gunn to Pidgeon, 1 Nov. 1932. For an opposite view, see Phyllis Airhart, *Serving the Present Age: Revivalism, Progressivism, and the Methodist Tradition in Canada* (Montreal and Kingston: McGill-Queen's University Press, 1992), epilogue. The persistence of this strain of popular evangelical belief has been suggestively examined by George Rawlyk, *The Canada Fire: Radical Evangelicalism in British North America, 1775–1812* (Montreal and Kingston: McGill-Queen's University Press, 1994), 211. This volume reached us as the manuscript was nearing completion.

89 UCA, United Church, Commission on Economic and Social Research, 82.032C, "Standing Commission," 27 Oct. 1937; "Minutes of Commission," 29 Oct. 1937, 14 Dec. 1937, 4 Jan. 1938, 10 Feb. 1938, 24 Feb. 1938; Ibid., "Industrial Organization and Collective Bargaining," A Report of the Economic and Social Research Commission, 1940, 10. This commission generally supported proposals for contributory unemployment insurance. See, for example, UCA, United Church, Board of Evangelism and Social Service, box 64, file 321, J.R. Mutchmor to Mackenzie King, 30 Nov. 1939; Ibid., Tom Moore, president, Trades and Labor Congress, to the Rev. D.N. McLachlan, 7 Oct. 1932; UCA, Mutchmor Papers, Mutchmor Journal, 4 Jan. 1938, 24 Nov. 1938, 26 Nov. 1938. The commission also supported national health insurance but was reluctant to endorse the idea of compulsory collective bargaining as proposed by the CIO. Hugh Dobson was one of the few clergymen to sit on the commission. For his views on these issues, see UCA, Dobson Papers, box 19, Dobson to the Rev. E.W. McKay,

27 Feb. 1935, Dobson to the Rev. H.G. Cairns, 15 Jan. 1935, Dobson to Harry Cassidy, 30 Dec. 1935, Dobson to J.R. Mutchmor, 26 Aug. 1937, J.R. Mutchmor to Dobson, 8 Dec. 1937, Dobson to Mutchmor, 23 Dec. 1937. Dobson believed that the commission should address all matters of social security, including unemployment insurance, health insurance, old-age pensions, low-cost housing, and the right to collective bargaining. However, Dobson agreed with T.A. Crerar, one the most the most conservative members of the Liberal cabinet, that there were limits to state encroachment on individual rights and he feared the overcentralization of the management of social welfare in the hands of the federal cabinet.

90 UCA, Commission on Economic and Social Research, "Minutes," 24 Feb. 1938.

91 These campaigns were the creation largely of Richard Roberts who, after the waning of the Oxford Group movement, became absorbed in the story of Group Evangelism, as told in *The Finger of God* by a British Methodist, Frank Raynor. In 1935 five British evangelists conducted these campaigns which, after their first successes in Montreal, spread through almost every town and city throughout Canada. See UCA, Pidgeon Papers, box 9, file 179, Roberts to Pidgeon, 10 Aug. 1934, with enclosed statement by Roberts penned 25 July 1934; Ibid., box 9, file 181, "Committee on a Service of Witness," Maple Leaf Gardens, 5 March 1935. On the success of the revival meeting at the Montreal Forum, where 17,000 people attended, see Leslie Pidgeon to George Pidgeon, 23 Jan. 1935. George Pidgeon encouraged ministers all across Canada to undertake similar revivals. See, for example, his letters on 6 Feb. 1935 to the Rev. D. McIvor, W.G. Wilson, J.G. Brown, McGregor Grant, and George Macdonald, who preached in Victoria, Vancouver, Brandon, and Edmonton. The socialist mayor of Toronto, Jimmy Simpson, wrote to Pidgeon on 11 Feb. 1935 expressing his regret that they could not hold a service of "Witness" in Toronto, but he advocated a day of prayer. These revivals were still occurring during the late 1930s. See UCA, Dobson Papers, box 19, undated memorandum, 1938, in which a clergyman from New Brunswick reported that 4,500 people had attended one such revival meeting.

CONCLUSION

1 UCA/UW, Cormie Papers, "Draft Report of the General Council's Commission on Urban Problems, 1938." So impervious was Canadian Christianity to the penetration of secular values that only by the late 1930s were the churches beginning to exhibit anxiety over declining church attendance, and incredibly their concern focused not upon a loss of faith among the majority of ordinary Canadians but upon the fact that middle-class Christians, though they continued to attend morning services on Sunday, were no longer attending the evening service in large numbers.

2 UBCA, Mackenzie Papers, box 31, folder 4, William Creighton Graham to Mackenzie, 20 March 1948; Ibid., box 103, folder 8/10, "Address by Dr. N.A.M. Mackenzie," 3 Oct. 1948.

3 For an examination of this process, see Robert K. Burkinshaw, *Pilgrims in Lotus Land: Conservative Protestantism in British Columbia, 1917–1981* (Montreal and Kingston: McGill-Queen's University Press, 1995), chapters 9 and 10. See also Bruce Hindmarsh, "The Winnipeg Fundamentalist Network, 1910–1950: The Roots of Transdenominational Evangelicalism in Manitoba and Saskatchewan," and Robert Burkinshaw, "Evangelical Colleges and Seminaries in Twentieth Century Canada," Papers presented to the Conference on the Canadian Evangelical Experience, 10–14 May 1995, Kingston, Ontario.

Manuscript Sources

ARCHIVES OF ONTARIO (TORONTO)
Ontario Welfare Council Papers
Office of the Premier
E.C. Drury Papers

BILLY GRAHAM CENTER ARCHIVES (WHEATON, ILL.)
J. Wilbur Chapman Papers

BRITISH LIBRARY OF POLITICAL AND ECONOMIC SCIENCE (LONDON)
Edwin Cannan Papers

McCORD MUSEUM (MONTREAL)
Canadian Patriotic Fund Papers

McGILL UNIVERSITY ARCHIVES (MONTREAL)
President's Papers, Sir Arthur Currie
Minutes of the Board of Governors

NATIONAL ARCHIVES OF CANADA (OTTAWA)
Canadian Association of Social Workers
Canadian Council of Churches
Canadian Council on Social Development
W.C. Good Papers
C.B. Sissons Papers

Charlotte Whitton Papers
James Shaver Woodsworth Papers

OXFORD UNIVERSITY, BODLEIAN LIBRARY
Oxford Economic Society Papers

PROVINCIAL ARCHIVES OF MANITOBA (WINNIPEG)
C.W. Gordon Papers
Valentine Winkler Papers

SASKATCHEWAN ARCHIVES BOARD, UNIVERSITY OF SASKATCHEWAN (SASKATOON)
Violet McNaughton Papers
J.B. Musselman Papers
Saskatchewan Grain Growers' Association

UNITED CHURCH OF CANADA ARCHIVES (TORONTO)
Albert Carman Papers
Samuel Dwight Chown Papers
Hugh Dobson Papers
George Dorey Papers
John Maclean Papers
Methodist Church, Army and Navy Board
Methodist Church, Department of Evangelism and Social Service
James Mutchmor Papers
George Campbell Pidgeon Papers
Presbyterian Church, Board of Moral and Social Reform
James Robertson Memorial Lectures
C.E. Silcox Papers
A.E. Smith Papers
United Church of Canada, Board of Home Missions
United Church of Canada, Commission of Christianizing the Social Order
United Church of Canada, Commission on Courses of Study Records
United Church of Canada, Commission on Economic and Social Research
United Church of Canada, General Council Committee on the Tenth Anniversary of Church Union
United Church of Canada, Recruits for the Ministry

UNITED CHURCH OF CANADA ARCHIVES, UNIVERSITY OF WINNIPEG
All People's Mission Papers
John A. Cormie Papers

UNIVERSITY OF BRITISH COLUMBIA DEPARTMENT OF SPECIAL COLLECTIONS (VANCOUVER)
Norman A. Mackenzie Papers

UNIVERSITY OF GUELPH ARCHIVES
President's Papers
President J.B. Reynolds

UNIVERSITY OF MANITOBA ARCHIVES (WINNIPEG)
Faculty of Agriculture, Rural Sociology Department
C.W. Gordon Papers

UNIVERSITY OF TORONTO ARCHIVES
Harry Cassidy Papers
S.D. Clark Papers
H.J. Cody Papers
Department of Graduate Records
Department of Political Economy Papers
Robert Falconer Papers
Harold Innis Papers

UNIVERSITY OF TORONTO, THOMAS FISHER RARE BOOKS LIBRARY
Robert S. Kenny Collection
James Mavor Papers

UNIVERSITY OF WATERLOO, DEPARTMENT OF SPECIAL COLLECTIONS
Elizabeth Smith Shortt Papers

Index

Academic freedom, 149–50. *See also* MacIver, R.M.
Adams, Thomas, 175–7
Adcock, Rev. W.H., 184
Addams, Jane, 107, 178, 246
Airhart, Phyllis, 42, 60
All People's Mission, 50–1
Allen, Richard, 87–8, 113, 131, 160; on social gospel, xiii
Andrews, Rev. W.W.: on evolution and religion, 80–1
Anglican Church, 160, 167, 184, 200–1, 216–18
Armstrong, Christopher, 165
Ashley, W.J., 83–4, 91

Baptist Church, 84, 89, 205–6, 214
Barnett, Canon Samuel: and Toynbee Hall, 151; influence on E.J. Urwick, 151. *See also* Urwick, E.J.
Bennett, R.B., 215, 243
Bentley, Rev. J.F., 103
Beveridge, Sir William, 213
Biss, Irene: and Machine Age Series, 167, 218–19; and Commission on Christianizing the Social Order, 239–40. *See also* Machine Age Series; United Church, Commission on Christianizing the Social Order
Bland, Rev. C.E., 239
Bland, Rev. Salem: and rural problems, 172; and social service, 24; and socialism, 16; and support for J.A. Dale, 149
Blatz, W.E.: and Social Service Council of Ontario, 214
Board of Evangelism and Social Service (United Church), 224, 235, 238; and redefinition of evangelism, 242
Board of Social Service and Evangelism (Presbyterian Church): formation of, 3; on social science, 89
Bott, E.A., 214; participation in Oxford Group, 348n44
Bowman, Isaiah: and concept of pioneer fringe, 190; influence on the Rev. R.W. Murchie, 193
Bracken, John, 193
Brady, Alexander, 194–5
Brigden, Beatrice, 22, 96, 101; background, 42; and modern culture, 15; and relations with local clergy, 25–30, 55; and social evangelism, 28–30, 43, 49, 51–3; and social purity, 15, 26–7, 49; and socialism, 20; and Winnipeg General Strike, 31–4; and working class, 54
Britnell, George, 218–19. *See also* Machine Age Series
Brotherhood Movement, 96–7
Bryce, Rev. Peter, 148, 184; and Canadian

Association of Social Workers, 157; and child welfare, 129–30; and evolution, 81; and old age pensions, 217. *See also* Canadian Association of Social Workers; child welfare; evolution
Burgess, Ernest: influence on the Rev. Carl Dawson, 136–9
Burwash, Rev. Nathanael: and social science, 82

Caldwell, William, 133
Canadian Association of Social Workers: formation of, 157–8; and Social Service Council of Canada, 160–2
Carman, Rev. Albert, 109; and Social Service Council of Canada, 21–2, 210
Cassidy, Harry, 164, 220, 246; and Social Service Council of Ontario, 218; on unemployment, 218
Chapman, Rev. J. Wilbur, 61–2; appeal of 64; and Toronto revival, 59–60
Child welfare, 23, 78, 111, 124–7, 201–2, 206; leadership of Protestant churches in, 107
Child welfare exhibits, 127–30. *See also* Dobson, Rev. Hugh
Chown, Alice, 3
Chown, Rev. Samuel Dwight: attitude to immigrants, 188; career, 41; and Christian socialism, 16–17; and critique of theology, 5–7; and Department of Evangelism and Social Service, 21–2, 35; on modern culture, 14; and Oxford Group, 229; on relations of church and state, 200; on revivalism, 71; and social reform, 15–16; and social sciences, 82, 84–6; and Social Service Council of Canada, 209–10; on status of clergyman, 98–9; on unemployment, 201. *See also* Department of Evangelism and Social Service; Methodist Church; Oxford Group; Social Service Council of Canada
Christian socialism, 16–17
Church and state relations, xiv, 105–6, 111–12, 148–50, 183–4, 199–200, 203–4, 207. *See also* Social Service Council of Canada; Social Service Council of Ontario; Chown, Rev. Samuel Dwight; Gordon, Rev. C.W.; Pidgeon, Rev. George C.
Church attendance, 224–6; 231. *See also* Social surveys
Clark, William L., 22. *See also* Social purity
Clergy: female, 78; modern role of, 246; status of, 98–9
Cochrane, Rev. R.B., 235; critique of social evangelism, 238
Commission of Conservation, 170, 175–7. *See also* Adams, Thomas; Sifton, Sir Clifford
Commission on Christianizing the Social Order (United Church), 239–41. *See also* Biss, Irene; Falconer, Sir Robert; Line, Rev. John; United Church; Urwick, E.J.
Commission on Economic and Social Research (United Church), 242. *See also* Rowell-Sirois Royal Commission
Commission on the Church and Industry (United Church), 235
Commons, John R., 93–4
Communism, 225, 234–6, 239
Conference on Charities and Corrections, 212. *See also* Social reform
Cook, Ramsay, xi, 76
Cooke, Rev. A.E.: on unity of science and religion, 79–80
Co-operative Commonwealth Federation (CCF), 235, 237, 243, 248
Cormie, Rev. J.A., 99, 174; and family farm, 166, 171; on immigration, 191
Creighton, Rev. W.B.: attitudes to Oxford Group, 229; and communistic ideas, 226
Currie, Sir Arthur: formation of McGill University Department of Social Service, 134–5. *See also* Dawson, Rev. Carl

Dale, J.A., 143; and Canadian Association of Social Workers, 157; education of, 147; on social service, 147–8; and Social Service Council of Ontario, 214; and Toronto municipal politics, 148–9. *See also* Falconer, Sir Robert; Social Service Council of Ontario; Social work; University of Toronto, School of Social Service
Dawson, Rev. Carl A., 132, 246; and Canadian Frontiers of Settlement Series, 192–5; education of, 135–41; and formation of Canadian Association of Social Workers, 157; ideas of Christian social reform, 136–42; on pioneer settlement, 190; on social evange-

lism, 101–2; and Social Service Council of Canada, 217. *See also* Burgess, Ernest; Currie, Sir Arthur; Leacock, Stephen; McGill University, Department of Social Service; Mackintosh, W.A.; Murchie, Rev. R.W.; Park, Robert; Social Service Council of Canada; social surveys
Dean, Rev. S.W., 51
Democracy, 15, 66–7
Department of Evangelism and Social Service (Methodist Church): and challenge to theology, 9; creation of, 3, 21–2; and immigration, 190; and rural sociology, 167, 174; and social legislation, 206; and social science, 89; and social surveys, 178–87. *See also* Chown, Rev. Samuel Dwight; Dobson, Rev. Hugh; Moore, Rev. T. Albert
Dobson, Rev. Hugh, xiii, 3, 24, 214; attitude to immigrants, 188–9; background of, 42; and child welfare, 23, 111, 124, 128–9; critique of social evangelism, 237; on decline of Social Service Council of Canada, 221–2; on evolution, 81; on labour question, 33–4, 112–13; and links with American social reform, 125–6; on modern culture, 13–14, 35, 44–5; opposition to, 26; and Progressive Party, 104–5; on relationship of church and state, 105–6, 183–4, 199, 203–4; on rural problems, 176–7; on social evangelism, 51, 55–6, 73–4; on social legislation, 201, 206, 216; and social reform, 107–8; and social sciences, 86, 89–90; and social surveys, 179–80, 186–7. *See also* child welfare; child welfare exhibits; Department of Evangelism and Social Service; Methodist Church; Moore, Rev. T. Albert; social evangelism; social surveys
Dorey, Rev. George, 103–4
Dow, Rev. John: and Commission on Christianizing the Social Order, 239–40
Drummond, W.M., 218–19. *See also* Machine Age Series
Drury, E.C., 113; and Social Service Council of Canada, 148

Ely, Richard T., 93
Eugenics, 81
Evangelicalism: fragmentation after World War II, 250; J.S. Woodsworth and, 9–13; and popular culture, 38–40; theology of, 5–6
Evolution: ideas of among Protestant clergymen, 78–81

Falconer, Sir Robert, 144, 156; and Commission on Christianizing the Social Order, 240–1. *See also* Dale, J.A.; MacIver, R.M.; University of Toronto, School of Social Service
Falk, J.H.T., 109, 222; and Canadian Association of Social Workers, 157; and McGill University, Department of Social Service, 132; resignation from McGill University, 134
Fascism, 225, 234, 239
Fellowship for a Christian Social Order, 225
Ferguson, Barry, 194
Ferguson, G. Howard: and social sciences, 149–50. *See also* academic freedom
Flett, Rev. J.W., 5
Flett, Rev. M.C., 31–2. *See also* Smith, Rev. A.E.; Winnipeg General Strike
Foght, H.W., 186
Forsey, Eugene: on immigration policy, 111; and Machine Age Series, 167, 218–19. *See also* Machine Age Series
Fundamentalism: and evolutionary thought, 80

Good, W.C., 209
Gordon, Rev. C.W.: critique of theology, 5, 7; and labour question, 20; novels, influence of, 37–8, 47–8; on relationship of church and state, 199, 203; on revivals, 52, 56–7, 69–70; on social reform, 22; and Social Service Council of Canada, 199; views on democracy, 15. *See also* church and state relations; Presbyterian Church; revivalism; revivals; Shearer, Rev. J.G.
Gordon, Rev. King: critique of Oxford Group, 232
Graham, Rev. William Creighton, 161; on influence of religion on modern culture, 249–50
Great Depression, 248; and CCF, 235; effect on church progressives, 235, 237; and financial

problems of Social Service Council of Canada, 217–18; as spiritual crisis, 224, 236

Hatch, Nathan O., 38–9, 41
Harkness, D.B., 157, 159, 164; and Social Service Council of Ontario, 184. *See also* Cassidy, Harry; Social Service Council of Ontario
Henderson, Charles R., 94, 134; influence on Rev. Carl Dawson, 136. *See also* Dawson, Rev. Carl A.
Hobson, J.A.: influence on E.J. Urwick, 151; and new liberalism, 91, 214. *See also* new liberalism
"Human Personality": concept of, 240

Immigrants: attitudes of Methodist and Presbyterian churches to, 187–92; social surveys of, 184–8. *See also* Dobson, Rev. Hugh; Moore, Rev. T. Albert; Murchie, Rev. R.W.; social surveys; Whitton, Charlotte
Immigration policy, 189–91, 215
Individual piety: and Great Depression, 224, 229. *See also* Oxford Group; personal evangelism; revivalism
Industrialization, impact of, 14–16, 235. *See also* Machine Age Series
Ivens, Rev. William: on Christian socialism, 17; and Labor Churches, 17; on radicalism, 33; on social evangelism, 51; on socialism, 16, 58. *See also* Smith, Rev. A.E.; Winnipeg General Strike; Woodsworth, Rev. J.S.

Jackman, W.T.R., 215
Jackson, Gilbert, 135, 214, 224; on immigration, 215. *See also* Social Service Council of Canada
Johnson, Franklin, 145
Joint Commission on Evangelization of Canadian Life (United Church), 228, 234. *See also* United Church

Keal, Rev. William, 16
Keirstead, Rev. W.C., 214–15, 290
Kemp, Hubert, 215, 220; on old age pensions, 216
Keynesianism, 198–9
King, Mackenzie, 87, 107–8, 214, 243. *See also* church and state relations
King, William McGuire, 88
Kirkwood, Mossie May, 218–20. *See also* Machine Age Series

Labor Churches, 17
Labour question, 18, 20–1, 33–4, 112–13, 209, 245. *See also* Dobson, Rev. Hugh; Methodist Church; Presbyterian Church
Leacock, Stephen: and McGill Department of Social Service, 133–4; and new liberalism, 92. *See also* Currie, Sir Arthur; Dawson, Rev. Carl; McGill University, Department of Social Service
League for Social Reconstruction, 87, 167, 198, 220, 226, 240
Liberalism: influence of collectivist ideas upon, xiv, 18, 90–2, 145–7, 151, 198, 201. *See also* new liberalism
Line, Rev. John, 214, 220, 239; and Commission on Christianizing the Social Order, 239–40; on evangelization, 226. *See also* Commission on Christianzing the Social Order; Fellowship for a Christian Social Order
Lucas, Sir Charles: and Indian land claims, 209

McClung, Nellie, 214
McCrimmon, Rev. A.L., 214; education of, 84, 89
MacDougall, Rev. John, 168, 183, 215
McGill University, Department of Social Service, 102, 131; creation of, 132–5; demise of, 142–3; relations with Protestant churches, 132–3; and sociology, 89. *See also* Currie, Sir Arthur; Dawson, Rev. Carl; Leacock, Stephen
MacGregor, D.C., 218–19
Machine Age Series, 167, 205, 218–21. *See also* Biss, Irene; Britnell, George; Drummond, W.M.; Forsey, Eugene; Kirkwood, Mossie May; Ritchie, D.L.
MacIver, Robert M., 19, 143; on Christianity and new liberalism, 92; education of, 145–6; on social evangelism, 89; and Social Service Council of Canada, 212; social thought of, 145–8. *See also* academic freedom; Falconer, Sir Robert; new liberalism; social sciences
Mackenzie, Norman: and American culture, 249. *See also* Creighton, Rev. W.B.
Mackintosh, W.A., 215; and Canadian Frontiers

of Settlement Series, 193–4. *See also* Dawson, Rev. Carl; Murchie, Rev. R.W.
McLachlan, Rev. D.N., 14–15, 67; attitudes to immigrants, 188; on evangelization, 227; on Great Depression as spiritual crisis, 240; on labour question, 18; and Oxford Group, 229–30; on revivals, 225; on social evangelism, 72. *See also* Oxford Group; revivals
MacLaren, Alexander: and rural sociology, 167–8
Maclean, Rev. John: and working-class revivalism, 59
McLeod, Rev. G.P.: and personal evangelism, 237–8
Macmillan, Rev. J.W.: career, 83–4; on minimum wage legislation, 121; on rural problems, 177; on social evangelism, 89, 100; and Social Service Council of Ontario, 214
MacMurchy, Dr Helen, 108
McNaughton, Violet, 118, 170, 185; and Rev. J.S. Woodsworth, 119–20. *See also* maternal feminism
McPherson, Aimee Semple, 59
Marshall, Alfred, 86, 90–1; influence on E.J. Urwick, 151
Marshall, David, xi
Marxism: critique of, 15
Mass culture, 249
Maternal feminism, xiv, 247; alliance with Protestant churches, 77, 108, 114–16; influence on social reform, 116–18; and rural problems, 169–70; on social evangelism, 78. *See also* child welfare; Dobson, Rev. Hugh; McNaughton, Violet; National Council of Women; social legislation
Mathews, Shailer, 89
Mavor, James, 82
Methodist Church: and child welfare, 78, 124; and immigration, 187–92; and labour question, 20, 112–13, 209; leadership in social reform, 107–8; and maternal feminism, 116; and relationship of church and state, 111–12; and progressivism, 13–14; and revivals, 52; and social evangelism, 245; and social legislation, 202–3; and social purity, 53–4; and social science, 82–3, 90; and social surveys, 178; and social work, 148; and theology, xii, 25; and Winnipeg General Strike, 31–4. *See also* Brigden, Beatrice; Chown, Rev. Samuel Dwight; Department of Evangelism and Social Service; Dobson, Rev. Hugh; Moore, Rev. T. Albert; social evangelism
Michell, Humphrey: and Social Service Council of Ontario, 214
Milne, Rev. J.W.H.: and Ottawa revivals, 226–7; and Oxford Group, 228, 231
Minimum wage legislation, 120–1. *See also* Macmillan, Rev. J.W.
Modern culture, 13–15, 35, 37–8, 39–41, 44–5, 47–8, 68–71, 247
Modernization: of Protestant churches, 8, 35, 247
Moore, Rev. T. Albert, 100; attitude to immigrants, 188; on democracy, 66; denounces Marxism, 15; and Department of Evangelism and Social Service, 22–3; on individual piety, 224–5; on labour question, 18–19; on modern culture, 44–5; on modernization of church, 8, 35; and Oxford Group, 229; on relations of church and state, 203, 207; on revivalism, 12, 42, 61, 63–4, 69; on social evangelism, 31, 51, 73; on social legislation, 202–3; on social purity, 53; on social science, 89; and Social Service Council of Canada, 210–11; and Winnipeg General Strike, 32–4. *See also* Brigden, Beatrice; Department of Evangelism and Social Service; Dobson, Rev. Hugh; Methodist Church
Morton, W.L., 118–19
Murchie, Rev. R.W.: and Canadian Frontiers of Settlement Series, 192–5; education of, 193; on rural surveys, 166, 186–7. *See also* Dawson, Rev. Carl; social surveys; sociology
Murphy, Judge Emily: on rural delinquency, 169
Mutchmor, Rev. J.R., 159, 164; and Charlotte Whitton, 159; education of, 41–2; on social science, 102; on social security, 223; on unemployment, 215

National Council of Women: alliance with

Protestant churches, 107, 114–15, 212; attitude to immigrants, 189. *See also* maternal feminism
Nelles, H.V., 165
New liberalism, 91–2, 151–5, 214, 245. *See also* liberalism; MacIver, R.M.
New Outlook, 229, 233; on Communism, 236
Nicholson, Rev. J.W.A., 226
Niebuhr, Reinhold, 220

Old age pensions, 216–17
Oliver, Rev. French: on fundamentalism and evolution, 80
Ontario Agricultural College, 168
Ontario Royal Commission on Unemployment, 213
Orr, Rev. James, 12–13, 96
Owram, Doug, xiii, 109, 177, 197
Oxford Group, 227, 228–30; appeal of to middle class, 230–2. *See also* personal conversion; personal evangelism

Park, Robert, 246; influence on Rev. Carl Dawson, 136–9
Parlby, Irene, 118
Pentecostalism, 59
People's Church (Brandon), 17
People's Forum, 50–1
Personal conversion: J.S. Woodsworth on, 12; reassertion of in Great Depression, 242, 248; relationship to social evangelism, 42–3, 55–6
Personal evangelism, 228–9, 234, 237–8, 243–5, 248; appeal of to men, 57; appeal of to working class, 57–60; and Commission on Christianizing the Social Order, 240–1; and demise of social evangelism, 239, 241; relationship to social evangelism, 29–30, 36, 70–1. *See also* Oxford Group; revivalism; revivals
Pidgeon, Rev. George: critique of social evangelism, 237, 238–9; and Oxford Group, 228–34; on secularism, 235; on social legislation, 202
Pidgeon, Rev. Leslie: and Oxford Group, 231
Pierce, Rev. Lorne, 172–3, 184
Popular religion, 245; influence on evangelism in Great Depression, 234, 237–9; relationship to cultural mainstream, 250; renewal of in Great Depression, 224–7. *See also* Oxford Group; revivalism; revivals
Practical Christianity: demise of in United Church, 227. *See also* social evangelism
Presbyterian Church: and democracy, 67; and immigration, 187–92; and labour question, 20–1, 113, 209; and progressivism, 13–14; and revivals, 52; and social evangelism, 51–2, 245; and social purity, 53; and social reform, 35, 106; and social science, 81–3; and social surveys, 178; and social work, 148; and theology, xiii; and working class, 51–2. *See also* Board of Social Service and Evangelism; Gordon, Rev. C.W.; Shearer, Rev. J.G.
Progressive Party, 104–5
Progressivism: collapse of urban, xi, xiv, 107, 247–8; definition of, 109, 121–2, 129, 165; in Methodist and Presbyterian churches, 13–14; and social sciences, 77, 148–50; and social sciences in the United States, 92–5; in the United States, 246. *See also* liberalism; new liberalism; social evangelism
Psychology, 75, 245
Public confession: critique of, 229. *See also* Oxford Group

Radicalism, 33; in religious thought, 8–9
Ramsay, E. de B., 37, 41
Ratte, Miss M.C., 22, 53. *See also* social purity
Rawlyk, George, 39–40
Reekie, Rev. W.P.: and conflict with Social Service Council of Canada, 210–11. *See also* Social Service Council of Saskatchewan
Reid, Helen: and McGill University, Department of Social Service, 133
Revivalism: comparison with United States, 42–5, 71–2; definition of, 60–1; organization of, 66–7; and popular culture, 39–41, 225; and progressivism, 43; relationship to social evangelism, xi–xiii, 42–3, 62–3, 72–4
Revivals, 48–9; and Great Depression, 226, 243; and social evangelism, 49; and working class, 57–60. *See also* personal evangelism
Riddell, W.A., 184. *See also* social surveys

Ritchie, D.L., 218. *See also* Machine Age Series
Roberts, Rev. Richard, 214; background of, 42; and Commission on Christianizing the Social Order, 239–40; and Oxford Group, 229; and social science, 100–1
Robinson, Rev. T.R., 102, 144; and Christian social reform, 109; on social insurance, 213; and Social Service Council of Ontario, 115, 214
Ross, E.A., 89, 94–5; influence on Rev. Carl Dawson, 141
Rowell-Sirois Royal Commission: and United Church, 242
Rural Community Life Movement, 169
Rural problems, 7, 166–77.
Rural sociology, 167–8, 171, 173–4. *See also* social surveys

Scott, F.R., 220
Secularism, 225, 244; and Great Depression, 235; effect of World War II upon, 250
Secularization thesis, xi–xii, 4–5, 45, 246–50
Shaver, Rev. J.M., 214; and Oxford Group, 229
Shearer, Rev. J.G., 47, 170; on child welfare, 206; on labour question, 20; on revivalism, 42, 61–2, 64; on social evangelism, 51; on social purity, 53; on social reform, 22; on social science, 89–90; and Social Service Council of Canada, 210; and Social Service Council of Ontario, 214; and Social Service Council of Saskatchewan, 210–12; and *Social Welfare*, 36; and unemployment, 201. *See also* Board of Social Service and Evangelism; Gordon, Rev. C.W.; Presbyterian Church
Shore, Marlene, 135, 194
Shortt, Adam, 86–7; and social evangelism, 89
Sifton, Sir Clifford, 108, 170. *See also* Commission of Conservation
Silcox, Rev. Claris, 4; education of, 103; and Social Service Council of Canada, 161–2, 221–3; and Great Depression, 235; on social surveys, 173
Simpson, Jimmy, 209, 215
Singleton, Rev. J.M., 15
Sissons, C.B., 9
Skelton, O.D., 87; on relations of church and state, 199–200; on social evangelism, 89, 108
Small, Albion, 89, 94
Smith, Rev. A.E., 12, 191, 238; background of, 41; on revivalism, 17, 58; and Winnipeg General Strike, 31–4; on working-class religion, 17
Smith, Rev. W.H., 7
Social evangelism, xi, 51–2, 245–9; definition of, 4, 24–5, 31; effects of Winnipeg General Strike on, 31–4; male influence in, 95–6; and mass culture, 68–71; and new liberalism, 91–2; relationship to American Progressivism, 35, 106–7; relationship to secularization, xii; and revivalism, xiii, 49, 56–7; and role of state, xiv, 148–50; and social sciences, 130–2; and social work, 148, 156–62; women's influence on, 119–21; and working class, 54–5. *See also* practical Christianity; progressivism
Social insurance, 212–13
Socialism, 16–17, 20, 58
Social legislation, 197–8, 201–3, 206–16
Social purity, 15, 22–3, 53–4. *See also* Brigden, Beatrice; Clark, William; Ratte, Miss M.C.
Social reform, 15–16, 22, 25, 35, 62–3, 72, 106–8, 136–42, 246; links with American reform, 107, 125–6, 178–9
Social research: and Social Service Council of Canada, 166–8, 172–3, 178, 199, 213–21; and Social Service Council of Ontario, 192, 213–14; and United Church, 235, 242
Social science: and church colleges, 89–90; and evolution, 81; and Protestant churches, 75–6, 81–2; and social evangelism, 86, 89; and training of clergy, 76–7, 98–9, 101–4
Social security, 223, 240, 247
Social Service Council of Canada, xiii, 77–8, 126, 247–8; and child welfare, 123, 127, 201–2, 206; creation of, 21–2, 205, 208–10; and immigration, 189, 215; and maternal feminism, 114–15; problems of during Great Depression, 217–18; relationship to Canadian Association of Social Workers, 157–8, 160–2; and rural problems, 170–1, 175; and social legislation, 197–8; and social reform

movements, 110–11, 211–13; and social research, 166–8, 172–3, 178, 199, 213–21. *See also* Shearer, Rev. J.G.
Social Service Council of Ontario; function of, 205; and rural problems, 167–9; and social insurance, 212–13, 216; and social research, 192, 213–14. *See also* Robinson, Rev. T.R.
Social Service Council of Saskatchewan, 205–6; conflict with Rev. J.G. Shearer, 210–11. *See also* Reekie, Rev. W.P.
Social surveys, 178–87; and modern state, 195–6; and Protestant churches, 111; relationship to U.S. surveys, 178–9; and Social Service Council of Canada, 166; and universities, 192–6
Social Welfare, 36
Social work, xiii, 75; definition of, 152–5; and McGill University, 132–43; and University of Toronto, 143–8
Sociology, xiii, 75–6, 245; definition of, 146–7; and McGill University, 89, 132–5; and Protestant churches, 83; and rural sociology, 167–8, 173–4; and United Church, 89
Stapleford, Rev. Frank: and Neighbourhood Workers' Association, 145, 148, 157
Stelzle, Rev. Charles, 20; and revivals, 51, 72
Stephens, Rev. H.L., 62
Stevenson, John: definition of Canadian progressivism, 122, 165
Stewart, Bryce: and Port Arthur Survey, 182–3
Struthers, James, 113–14
Sunday, Rev. Billy, 4, 61

Taylor, Griffith: and concept of pioneer fringe, 190
Taylor, W.R.: and Commission on Christianizing the Social Order, 239
Theology, 48; critique of, 5–7, 9, 244
Thomas, Rev. Ernest, 4, 156; and attitude to Oxford Group, 229; background, 42; and Commission on Christianizing the Social Order, 239; and female clergy, 78; and industrialization, 14, 16; on liberalism, 201; and personal evangelism, 225–6, 237; and relation of church and state, 199; and social evangelism, 25, 217; and working classes, 52. *See also* Department of Evangelism and Social Service; Methodist Church
Trades and Labor Congress: and Social Service Council of Canada, 108, 113, 211–12
Tucker, Rev. Canon: relation of church and state, 200; and unemployment, 201. *See also* Social Service Council of Canada

Underhill, F.H., 220
Unemployment, 201, 213–15, 218
United Church: Commission on Christianizing the Social Order, 150, 239; Commission on Courses of Study, 89–90; Commission on Economic and Social Research, 242; Commission on the Church and Industry, 235; Joint Commission on Evangelization of Canadian Life, 228, 234; and Oxford Group, 228–9, 234; and Rowell-Sirois Royal Commission, 242
United Theological Colleges (McGill University): and social work, 132–3, 142–3
University of Chicago, 89, 94, 135–41, 178
University of Toronto, School of Social Service, 44, 89, 122–3, 131, 143–8, 155–6
Urwick, Edward Johns, 131–2, 144, 222, 246; and Canadian Association of Social Workers, 157; and Commission on Christianizing the Social Order, 150, 239–40; education of, 151–4; influence of religion upon, 155, 162–3; and Social Service Council of Canada, 215; and Social Service Council of Ontario, 214; social thought of, 150, 152–5; and University of Toronto, 155–6. *See also* University of Toronto, School of Social Service

Valverde, Mariana, xiii, 187–8
Vernon, Rev. Canon C.W., 160, 169, 184, 218; and social research, 216. *See also* Social Service Council of Canada

Watts, Rev. Dr John R., 169, 171–2
Whitely, Rev. H., 13
Whitton, Charlotte, 143, 158, 222, 246; and immigration policy, 189–91, 215; and Rev. J.R.

Mutchmor, 159; and social evangelism, 124; and Social Service Council of Canada, 202; and social surveys, 179–80
Winnipeg General Strike: and Protestant churches, 16, 31–4; and working-class revivalism, 59
Wood, Henry Wise, 104–5, 171
Woodsworth, Rev. J.S., 70, 244; and All People's Mission, 50–1; and immigrants, 185–6, 188, 191–2; influence of American and British social thought on, 88; and Regina Survey, 181–2; relationship to evangelical tradition, 9–13; and role of clergyman, 99–101; and rural problems, 169–70, 172–4; on social evangelism, 51, 110; on socialism, 16; on social work, 156; on theology, 48; and Violet McNaughton, 119–20; and Winnipeg General Strike, 33. *See also* All People's Mission; McNaughton, Violet
Working class: influence of religious novels upon, 38; and Presbyterian Church, 51; and religion, 17–18, 40–1, 54, 59, 245; and revivals, 49–50, 57–60
World War II: and religious diversity, 250